TREK NAVIGATOR

D0247168

Captains' Logs: The Unauthorized Complete Trek Voyages

Captains' Logs Supplemental: The Unauthorized
   Guide to the New Trek Voyages

TREK NAVIGATOR
THE ULTIMATE GUIDE
TO THE ENTIRE
TREK SAGA
MARK A. ALTMAN
AND EDWARD GROSS

B▓XTREE

First published in America in 1998 by Little Brown & Company
Limited and simultaneously in Canada by Little, Brown &
Company (Canada) Limited

This edition published 1998 by Boxtree
an imprint of Macmillan Publishers Ltd
25 Eccleston Place, London, SW1W 9NF
and Basingstoke

Associated companies throughout the world

ISBN 0 7522 2457 3

1 2 3 4 5 6 7 8 9 10
A CIP catalogue record for this book is available from the British
Library.

Designed by Barbara Werden
Printed and bound by Mackays of Chatham plc, Chatham. Kent

Front cover photography by Fotos International/Archive Photos
Back cover photograph by David Bartolomi

DEDICATIONS

MARK A. ALTMAN   I dedicate this book to my grandmother, Rebecca Isserson, for encouraging me to believe in the future; as well as my brother, Ira, whom I forgot to thank in the last book. In addition, I extend my deep appreciation to everyone else who has ever been touched by the spirit of *Star Trek* — and shelled out the bucks to pick up this book. I'd also like to thank my coauthor for sharing the dream and all my future ex-wives for dressing up as Green Orion Slave Girls for my perverse amusement. And, perhaps most of all, I'd like to thank Gene Roddenberry and Gene L. Coon for making it all possible. You were the best. Still are.

EDWARD GROSS   I'd like to dedicate this book to my coauthor, whose screaming matches with me between the coasts served as the seed that spawned this book; to my sons, Teddy, Dennis and Kevin — three joyous gifts who have had to put up with a grumpy, stressed-out father more than they should have to; and, most of all, to my wife, Eileen, the love of my life, who is also my inspiration and my best friend.

Additionally, we would like to thank our editor, Geoff Kloske, and our agents, Laurie Fox and Linda Chester.

ABOUT THE AUTHORS

MARK A. ALTMAN was the editor in chief of the influential genre magazine *Sci-Fi Universe* for four years. He is a former Los Angeles bureau chief for *Cinefantastique Magazine* and has written for the *Boston Globe, Film Threat, Starlog Magazine, The Manchester Guardian, Femme Fatales* and many other publications, as well as DC Comics and Malibu Comics. He is a member of the TV Critics Association, the Authors Guild and the International Film Press Academy and is a regular commentator on the Sci-Fi Channel's *SF Vortex*. He has been featured on *A&E Biography*, Fox News, KCOP Evening News, KIRO and E! Entertainment Television. In addition, Mr. Altman is editorial consultant for the online science-fiction magazine *Planet X*, from Centropolis Entertainment and the creators of *Sci-Fi Universe*. He is currently cowriting and producing his first movie, for Triad Studios, and lives in Beverly Hills, California.

EDWARD GROSS is senior editor of *Cinescape Magazine*. A former New York correspondent for *Starlog Magazine*, he has written for publications such as *Cinefantastique Magazine, Comics Scene, Fangoria, Nightlife, Total, Not of This Earth* and *Premiere*. His numerous nonfiction books covering the film and television media include *Secret File: The Making of Wiseguy, A 25th Anniversary Odd Couple Companion, The Making of the Trek Films, Rocky and the Films of Sylvester Stallone, The LA Lawbook, The Secret of Michael J. Fox's Success* and the forthcoming *Alien Nation Companion*. He lives on Long Island with his wife, Eileen; their three sons, Teddy, Dennis and Kevin; and a mutt named Clifford.

CONTENTS

AN INTRODUCTION

DO YOU LIKE TO WATCH? Twenty years ago there couldn't have been a book like this. *Star Trek* was over, and *Star Wars* was all the rage.

Sure, *Trek* continued to perform well in syndication, and talk of a feature-film spin-off ran rampant through the halls of Paramount, but it would be hard to conceive of the fact that nearly two decades later, *Star Trek* would be so ubiquitous that anywhere you go, you'll probably find some aspect of the *Trek* universe represented. It was a cult — a vociferous cult, but a cult nonetheless. We were Trekkies. Now we're a phenomenon. So whether it's a bookstore, a music store, Toys "R" Us, surfing cable, the op-ed pages or just walking down the street, you'll find *Star Trek* everywhere.

And why not? Classic *Trek* and the three series it has spawned are among some of the best television entertainment ever to grace the airwaves. Why else devote a book such as this to its many episodes? People have attempted to explain the ap-

peal of the series, but explanations always seem to miss the point. We've heard about how it represents an optimistic future, a family in a world in which the traditional nuclear family structure had been shattered; how it tapped into humankind's fascination with outer space, our pioneering spirit. But whether you agree with any of these reasons or none of them, it always seems to come back to one thing: *Star Trek* entertains us. In any of its incarnations, *Star Trek* isn't mundane; it's challenging, exciting, fun and, to steal a phrase, fascinating. That's why we watch.

In 1966, when *Star Trek* premiered on NBC, there had never been a science-fiction show like it. Intelligent, prescient and provocative, it was a trip into the fantastique unlike any other. What's amazing is that despite what some decry as the now hokey production values and dated effects, the original *Star Trek* holds up remarkably well. The fact that these effects were so close to the mark is a testament to the creativity of those involved. Things such as sliding doors, cell phones, diagnostic beds and computer disks were all sagely predicted in the original series. What we now take for granted was exclusively the purview of fantasy back in the late sixties.

Indeed, some of the social allegory we now look at as heavy-handed was remarkably daring and cutting-edge when it first aired. Whether it was the first interracial kiss in "Plato's Stepchildren," examining the Vietnam War through the lenses of the Klingon/Federation conflict in "A Private Little War" or something as seemingly innocuous as having an African-American communications officer, *Star Trek* was daring and groundbreaking at the time. Perhaps that is why the show holds up so well today. Its stories are mature and always eminently watchable.

Classic *Trek* created a template for quality science fiction, combining exciting action/adventure with distinctive and original characters. It also created the dramatic vocabulary that would come to characterize all the *Trek* series, creating a futuristic lexicon of gadgetry ranging from warp speed to transporters to cloaking devices. (Even the holodeck was introduced in the animated series episode "Practical Joker," not *The Next Generation* as is widely assumed.) The bridge of the *Enterprise* was staffed by a diverse and charismatic cast of characters, and each week this family found themselves in the most remarkable of circumstances.

More than any other series in the franchise, Classic *Trek* captured the wonder of the universe, the dangers of space and the family spirit created by working together in confined quarters. It didn't hurt that some of the best science-fiction writers of the era lent a hand to Gene Roddenberry, Gene Coon and their confederates in crafting their weekly adventures. Nor did it hurt that matinee idol Jeffrey Hunter eschewed an offer to return to space duty when offered the second *Star Trek* pilot, making room for William Shatner.

More than any other person, Shatner was able to create the *Star Trek* mystique. Imbuing Kirk with the perfect mix of bravado, courage, intelligence and wit, he created an archetype that will probably endure until the twenty-third century. Along with Leonard Nimoy (Mr. Spock) and DeForest Kelley (Dr. Leonard "Bones" McCoy), they created perhaps the most memorable troika of characters ever to form the nucleus of a television series. Their on-screen chemistry and distinctive character traits helped make the original *Star Trek* a classic and led to a series whose brilliance has yet to be matched even by its successors.

In the early 1970s, Filmation continued the curtailed five-year voyage of the *Enterprise* by producing the animated series. Featuring the return to duty of the entire original cast sans Walter Koenig's Chekov, the animated series has become a forgotten part of *Trek* history. Not considered canon by the studio, the cartoon is rejected as part of the mythology of the *Trek* universe. This is ironic, considering it was overseen by Gene Roddenberry himself and featured scripts from many of the same writers who worked on the original series. It was one of the most adult Saturday morning series ever produced for television and stayed true to the spirit of the original. As authors who respect the series, we have chosen to include the animated series as part of our *Trek Navigator* and hope we will encourage our readers to revisit this overlooked part of *Trek* history.

Certainly not overlooked is the 1987–1994 series *Star Trek: The Next Generation*. Miraculously, *The Next Generation* was able to capture the spirit of the original series with an entirely new cast of characters. Although the dramatic structure was the same as the series that had spawned it, this was a different kind of *Trek*. After a bumpy first-season voyage that, to a large degree, unsuccessfully took its cues from the earlier series, *The Next Generation* began to strike out in its own direction. It was less an action/adventure show and more a drama with state-of-the-art visual effects and an accomplished cast led by English actor Patrick Stewart, who brought a powerful presence to the bridge of the *Enterprise*. As Bill Shatner did with Kirk, Stewart soon made the role of Picard his own.

By the 1980s, the television environment had changed radically. In the wake of comedies of Norman Lear and Larry Gelbart and the dramas of Steven Bochco, science-fiction allegory almost seemed a dated concept. Who needed to deal with social issues through the lens of fantasy when it was being dealt with head-on in the compelling dramas already airing on the networks? So *The Next Generation* had to reinvent

itself for a contemporary audience, and it did. Not at first, maybe, when the battles behind the scenes between warring writers and producers resulted in an on-screen schizophrenia in the shows themselves, aided and abetted by a crippling writers strike during the second season. Eventually, though, *The Next Generation* embraced the high-concept science-fiction story while also giving depth to its less than three-dimensional characterizations.

The Next Generation also began to define its own universe. Whereas the original *Star Trek* often explored the unknown, taking place out there in the deepest reaches of the cosmos, far from the world of the Federation and unable to reach Starfleet on subspace, *The Next Generation* used the building blocks of *Trek* mythology (the Klingons, Romulans and Vulcans, for example) to flesh out a universe. It also, for better or worse, embraced the mumbo jumbo of technobabble in an effort to beef up its occasionally silly stories.

If the original *Star Trek* could be accused of hammering home its drama with sometimes blatantly obvious allegory (for instance, the black/white prejudice of "Let That Be Your Last Battlefield"), bright NBC Technicolor planets and costumes, sexy space sirens and the delectably passionate acting of its principals, *The Next Generation* brought down the decibel level in more ways than one. Patrick Stewart was muted in comparison to his counterpart, William Shatner, which carried over to most of the *Enterprise D*'s complement. And filling the shoes of Gene Roddenberry as the *Enterprise*'s new helmsman in Paramount's Cooper Building was executive producer Rick Berman, who equated the bombast of the original with hokeyness. The lyrical and stirring music, the revealing costumes, the great guest stars, the fabulous monster makeup and the vivid cinematography were all reduced from the Woodstock-like fever pitch of the sixties to a more appropriate Kenny G–like timbre for the eighties.

By the nineties, with the unprecedented success of *The Next Generation*, *Star Trek* spawned two more space sagas on which the history books are not yet closed. *Deep Space Nine* was the most daring — and, by extension, the most provocative — of the two. Eschewing the starship-based milieu of previous shows, it attempted to redefine the *Trek* mythos. *Voyager*, while paying lip service to boldly going where no one had gone before, has regrettably gone where previous *Trek*s did go before. While *Deep Space Nine* has continued to evolve, stumbling at times, it has produced some of the best *Star Trek* drama ever. *Voyager*, still young to be sure, began promisingly but has languished in a sea of *Star Trek* clichés and betrayed a malaise among its creative team, who have worked in the *Trek* trenches for too many years. To be fair, the show, now in its fourth year, has started to show promise for the future.

It's no secret that for the two of us, the original *Star Trek* was the best series. It hit the highest highs (and maybe the lowest lows), but it was rarely boring: always fun, always entertaining, often provocative. *The*

Next Generation, created in the image of the show that spawned it, eventually found its identity. It had its ups and downs but emerged as impressively well realized and as a well-produced series with some fine episodes over its seven-year run. But *Deep Space Nine* may be the most interesting series of all. Never really embraced by the masses, *Deep Space Nine* has become completely enthralling television. It's surprising and different, and it dares to break with *Trek* convention. It has followed serialized story lines and crafted some epic tales. In establishing the Dominion and continually redefining the Cardassians, it has created a vast tapestry for its action, which is ironic considering that it appears to be the most confined in its concept. It's also an incredibly adult show marked by some superb performances.

Since shearing his hair, Avery Brooks has nailed the character of Sisko, turning his captain into a force to be reckoned with and joining the pantheon of classic *Trek* captains. In addition, his nuanced and loving relationship with his son, Jake, is unlike any relationship we've seen before on *Star Trek,* and his continuing affair with Kasidy Yates (Penny Johnson), with whom he's shared some ups and downs, is notable. *Deep Space Nine* also features an incredibly rich supporting cast, from Garak to Rom to Leeta and even Morn, the mute alien barfly. It is great television, which still goes unrecognized.

So now, in the wake of the *Star Trek* thirtieth anniversary celebration, a crass commercial milestone that is less significant than the continuing quality of the stories still being mined from Gene Roddenberry's creation thirty years after its birth on his manual typewriter, we look back at the adventures that span the corners of our galaxy and reflect on a product of American popular culture that is unlike any other. This science-fiction franchise has transcended the genre that spawned it and become a legend of the television medium.

We've written about *Trek* before, but never from such a subjective perspective. In a way, this book is a love story — an ode to a show that has meant so much to us through the years. *Star Trek* has been an ever-present and welcome part of our lives — and, we suspect, of yours as well. So as you embark on your journey through the hundreds of hours of *Star Trek* that have aired on television in the past thirty years, we wish you a good voyage. Whether you use this book as a reference while watching your favorite series in syndication or devour it from A to Z (or Atoz), enjoy! Those are our orders, dear reader. Engage — and, of course, live long and prosper.

MARK A. ALTMAN
EDWARD GROSS
March 1997

ABBREVIATIONS AND SYMBOLS

TOS	The Original Series
TAS	The Animated Series
TNG	The Next Generation
DS9	Deep Space Nine
VOY	Voyager
TMS	The Movie Series

RATINGS

****	Classic!
***1/2	Great
***	Good
**1/2	Average
**	Mediocre
*1/2	Poor
*	Lousy
1/2*	Abysmal
No stars	"Brain? What is brain?"

THE EPISODES

A

ABANDONED, THE

(DS9)
Original Airdate 11/5/94
Written by Thomas Maio and Steve Warnek
Directed by Avery Brooks

An infant Jem'Hadar is discovered on the station and begins aging rapidly. Odo, feeling an obligation to the growing child, tries to teach him to control his aggression and realize that he doesn't have to be a killing machine enslaved by the Founders.

ALTMAN (**1/2): Although there are strong echoes of "I, Borg" in the episode as the crew attempts to convince an adversary of the errors of his ways, there's much to recommend it, including the atypical ending, in which the Jem'Hadar cannot deny his heritage and returns to his people. Avery Brooks's freshman directorial outing is assured, and Rene Auberjonois turns in yet another strong performance as Odo.

GROSS (***): The passion of Rene Auberjonois is the locomotive behind this episode, as he takes on the task of rechanneling a Jem'Hadar's aggressive nature. You can almost feel his desperation as he tries to explain that the child does not have to be like his peers, although, in reality, he does. Avery Brooks does an impressive job behind the camera.

ACCESSION

(DS9)
Original Airdate 2/22/96
Written by Jane Espenson
Directed by Les Landau

A ship materializes from the wormhole, leading the Bajorans to believe that its sole occupant, Akorem Laan (Richard Libertini), is the true Emissary, which suits Sisko just fine until Akorem Laan decides to become a Bajoran isolationist.

ALTMAN (***): Thoughtful and engaging, "Accession" may not have the fireworks of other episodes, but it is certainly a provocative bottle show featuring a great performance by the always lively Richard Libertini. In examining Sisko's role in Bajoran culture, "Accession" not only manages to service the character of Sisko well but also provides Avery Brooks with a chance to turn in one of his most modulated performances.

GROSS (***): As is the norm on *DS9*, the characters are perennially evolving, and "Accession" takes Sisko a long way from where he began in "Emissary," where the Bajoran prophets detailed what he would represent to the people of Bajor. For much of the series, Sisko has avoided this imposed responsibility, but by the end of this episode, he comes to grips with it and actually seems to be relishing his position. Avery Brooks finds the proper balance here as Sisko.

ADVERSARY, THE

(DS9)
Original Airdate 6/24/95
Written by Ira Steven Behr and Robert Hewitt Wolfe
Directed by Alexander Singer

Starfleet sends Sisko and his crew on a mission aboard the Defiant, *during which they learn that the admiral accompanying them is actually a changeling and has seized control of the starship in an attempt to start a war.*

ALTMAN (**1/2): The promotion of Sisko to captain proves to be much ado about nothing, and a disproportionate amount of time is spent on his ascension in the ranks. The real juice here is the story of a saboteur aboard the *Defi-*

ant. And while the claustrophobia and mounting tension work to a point, the episode is wildly derivative, particularly in a blood test scene that mimics John Carpenter's remake of *The Thing* note for note.

GROSS (***1/2): Despite the fact that this is a bottle show taking place on the *Defiant*, "The Adversary" manages to convey the sense of movement and urgency that a starship-based adventure should. The element of paranoia that began infiltrating *DS9* in the third season is turned up a notch here, bearing some resemblance to such genre classics as *The Thing* and *Alien*.

ALBATROSS

(TAS)
Original Airdate 9/28/74
Written by Dario Finelli
Directed by Hal Sutherland

When the Enterprise *delivers medical supplies to Dramia II, McCoy is arrested and charged with the murders of millions of inhabitants in a plague twenty years earlier, prompting Kirk to launch an investigation to prove the doctor's innocence before he is convicted.*

ALTMAN (**): Although there are some gaping holes in the plot (such as why the Dramians are so set on preventing the *Enterprise* crew from exonerating McCoy), there are a couple of notable moments in the show, particularly in the final banter between Spock and McCoy, which prompts the first officer to note to McCoy, "Hippocrates would not have approved of lame excuses." Otherwise, "Albatross" is largely a pastiche of plot points that were handled better in the live-action show in episodes ranging from "Miri" to "The Naked Time." The revelation that the plague is caused by a nearby aurora is the final nail in the credibility coffin.

GROSS (**1/2): An interesting story that scores so high in the ratings simply because it was a Saturday morning cartoon that was attempting to be about something. One of your leads accused of mass murder? *Pufnstuf* it ain't!

ALL GOOD THINGS

(TNG)

Original Airdate 5/23/94

Written by Ronald D. Moore and Brannon Braga

Directed by Winrich Kolbe

Seven years of starship voyages come to an end as Picard confronts a juxtaposition of time lines in an attempt to solve a puzzling galactic mystery that Q threatens will lead to the destruction of humanity. Propelled through the past, present and future, Picard joins with the crew of the Enterprise *in each time period to prevent humanity's annihilation.*

ALTMAN (***1/2): For its first hour, "All Good Things" is truly remarkable entertainment. Boasting a broad scope and some exceptional performances (Patrick Stewart, John de Lancie and Brent Spiner, who remarkably captures the subtle nuances of his character in the *TNG* pilot, "Encounter at Farpoint"), this episode features an intricate tale whose brilliance is in the simplicity of its premise and compelling extrapolations on established character arcs. The production values also are top-notch.

Unfortunately, whereas the first hour of the show represents this show at its best, it is only appropriate that the closing acts mar an otherwise inventively ingenious episode with the ever-insidious technobabble in which converging tachyon beams jeopardize the universe. Nonetheless, the show's coda involving a final poker scene is both genuinely moving and deftly executed, proving a more than satisfying cap to an illustrious series.

GROSS (****): OK, all that technobabble about tachyon beams and pulses and whatever else they are talking about gives me a migraine (damn, it's starting again just thinking about it), but "All Good Things" works because it shifts back and forth between nostalgia, a desire to uncover the mystery and fascination over the directions in which the lives of the ship's crew might go over the next twenty-five years. The sequences taking place prior to the Farpoint mission are intriguing because they provide an insight into what may have been happening to different crew members before we were allowed to tune in seven years earlier, as well as their various reactions to the *Enterprise*'s new captain. In the future, we learn that Picard and Beverly Crusher finally do what everyone thinks they should: They get married — only to get divorced some time later. Worf's dating Deanna Troi creates a rift between the Klingon and Riker that is only accentuated when Troi dies. It just goes on and on. The real strength of the show comes from Patrick Stewart, whose Picard rapidly goes from befuddled to assured as he begins to put the pieces of the puzzle together. His sequences with de Lancie's Q are among the best these two have had together, and by episode's end you truly get a sense of the affection that Q feels for Picard — although he'd never admit it, of course. Just a wonderful end to a terrific series. It's a shame the original series didn't have a chance to wrap things up like this.

ALL OUR YESTERDAYS

(TOS)
Original Airdate 3/14/69
Written by Jean Lisette Aroeste
Directed by Marvin Chomsky

A landing party beams down to Sarpeidon to remove the inhabitants before the planet is destroyed by a supernova, and they find a massive library administered by Mr. Atoz (Ian Wolfe), a librarian who has sent the planetary's population back in time through the planet's long history. Kirk, Spock and McCoy all find themselves inadvertently thrust back into the past, where Spock falls in love with Zarabeth (Mariette Hartley), a woman trapped there during the planet's ice age.

ALTMAN (***): Although this episode may give the so-called Mary Sue fandom chills as Spock melts in the hands of a half-naked Mariette Hartley (OK, so that gave me chills, too), a fabulously inventive sci-fi premise is squandered as the episode fails to explore the most interesting aspects of its essential premise: sending a plane-tary populace back in time before obliteration. Kirk's actions during Sarpeidon's equivalent of the Salem witch trials may not be particularly inventive but boasts some fanciful swordplay. The always reliable sparring between Spock and McCoy as they face an uncertain future helps keep the episode afloat.

GROSS (***): Once you get beyond the notion that just because he's gone back in time, Spock won't necessarily revert to his society's more barbaric past, this is a third-season highlight. Much of that has to do with the relationship between Spock and McCoy, particularly the less inhibited Spock's grabbing the doctor's throat and protesting McCoy's oft-spoken criticisms of the Vulcan. The idea of librarian Mr. Atoz (A to Z — get it?) sending people back to the planet's past before their world was destroyed is inspired and would have been worthy of an episode in and of itself. Hartley is surprisingly good as a woman who has been alone for years and wants Spock to stay with her — no matter what.

ALLEGIANCE

(TNG)
Original Airdate 3/24/90
Written by Hans Beimler and Richard Manning
Directed by Winrich Kolbe

Picard is abducted by aliens as part of a futuristic lab experiment and is replaced by a duplicate who acts in an atypical manner: seducing Dr. Crusher and singing drinking songs with the crew in Ten-Forward. Meanwhile, Picard joins with three other captured aliens in an attempt to escape from captivity, discovering that one of them is actually the lab keeper.

ALTMAN (***): A staple series plot combines the premises of a number of Classic *Trek* installments, including "The Empath" and "The Cage," and blends them into a tantalizing mix. Picard's routine encounters with his fellow inmates are overshadowed by the amusing antics on board the *Enterprise* as his alter ego wreaks havoc. While the senior staff's decision to mutiny is reminiscent of the inferior *TNG* first-season show "Lonely Among Us," it doesn't mar an otherwise enjoyable episode.

GROSS (**): Patrick Stewart's lively performance as the "other" Picard keeps things moving along fairly well, but "Allegiance" is too derivative to be thoroughly enjoyable. The plot is influenced not only by the first season's "Lonely Among Us" but also by Rod Serling's "Five Characters in Search of an Exit" *Twilight Zone* episode.

ALLIANCES

(VOY)
Original Airdate 1/22/96
Written by Jeri Taylor
Directed by Les Landau

After sustaining an attack by the Kazon that results in the death of a crew member, Chakotay prompts Janeway to seek alliances in the Delta Quadrant. This leads to the captain's seeking the aid of the Trabe, who are bitter enemies of the Kazon but secretly plan to sabotage their peace negotiations.

ALTMAN (**): Jeri Taylor's antipathy toward the Kazon arc is abundantly clear in her less than stellar script. "Alliances" aspires to the mythic quality of *The Godfather* films, as Janeway assembles all the Kazon leaders to negotiate peace, until her plans are undermined by the Trabe, who strafe the room with phaser fire. What works so well in the gangster milieu seems derivative and silly in a science-fiction setting. There's nothing remotely noble about the Kazon, and the entire scene seems rushed and without any mythic import. Even the episode's dilemma, in which Janeway must reluctantly embrace an alliance in the Delta Quadrant, seems contrived and is made even less palatable by the heavy-handedness of its Maquis proponents. Ultimately, the episode ends with Janeway engaged in the kind of soapbox polemic that hasn't been heard since the early days of *TNG*.

GROSS (***): Chakotay's impassioned request that Janeway look at the possibility of setting up alliances is logical. Indeed, if *Voyager* had been successful, it could have played an integral role in forming what might have become a Delta Quadrant version of the Federation. But this idea is nullified by the Trabe. Not everything about this episode works, with some of it seeming rather contrived, but its intent is quite legitimate, and Janeway's initial reluctance to try an alliance is understandable.

ALTERNATE, THE

(DS9)
Original Airdate 1/10/94
Teleplay by Bill Dial
Story by Jim Trombetta and Bill Dial
Directed by David Carson

Odo is reunited with Bajoran scientist Dr. Mora Pol (James Sloyan), who studied the shape-shifter when he was first discovered. Pol lures Odo to a planet where he's exposed to a mysterious gas that causes him to metamorphose into a rampaging creature.

ALTMAN (**): Playing like a bad 1950s mutant slime movie, "The Alternate" works primarily because of the story of Odo's relationship with his caretaker, the overbearing scientist played marvelously by James Sloyan. Although the gag that Odo is actually the destructive creature menacing DS9 is a little difficult to fathom, Rene Auberjonois gets another chance to shine as Odo. In addition, there are some enticing glimpses into his fascinating backstory.

GROSS (***): Although there are a number of horror science-fiction film trappings about this episode, it is rooted firmly in reality by the performance of Rene Auberjonois, whose Odo never truly loses his humanity (as strange as that may sound). Particularly intriguing is the exploration of the past and current relationships between Odo and Dr. Pol, in which Pol and his refusal to accept Odo as more than an experiment reveal the doctor to be the true monster. There are certain similarities between the two characters that hark back to Data's struggle to prove his

sentience in "The Measure of a Man." Director David Carson delivers his usual sterling effort, enhanced by Michael Westmore's creature makeup during Odo's transformation.

ALTERNATIVE FACTOR, THE

(TOS)
Original Airdate 3/30/67
Written by Don Ingalls
Directed by Gerd Oswald

The Enterprise encounters two versions of a man named Lazarus (Robert Brown), one of them seeming perfectly rational, the other insane. We learn that the insane Lazarus is planning on opening a rift between two dimensions that will destroy both. It's up to Kirk to trap the two versions of Lazarus together between dimensions and thus save both universes.

ALTMAN (*): Despite a great teaser in which the *Enterprise* encounters a sector of space that literally winks out of existence, "The Alternative Factor" is easily one of the worst *Trek* episodes ever. It includes not only a disappointing performance by Robert Brown but also a plot that is largely incomprehensible. It also seems ridiculous that Lazarus so easily disables the ship and steals the *Enterprise*'s dilithium crystals. In addition, his time ship is one of the silliest *Trek* vehicles ever visualized.

GROSS (1/2*): This episode gave me a headache when I was six, and three decades have done nothing to lessen the pain. The story makes absolutely no sense, the effects — hokey even by *Star Trek* standards — are repeated ad nauseam and everyone is overacting so ridiculously that it's difficult to watch. The dopiness goes on right until the episode's conclusion, when Kirk and Spock discuss the fact that the universes have been saved. "But what of Lazarus?" Kirk asks solemnly. "What of Lazarus?" Who cares?

AMBERGRIS ELEMENT, THE

(TAS)
Original Airdate 12/1/73
Written by Margaret Armen
Directed by Hal Sutherland

While exploring the underwater world of Argo in the aqua-shuttle, Kirk and Spock are attacked by a vicious sea beast, only to be saved by the planet's inhabitants, who have transformed them into water breathers. While Kirk and Spock attempt to reverse their predicament, the Aquans grow suspicious of their motives.

ALTMAN (**1/2): In an episode that could have been told only on the animated series, Kirk and Spock boldly swim where they've never swum before as water breathers. Surprisingly, the concept isn't nearly as untenable as it sounds. Even Kirk pokes fun at his predicament when he tells McCoy, "I can't command my ship from inside an aquarium." Ultimately, the positive message of the episode overshadows the sheer hokeyness of Kirk and Spock as gilled ocean dwellers. Hey, it sounds as if it's rife with remake possibilities as a Brannon Braga *Voyager* episode.

GROSS (**): An intriguing premise that could have been done only in animation. A middle-of-the-road episode for the series, although the notion of a race of ocean dwellers is intriguing. The concept of this race's initially helping Kirk and Spock and then growing suspicious of the type of beings they are could have been interesting, but there's no explanation of their feelings.

AMOK TIME

(TOS)
Original Airdate 9/15/67
Written by Theodore Sturgeon
Directed by Joseph Pevney

Spock begins to lose control of his emotions as he is overtaken by the pon farr, the Vulcan mating cycle that occurs every seven years. During this time, the Vulcan male must return home to Vulcan to mate or die. When Kirk learns of Spock's predicament, he violates orders to return Spock home but finds himself pitted against his first officer in a deadly battle to the death.

ALTMAN (****): A truly outstanding episode that is both cerebral and action-packed. Leonard Nimoy has rarely been better, as his logical Vulcan veneer is stripped away by the mating urge of the pon farr. Kirk and McCoy's bemusement over the strange Vulcan customs is on the mark until Kirk must fight Spock in battle. The fisticuffs are brilliantly executed, the music is unforgettable and McCoy's final solution and the show's witty coda in sick bay are the stuff that made *Star Trek* a legend.

GROSS (****): This is probably the first episode to drive home the depth of the friendship between

Kirk and Spock, as the good captain risks everything to help his first officer, and also the first time we've been brought so deeply into the Vulcan culture. The acting is among the best ever featured in the series, and Joseph Pevney's direction draws the audience right in, particularly during the battle to the death between Kirk and Spock, which includes a variety of bizarre camera angles. The sparks between William Shatner, Leonard Nimoy and DeForest Kelley are a sight to behold, and make sure to check out the indisputable joy — quickly veiled — on Spock's face when he learns that Kirk is still alive.

AND THE CHILDREN SHALL LEAD

(TOS)
Original Airdate 10/11/68
Written by Edward J. Lasko
Directed by Marvin Chomsky

The Enterprise *retrieves a group of orphaned children on Triacus who are being manipulated by "Gorgon, the Friendly Angel" (Melvin Belli). Gorgon turns out to be anything but friendly as he attempts to use the children to commandeer the ship.*

ALTMAN (*): If not the worst *Star Trek* episode of all time, it's certainly among them. Attorney Melvin Belli is woefully miscast as Gorgon, who tempts a bevy of bratty kids to take over the *Enterprise*. It's hard to watch as Kirk is reduced to playing baby-sitter to the children, who, until the end, are oblivious to the deaths of their parents. Admittedly, some of the sadistic fun the children have in

disabling the *Enterprise* crew is mildly inventive, but otherwise the episode is insipid.

GROSS (*): Adults surrounded by maniacal children can be a chilling thing, as witnessed by *Village of the Damned* and even *Trek*'s "Miri," but there's nothing threatening about this bunch of brats, except for the fear that they might go on to other roles. Just a terrible episode. What genius thought the casting of Belli was a good idea?

ANGEL ONE

(TNG)
Original Airdate 1/23/88
Written by Patrick Barry
Directed by Michael Rhodes

Searching for survivors of a freighter ship named the Odein, *the* Enterprise *arrives at Angel One, a matriarchal society in which men are deemed to be a lower life-form. Riker leads an Away Team in an attempt to locate the crew of the missing ship, while a holodeck malfunction leads to a virus that swiftly infects the* Enterprise *crew.*

ALTMAN (**): A halfway intriguing story with echoes of Gene Roddenberry's own failed pilot, *Planet Earth,* is destroyed by a ludicrous and credulity-straining B story of a deadly holodeck-created virus that has absolutely no place in the episode. Some of the lascivious Riker's come-ons are fun as he seduces the planet's pulchritudinous leader, Ariel (Patricia McPherson), smirking, "Will you still respect me in the morning?" in the finest Kirk-ian tradition, but the show's quick wrap-up is a disappointment. Ironically, this episode, which condemns sexism, is probably one of the most sexist since the original series' "Turnabout Intruder."

GROSS (**): How do you instantly date *The Next Generation*? Do an episode about a planet ruled by women and treat it exactly the same way that Gene Roddenberry treated it in his *Planet Earth* pilot some thirteen years earlier. Definitely an attempt to recapture the feeling of the original series, "Angel One" offers little of interest, with the exception of a final speech about the flames of revolution that would have done James Tiberius Kirk proud. What should have been an indictment of apartheid is, instead, silly and meaningless. The B story about a virus on the *Enterprise* is a waste of time, showing once again a malfunctioning holodeck.

APPLE, THE

(TOS)
Original Airdate 10/13/67
Written by Max Ehrlich and Gene L. Coon
Story by Max Ehrlich
Directed by Joseph Pevney

The Enterprise *encounters a primitive world in which humans are overseen by an ancient computer creature called Vaal. In this idyllic world, the people are exactly like children, with no cares or concerns, as Vaal maintains the paradise until the* Enterprise *landing party interferes in an attempt to allow the inhabitants to grow and learn.*

ALTMAN (***1/2): Although the premise is hardly fresh, the show's indictment of cultlike values, as well as some classic humor, makes

"The Apple" a winner. This episode also is notable for its wholesale slaughter of red-shirted security guards, a Classic *Trek* tradition. And there are some eerily effective moments, such as Akuta's (Keith Andes) primer in murder. The show's finale — in which Kirk, Spock and McCoy muse about Kirk being the snake who drove the worshipers of Vaal out of paradise, and Kirk responds acerbically that *he's* not the one who resembles Satan — includes first-rate banter from the pen of Gene Coon. Look for guest star David Soul as one of the tribesmen.

GROSS (***): One of the numerous occasions when the *Enterprise* encounters a paradise-like situation. The difference between Kirk's visits to such places and Picard's is that Kirk often (as in the case of "The Apple") unilaterally decides that he doesn't like the way a society is run, and he changes it, ignoring the Prime Directive. The episode has some great character bits, including the coda cited above.

AQUIEL

(TNG)
Original Airdate 1/23/93
Written by Brannon Braga and Ron Moore
Story by Jeri Taylor
Directed by Cliff Bole

Geordi LaForge falls for a presumably murdered woman while studying her journals and deduces that the Klingons were involved in her death. When the woman turns up alive, she becomes the prime suspect in another gruesome killing aboard a subspace relay station.

ALTMAN (*1/2): Initially, "Aquiel" appears to have everything going for it: some nifty new sets, a great Klingon subplot and, most importantly, a chance for the appealing LeVar Burton to finally stop speaking technobabble and show some genuine emotion. There's even a great confrontation between LaForge and Riker. But alas, as is the case with much of *TNG*'s sixth season, it suffers from the gratuitous science-fiction twist. "Aquiel" falls apart in its last ten minutes, when Dr. Crusher attempts to deliver a convoluted explanation of some alien being that absorbs people. I'm not quite sure what that means, and neither, apparently, is Michael Dorn, who speaks his lines with such bemused detachment that he's unintentionally hysterical. Ultimately, LaForge discovers (à la "The Man Trap") that his lover's dog is the real evil-doer, as it transforms itself into a killer entity that he fends off with his phaser. Any way you cut it, "Aquiel" is a real dog.

GROSS (**1/2): LaForge's lack of luck with the ladies continues. Here he immerses himself in a presumed dead woman's world, actually falling for her, and then finds out that she's very much alive but a murder suspect. LeVar Burton's earnestness is contagious, but you want to slap the chief engineer because he's so damn gullible, offering Aquiel every benefit of the doubt no matter what the evidence says. Then again, the laugh turns out to be on us when we find out who the real killer is. The confrontation between LaForge

and Riker is a rarity for *TNG*, though a staple of the original series.

ARENA

(TOS)
Original Airdate 1/19/67
Written by Gene L. Coon
From a story by Fredric Brown
Directed by Joseph Pevney

When a Federation starbase is destroyed, the Enterprise sets off in pursuit of the attackers. En route, they enter an uncharted sector of space where Kirk and the commander of the other vessel, the lizardlike Gorn, are pitted in mortal combat to determine the fate of their respective ships.

ALTMAN (****): An extraordinary episode that features not only large dollops of Classic *Trek* humanism but also some wonderful action set pieces. The teaser, in which the *Enterprise* crew arrives and learns of the base's destruction, and the subsequent action in the charred remains of the starbase at Cestus III, are among the best executed and most imaginative action sequences that any of the *Trek* series has yet produced. Kirk's obsession with destroying the Gorn and his admonition to Spock, who questions his decision — "Do I make myself clear — I'm delighted" — is classic Kirk. Later, his novel solution in fending off the Gorn and his subsequent epistle to the Metrons that he will not slay the Gorn captain make "Arena" vintage *Trek*. The depiction of the Gorn, designed by Wah Chang (voice by Ted Cassidy), is equally creative.

GROSS (***1/2): Only Gene L. Coon could pen a *Star Trek* script in which two characters can beat the hell out of each other for most of the episode, and then one of them is redeemed by the fact that he wouldn't deliver the fatal blow. This is Classic *Trek* at its best, mixing equal amounts of action and character and demonstrating why this series succeeded where so many have failed.

ARMAGEDDON GAME

(DS9)
Original Airdate 1/31/94
Written by Morgan Gendel
Directed by Winrich Kolbe

O'Brien and Bashir attempt to help a race elimi-nate a biomechanical weapon that has been used in an ongoing war between the Kellerun and the T'Lani. When they do, they are exposed to the weapon and must fight for their lives, as the aliens are afraid that the humans will attempt to dupli-cate the Harvester technology. At the same time, Dax and Sisko investigate the supposed deaths of their fellow officers.

ALTMAN (**): Unfortunately, there's nothing particularly fresh about a *Star Trek* story in which its lead characters are mistakenly pre-sumed dead, with the requisite hand-wringing milked for all the pathos it's worth. The rationale for the alien race wanting O'Brien and Bashir dead strains one's credulity, to say the least, as does Keiko's rea-son for believing that O'Brien may still be alive. The usually reliable Bashir/O'Brien combo also plays strangely flat, relying on clichéd male bonding rather than com-pelling exploration of character. By the time Sisko and Dax come to the rescue, the sheer stupidity of the premise is hard to dismiss.

GROSS (**1/2): When *DS9* began, everyone carried on about the Quark/Odo relationship, but as "Armageddon Game" once again proves, the real strength of the se-ries is the dynamic of the O'Brien/Bashir pairing. You could never imagine these two guys hanging out with each other, but they are continually thrust into situations like this one, forced to work together and, perhaps de-spite themselves, forging a firm friendship. The alien Harvester plot line is adequate, although it's difficult to identify with the crew of DS9, who believe that their friends are dead.

ARSENAL OF FREEDOM, THE

(TNG)
Original Airdate 4/9/88
Written by Richard Manning and Hans Beimler
Story by Maurice Hurley and Robert Lewin
Directed by Les Landau

When the USS Drake *disappears in orbit around the planet Minos, the* Enterprise *investigates by sending down an Away Team, which is attacked by the planet's defensive weapons system, injuring Dr. Crusher. Meanwhile, Geordi LaForge, who has been left in command, must defend against the or-bital defensive weapon, which they learn is for sale from a weapons dealer played by Vincent Schi-avelli.*

ALTMAN (**): Another overly am-bitious episode that attempts too much in too little time. The idea of the *Enterprise* encountering a desolate world inhabited by arms merchants is intriguing but ineptly handled. The same can be said of the routine story line, in which Dr. Crusher is injured while Riker and company fend off killer robots. Rather than exploring the dynamics of a simple idea, the show is overburdened with too many divergent story lines.

GROSS (***): Lighten up, Altman. This is a rousing adventure on two fronts, giving LeVar Burton the opportunity to call the shots as Geordi LaForge on board the *Enterprise,* while much of the rest of the primary crew is trapped on the planet the ship is orbiting, defending themselves against automatically activated weapons systems. The episode also drives home the idea that having a captain *and* his first officer beam down into a hostile situation truly *is* ludicrous, and one begins to wonder how it was so freely accepted on the original series. As usual, the special effects are impeccable, and the idea that this planet is serving as a live-action commercial for intergalactic arms dealers is a fitting commentary on modern-day foreign affairs policies.

ASSIGNMENT: EARTH

(TOS)
Original Airdate 3/29/68
Written by Art Wallace
Story by Gene Roddenberry and Art Wallace
Directed by Marc Daniels

In this pilot for an aborted spin-off series, the En-terprise researches Earth in the twentieth century. The crew encounters Gary Seven (Robert Lansing), a man who has been captured by alien beings and has been trained to save humankind from destroy-ing itself during the tumultuous period of the late 1960s.

ALTMAN (***): Although the episode betrays its origins as a backdoor pilot for a never-realized series spin-off, Robert Lansing as Gary Seven, along with his well-stocked bag of tricks, is engaging, as is his sidekick, Roberta Lincoln (Teri Garr). Kirk and Spock, confronted with the dilemma of whether to trust the enigmatic Seven, play second fiddle. Although it's a little difficult to buy the concept of the *Enterprise* routinely traveling back in time for scientific observations of the past, this episode is a fun, if slight, capper to the original series' second season.

GROSS (***): Unlike most backdoor pilots, which relegate series regulars to little more than cameos so that the newcomers can be highlighted, "Assignment: Earth" manages to tread the line perfectly. It provides us with enough of an idea of what the new series will be like, while keeping Kirk, Spock and the *Enterprise* at the center of the story. The notion of the starship coming back in time for scientific observations is actually a logical one, and it's unfortunate that it's not taken further. Robert Lansing and newcomer Teri Garr work well together, and the potential for a successful spin-off was there. The show's budget constraints are particularly evident in the attempt to re-create the Kennedy Space Center with both actual NASA footage and sound-stage footage. Other *Trek* sojourns to the present or near future include "Tomorrow Is Yesterday," *Star Trek IV: The Voyage Home* and *Star Trek VIII: First Contact*.

ATTACHED

(TNG)
Original Airdate 11/8/93
Written by Nicholas Sagan
Directed by Jonathan Frakes

Picard and Dr. Crusher are kidnapped and, through a telepathic link, discover their true feelings for each other. Meanwhile, two feuding races ask to have their dispute mediated by Commander Riker.

ALTMAN (***): The episode boasts a surprisingly strong performance by Gates McFadden and is another fine directorial outing for Jonathan Frakes. Although action/adventure is highlighted in lieu of the long-awaited Picard/Crusher romance, which is given short shrift, the episode is an interesting change of pace for the series, addressing a long-overdue character issue. The mind probe is a plot contrivance that never pays off, but the two feuding alien cultures are well drawn, and in its best moments, the show even reminds me of Classic *Trek*'s "A Taste of Armageddon."

GROSS (***): During the earliest days of *TNG*, the big question was when Captain Picard and Dr. Crusher would "get it on" (or, as Bruce Willis used to say in *Moonlighting*, "get horizontal"). The question was seldom broached after the first season, and this seventh-season episode goes quite a way in explaining why. Forget the aliens plot; it's only a MacGuffin. Just sit back and watch Patrick Stewart and Gates McFadden strut their stuff, exploring feelings telepathically that neither has had the nerve to voice. At episode's end, there's an indication that the two *might* pursue something of a relationship, but the notion was never explored in the series' last season and has been completely ignored in the features.

BABEL

(DS9)
Original Airdate 1/25/93
Teleplay by Michael McGreevey and Naren Shankar
Story by Sally Caves and Ira Steven Behr
Directed by Paul Lynch

A Bajoran weapon designed to be used against the Cardassians is triggered on DS9, and the result is a disease that sweeps through the station, rapidly infecting the crew and making them think and speak in gibberish.

ALTMAN (*1/2): The old reliable *Star Trek* cliché, in which a virus imperils the crew, is resurrected unsuccessfully when the entire complement of the space station is threatened by a genetically engineered virus that creates an aphasia-like condition leading to death. The clichéd virus story is a tired premise that is resolved too quickly. Miraculously, an antidote is found and administered during the commercial break. The only element that keeps the story interesting is the always lively banter between Quark and Odo. Armin Shimerman quickly distinguishes himself as one of the ensemble's most interesting actors, endowing Quark with a perverse sense of twisted, greedy nobility.

GROSS (**): Some humorous Odo/Quark moments, as well as O'Brien's attempts to hold the station together, just aren't enough to overcome the weaknesses. *Star Trek* seems to have created a genre unto itself in the "disease of the week" category. In this case, the disease is clearly inspired by an episode of *The Twilight Zone* (the new series), in which Robert Klein was offered dinosaur instead of breakfast by his wife, who, like the rest of the world, seemed to be speaking gibberish to him. Although the *notion* of the disease is interesting, in that it has been created as a Bajoran weapon against the Cardassians, the cure for it, which Kira finds someone developing eighteen years later, stretches one's credulity to the next star system.

BALANCE OF TERROR

(TOS)
Original Airdate 12/13/66
Written by Paul Schneider
Directed by Vincent McEveety

After a series of bases along the Neutral Zone are attacked, the Enterprise *engages in an interstellar game of cat and mouse with the flagship of their unseen adversaries, the Romulans, whose ships have the ability to cloak themselves in an invisibility shield. Kirk is intent on destroying the Romulans before they can report on their victories and initiate another war against the Federation.*

ALTMAN (****): Although some of the literal transpositions of the dynamics of submarine warfare to outer space don't quite work (for example, Kirk ordering silence aboard ship so as to elude detection), almost everything else does, including a knockout teaser in which Kirk presides over a wedding that is interrupted by the Romulan attack and bookended by the officer's funeral in the show's coda. Mark Lenard is sensational as the Romulan commander, and there's some genuine suspense and brinkmanship in the episode. Although one wonders why Spock is cruising the corridors of the *Enterprise* at such a crucial moment in the show's conclusion (when he saves the ship), why quibble with an otherwise brilliant show?

GROSS (****): One of the most suspenseful episodes of *Trek* ever created, as the *Enterprise* and the Romulan warbird stalk each other in space. Indeed, this sequence clearly had an influence on a similar situation between the starship and the Khan-commanded *Reliant* in *Star Trek II: The Wrath of Khan*. Like many early *Trek* episodes, this show manages to bring us into the daily life of the ship's crew, with Kirk presiding over a wedding and then, tragically, the groom's funeral. There's also an interesting bit of racism in the twenty-third century, as one of the crewmen challenges Spock's loyalty based on the fact that the Romulans are an offshoot of the Vulcan race. Kirk delivers a wonderfully terse, "There's no room for prejudice on this bridge, mister!" Mark Lenard is terrific as the Romulan commander, and at episode's end, when he tells Kirk, the man who has proven himself his equal, "In another reality, I might have called you friend," you sense that both men regret that it can't be so. Check out an early sequence in which a starbase is destroyed. Now *that's* emotional power.

BAR ASSOCIATION, THE

(DS9)
Original Airdate 2/17/96
Teleplay by Robert Hewitt Wolfe and Ira Steven Behr
Story by Barbara J. Lee and Jennifer A. Lee
Directed by LeVar Burton

Quark's abusive behavior toward his employees, particularly his brother Rom, prompts the employees of the bar to go on strike. At first Quark is resistant, but when Sisko intercedes, the frugal Ferengi must relent, which leads to Rom striking out on his own while Worf comes to terms with life aboard a space station.

ALTMAN (***): The Ferengi are at it again in an episode that boasts a terrific performance by Max Grodenchik, who emerges from his brother's shadow and, in flagrant violation of Ferengi law, strikes against Quark. Chase Masterson also shines as the ditzy D'abo girl Leeta, imbuing her busty Bajoran beauty with a Gracie Allen–like charm. The episode also features some sly digs at *TNG*, as Worf tries to acclimate to life on DS9 and cites the *Enterprise*'s plush comforts, only to realize that its sleek, streamlined life is no match for the moodier, more challenging life of Deep Space Nine. Hmmm.
GROSS (**1/2): Worf starts to fit into the groove of Deep Space Nine as best he can. The core of the episode is Rom's battle for independence from Quark, and there's a lot of humor and actually a few touching moments here. Not one of the best efforts the series has to offer, but not bad either. What's most amazing is how palatable the Ferengi remain on this show.

BASICS, PART I

(VOY)
Original Airdate 5/19/96
Written by Michael Piller
Directed by Winrich Kolbe

The Voyager *receives an emergency message from Seska (Martha Hackett), who reveals that Chakotay's and her newborn son is going to be banished by the Kazon leader, Culluh (Anthony DeLongis), to a servant colony. This prompts the ship to attempt a rescue, only to be captured and stranded* on an inhospitable alien planet with only the doctor and the psychotic Ensign Suder left on board.

ALTMAN (**1/2): I must begrudgingly admit that "Basics, Part I" is the best cliff-hanger since "Best of Both Worlds." Regrettably, this isn't achieved through well-written character drama, scintillating dialogue or inspired direction. Rather, it's just a kick-ass action show. Fortunately, the pace is so breakneck that it's easy to overlook the soap opera–like underpinnings and sheer incompetence of the crew in allowing their ship to be seized by Seska and her Kazon confederates. Let's face it, this all happens because Seska has lured them with the fact that she has Chakotay's secret love child! Is this *Voyager* or *Melrose Place*? Admittedly, the episode's cliff-hanger, which plays like *Land of the Lost* meets *Lost in Space*, stretches one's credulity, but the scope and intensity of the finale are truly engrossing.

GROSS (***): Director Rick Kolbe punches up the action in this episode, which is designed to be little more than an all-out adventure and a climactic battle between *Voyager* and the Klingon wannabes, the Kazon. One question that comes to mind while watching some of the battle sequences is, Considering the number of times the *Voyager* bridge has been blasted apart in battles, how do they keep putting it back together? Additionally, the starship's falling into Kazon hands so easily makes

Janeway and Chakotay look extremely naive. The ending does have some visceral impact, as the crew members watch their starship take off for space. I'm still trying to figure out some logic in terms of Culluh telling Janeway, "You would not share your technology. Let's see how you live without it." There's always been this anger about *Voyager* not sharing its technology, but the Kazon aren't exactly primitives, given their vessels, warp speed capabilities and weapons. Look for an early scene between Tuvok and Ensign Suder (Brad Dourif), which picks up plot threads from "Meld" and shows the steps that Suder has made toward sanity. His madness, we learn, is probably not very far from the surface, given his explosive reaction to Janeway's not giving him an immediate answer to a request.

BASICS, PART II

(VOY)
Original Airdate 9/4/96
Written by Michael Piller
Directed by David Livingston

The marooned crew members fend for themselves against primitive Neanderthals and hulking lizardlike creatures, while Suder and the doctor launch an attempt to retake the ship from the Kazon.

ALTMAN (1/2*): The episode exists on a precarious perch between sci-fi adventure and self-parody, with CGI lizard creatures looking like something out of the Universal Studios tour. Although there's a glimmer of inventiveness in the doctor and Suder's predicament as they attempt to retake *Voyager* and the doctor spars with the always enjoyable scenery-chewing villainy of Seska, the rest of the show's a turkey of the first order. When Kes is kidnapped by primitive tribesmen after Ensign Hogan is eviscerated by one of the creatures (or what appears to be an out of control camera dolly), I screamed uncle. It doesn't get much worse than this.

GROSS (**1/2): What primarily works about the planetside portion of the episode is the *Voyager* crew's attempts to start acclimating themselves to a possible life on this planet, interacting with the locals and, by saving the life of one of them, establishing the possibility of peace and friendship. The real heat comes from the shipboard story with the doctor and Suder. Brad Dourif as Suder is the standout here. He has come to grips with his violent, psychopathic nature (thanks to an earlier mind-meld with Tuvok), but he must reimmerse himself in the world of madness he once ruled. There's something tragic about watching him kill for the first time since that mind-meld and seeing how his skills as a killer are what allow *Voyager* to return to its proper commanders. Thankfully, this episode also marks the end of the overused, underdeveloped Kazon.

BATTLE, THE

(TNG)
Original Airdate 11/14/87
Written by Herbert Wright
Story by Larry Forrester
Directed by Rob Bowman

Ferengi DaiMon Bok (Frank Corsentino) offers a gift to Picard: his former ship, the Stargazer. *Unbeknownst to Picard, the gift is all part of a plan to seek vengeance against him for the death of Bok's son. Bok plans to use an alien mind-control device to force Picard to relive his final battle aboard the* Stargazer, *with the Ferengi vessel being replaced by the* Enterprise.

ALTMAN (*1/2): The Ferengi are seen at their worst in this standard revenge epic. The only thing that works is the relationship between Riker and his opposite number aboard the Ferengi marauder, First Officer Kazago (Doug Warhit). Otherwise, it's sci-fi by the numbers and stupidity by the shovelful. Patrick Stewart is reliable as always, but even he can't salvage this interminable mess. *Moby Dick* it's not.

GROSS (***): There is something inherently fascinating about the past catching up with someone years later. In *Star Trek* mythos, we see it happen to Captain Kirk when Khan resurfaces in *Star Trek II: The Wrath of Khan* and, to a lesser degree, to Picard in "The Battle." This is an effective episode, providing more layers to the captain's character and some depth to the Ferengi. A true highlight is Patrick Stewart's solo performance on the bridge of the *Stargazer,* interacting with the ghost images of that vessel's former crew. Kudos to writer Herb Wright and director Rob Bowman. See also "Bloodlines."

BATTLE LINES

(DS9)
Original Airdate 4/26/93
Teleplay by Richard Danus and Evan Carlos Somers
Story by Hilary Bader
Directed by Paul Lynch

Sisko, Kira and Bashir take Kai Opaka (Camille Saviola) on a trip through the wormhole. When they are stranded on an alien world, the Kai dies. As the survivors attempt to communicate with DS9, they encounter two warring factions engaged in a seemingly endless conflict in which they never die.

ALTMAN (**): "Battle Lines" begins with an enjoyable teaser in which the Kai pays an unexpected visit to the station, while Kira comes to terms with being a "minor terrorist," according to the Cardassians. The more rousing elements of the show's first thirty minutes are offset by a less than satisfying resolution. Most notable is how inconsequential the Kai's role is in the episode. When a resurrected Opaka is stranded on the planet, it serves very little dramatic purpose in the episode, except to allow for future episodes that address the power vacuum created by her exile. Kira's moments with the Kai are overly melodramatic, although Bashir finally gets to show his teeth.

GROSS (***): Nice to see — at last — a tie-in to the pilot in terms of the Kai's appearance. It's also about time the wormhole is used to take us to a new planet and adventure. It's too bad that the world happens to exist in a *Star Trek* re-run. Despite story similarities to the original show's "Day of the Dove," "Battle Lines" works rather well, helped considerably by the fact that the warring factions are motivated by a determination to vanquish their opponents — despite the futility of their efforts — rather than being influenced by an alien presence. Even when Bashir can potentially offer them freedom by death, their first impulse is to use the doctor's theory as a weapon against the enemy. The coda, in which Sisko leaves them to fend for themselves, is a rather downbeat conclusion for *Star Trek*. There are a couple of nice character moments, particularly between Kira and the Kai, with Kira coming to grips with the position she currently occupies, as opposed to being a Bajoran terrorist. Also, there's a wonderful scene between Sisko and Bashir regarding the Prime Directive, which sounds as if it could have taken place between Kirk and McCoy. See also "Emissary," "The Collaborator" and "Accession."

BEM

(TAS)
Original Airdate 9/14/74
Written by David Gerrold
Directed by Hal Sutherland

Bem, an observer from the planet Pandros, joins a landing party mission to determine whether the Federation is worth allying with. To achieve his aims, he manipulates a series of circumstances on Delta Theta III, where a mysterious entity oversees the evolution of a race of primitive lizard creatures.

ALTMAN (***): A thoroughly engaging animated episode in which a mysterious ambassador manages to frustrate Kirk to the point where the veteran *Trek* captain says with a sigh, "There are times, Mr. Spock, when I think I should have become a librarian." Incarcerated in cages by aboriginal aliens, Kirk bemoans their situation by noting wryly, "How come we always end up like this?" It's a nice self-reflexive bon mot that helps elevate this routine *Trek* adventure with its simple but effective moral message. The colony-like alien ambassador foreshadows the alien Mark Lenard played in the second year of *Buck Rogers in the 25th Century*.

GROSS (***): David Gerrold, who brought humor to *Star Trek* in "The Trouble with Tribbles," manages to include a healthy dose of humor in this animated episode that successfully captures the feeling of the live-action series. Bem is a bizarre alien, able to split his body and have the various pieces operate independently of each other — an achievement that would have been impossible without animation. One question: Why is Kirk constantly identifying himself as "James *Tiberius* Kirk"? Once would have been sufficient.

BEST OF BOTH WORLDS, PART I

(TNG)
Original Airdate 6/18/89
Written by Michael Piller
Directed by Cliff Bole

Borg expert Shelby (Elizabeth Dennehy) hopes to become first officer on board the Enterprise *when Riker is offered a promotion to captain of the Melbourne after the Enterprise encounters the destroyed Federation colony Jure 4, the victim of a Borg attack. When the ship tracks down the Borg cube that is responsible, Picard is abducted and transformed into the Borg drone Locutus, charged with assimilating Earth.*

ALTMAN (****): The Borg are back in a knockout script from Michael Piller that is almost ruined by Cliff Bole's uninspired direction. Despite lacking the stylish mise-en-scène of Rob Bowman's "Q Who," this episode holds up as a *Trek* masterpiece thanks to its atypically violent and fatalistic premise and its riveting character moments. Elizabeth Dennehy delivers a dynamic guest turn as the ambitious Shelby, forcing Riker to rise to the occasion. Ron Jones's powerhouse score is one of *TNG*'s best, and the cliff-hanger is a classic.

GROSS (****): Perhaps one of the most exciting cliff-hangers ever filmed for television. The return of the Borg is one of the best *Trek* adventures ever (following "City on the Edge of Forever" and "Yesterday's Enterprise"). It effortlessly combines great characterization (particularly Riker's exploration of where he's going in life and the adversarial sparks struck between Jonathan Frakes and guest star Elizabeth Dennehy), superior special effects and the best efforts of writer Michael Piller and director Cliff Bole. Check out the chilling Picard-turned-Locutus. It doesn't get any better than this. See also "Best of Both Worlds, Part II," "Emissary" and *Star Trek VIII: First Contact*.

BEST OF BOTH WORLDS, PART II

(TNG)
Original Airdate 9/24/89
Written by Michael Piller
Directed by Cliff Bole

In the season premiere and conclusion of "Best of Both Worlds, Part I" Riker's plan to use the ship's deflector dish to disable the Borg ship fails, and the alien vessel continues on its direct path toward Earth, destroying a fleet of forty-eight starships. The Enterprise *sets out to rescue Picard and stop the Borg before they can assimilate Earth.*

ALTMAN (***): Part II is the follow-up to one of the greatest *Trek* episodes ever and is a profound disappointment. Then again, it would have been extremely difficult to match the dramatic impact and power of the first part of "Best of Both Worlds," in which the *Enterprise* once again encounters the all-powerful Borg and Picard is abducted and turned into a member of the alien totality. Despite an outstanding teaser, some great character moments, a sensational Ron Jones score and a spectacular battle sequence in which the remnants of the destroyed Federation fleet are vividly brought to the screen by Rob Legato and his able visual effects team, "Best of Both Worlds, Part II" is a bummer. It is intimate when it should be epic (the conclusion takes place in Data's lab rather than in space, where it belongs) and is filled with myriad inconsistencies. The most annoying one occurs when the entire Starfleet is annihilated but the *Enterprise* mysteriously survives its numerous encounters with the Borg. Worst of all, the episode is filled with technobabble, that mumbo jumbo that all too often is used to buttress a writer's floundering fiction. This time out, Cliff Bole's dull direction sabotages a story that suffers from a quick wrap-up and some unsatisfying plot contrivances. In the hands of a more capable visual director, Data's putting the Borg to sleep by way of an interspatial communications hookup through Picard may have worked, and the show's ambiguous conclusion could have been a real knockout. Instead, the overlit and thoroughly unstylish mise-en-scène falls flat.

GROSS (***1/2): Though not as effective as the first part, the conclusion is a thoroughly enjoyable excursion. The often adversarial repartee between Jonathan Frakes and Elizabeth Dennehy still sizzles, and Patrick Stewart continues his ominous ways by speaking in the monotone voice of the Borg liaison. The thematic point of trying to reach the human part of Picard that still exists within Locutus seems a bit too similar to Commander Decker's attempts to reach the real Lieutenant Ilia through the probe that has taken her form in *Star Trek: The Motion Picture*. The conclusion is a letdown in comparison to its predecessor's, but there is a dark moody feeling to the final moment, when Picard is alone in his ready room, reliving what he's been through. Watch both parts in one sitting for the story's full impact. See also "Best of Both Worlds, Part I," "Family,"

"Emissary" and *Star Trek VIII: First Contact*.

BEYOND THE FARTHEST STAR

(TAS)
Original Airdate 12/22/73
Written by Samuel A. Peeples
Directed by Hal Sutherland

The Enterprise *is captured by the gravity of a black hole known as Questar M-17. There the crew discovers a starship whose sole occupant is an evil and formless creature that has been stranded on the alien ship for millennia. The force manages to take control of the* Enterprise, *but Kirk and Spock have other plans for the sinister space anomaly.*

ALTMAN (**): Veteran sci-fi writer Samuel Peeples contributes an unspectacular entry to the animated series. Although there are some nice touches, including the use of life-support belts to replace the unwieldy environmental suits in the live-action series, the story is unremarkable. We've seen alien beings hijack the *Enterprise* for their own nefarious reasons ad nauseam, and there's nothing new other than the original design of the ancient alien vessel encountered by the *Enterprise*. It's enough to leave one longing for Sybok and *Star Trek V: The Final Frontier*.

GROSS (**1/2): Granted, there is much about this episode that we've seen before, but Samuel Peeples, writer of *Trek*'s second pilot, "Where No Man Has Gone Before," has taken the animated format and attempted to concoct a script whose sheer scale is unlike anything that could have been ac-

complished in the live-action show back in the 1960s. At episode's end, the alien's plea not to be left alone because of eternal loneliness, after it has been tricked by Kirk and Spock, is a bit touching, but too little too late after what it has put the *Enterprise* through.

BIG GOODBYE, THE

(TNG)
Original Airdate 1/9/88
Written by Tracy Torme
Directed by Joseph Scanlan

Captain Picard decides to engage in some holodeck relaxation while preparing for the first contact with the alien Jarada in twenty years. In the holodeck, he re-creates the fictional world of 1940s detective Dixon Hill and the detective adventure "The Big Goodbye," only to face real danger when the holodeck malfunctions, pitting him against vicious gunmen and molls.

ALTMAN (***): This Peabody Award–winning classic is a delightful homage to film noir. Writer Tracy Torme exploits the gangster milieu for all it's worth, and Patrick Stewart is wonderful as the fictional detective Dixon Hill. Also kudos to casting director Junie Lowry for casting Dick Miller in a cameo as a newsstand vendor and the always menacing Lawrence Tierney (*Reservoir Dogs*) as the evil Sirus Redblock, a Sidney Greenstreet–inspired villain. More time in the holodeck and less following Picard's attempts to master alien linguistics would have served the episode better, but it's still one of

TNG's best and most beloved early offerings.

GROSS (***): "Haven" was a promising *Star Trek* debut for former *Saturday Night Live* and *SCTV* writer Tracy Torme, who went on to create *Sliders*, but he comes into his own with "The Big Goodbye." Demonstrating a natural flair for film noir, his 1940s material in the holodeck is just terrific, and Patrick Stewart, Brent Spiner and Gates McFadden all seem to be having a ball as a trio of twenty-fourth-century citizens trying to adapt to a very different time. Although the rationale behind having events in the holodeck suddenly become real is never explained to satisfaction and the Jarada situation is nothing more than a MacGuffin, this episode ranks alongside "The Trouble with Tribbles" in effectively combining comedy and drama. Director Joseph Scanlan successfully walks the fine line between re-creating the past and never letting the audience forget that they're aboard the *Enterprise*.

BIRTHRIGHT, PART I

(TNG)
Original Airdate 2/22/93
Written by Brannon Braga
Directed by Winrich Kolbe

On a visit to Deep Space Nine, Worf learns that his father may still be alive in a Romulan prison camp, prompting him to investigate. A power surge results in Data's experiencing a mysterious vision left to him in his original programming by Dr. Noonian Soong.

ALTMAN (***1/2): "Birthright, Part I" is solidly entertaining *Trek*. It makes good use of the expanded format by telling a captivating, surreal Data story, while also slowly laying the groundwork for Worf's quest. Alexander Siddig lends an able assist (proving more interesting in *TNG* than in *DS9*), and Winrich Kolbe's dream imagery for Data's vision makes it one of the most visually arresting sequences of the year. Brannon Braga seamlessly blends two divergent story lines into an intoxicating tale featuring strong character development and action/adventure but eschewing the standard *Trek* clichés.

GROSS (***): The interaction of *DS9* characters with those of *TNG* is enjoyable, particularly the Data/Dr. Bashir pairing, and Worf's search for his father is fairly interesting. Data's first dream, which is both surreal and intriguing, works well. Most interesting is the android's attempt to unravel exactly what each image represents and his ultimate meeting with his father, Dr. Soong. With this dream, Data takes yet another step toward humanity.

BIRTHRIGHT, PART II

(TNG)
Original Airdate 3/1/93
Written by Rene Echevarria
Directed by Dan Curry

Worf attempts to instill a sense of heritage in the Klingons living in the Romulan prisoner of war camp, while also trying to execute an escape and rendezvous with Shrek (James Cromwell) to return to the *Enterprise*.

ALTMAN (***): Give *TNG* an A for effort (or three stars in this case) in producing such an ambitious and refreshingly different installment, which addresses everything from civil disobedience to the need to preserve a species culture to race relations in a sort of twenty-fourth-century *Jungle Fever*. With its focus on Worf, reducing the *Enterprise* to supporting status, "Birthright, Part II" is unpredictable and captivating. Although it borders several times on the derivative — including its intergalactic equivalent of the French "Marseillaise" scene in *Casablanca*, in which the Klingons chant a warrior battle hymn, drowning out the sadly out-of-place Romulans — it is different enough from the average *Trek* fare to make it a worthy installment in the canon, with above-average performances.

GROSS (***): It's interesting to see Worf, usually the only Klingon among humans, as the only *true* Klingon among other members of his race. His dedication to honor and heritage peaks in this episode, as he attempts to instill a sense of cultural pride in the Klingons residing in this camp. The episode offers plenty of intrigue, as he teaches them while attempting to make his escape back to the *Enterprise*. Also worth noting is the fact that the Romulans believe this is a paradise, refusing to accept that a fur-lined prison is still a prison. A truly significant Worf episode.

BLOOD OATH

(DS9)
Original Airdate 3/28/94
Written by Peter Allan Fields
Directed by Winrich Kolbe

Three of Classic Trek's most endearing Klingon baddies — Kor (John Colicos), Kang (Michael Ansara) and Koloth (William Campbell) — reunite on DS9 to avenge the death of Kang's son at the hands of the evil Albino (Bill Bolender). Dax must decide whether to assume the "blood oath" made by Curzon.

ALTMAN (****): The show unfolds on a large canvas, beginning at DS9 and finally culminating in a big action scene at the compound of an alien nasty. The episode's broad scope ensures that nostalgia isn't the only reason "Blood Oath" works so splendidly. Admittedly, it would have been nice to hear the three Klingons pay homage to Kirk during their barroom meditations, but it was not to be. John Colicos as Kor chews the scenery with his usual aplomb, and Michael Ansara is absolutely riveting as Kang, proving once and for all that we need no urging to love Klingons. Terry Farrell holds her own and turns in one of her wittiest and most endearing performances as Dax.

GROSS (****): A true second-season triumph that not only allows Terry Farrell to soar as Dax but also ties in wonderfully with the original *Star Trek*, as John Colicos, William Campbell and Michael Ansara reprise their Klingon roles. Everything about this story rings true, much of it having to do with the fact that Farrell makes you believe that more than one person is living inside her. In other words, she makes it totally viable that she has lived several lifetimes and the "blood oath" remains a very serious thing to her. Director Winrich Kolbe serves up the episode in a splendid manner, with lots of humor and action during the climax. One complaint: Why didn't the Klingons toast the memory of their greatest adversary, James T. Kirk? See also "Errand of Mercy," "Day of the Dove," "The Trouble with Tribbles," "More Tribbles, More Troubles" and "The Sword of Kahless."

BLOODLINES

(TNG)
Original Airdate 5/2/94
Written by Nicholas Sagan
Directed by Les Landau

DaiMon Bok returns to exact revenge on Picard for the death of his son (again!) by genetically engineering Jason Vigo (Ken Olandt) to appear to be Picard's illegitimate child. By creating a son for Picard and convincing him of his veracity, Bok then plans to kill Vigo and finally get his long-simmering vengeance on the captain.

ALTMAN (**): This utterly pointless sequel to "The Battle" is redeemed only by a strong and lively performance by Ken Olandt as Picard's would-be son Jason, who in one of the show's more amusing moments attempts to seduce Troi in the middle of her attempts to counsel him. A rewrite by Rene Echevarria, along with an emotional performance from Patrick Stewart, helps elevate this otherwise mundane episode by injecting some well-needed character nuance, but the premise is still rather slim.

GROSS (**1/2): This sequel to "The Battle" comes out of nowhere and makes little sense. What is truly wonderful about this episode, however, is watching Picard trying to deal with the possibility that he has a son. The character arc he goes through in the feature film *Star Trek VII: Generations* provides a great deal more poignancy to this episode. One complaint is the revelation that Bok has manipulated the young man's DNA so that he would *seem* to be Picard's son. The writers should have had the guts to make them blood relations so that Picard would have to deal with this issue for the rest of his life. Instead, when he tells Jason that he'll drop in to see him again, you know he's full of it. See also "The Battle."

BODY PARTS

(DS9)
Original Airdate 6/10/96
Teleplay by Hans Beimler
Story by Louis DeSantis and Robert Bolivar
Directed by Avery Brooks

Quark thinks he's dying and unknowingly auctions off his corpse to his old adversary, Brunt (Jeffrey Combs). When Quark finds out that he was misdiagnosed, he realizes that he'll have to honor his contract or be excommunicated by civilized, capitalistic Ferengi society.

ALTMAN (**1/2): "Body Parts" is arguably one trip to the well too many for a Ferengi story (the Ferengi work much better as comic foils than as the focus of an episode), but nevertheless there's much to recommend this episode. With the exception of a mundanely lensed dream sequence, Avery Brooks does a fine job in the director's chair, and all the performances are first-rate. Not only does guest star Jeffrey Combs turn in yet another strong performance (it's no wonder they keep casting him), but both Armin Shimerman and Max Grodenchik also bring far more to the stage than was on the page. They are among two of the show's best assets. Although the story unfolds fairly routinely with few twists (sans a visit by Quark to Garak to arrange for his own murder), the denouement, though extremely saccharine, manages to capture the warm family feeling of the original series and *TNG*'s "All Good Things" better than virtually any other episode of this show.

GROSS (***): If nothing else, throughout the run of *DS9*, Quark has proven himself to be an honorable Ferengi (is that an oxymoron?), always doing the right thing according to the customs of his people. In "Body Parts," he is prepared to do the same but ultimately finds that he cannot. Instead of coming up with some little twist of the rules that will allow things to go back to the way they were, Quark elects to live despite the fact that he is stripped of all his rights as a Ferengi. The climax, when members of the station refurbish the stripped-away bar, is so touching that you almost expect to see Jimmy Stewart and Donna Reed enter and inform Quark that a Ferengi with friends is a rich Ferengi indeed (not that Quark would buy *that* one).

BONDING, THE

(TNG)
Original Airdate 10/21/89
Written by Ronald D. Moore
Directed by Winrich Kolbe

The son of a crew member, Jeremy Aster (Gabriel Damon), must cope with the death of his mother on an Away Team mission, leading Worf to play surrogate father, since he led the mission. When the mother, Marla (Susan Powell), is found alive and well on board, the crew learns that she is a re-creation of the guilt-ridden alien race that was responsible for her death.

ALTMAN (***): Ron Moore's script marks the assured debut of the young scribe in the *Trek* universe. This is a strong bottle show providing some deft musings on death and loss. Gabriel Damon gives a good performance as the grief-stricken youth, and having orphan Worf bond with the youngster is a nice touch.

GROSS (***): "The Bonding" works so effectively because of the shared experiences of family loss between Jeremy Aster, Wesley Crusher and Worf. Even Picard gets in the act, as he was the one who informed Wesley and his mother that Jack Crusher had been killed, much as Worf has to do regarding Jeremy's mother. The acting is above average, and the final moment (a time of bonding between Worf and Jeremy) is quite touching. Now if only Worf felt as comfortable with his own son . . .

BOOBY TRAP

(TNG)
Original Airdate 10/28/89
Written by Ron Roman, Michael Piller and Richard Danus
Directed by Gabrielle Beaumont

The Enterprise *is trapped in a futuristic minefield that drains the ship's power, prompting LaForge to enlist the help of a holographic aide, designer Dr. Leah Brahms (Susan Gibney). He re-creates her and the* Enterprise *design labs to devise a means to navigate the ship to safety before it's destroyed.*

ALTMAN (***): The science may be slim, with an unhealthy helping of technobabble complicating matters, but the drama is engaging, with the sparks between Dr. Brahms and LaForge providing most of the heat. It's also a more clever use of the holodeck as an educational tool, as opposed to a recreational area that serves only for disaster. Susan Gibney gives a fetching performance as Brahms, and the *Enterprise*'s entrapment in the minefield is skillfully executed.

GROSS (***1/2): A series of great concepts makes this an outstanding episode of *TNG*. The idea of a thousand-year-old vessel actually being a sophisticated booby trap is brilliant, as is LaForge's inspiration to team up with the woman who designed the *Enterprise*'s engines as a means of getting them out of there. Ultimately, this is a wonderful foreshadowing of a later episode that unites LaForge with

the real-life Dr. Brahms. "Booby Trap" also drives home the fact that LaForge just doesn't have any luck with the ladies. See also "Galaxy's Child."

BREAD AND CIRCUSES

(TOS)
Original Airdate 3/15/68
Written by Gene Roddenberry and Gene L. Coon
Story by John Kneubuhl
Directed by Ralph Senensky

On planet 892 IV, the Enterprise *discovers a society that resembles Earth in the twentieth century, although it is based on the tenets of ancient Rome, and gladiator games are televised as a spectator sport. The crew also finds Merik (William Smithers), the captain of a stranded expedition who has watched his crew die in the arena and now expects the crew of the* Enterprise *to do the same.*

ALTMAN (***1/2): Although the whole idea of Hodgkin's Law of Parallel Planetary Evolution is pretty goofy, "Bread and Circuses" is a terrific episode because of its scathingly cogent observations about television and extraordinarily choreographed fisticuffs. Clearly, Roddenberry and Coon invested their script with some of their own misgivings about the medium, and when one gladiator shouts, "Fight, Flavius, or we'll do a special on you," it's a sidesplitting moment. In addition, there are some classic Kirk interludes, especially when Claudius Marcus grants the captain a night with his voluptuous servant girl, Drusilla (Lois Jewell), prompting Kirk to quip later, "They threw me a few curves." There is also some compelling banter between McCoy and Spock. Most powerful is the ending, in which Merik sacrifices his life to save Kirk when he tries to reclaim his lost honor.

GROSS (***1/2): Only *Star Trek* could make fun of the television industry — indeed, the very people who seemed eager to cancel the series — and get away with it. The script by Roddenberry and Coon is marvelously wry, providing character interplay, terrific action and some interesting exchanges between McCoy and Spock. It's surprising that Roddenberry, who often proclaimed that he didn't believe in the traditional concept of God, had his name on a script that deals with the notion of Christianity reaching this star system more than two thousand years after it appeared on Earth. It's kind of neat that Uhura is the one who has to open Kirk's, Spock's and McCoy's eyes to the idea that the "son" the people of this world continually refer to is not the sun in the sky, but the son of God.

BROKEN LINK

(DS9)
Original Airdate 6/17/96
Written by Robert Hewitt Wolfe and Ira Steven Behr
Directed by Les Landau

Rapidly losing his powers, Odo returns home and is tried by his fellow changelings in the Great Link, who, punishing him for killing one of their own, condemn him to life as a mortal, stripped of his shape-changing abilities. In the episode's coda, Odo reveals that he has learned that Chancellor Gowron is a changeling as well.

ALTMAN (**1/2): I haven't thought much of the Odo arc since it was established that Odo was a Founder in the dreadful "Search" two-parter. The quest for his identity seemed an essential part of the character, and that was pretty much destroyed with the revelation that he was part of the ooze that spawned the Federation's most feared changeling foes. Regrettably, "Broken Link" plunges ever deeper into this aspect of the mythology in a fairly routine way. We never really see what Odo is forced to face, only its aftermath, and most of the dialogue is trite, poorly written and surprisingly out of character. There are exceptions, however. There's a terrific, but badly directed, scene between Worf and Garak as Garak tries to sabotage the *Defiant* and obliterate the Founders' homeworld. Sisko also has several moments in the sun as he confronts the changeling leader, played splendidly by Salome Jens (although one has to wonder why she looks just like Odo if he was supposedly trying to take the form of the Bajorans when he first appeared in the Alpha Quadrant; the changelings didn't seem to have any trouble duplicating Gowron). Jens also has a savage, highly charged confrontation with Garak, which may be the best moment in the episode. Jens goes from being warmly sympathetic to Odo's plight to a menacing and sinister adversary, provoked into a genocidal rage with the mealymouthed Cardassian. Ultimately, though, Odo's dilemma of being trapped in a human body doesn't have much resonance. (Not only does he not do much shape-changing on the show, but it has always seemed like a gimmick to me.)

GROSS (***): As executive producer Ira Steven Behr has often said regarding *DS9,* the events of one episode have the tendency to bite the characters in the ass down the line, and that is certainly true in "Broken Link," which thematically picks up where "The Adversary" left off. Because Odo has killed a changeling — the first time that's ever happened — he has been tried and punished by his fellow Founders. Rene Auberjonois's pain and sense of loss as Odo make the audience sympathetic to his plight. While his shape-shifting abilities separated him from those around him, they also made him unique, and this loss is a profound one. Mr. Altman's comments about Salome Jens's makeup are valid. See also "The Search, Parts I and II" and "The Adversary."

BROTHERS

(TNG)
Original Airdate 10/8/90
Written by Rick Berman
Directed by Rob Bowman

Data commandeers the Enterprise *and beams down to a mysterious planet. He has been summoned by his creator, Dr. Soong (Brent Spiner),* *who intends to plant a chip in his electronic circuitry that will give him humanity. When Lore (Spiner again), Data's evil twin brother, arrives, he deceives Soong into planting the chip in him, depriving Data of his chance to be human. When the Away Team beams down, they find Lore gone and Soong dying.*

ALTMAN (**1/2): "Brothers" succeeds more in technical proficiency than in storytelling, but it is filled with great moments nonetheless. The opening, in which Data seizes the ship and expels the bridge crew, taking control of the *Enterprise,* is the most exciting action scene since Kyril Finn tried to blow up the *Enterprise* in "The High Ground." The ending, in which Lore escapes with Soong's chip in his head, is unsatisfying, though, and the episode lacks closure as a result. The directing, motion-control work and a tour de force performance by Spiner as three characters are sensational, however.

GROSS (***): Mirroring the type of special effects used in *Back to the Future II,* the *Next Generation* team is able to create some splendid magic by flawlessly presenting three versions of Brent Spiner in one scene. The actor makes you believe that he is actually three different people. Not a bad first effort for executive producer turned writer Rick Berman, and it was nice to have Rob Bowman return to the directorial chair after an extended absence. See also "Datalore" and "Descent, Parts I and II."

BY ANY OTHER NAME

(TOS)
Original Airdate 2/23/68
Written by D. C. Fontana and Jerome Bixby
Story by Jerome Bixby
Directed by Marc Daniels

Members of the Kelvan race take human form and assume control of the Enterprise *by turning the majority of the crew into tetrahedrons. Their goal: return to Andromeda and report that the Milky Way is ripe for colonization. Kirk, Spock, McCoy and Scotty have other plans for the Kelvans, turning their newly acquired human emotions against them.*

ALTMAN (***): A lot of Classic *Trek* bits surface in this episode, including Spock's use of the Vulcan mind-meld, Kirk's seduction of an alien (in this case, Barbara Bouchet's Kelinda), the *Enterprise* being taken over by a superior alien force and Kirk convincing everyone that it's all been one big misunderstanding. Although the plot itself is familiar and cliché-ridden, the various vignettes are delightful, including the Kelvans transforming the crew into tetrahedrons on the planet's surface and crushing one of the landing party as a horrified Kirk looks on. Later, as Scotty gets into a drinking contest with one of the Kelvans, the show's unique charms are hard to dismiss.

GROSS (**): A very goofy second-season episode that has some undeniably appealing elements (noted in the above review). In addition, the notion of crewmen becoming blocks has become a series icon. Generally, though, a middle-of-the-road show.

CAGE, THE

(TOS)
Original Airdate: None (added to syndication package in the early 1980s)
Written by Gene Roddenberry
Directed by Robert Butler

The Enterprise, *led by its captain, Christopher Pike (Jeffrey Hunter), answers a distress call of stranded colonists from the planet Talos IV, which they learn is an illusion to trap the captain. Incarcerated by telepathic beings called Talosians, Pike tries to escape his captivity.*

ALTMAN (****): An extraordinary pilot by Gene Roddenberry that introduces the world to the starship *Enterprise* and its crew, albeit a very different one than would hit the airwaves in the fall of 1966. Jeffrey Hunter is far more laconic and world-weary than William Shatner as Kirk, and although he probably wouldn't have proved Shatner's equal in a continuing series, he shines in his sole *Star Trek* outing. Likewise, Majel Barret is terrific as Number One, the ship's second-in-command. "The Cage" betrays the influence of MGM's 1950s sci-fi film *Forbidden Planet*, but it also is the most consistently intriguing and cerebral sci-fi creation made for television up to that time, and probably even to this day.

GROSS (****): This is Gene Roddenberry's first take on *Trek*, and, particularly coming at the time it did (1964), the results are extremely impressive. The special effects, as primitive as they look today, probably represented the best the medium had to offer at the time, but the real joy lies in the literate plot line and diverse characters, which also were atypical of the genre. The Talosians are a terrific alien race, mysterious and just plain weird-looking. The cast deserves high praise for making the story believable. Jeffrey Hunter is a bit stiff as Captain Pike, but he's an effective enough progenitor of William Shatner's James T. Kirk. Check out Leonard Nimoy's Spock, who actually *smiles* on several occasions and practically shouts out his discoveries on the bridge. Interestingly, much of what this pilot offers in terms of the show's format and technology remains in the various spin-offs and feature films. A winner right out of the gate, this pilot is a testament to Roddenberry's genius, for coming up with the concept of this series, if nothing else.

CAPTAIN'S HOLIDAY

(TNG)
Original Airdate 3/31/90
Written by Ira Steven Behr
Directed by Chip Chalmers

Picard reluctantly takes a vacation on Rysa, the Club Med of the cosmos, where he becomes an unwitting pawn of the unscrupulous Vash (Jennifer Hetrick), who is seeking the legendary tax-u-tat treasure and is being trailed by former Ferengi ally Sovak (Max Grodenchik). Also searching for the lost and powerful treasure are two unsavory Vorgon time travelers from the twenty-seventh century, Ajor (Karen Landry) and Boaratis (Michael Champion).

ALTMAN (***): Some truly silly moments and incomprehensible plot lines involving the Vorgons make "Captain's Holiday" an imperfect episode, but it's the closest *TNG* comes to equaling the comedy classics of the original series. Watching Picard relax on shore leave in a twenty-fourth-century Speedo while a Ferengi, who seems to have borrowed Don Johnson's *Miami Vice* wardrobe, harasses him is a hoot. Grodenchik is delightful in this pre-Rom role, and Jennifer Hetrick is perfectly cast as the comely Vash, a sexy and ambitious explorer who allows Picard to play Indiana Jones and take her to bed all in one day. Even Kirk would be jealous.

GROSS (***): Forget the time-travel elements of this episode (they're downright silly), but relish the comic relief provided by the Ferengi and the chemistry between Patrick Stewart's Picard and Jennifer Hetrick's Vash. This episode is designed to do little more than entertain, and it succeeds nicely. See also "Q-pid" and "Q-Less."

CAPTIVE PURSUIT

(DS9)
Original Airdate 2/1/93
Teleplay by Jill Sherman Donner and Michael Piller
Story by Jill Sherman Donner
Directed by Corey Allen

An alien being named Tosk (Scott MacDonald) appears through the wormhole. The crew later learns that Tosk is genetically bred prey in an intergalactic "most dangerous game" taking place in the Gamma Quadrant.

ALTMAN (***): Corey Allen's direction is somewhat lackluster, and the station continues to feel claustrophobic in this early first-season episode, but it's the first opportunity for O'Brien to shine, and Colm Meaney is up to the challenge. The requisite phaser fights aren't all that well executed, and the dramatic confrontation between Sisko and O'Brien serves as the primary source of incendiary conflict in the more than satisfying coda.

GROSS (***1/2): All the elements of *DS9* come together in this fascinating fox-on-the-run tale with a twist (that the "fox" has been created specifically to serve as the hunted, and that it's a position of honor) that would make Rod Serling proud. Sure, there are phaser battles and some effective suspense in the course of the hunt, but the core of the episode is the wonderful relationship between O'Brien and Tosk. By the time the hour is up, it is completely believable that these two characters have gone from members of two races encountering each other for the first time to genuine friends. Kudos to Colm Meaney and Scott MacDonald for pulling it off.

CARDASSIANS

(DS9)
Original Airdate 10/25/93
Teleplay by James Crocker
Story by Gene Wolander and John Wright
Directed by Cliff Bole

*A Cardassian orphan is revealed to be the son of a leading Cardassian civilian, and the plight of Car-*dassian orphans is examined as part of the complex political machinations of feuding Cardassians who once occupied Bajor.*

ALTMAN (***): This emotionally wrenching episode also marks the return of Garak, and it is certainly worth the wait. This "tinker, tailor, soldier, spy" not only plays a key role, thanks to a terrific star turn by Andrew Robinson and a witty yet weighty teleplay by James Crocker, but it also helps to provide Bashir's character with some much-needed resourcefulness. It is a compelling mystery, in contrast to the usual predictable story lines, which mitigates its fleeting similarity to *TNG*'s fourth-season episode "Suddenly Human."

GROSS (***1/2): A frustrating aspect of *TNG* is that it seldom deals with any of the "big" issues, often choosing to focus on Worf's being a single father and stories of a similar ilk. Conversely, "Cardassians" is an extremely powerful look at the plight of war orphans. The emotions here are real, with Siddig El Fadil and Andrew Robinson both fully able to handle having the spotlight firmly on them.

CARETAKER

(VOY)
Original Airdate 1/16/95
Teleplay by Michael Piller and Jeri Taylor
Story by Rick Berman, Michael Piller and Jeri Taylor
Directed by Winrich Kolbe

The newest Star Trek *series debuted gloriously with a knockout premiere in which the starship* Voyager *travels to the distant reaches of the galaxy while pursuing a missing Maquis ship and finds itself victimized by an alien force that has abducted members of its crew.*

ALTMAN (***1/2): "Caretaker" introduces a remarkably cast *Trek* ensemble, which makes a striking first impression. Each and every one (even Neelix) proves immediately engaging. Most delightful of all is the telefilm's tone, which harks back to that of the original *Star Trek*, including the crew's befuddled reaction to an Earth-like farmhouse aboard an enigmatic array and a delightfully preposterous coda involving a guilt-ridden alien entity that echoes such classic creatures as the Organians in "Errand of Mercy." Unfortunately, the show has yet to recapture the magic of its premiere.

GROSS (****): Every time they do a *Star Trek* pilot, it seems to improve on its predecessor, and "Caretaker" is no exception. Based on this two-hour film, the series was born fully gestated. Usually a premiere such as this has an episodic feeling as the various characters are pulled together, but here their introductions are handled logically and flawlessly. Kate Mulgrew immediately proves that she has the stuff to join the ranks of Shatner, Stewart and Brooks. Make no mistake about it, the lady's in charge. Tim Russ (Tuvok) does the best Spock impersonation ever seen (that's actually a compliment), and each member of the ensemble seems perfectly cast, with the group jelling on camera almost immediately. The notion of the Caretaker is as good a MacGuffin for getting them into the Delta Quadrant as any. The idea of the Caretaker bringing *Voyager* into its reality as represented by what could easily be Mayberry works nicely, although creating a reality that the crew could relate to would become a series cliché by the third season. Winrich Kolbe, who directed the series finale of *TNG* ("All Good Things"), among other episodes, rises to the occasion and sets the newest spoke of Paramount's franchise wheel on the right path from the get-go. See also "Cold Fire."

CATHEXIS

(VOY)
Original Airdate 5/1/95
Teleplay by Brannon Braga
Story by Brannon Braga and Joe Menosky
Directed by Kim Friedman

Returning from exploring a black nebula, Tuvok and Chakotay are injured as an alien presence is unleashed, seemingly leaping from crew member to crew member and attempting to manipulate the ship. It turns out that this "alien" is actually Chakotay's subconscious mind trying to save the Voyager from the nebula.

ALTMAN (*1/2): A thoroughly ineffective retread of first-season *TNG*'s "Lonely Among Us," in which a mysterious alien force possesses members of the crew while Chakotay lies in a coma. The biggest misstep in the episode is the lack of genuine suspense and paranoia. Everything is laid out immediately, with the audience anticipating the few twists and turns before they happen. There's no sense of foreboding in the *Body Snatchers*–like premise, which begs the question, Who can you trust? Unfortunately, this potentially intriguing nugget is rejected. Instead, the clichéd technomystery, involving what Kim dubs "strange energy beings living inside the nebula" that feed on the crew's neural energy, is explored. Frankly, the pointless Jane Eyre teaser in the holodeck (where did this come from?) and the hokey Indian mysticism don't help either.

GROSS (**): The first thing this episode has against it is the fact that we've seen the body-to-body transference way too many times in the history of *Trek*. Second, whether or not this is Chakotay's subconscious mind doesn't matter. There's nothing for the audience to lock onto or identify with. Obviously, this is an attempt to provide a little bit of insight into *Voyager*'s first officer, but it just doesn't work.

CATSPAW

(TOS)
Original Airdate 10/27/67
Written by Robert Bloch and D. C. Fontana
Directed by Joseph Pevney

Beaming down to Pyris VII, Kirk, Spock and McCoy confront Sulu and Scotty, who have been transformed into zombies by the aliens Sylvia (Antoinette Bowers) and Korob (Theo Marcus). The aliens are intent on conquering the universe, and they marshal the icons of Halloween to enlist Kirk's help.

ALTMAN (***): Although it's a decidedly high-concept gimmick show, "Catspaw" isn't a total turkey, thanks to the sense of dread and menace invoked in its set pieces. Sylvia is suitably seductive, and the finale, in which Kirk destroys the source of their power, only to reduce the two alien invaders into strange, small, tentacled miniature creatures, is the kind of wildly inventive storytelling that no subsequent *Star Trek* series has achieved.

GROSS (**): Although there are some unsettling moments, unlike most episodes of the original series, this one is hurt by poor special effects. Among them are a supposed giant black cat that looks like the kind of effect often seen on *I Dream of Jeannie* and the *Enterprise* supposedly being shrunk down to pendant size and swung over a flame. A Robert Bloch script that just doesn't work.

CAUSE & EFFECT

(TNG)
Original Airdate 3/23/92
Written by Brannon Braga
Directed by Jonathan Frakes

The Enterprise *becomes trapped in a time warp, in which the crew is forced to repeat endlessly the same experience from the past: The ship faces inevitable destruction after a collision with another starship, the USS* Bozeman.

ALTMAN (**1/2): One of *TNG*'s most sensational teasers, in which the *Enterprise* is obliterated in an outer space collision, sets off a strange chain of events in this visually stunning, but dramatically uneven, episode. Braga's story boasts an impressive sci-fi nugget, but like many of his episodes, it involves a resolution with a less than credible deus ex machina to extricate the crew from their vexing dilemma. I would have liked to see more of Kelsey Grammer and the *Bozeman*, but ultimately this show is only a vastly improved version of the second season's "Time Squared."

GROSS (**): A hell of an opening, but it goes downhill from there. Director Jonathan Frakes does his best to keep things moving and the mystery mounting, and for a while he succeeds. But when each commercial break is initiated by the *Enterprise* blowing up, it starts to look like something out of *Airplane*. Maybe it's me, but I still don't get how Data is able to send a message back to himself while trapped in this time loop. Additionally, although *Frasier*'s Kelsey Grammer is always welcome in the twenty-fourth century, that whole business of the *Bozeman* is just a lame takeoff on the far more effective time-travel episode "Yesterday's Enterprise."

CHAIN OF COMMAND, PART I

(TNG)
Original Airdate 12/14/92
Teleplay by Ron Moore
Story by Frank Abatemarco
Directed by Robert Scheerer

When hostilities flare with the Cardassians, Picard is reassigned on a secret mission to investigate the Cardassian construction of a metagenic weapon, while Edward Jellico (Ronny Cox) is assigned to the Enterprise as its new captain. Ultimately, Picard is captured as part of a Cardassian plot to lure him into captivity.

ALTMAN (***1/2): Ron Moore delivers another powerhouse installment in which he shakes up the command hierarchy, resulting in some of the most exciting interpersonal conflict aboard the *Enterprise* since Spock relieved Matt Decker in "The Doomsday Machine." Ronny Cox turns in a marvelous performance as the hyperkinetic Jellico, who takes an immediate disliking to Riker and inspires loathing among most of the *Enterprise* crew. Equally impressive is some ambitious action/adventure plotting on Celtris III, where Picard leads Worf and Dr. Crusher into a Cardassian trap. Ultimately, what makes "Chain of Command" so rewarding are the subtle touches, including the change-of-command ceremony and Jellico's admonition to Riker, "Get that damn fish out of my ready room."

GROSS (***): For those of you who think that Picard is a bit of a stern taskmaster, check out Captain Edward Jellico. If this guy smiled, his face might crack. Guest star Ronny Cox certainly shakes things up as the visiting commander of the *Enterprise*, and his interactions with various crew members (from disliking Riker's attitude as first officer to criticizing Troi's uniform) are dynamite. The espionage mission of Picard, Worf and Crusher is well done, but the best is yet to come.

CHAIN OF COMMAND, PART II

(TNG)
Original Airdate 12/14/92
Written by Frank Abatemarco
Directed by Les Landau

Picard is brutally tortured by a Cardassian inquisitor, Gul Madred (David Warner), who attempts to obtain the Federation's defense strategy against a Cardassian takeover of a disputed quadrant. On the Enterprise, *Captain Jellico (Ronny Cox) attempts to stop the invasion by recruiting Riker to mine the hulls of the Cardassian warships.*

ALTMAN (***1/2): An uncredited Jeri Taylor deserves the real kudos for this exceptionally ambitious off-concept show, in which Patrick Stewart gives a magnificent and gutsy performance as he slowly caves in under the pain of Cardassian torture. Although Gul Madred (David Warner) is a little too easy to provoke in the end, a potentially impotent story line in Taylor's capable hands proves extremely intense. Less satisfying, primarily due to budget overages, is the resolution of the Cardassian/Federation standoff, in which most of the brinkmanship takes place off camera. Ronny Cox continues to be impressive in a story line that could have easily lent itself to a whole other episode exploring the dynamics of his relationship with the *Enterprise* crew. The crosscutting between the *Enterprise* and Picard also dilutes the power of Picard's physical and psychological abuse, relieving the pressure of the Cardassians' prolonged verbal and mental assault.

GROSS (****): The *Trek* exception: the second part of a two-part episode that's actually more fully realized than its predecessor. The fact that Patrick Stewart did not even get an Emmy nomination for his performance is incomprehensible. In one of the actor's best efforts, his sequences with David Warner's Gul Madred are sheer magic. During the torture scenes, the good captain is at both his most vulnerable and his strongest, initially refusing to give in to the demands of his keeper, but doing so ever so slightly when Gul Madred continues to move the line in the sand. Picard conveys the sense that he's always a moment away from handing himself over emotionally, but he pulls back at the last second. Writers Frank Abatemarco and Jeri Taylor and director Les Landau deserve kudos for helping to present a *Trek* that is a little bit deeper and richer than most.

CHANGELING, THE

(TOS)
Original Airdate 9/29/67
Written by John Meredyth Lucas
Directed by Marc Daniels

The Enterprise *transports a deadly probe on board. The probe, Nomad (voice of Vic Perrin), believes that Captain Kirk is actually its creator, Jackson Roykirk. In a Vulcan mind-meld, Spock learns that the machine was an Earth probe that was lost in space centuries earlier, has combined with another alien probe, Tan Ru, and now seeks to sterilize and destroy all things impure.*

ALTMAN (***1/2): Writer John Meredyth Lucas should get royalties from the video sales of *Star Trek: The Motion Picture,* a movie that literally rips off his teleplay for "The Changeling" without giving it any new life. The conceit that Nomad believes Kirk is his creator is cleverly executed, and Nomad, effectively visualized as a floating robot, proves to be a worthy antagonist for the *Enterprise* crew. It may once again fall to Kirk to talk another computer to death, but it works a lot better than it did with Landru.

GROSS (***): Nomad makes quite a formidable opponent for Kirk, and the power that this little metallic cylinder has at its disposal is impressive. The real strength of the episode comes from William Shatner's Kirk, who has to try to manipulate the mechanical device to his own way of thinking and away from its more destructive directives. When things don't go his way, Kirk pulls the ace from his sleeve: using verbal logic to destroy that which can withstand any energy weapon. Add this to similar efforts in "What Are Little Girls Made Of?," "The Return of the Archons," "I, Mudd" and, later, "The Ultimate Computer," and you have an impressive track record. There are a couple of annoyances. First, Scotty is killed by Nomad and then resurrected (similar to McCoy in "Shore Leave"). More ridiculously, Uhura's memory is wiped clean by the device, but by episode's end, her reeducation has

already reached the junior high school level. Things are good in the twenty-third century, but they aren't *that* good.

CHARLIE X
(TOS)
Original Airdate 9/15/66
Written by D. C. Fontana
Story by Gene Roddenberry
Directed by Lawrence Dobkin

Shortly after the captain of the Antares *drops adolescent Charlie Evans (Robert Walker, Jr.) off on the* Enterprise, *the* Antares *is mysteriously destroyed. Following other unexplained events, the blame falls on Charlie, who then reveals his incredible telekinetic abilities to alter matter and cause people to vanish, which he learned from the Thalasians.*

ALTMAN (**1/2): In a story reminiscent of *The Twilight Zone*'s "It's a Good Life," "Charlie X" boasts moments of surreal horror, as Charlie is let loose on board the *Enterprise,* torturing its crew with his seemingly unstoppable powers. Ultimately, it's a simplistic story about immaturity, but some of Kirk's admonitions about "the birds and the bees" are enough to make any viewer cringe. Walker is good in the role of the hormone-driven youth, and it's certainly Grace Lee Whitney's best chance to shine as Yeoman Rand.

GROSS (***): Seeing Kirk in a mentor/student, father/son relationship with Charlie is worth the price of admission. The real force here is guest star Robert Walker, Jr. (who bears a startling resemblance to his father, costar of Hitchcock's *Strangers on a Train*), whose Charlie is concurrently naive and all-threatening, making crewmen disappear and Uhura lose her voice and turning others into lizards. Probably the most unsettling moment in *Star Trek* history occurs when Charlie describes his feelings to Rand, saying that when he's with her, he feels hungry all over. He moves in closer, more threateningly, and we cut away, leaving the following sequence to the imagination.

CHASE, THE

(TNG)
Original Airdate 4/26/93
Teleplay by Joe Menosky
Story by Ronald D. Moore and Joe Menosky
Directed by Jonathan Frakes

When a mentor of Picard's is killed, the captain pursues a trail of DNA fragments that leads the ship to a planet that has already attracted feuding Cardassians, Klingons and Romulans, all in search of the secret encoded in the DNA fragments.

ALTMAN (***): "The Chase" is an utterly delightful homage to Classic *Trek*, capturing the larger-than-life flavor and sometimes hokey messages of cosmic significance that typified the voyages of the original starship *Enterprise*. Who can forget "Arena" and "Errand of Mercy," to which "The Chase" owes a thematic debt, in which the Organians chastise the Klingons and the Federation for their warring nature, pointing out they will sometime in the future

become fast friends? It's odd that "The Chase" becomes such a romp, because the early scenes between Picard and Norman Lloyd (as the captain's former mentor, Dr. Galen) are among the most dramatically charged and effective character drama the show has ever done. Stewart is particularly good in the episode's first several acts, as is ever-reliable film and TV veteran Norman Lloyd. Picard's stinging rebukes to Riker and Troi as he pursues his obsession with solving the mystery of Galen's murder are memorably venomous.

GROSS (***1/2): One of the criticisms Gene Roddenberry received during the run of the original *Star Trek* was how many Earth-like planets and humanoids the *Enterprise* encountered. "The Chase," which is one of those episodes that wonderfully epitomize Roddenberry's philosophy concerning the future, offers a logical explanation: Aliens seeded many worlds, thus genetically relating such divergent species as Earthlings, Klingons, Romulans and Cardassians. The refusal of the Klingon and Cardassian representatives to accept this as fact is amusing, and it's thought provoking to see the Romulan commander share a more philosophical discussion with Picard. This episode has a wonderful premise that is beautifully executed by director Jonathan Frakes. A nice turn by *St. Elsewhere*'s Norman Lloyd as Picard's former mentor, Professor Galen.

CHILD, THE

(TNG)
Original Airdate 11/19/88
Written by Jaron Summers, Jon Povill and
Maurice Hurley
Directed by Rob Bowman

*Deanna Troi is impregnated by an alien presence
and comes to term with the child in a matter of
days. She gives birth to what appears to be a normal child, who begins aging rapidly and inadvertently affects the growth of a deadly organism
being held in the cargo bay.*

ALTMAN (*1/2): Despite Bowman's stylish opening crane shot,
"The Child" doesn't justify its impressive buildup. Its tired origins
show through like a sore thumb (it
was written for the aborted *Trek*
TV revival in the late 1970s), and
the second-season addition of
Katherine Pulaski as the ship's doctor is a genuine misstep, as she
chides Data as though she was
some long-lost relative of Dr. Mc-
Coy. Unlike the intellectually superior Spock, who could rebuke
McCoy with as little as a raised
eyebrow that revealed a devilish
Vulcan smirk, Pulaski's attacks on
Data are equivalent to a parent haranguing an innocent child. As for
Troi's child, what's the point of
Troi giving birth if we know the
child will be gone by the end of
the show? It *is* episodic television,
after all.

GROSS (**): A pair of story lines
that really don't come together
that effectively. In addition, we're
never given an explanation for
why this alien has impregnated
Troi or what the show is really
about. In its original conception as

a script for the *Star Trek Phase II*
series of the 1970s, *Enterprise*
navigator Lieutenant Ilia served
as the alien's first womb and the
Enterprise as its second. As such,
the story was more effective. One
positive aspect of the *Next Generation* version is a wonderful debate
over whether the child should be
born, with Troi stating categori-
cally that she will indeed give
birth. Very few television series
in 1988 would have been able to
pull off such a debate. And whose
idea was it to jettison Gates
McFadden for Diana Muldaur's
McCoy wanna-be, Dr. Pulaski?
Bad move.

CIRCLE, THE

(DS9)
Original Airdate 10/4/93
Written by Peter Allan Fields
Directed by Corey Allen

*The political manipulation begun in "The Home-
coming" continues as Minister Jaro (Frank Langella) has Kira reassigned to Bajor. The influence of
the Bajoran isolationist cult, the Circle, begins to
grow, leading Starfleet to order Sisko to evacuate
Deep Space Nine.*

ALTMAN (****): The episode begins with a riotously funny
opener, which compares favorably
to some of the classic screwball
comedies of the 1940s, as a departing Kira is visited and repeatedly
interrupted by all her friends, who
come to bid her adieu. Both witty
and foreboding, "The Circle" is
one of *DS9*'s finest hours. Kira's
strange and sexy encounter with a
Bajoran orb is executed with fi-

nesse, and the political jockeying for power on Bajor is riveting, spearheaded by two powerful performances by Louise Fletcher as Vedek Winn and an uncredited Frank Langella as Minister Jaro (apparently channeling the spirit of Bob Dole).

GROSS (***1/2): The politics thicken! As Li Nalas attempts to assume his new position on DS9, the political intrigue between Vedek Winn and Jaro intensifies. At the same time, the episode carries through on some themes established in the first-season finale, "In the Hands of the Prophets" (particularly the notion of a "Bajor for Bajorans"). There are some real emotions here, as Nana Visitor effectively brings forth Kira's feelings about adjusting to what seems to be a whole new life.

CITY ON THE EDGE OF FOREVER

(TOS)
Original Airdate 4/6/67
Written by Harlan Ellison
Directed by Joseph Pevney

The Enterprise *is studying strange time disturbances when McCoy accidentally injects himself with an overdose of cordrazine, sending him into a psychotic rage and leading him to the center of the time disturbances, the Guardian of Forever, which he passes through and in so doing changes history. In an attempt to set right what he has done, Kirk and Spock return to the year 1930 and encounter the focal point in time: social worker Edith Keeler (Joan Collins).*

ALTMAN (****): The most beloved episode in *Star Trek* history warrants every bit of its well-documented reputation. It is a brilliantly inventive story by legendary sci-fi author Harlan Ellison (rewritten by D. C. Fontana and Gene L. Coon), which boasts some of the most moving character drama the series has ever had. Kirk's dilemma, in which he must allow history to go unchanged at the expense of the woman he loves, is truly tragic, and his pained expression as he stops McCoy from changing history is a testament to the brilliance of William Shatner's acting.

GROSS (**** — and then some): It is so difficult for a one-hour drama to make you believe that one of its leads has fallen in love, but this episode manages to do so by bringing Kirk and Edith Keeler, a visionary of the twentieth century, together. Even after thirty years and countless voyages, this remains the best *Trek* adventure ever filmed. Beyond the strength of the romantic relationship, there's the creative ingenuity of the Guardian itself, as well as the humor and character interaction between Kirk and Spock, who must adapt to a relatively more barbaric time. The ending of the episode is extremely moving, from Kirk's emotional pain at allowing Edith to die to McCoy's demand, "Do you know what you just did, Jim?" and Spock's all-knowing reply, "He knows, Doctor. He knows." When the trio returns through the Guardian and Kirk says, "Let's get the hell out of here," I can't agree with him more. Incredible television.

CIVIL DEFENSE

(DS9)
Original Airdate 11/12/94
Written by Mike Krohn
Directed by Reza Badiyi

An automated Cardassian security system is accidentally activated, putting the station in a self-destruct mode that seems impossible to stop. Gul Dukat arrives, gloating over the situation, until he finds himself trapped as well and must work with Sisko to stop DS9 from being destroyed.

ALTMAN (***): An ingenious premise is well realized, particularly in light of the strong character moments between Sisko, Dukat and Garak. It's a chance to see more of the station than ever before, and despite the episode's similarities to *TNG*'s "Disaster," it works slightly better, thanks to the moments of conflict between the feuding characters and its sparse technobabble.

GROSS (***): Once again, *DS9* proves that it can take a premise that works only moderately well in one of its sister series and make it work like gangbusters. The idea of an accidentally activated booby trap is brilliant, particularly the fact that every time a solution is put into action, a new wrinkle develops. Marc Alaimo's Gul Dukat is just *so* arrogant when he first appears, ready to let everyone die, until he himself becomes a potential victim. It's great watching him argue with video images of himself from years past. A surprisingly suspenseful episode.

CLOUD, THE

(VOY)
Original Airdate 2/13/95
Teleplay by Tom Szollosi and Michael Piller
Story by Brannon Braga
Directed by David Livingston

The Voyager *inadvertently injures an alien life-form that the crew mistakes for a nebula, and they are intent on repairing the damage they have caused.*

ALTMAN (***): Although the plot is nothing new — a sort of high-concept hybrid of "The Immunity Syndrome" and "Galaxy's Child" — it sets the stage for one of *Voyager*'s most agreeable installments. What helps distinguish the show from its predecessors in the *Trek* universe is its acerbic, sarcastic and often self-reflexive wit. Rather than deal with its techno-babble-ridden MacGuffin with earnest and dour conversation (à la *TNG*), Neelix and the doctor echo the audience's sentiments when they poke fun at the fact that *Voyager* consistently finds itself in outrageously hokey situations involving spatial anomalies. "These people are natural-born idiots if you ask me," Neelix remarks. Unfortunately, the episode does make one giant and offensive misstep by giving apparent credence to Chakotay's mystical mumbo jumbo involving a spirit-animal guide.

GROSS (***): Janeway's reaction to injuring this being and her commitment to doing something about it would have made Picard proud and certainly continues the tradition of Gene Roddenberry's vision for the future. Neelix's comments are hysterical, and one almost expects him to look right at the camera and wink. A strong early episode for the series.

CLOUD MINDERS, THE

(TOS)
Original Airdate 2/28/69
Written by Margaret Armen
Story by David Gerrold and Oliver Crawford
Directed by Jud Taylor

The Enterprise *arrives at Ardana to obtain a zienite consignment to cure a plague on Merak II. They find a divided race, with the elite living in a city in the clouds and the Troglytes on the planet's surface, their mining duties having led them to madness.*

ALTMAN (**): Despite its clever depiction of a cloud city (years before George Lucas had dreamed of Bespin) and some interesting production design, "The Cloud Minders" is a pretty goofy episode that clunkily addresses the issue of socioeconomic division. In one of its most ludicrous scenes (often cut from syndication), Spock meditates on the nature of the conflict between the sky and mine dwellers, as well as the beauty of the "lovely Draxine." It's a hoot. Acting teacher Jeff Corey turns in a solid performance as Stratos's leader, who is thrust into a fistfight with Captain Kirk.

GROSS (*1/2): What could have been a fascinating exploration of the division between those who have and those who have not degenerates into a shouting match between Kirk and Stratos's leader, culminating in an over-the-top

Kirk holding a phaser on the man in the mines, demanding, "I said dig!" The solution — more or less to get the miners gas masks for protection — ignores the central issue that the episode is purportedly addressing, offering little in the way of a solution.

CLUES

(TNG)
Original Airdate 2/11/91
Teleplay by Bruce D. Arthurs and Joe Menosky
Story by Bruce D. Arthurs
Directed by Les Landau

The crew of the Enterprise *slowly begins to discover that they have lost twenty-four hours since encountering a mysterious wormhole in space, and Data begins to exhibit suspicious signs pointing to a cover-up. Following the clues, Picard learns that the* Enterprise *crew's memories were erased by a xenophobic race intent on preserving their solitude. When the ship returns, the aliens threaten to destroy the* Enterprise *unless the crew can assure them of success in erasing all knowledge of their existence.*

ALTMAN (**): Landau's stylized direction helps a pedestrian teleplay in which the opening Dixon Hill adventure, where Guinan and Picard embark on a new mystery in the holodeck, proves far more fascinating than the story that follows. I find it hard to believe that Picard would consent to having the memories of the crew erased, although some of the intricacies of Data's tightly plotted conspiracy do prove interesting.

GROSS (***): An episode that deserves applause for its ingenuity, as the crew of the *Enterprise* valiantly attempts to unravel the mystery of a missing day in their lives. Things unfold gradually, with each new clue plunging Picard and the other main characters into a real-life Dixon Hill adventure, until all is revealed and history essentially repeats itself. A good conspiracy episode that would make Oliver Stone proud.

CODE OF HONOR
(TNG)
Original Airdate 10/19/87
Written by Katharyn Powers and Michael Baron
Directed by Russ Mayberry

The Enterprise *is in the midst of negotiating an invaluable vaccine from the people of Ligon II, when the world's leader, Lutan (Jessie Lawrence Ferguson), kidnaps Tasha Yar and decides that he wants to keep her as his concubine. In response, Lutan's wife, Yareena (Karole Selmon), challenges her to a battle to the death.*

ALTMAN (**): "Code of Honor" is not only one of *TNG*'s most racist episodes, casting all African-Americans in the role of Ligon II's tribelike race, but it also is among its most derivative, replaying many of the same beats as the original series' "Amok Time." "Code of Honor" vividly illustrates *TNG*'s first-season propensity for cannibalizing old *Trek* plots. Despite the episode's many failings, the fisticuffs are well done, and it's one of the few episodes that actually gives Tasha Yar something to do.

GROSS (*1/2): This is probably the most racist episode of *Star Trek* ever produced, and the only one

that could be perceived as insulting to African-Americans. Despite this, an interesting culture is presented, and the battle to the death between Tasha Yar and Ligon's Yareena is effective. At this early stage of *TNG*'s run, it's obvious that the show's creators are still searching for a direction, trying to establish their own identity while not straying too far from the original *Trek*. This is particularly noticeable in the aforementioned battle, which does indeed bear some striking similarities to the Spock/Kirk duel in "Amok Time."

COLD FIRE
(VOY)
Original Airdate 11/13/95
Teleplay by Brannon Braga
Story by Anthony Williams
Directed by Cliff Bole

The Voyager *discovers the female Caretaker and comes to learn that she has an ax to grind with Janeway, believing that the crew is responsible for her mate's death. She exploits an expatriate Ocampa colony to assist in her revenge.*

ALTMAN (*1/2): The problem with "Cold Fire" is that although it has a potentially captivating premise, the story is executed with absolutely no finesse. Quite simply, the episode isn't about anything. The show meanders endlessly, and quite pointlessly, until it culminates in some gory pyrotechnics, which are among its most original elements. The big problem here is Brannon Braga's continuing efforts to turn *Trek* into something it's not. He continues to try to make the series weird for weirdness' sake, and such homages as calling the Caretaker Suspiria and Gary Graham's telekinetic Ocampa Tanis only exacerbate the cheesy, by-the-numbers derivativeness of his work. Braga is a good writer, but he's trying to fit a square peg into a round hole.

GROSS (*1/2): This episode features a pair of story lines that are supposedly connected but really have little to do with each other. Gary Graham's (star of TV's *Alien Nation*) Tanis reaching out to teach Kes how to develop her powers could have been an episode in itself, as could a story dealing with the female Caretaker. The problem with the latter is that it's all buildup and no payoff. Janeway manages — as unlikely as it may seem — to corner the Caretaker but refuses to injure it. "Even after all I have done to you and your ship?" muses the Caretaker, who vanishes without another word. Oh, I get it. Janeway shows mercy, so she must be advanced. Good lesson. Learned it myself from Captain Kirk thirty years ago in "Arena." See also "Caretaker."

COLLABORATOR, THE

(DS9)
Original Airdate 5/23/94
Teleplay by Gary Holland, Ira Steven Behr and Robert Hewitt Wolfe
Story by Gary Holland
Directed by Cliff Bole

Vedeks Winn and Bareil run against each other in the Bajoran election that will determine who will become the Kai of Bajor. Winn obtains information indicating that Bareil may have revealed the location of Bajoran rebels to the Cardassians, leading to the rebels' deaths during the occupation.

ALTMAN (**1/2): The developing relationship between Vedek Bareil and Kira is one of the show's most interesting subplots. Although the slowly unraveling conspiracy is not among *Trek*'s most intricate mysteries, Vedek Winn's ascent to Kai helps contribute to the fascinating Bajoran political tapestry of the series, with the revelation that it was actually Kai Opaka who was responsible for revealing the rebels' location acting as a satisfying capper.

GROSS (***): From its first episode, *DS9* has been more about developing relationships than *TNG* was, and that point is brought home in "The Collaborator," as Kira must deal with the truth of her lover, Bareil. Some real emotions are at work here, all topped off with those tremendous sequences between Sisko and Vedek Winn in which there is so much more going on than what is being said. See also "Emissary," "Battle Lines," "In the Hands of the Prophets," "The Homecoming," "The Circle" and "The Siege."

COMING OF AGE

(TNG)
Original Airdate 3/12/88
Written by Sandy Fries
Directed by Michael Vejar

Wesley Crusher attempts to gain entrance to the Starfleet Academy by undergoing a series of written, psychological and behavioral examinations.

Meanwhile, Picard is offered a position as head of the Academy, while Admiral Quinn (Ward Costello) and his assistant Remmick (Robert Schenkkan) begin interrogating crew members to investigate a conspiracy within the Federation.

ALTMAN (**): Wesley Crusher's attempt to enter the Starfleet Academy and an investigation into Picard's competence to captain the *Enterprise* are both interesting story lines that don't really belong in the same episode. Although the show provides a prelude to "Conspiracy" (several episodes later), Crusher's overly melodramatic dilemma in attempting to gain entrance to the Academy offers few surprises, since the audience knows that he's not going anywhere — but wishes he would.

GROSS (***): Imagine, A, B and C stories that all work, although the idea of Picard being offered the position of head of the Starfleet Academy is the weakest link, primarily because everyone knows the answer before the question is asked. With all the references to the Academy that have been made in the various series, it's finally nice to see just what goes on there. Nicer still is that Crusher is treated like an adult instead of an obnoxious kid. The conspiracy theory and resulting interrogation of *Enterprise* personnel is great, with director Michael Vejar using some effective film tricks to segue from one person to the next. There are also some references to previous episodes, which adds to an overall sense of continuity. See also "Conspiracy" and "Final Mission."

CONSCIENCE OF THE KING, THE
(TOS)
Original Airdate 12/8/66
Written by Barry Trivers
Directed by Gerd Oswald

Anton Karidian (Arnold Moss), the head of a traveling Shakespearean troupe, is suspected of being Kodos the Executioner, the former governor of Tarsus IV who masterminded the deaths of millions during a famine. Kirk has agreed to provide transportation for the troupe to unearth the truth about Karidian.

ALTMAN (***): An engrossing episode with some strong performances by guest stars Arnold Moss and Barbara Anderson as Lenore Karidian, his vengeful daughter, who will do anything to protect his secret. There are some nice flourishes, including a Muzak version of the main *Trek* theme during a dinner party. Some of the romantic moments as Kirk puts the moves on Lenore, while also suspecting that her father is a murderer, are classic — particularly an exchange filled with racy double entendres in the ship's observation bay.

GROSS (***): Anyone who believes that Shakespeare wasn't discovered on *Star Trek* until Picard took command of the *Enterprise* should take a look at this episode, which has so many tragic elements that Shakespeare himself would be impressed. William Shatner is wonderfully restrained as Kirk, allowing the mystery of Karidian/Kodos to unfold slowly. Perhaps most intriguing is the way that Arnold Moss and director Gerd Oswald are able to make us feel as though we've been transported back to Tarsus IV and are reliving the memories of what happened there — without showing us a single frame of film to reinforce it. Truly an underappreciated episode that seldom makes anyone's "best of *Trek*" list.

CONSPIRACY

(TNG)
Original Airdate 5/7/88
Written by Tracy Torme
Story by Robert Sabaroff
Directed by Cliff Bole

The conspiracy hinted at in "Coming of Age" comes to fruition when Picard is mysteriously summoned by several other starship captains and is informed of a plot to infiltrate and subvert Starfleet, prompting the Enterprise *to proceed to Earth and Starfleet headquarters to investigate.*

ALTMAN (***): A graphically violent episode, which is superlative in its first few acts, as Picard is mysteriously summoned by his comrades and informed of the unfolding conspiracy. It doesn't get any better than this; it's truly chilling. The writing and characterizations are dead-on. But once the *Enterprise* arrives on Earth, the tightly knit plot begins to unravel, turning this paranoid *Invasion of the Body Snatchers* wanna-be into a shoot-'em-up with *Scanners*-like exploding heads. The complex story should have been at least a two-part episode, as it suffers from having too much crammed into its overstuffed coda. *DS9* managed to handle a similar story line far more

skillfully with its Dominion changeling arc years later.

GROSS (***1/2): Picking up thematic threads from "Coming of Age," this episode is a trip to the dark side of the twenty-fourth century, and it's a more than welcome journey. Tracy Torme brings *TNG* places it hasn't gone before, exploring a sense of paranoia that probably has more in common with *The Thing* and *Invasion of the Body Snatchers* than Gene Roddenberry's utopian view of the twenty-third century. Some pretty impressive effects, and some cheesy ones as well, highlight an episode whose ending is more unsettling than most in the *Trek* universe, implying that the threat is still out there.

CONTAGION

(TNG)
Original Airdate 3/18/89
Written by Steve Gerber and Beth Woods
Directed by Joseph Scanlan

A Federation ship, the Yamato, *is destroyed by a deadly computer virus that soon infects the* Enterprise *while also threatening a Romulan warbird. The clue to saving the ship lies on the legendary planet Iconia, where Picard and Data beam down in hopes of unraveling the superior technology of a long-dormant computer network of an ancient civilization.*

ALTMAN (***): Though thoroughly unintended, "Contagion" kicks off a surreal trilogy whose tone is atypical of the *TNG* series as a whole, capturing the strange mystery of space better than virtually any other episode of the new

Trek. It's a technically proficient story, with the Romulans serving as ancillary characters. The episode bears a slight resemblance to "The Last Outpost." The ending is rushed as usual, but the decidedly fatalistic tone and the intriguing design of the Iconian computer facility are nice changes of pace for the series.

GROSS (***): A great deal of mystery and some genuine suspense highlight this episode, which does bear some similarity to "The Last Outpost" and the original show's "All Our Yesterdays." Most enjoyable is the fact that this particular mystery unfolds gradually, and the audience has to unravel the clues along with the *Enterprise* crew, rather than being light-years ahead of them. The Romulan threat intensifies, paving the way for future episodes.

CONUNDRUM

(TNG)
Original Airdate 2/17/92
Teleplay by Barry M. Schkolnick and Joe Menosky
Story by Paul Schiffer
Directed by Les Landau

After being scanned by an unidentified ship, the crew members of the Enterprise *sustain a complete memory loss and are led to believe that they are at war with the Lysians, who they believe are responsible for causing their amnesia. They're unaware that they are being manipulated by the ship's executive officer, Keiran MacDuff (Erich Anderson).*

ALTMAN (***): A vast improvement over the previous season's "Clues," in which the crew is given amnesia to cover up the existence of a xenophobic alien race. What makes "Conundrum" so much better is that it combines great character drama and humor with a well-conceived sci-fi action/adventure plot. Having Worf believe that he is captain of the ship and taking command while a deferential Picard stands by is hysterical, as are the romantic sparks between Ensign Ro and Riker, while a jealous Troi keeps an eye on the lovebirds. The crew's final confrontation, once their memories are restored in sick bay, is a typical *Trek* coda, laced with humor and sarcasm. Director Les Landau mirrors the characters' uneasiness with an appropriately unsteady look, improving on the fine work he turned in with "Clues."

GROSS (***): My first impression was that we already saw this story in "Clues," but this episode is an enjoyable improvement. It's a lot of fun to see Worf in a command position — however briefly — and Picard's gradual shift back to the center seat. Additionally, without their memories, the crew's inhibitions are lowered, resulting in some sparks between Riker and Ro. The last ten minutes or so are terrific, with the morbidly fascinating view of *Enterprise*'s power unleashed against the inferior Lysian ships and Picard's gradual conclusion that this mission is morally wrong. Director Les Landau maintains a fair amount of suspense and mystery, and his cameras constantly being in flux conveys the disorientation of the crew. One question, though: If MacDuff was going to go through all the trouble of altering the computer databank anyway, why didn't he make himself captain so that no one would question his actions?

CORBOMITE MANEUVER, THE

(TOS)
Original Airdate 11/10/66
Written by Jerry Sohl
Directed by Joseph Sargent

The Enterprise *destroys a floating space buoy and is captured by an enormous space vessel, the Fesarius, which threatens it with destruction. As all attempts at escape fail, Kirk develops an ingenious plan to trick his opponent using the "Corbomite" bluff.*

ALTMAN (***1/2): The show that served as the template for many *Trek* yarns to come combines mystery, solar exploration, character, weird aliens and Kirk bluffing his way out of destruction. With brilliantly inventive visuals, including the *Fesarius,* which dwarfs the *Enterprise,* and the finale, in which a young Clint Howard plays Balok, who hides behind a more menacing facade, "The Corbomite Maneuver" is vintage *Star Trek* and compelling entertainment. Anthony Hall as Bailey stars as the audience's surrogate, and we share his sense of wonder, curiosity and trepidation as he confronts the alien ship.

GROSS (****): An episode that could just as easily have been the pilot for the series. Writer Jerry Sohl and director Joseph Sargent perfectly encapsulate Roddenberry's vision of tomorrow, while managing to explore a variety of issues. Check out some interesting tidbits, among them Spock shouting around the bridge (a habit he would finally break after this show) and, when Kirk criticizes the information he's been given, Spock actually starting to apologize. A wonderful, vintage episode.

COST OF LIVING

(TNG)
Original Airdate 4/20/92
Written by Peter Allan Fields
Directed by Winrich Kolbe

After destroying a deadly asteroid, the Enterprise *crew is unaware that a cloud of strange particles has attached itself to the ship's hull. Meanwhile, Troi's mother, Lwaxana, comes aboard, announcing her plans to wed Campio (Tony Jay), a man she's never met. She strikes up a friendship with Worf's son, Alexander (Brian Bonsall).*

ALTMAN (**): A wildly schizophrenic episode with a wonderful A story involving Lwaxana Troi, giving Majel Barrett some of the best writing she's ever had on the show. The B story, involving a threatening alien parasite, is completely unnecessary. It's an insipid jeopardy plot in which there's no sense of jeopardy. (We know the ship isn't going to blow up, so who cares?) Indeed, *TNG*'s propensity to mix character and jeopardy stories is one of its most notable failings. Fortunately, Peter Allan Fields's dialogue crackles with wit, intelligence and insight, but Lwaxana's marriage to Campio is given short shrift due to the B story about killer Jell-O destroying the

Enterprise. The ending, in which the lone Data pilots the ship into a meteor belt just in time to save the asphyxiating crew, is a joke.

GROSS (***): Like the fourth season's "Half a Life," "Cost of Living" has a touching Lwaxana Troi story line that allows the character to do her shtick without being as annoying as she was in her first few appearances. In fact, there's a certain sadness to the character, which is ultimately rectified by her relationship with Alexander. The episode is still a little too much like a soap opera for my taste, but the performances and the script by Peter Allan Fields make it effective. Forget the "ship in jeopardy" subplot; it doesn't offer anything worth talking about.

COUNTER-CLOCK INCIDENT, THE

(TAS)
Original Airdate 10/12/74
Written by John Culver
Directed by Bill Reed

The Enterprise's *first captain, Robert April, is being transported to his retirement ceremony when the ship is accidentally plunged into a nova in which everything works in a counterclockwise fashion. As a result, the people aboard the ship begin to grow younger. With the crew members reduced to children, April, now a thirty-year-old man, retakes command and must bring the* Enterprise *to safety before it's too late.*

ALTMAN (***): Though based on a seemingly ludicrous premise, "The Counter-Clock Incident" works far

better than it has a right to, thanks to its message that the elderly have a lot to teach us and can be productive members of society. This final voyage of the Saturday morning series features the same wit and intelligence that characterized the animated missions throughout its two-year run.

GROSS (***): The episode's positive message overshadows any story flaws. Interestingly, the notion of a society aging backward would become the subject of the "Innocence" episode of *Voyager.* For those interested in such things, Robert April was the captain character Gene Roddenberry conceived of when he wrote his first bible for *Star Trek.* See also "The Naked Time" and "Innocence."

COURT MARTIAL

(TOS)
Original Airdate 2/2/67
Written by Don M. Mankiewicz and Stephen W. Carabatsos
Directed by Marc Daniels

A computer malfunction implicates Kirk in the death of crewman Ben Finney (Richard Webb), and he is forced to stand trial for negligence. It is up to Spock and Kirk's lawyer, the formidable Samuel Cogley (Elisha Cook, Jr.), to prove his innocence and unveil the truth about Finney.

ALTMAN (**1/2): Although actor Elisha Cook, Jr. (*The Big Sleep*) is a welcome presence as the delightful Samuel Cogley, attorney-at-law, "Court Martial" strains one's credulity at times, as Finney engineers his own death, eventually finding himself in a situation where the entire crew has beamed off board and he can potentially destroy the ship single-handedly. Fortunately, the heated exchanges between Kirk and Finney, as well as Finney's daughter and a former paramour, litigator Areel Shaw (Joan Marshall), play far better, as does Cogley's passionate defense of books as a lost art form in the twenty-third century.

GROSS (**): An episode that misfires for a few reasons. First off, no one believes that Kirk would make as careless an error as he's accused of. Second, it's hard to believe that someone could manipulate the captain's log to present the false image that we're seeing. Third, the tracking down of Finney is just plain silly.

CROSSFIRE

(DS9)
Original Airdate 1/29/96
Written by Rene Echevarria
Directed by Les Landau

An intimate character drama, which only DS9 could do. First Minister Shakaar (Duncan Regehr) visits the station and kindles a romance with Kira, inflaming Odo's jealousy.

ALTMAN (***): Who can't relate to this universal story? It's hard not to like the first minister, played by Duncan Regehr, despite our natural sympathies with Odo over his plight. The show has one forced action scene, but it's the muted character drama that provides the real heat here. Beautifully written by Rene Echevarria and filled with strong performances throughout, particularly from *DS9*'s unsung hero, Rene Auberjonois, "Crossfire" examines several important character dynamics — including Odo/Worf, Quark/Odo and the Kira love triangle — better than virtually any other episode. Easily making up for the previous season's dreadful "Heart of Stone," this is mature, adult storytelling at its best.

GROSS (****): Character, character, character. Get the point? From beginning to end, "Crossfire" is a bottle show devoted to character, from a humorous precredit sequence in which we see Odo purposely going out of his way to annoy Quark by shape-shifting during the night in his quarters (which happen to lie right over the Ferengi) to Odo and Worf commiserating about unwanted guests, with Odo pointing out that you should never make such a visitor feel welcome. "Of course," says Worf, "otherwise they will come and see you again." Very funny stuff. The story takes a more serious and sadder turn when dealing with Odo's unrequited love for Kira, which monopolizes the rest of the episode. This sequence has some surprising, and touching, moments of friendship between Odo and Quark. Just another example of why *DS9* is the best *Trek* series since the original. See also "Shakaar."

CROSSOVER

(DS9)
Original Airdate 5/16/94
Written by Michael Piller
Directed by David Livingston

While traveling through the wormhole, Kira and Bashir find themselves in a parallel universe, where the Cardassians and Klingons have joined forces to dominate the human Terrans. Bashir is incarcerated under the Mirror Odo, while Kira kindles an uneasy alliance with her mirror self, the intendant running the duplicate Deep Space Nine.

ALTMAN (**): "Crossover" marks a most welcome return to the "Mirror, Mirror" universe, long thought to be only the purview of fanzine scribes and comic book writers. Unfortunately, this first return visit is a major disappointment, laying blame on Captain Kirk for the sad state of affairs for the humans in the Mirror universe. Despite being a fine writer, Michael Piller has no affinity for the original *Star Trek* milieu, and it shows. Director David Livingston creates a great look for the alternate DS9 universe, but the quality that made the original "Mirror, Mirror" great eludes the writers. "Mirror, Mirror" was about opposites, not shades of gray, and by trying to bring a degree of subtlety to both the characters and the story, these writers miss the point of the original episode (as well as its great dialogue and music). What does work here is Nana Visitor, who is terrific as Kira and her doppelgänger, a black leather–clad dominatrix-like thug. The intriguing lesbian subtext between the two Kiras is a delightfully offbeat

notion that works splendidly. Avery Brooks also growls appropriately as his doppelgänger.

GROSS (***): Though lacking the power of the original series' "Mirror, Mirror," "Crossover" is an effective follow-up. I disagree with the notion of blaming Kirk for the fall of the Empire/Federation in the alternate universe, but this does serve as an effective example of why the Prime Directive exists in the first place. The variations on the regular characters are interesting, as is the view of life on the alternate DS9, which probably represents what life on "our" station was like under Cardassian rule. Some of the scenes between the two Kiras are hot and will no doubt serve as the basis for a fanzine or two.

DAGGER OF THE MIND

(TOS)
Original Airdate 11/3/66
Written by Shimon Wincelberg
Directed by Vincent McEveety

While delivering supplies to the penal colony Tantalus Five, Kirk discovers that Dr. Tristan Adams (James Gregory) is using a revolutionary neural neutralizer to control and manipulate his patients, which he then turns on the captain himself.

ALTMAN (***): *The Manchurian Candidate*'s James Gregory is sufficiently sinister as Dr. Adams, who puts his invention to evil use. Morgan Woodward gives a kinetic performance as the unhinged Simon Van Gelder. What really works well is Adams forcing Kirk to fall in love with the beautiful Dr. Helen Noel (Marianna Hill), one of his crew members, whom the interstellar lothario loved and left at the *Enterprise* Christmas party.

GROSS (**1/2): An interesting look at memory manipulation and the possible directions in which criminal rehabilitation may go in the future. (We still haven't gotten there, though.) James Gregory's patently understated evil and the relationship (both real and forced) between Kirk and Helen really work. Note that Morgan Woodward's off-kilter performance is something he's continued to this day, recently appearing as a similarly deranged character on *The X-Files.* Like so many Classic *Trek* episodes, this one has a wonderful title.

DARK PAGE

(TNG)
Original Airdate 11/1/93
Written by Hilary J. Bader
Directed by Les Landau

Troi is forced to enter her mother's mind to discover the hidden trauma that is killing Lwaxana Troi. With the help of an alien delegate named Maques (Norman Large), Troi begins to explore her mother's mind, while Lwaxana desperately tries to keep secret the fact that her youngest daughter drowned when she was very young.

ALTMAN (**): Although this sappy story isn't particularly well suited to *Star Trek,* the show is well executed by director Les Landau and imbued with a strong performance by Marina Sirtis. As for the story's nightmare sequences, setting them aboard the *Enterprise* (unlike in "Phantasms," the episode that preceded this one) makes absolutely no sense and no doubt occurred because of budget exigencies. There are some genuine moments of pathos, which ultimately degenerate into melodrama.

GROSS (***): The seventh season of *TNG* was definitely a last-ditch effort to explore the characters in a bit more depth than they had been previously. "Dark Page" is no exception, bringing the audience, thanks to a trip through Lwaxana Troi's mind, to a part of the counselor's life that had been previously unknown even to her. The standout of this episode is guest star Majel Barrett, whose Lwaxana continues to amaze in a transformation from an annoyance to a fully fleshed-out human being. A very well done character drama.

DARMOK

(TNG)
Original Airdate 9/30/91
Written by Joe Menosky
Directed by Winrich Kolbe

The Enterprise *rendezvouses with a Tamarian warship to initiate a relationship with them. Unfortu-*

nately, the Enterprise crew does not understand the Tamarian language. When Picard is transported by the Tamarians to the surface of El Edrel, he finally learns that the Tamarians communicate using metaphor.

ALTMAN (***): An intriguing premise with some fine direction makes "Darmok" more than just a monotonous exercise in semantics. The universal translator's inability to function is a plot machination that stretches one's credulity, as it has functioned flawlessly through so many episodes of *Trek*. But the *Forbidden Planet*–ish id monster is better executed than the usual Trekkian clichés, and the performances are top-notch, despite some plot loopholes that are big enough to propel a starship through. Particularly poignant is a scene in which Patrick Stewart recites the *Gilgamesh Epic* to a dying Tamarian. Stunning location photography at Vasquez Rocks contributes to the vivid look, and veteran actor Paul Winfield (*Star Trek II: The Wrath of Khan*) turns in a solid performance.

GROSS (****): The perfect complement to season four's "First Contact." In that episode, the *Enterprise* reaches out to a civilization on the verge of space technology. In this episode, contact is made, but the two races need to learn to communicate with each other. What follows, in the tradition of "The Devil in the Dark," is a perfect encapsulation of the *Star Trek* philosophy, as the characters attempt to overcome their differences — be they cultural, philo-

sophical or linguistic — and work together. Despite the fact that Picard is a little too slow to grasp the notion that his alien counterpart does *not* want to fight him, the episode is highlighted by the fine performances of Patrick Stewart and Paul Winfield, as well as much-welcomed location shooting and well-executed *Predator*-like creature effects. Also of interest are events taking place in orbit between the *Enterprise* and the alien vessel. No doubt it's a humbling experience for Riker and the others when just a couple of blasts from the alien vessel wipe out all of the *Enterprise*'s defense screens. The ending, in which Picard becomes part of Tamarian legend, is rather moving. A real treat, thanks in part to writer Joe Menosky and director Rick Kolbe.

DATALORE

(TNG)
Original Airdate 1/16/88
Written by Robert Lewin and Gene Roddenberry
Story by Robert Lewin and Maurice Hurley
Directed by Rob Bowman

The Enterprise *returns to Data's homeworld, where they discover the remnants of an earlier version of Data. Once this version is reassembled, they learn it is Lore, an exact, evil duplicate who was responsible for destroying the colony and leads the* Enterprise *into a trap involving the crystalline entity that destroyed Omicron Theta.*

ALTMAN (**): A replay of Classic *Trek*'s "The Enemy Within" that lacks William Shatner's fiery histrionics but features the more muted intonations of Brent Spiner's Data and Lore. Rob Bowman adeptly handles the early passages on the planet, capably giving the lifeless world a strangely eerie quality. But once the crystalline entity shows up to devour the *Enterprise*, the story turns to substandard sci-fi contrivances that send it into oblivion, with the requisite brawl between Data and Lore, in which Data beams his brother out into space.

GROSS (***): Ever since Captain Kirk was split into good and evil during the original *Star Trek*, the notion of twinning a lead character has become a sci-fi cliché. Despite similarities to that story (for example, Lore gives Data a facial tick, as the evil Captain Kirk scratched the good one's face to match scratches given to him by Janice Rand), "Datalore" works thanks to a fast-moving script, Rob Bowman's sterling direction and Brent Spiner's performance, in which he actually makes you believe that Data and Lore are two different people (enhanced by superb special effects when the two are together on-screen). Additionally, Lore and his unlikely companion, the crystalline entity, create a real sense of menace, particularly when Lore phasers Beverly Crusher's arm, setting it ablaze. The series needed this lift badly at the time.

DATA'S DAY

(TNG)
Original Airdate 1/8/91
Story by Harold Apter
Teleplay by Harold Apter and Ronald D. Moore
Directed by Les Landau

A day-in-the-life episode that follows Data around the ship as he prepares for Chief O'Brien's (Colm Meaney) upcoming wedding, for which "dancing" Dr. Crusher teaches Data to tap. Meanwhile, a Vulcan ambassador beams aboard to lead secret negotiations with the Romulans, and when it appears that she has been killed in a transporter accident, Picard discovers that she was actually a Romulan spy coming in from the cold.

ALTMAN (***): The subtle nuances of life aboard the *Enterprise*, including Data's assuming duty at the end of a shift, help make "Data's Day" a winner. Less engaging is the subplot involving a Vulcan ambassador who turns out to be a Romulan spy. Sierra Pecheur gives a weak performance as T'Pel, but Alan Scarfe is sensational as the sinister Romulan admiral Mendak. The whimsical sequences in which Data and Crusher share dance steps (choreographed by Gates McFadden) are the highlight of the episode.

GROSS (***): On the surface, a day in the life of Data sounds hokey, but somehow everyone involved manages to pull it off, particularly Brent Spiner, who continues to impress with his interpretation of Data. An interesting insight into the daily operations of the *Enterprise*. The B story is just another day in the life of the Neutral Zone, and not a very interesting one at that.

DAUPHIN, THE

(TNG)
Original Airdate 2/18/89
Written by Scott Rubenstein and Leonard Mlodinow
Directed by Rob Bowman

Salia (Jamie Hubbard), an alien princess, beams aboard the Enterprise and must learn how to accept her responsibility as a mediator in a planetary dispute and sacrifice to live her own life. She is accompanied by her protector, Anya (Paddi Edwards), a shape-changing alien woman who warns an infatuated Wesley Crusher to stay away from the girl, fearing that she will be encouraged to stay aboard the Enterprise and relinquish her regal responsibilities.

ALTMAN (**1/2): What could easily have been a completely ludicrous costumed creature show actually turns into a surprisingly touching romance between Wesley Crusher and a princess, even if the acting ensign acts like a preadolescent geek rather than a postpubescent stud. Jamie Hubbard is charming as the visiting princess, and the scenes with Worf and Anya, her protector, are well written. The best moments in the show are a throwaway scene in which Riker uses Guinan to teach Crusher about courtship and a scene in the holodeck in which Crusher creates a visually striking space odyssey for his date. Talk about taking a girl to the drive-in!

GROSS (**): An opportunity for Wesley Crusher (Wil Wheaton) to have a romance, where he gets to act like a teenager rather than the Doogie Howser of the twenty-fourth century. Unfortunately, the episode is marred by the fact that the shape-changing element is too reminiscent of the 1966 episode "The Man Trap." Some pleasant performances, particularly by guest star Jamie Hubbard as the Dauphin.

DAX

(DS9)
Original Airdate 2/15/93
Teleplay by D. C. Fontana and Peter Allan Fields
Story by Peter Allan Fields
Directed by David Carson

In this "measure of a Trill," Dax is charged with murder, and an extradition hearing is convened to determine whether the host body of the Trill can be held responsible for the alleged crimes of the symbiont.

ALTMAN (**): With the exception of a sentimental coda, "Dax" offers nothing we haven't seen numerous times before in *Star Trek*'s voluminous history. The episode is marked by a number of lively guest performances, with Anne Haney's Judge Els Renora the standout. The Trill backstory is interesting and the courtroom jousting adeptly written, but one moment that strains one's credulity is when Odo cons Quark into turning over the bar for the extradition hearing. It's hard to believe that a station the size of Deep Space Nine doesn't have a conference room. The obvious impetus for this was to save money on not building a new set. It's disturbing when such plot points are forced by budget exigencies.

GROSS (**): The episode starts with a bang, as Dax is captured and Bashir attempts to save her. The suspense continues through the beginning of the first act, when the abductors launch their vessel and are captured at the last possible moment by a tractor beam. Having accomplished these scenes, director David Carson could have called it a day. Although the notion of one of the main characters being accused of murder has grown tired ("Court Martial," "Wolf in the Fold," "A Matter of Perspective" and "A Man Alone"), the nature of a Trill lends a bit of innovation. Unfortunately, it's not enough.

DAY OF THE DOVE

(TOS)
Original Airdate 11/1/68
Written by Jerome Bixby
Directed by Marvin Chomsky

An energy force that feeds on anger, hatred and hostility arms both the Klingons and the Enterprise crew with swords, then sets them at each other's throats on board the ship. Feeding off the hostility that is created by their conflict, the force heals all wounds so that the battle can continue for eternity.

ALTMAN (***): Although the premise is hokey, the derring-do and character conflict are enough to sustain this high-concept episode. The fencing scenes were shot superbly by director Chomsky, and the high energy never flags, culminating in one of the show's most memorable climaxes: A slaphappy Kang, played powerfully by Michael Ansara, and Kirk chastise the creature, laughing amiably and driving it off the ship and into space in an iconic final image.

GROSS (****): Easily the best episode of the third season, offering one of the show's most memorable portrayals of a Klingon (Michael Ansara's Kang). The notion of an alien force arming both sides with weapons so that they can engage in battles to the death, then healing all wounds so that the battle can continue — thus feeding the force — is terrific. It's interesting to watch the characters try to figure out what's going on while also being manipulated by the alien. Their bloodlust — and, more disturbingly, their racial intolerance — is brought to the forefront. *Deep Space Nine* borrowed elements from this episode when it produced its first-season episode "Battle Lines."

DEADLOCK

(VOY)
Original Airdate 3/18/96
Written by Brannon Braga
Directed by David Livingston

The Voyager *enters a plasma cloud to elude the Vidiians and discovers a duplicate starship with an identical crew. With not enough antimatter in their engines to sustain both vessels and the Vidiians pressing a deadly attack, only one ship can survive.*

ALTMAN (***1/2): One of *Voyager*'s best episodes. An extraordinarily effective sci-fi story that is notable for its labyrinthine story twists and deft writing by Brannon Braga. Aided by David Livingston's kinetic direction, "Dead-lock" is Braga's most inventive technothriller to date. Even Kate Mulgrew rises to the occasion, turning in a strong, tortured performance. Surprisingly sparse on technobabble, this episode should serve as the template for other shows that attempt to combine compelling character drama and inventive science-fiction concepts.

GROSS (***1/2): One of the best space anomaly shows that *Trek* has ever produced — and it's produced plenty. The inventiveness of these two alternate *Voyager*s is a joy to watch — one vessel seeming to be in its death throes, the other apparently just fine. Yet the Vidiians attack the perfectly functioning ship, which is where the battle takes place. By episode's end, the dead among the regular characters manage to live again as they transverse one universe to the next and everything is set right. A creative pleasure, thanks to writer Brannon Braga, director David Livingston and the acting of the regular cast — both of them.

DEADLY YEARS, THE
(TOS)
Original Airdate 12/8/67
Written by David P. Harmon
Directed by Joseph Pevney

While on the surface of Gamma Hydra IV, Kirk, Spock, McCoy and Scotty are infected with a disease that causes premature aging. Chekov, who also was present, is not affected and holds the key to curing the virus before the entire senior staff dies of old age.

ALTMAN (***): Another hokey high-concept story is redeemed by some strong performances and the sparring between beloved characters. The old-age makeup is effective, as are the performances underneath, particularly Kirk slowly giving in to senility and having his command competence questioned. The show's coda, in which Kirk, his youthful virility restored, takes back command from the mealymouthed diplomat Commodore Stocker (Charles Drake) and saves the ship from the Romulans by using a brilliant piece of strategy, is as unforgettable as it is ingenious.

GROSS (***1/2): A powerful look at the aging process, successfully managing to encapsulate the experience of losing control of one's faculties. McCoy, who becomes more of a southern country doctor than ever, and Spock age pretty much as we would expect (check out DeForest Kelley's cameo in *TNG*'s "Encounter at Farpoint" and Leonard Nimoy's appearance in "Unification, Part II"), but watching Kirk sink into senility is damn depressing. As noted above, however, when a cure is found and he is restored to normal, the sequence in which he takes back command of the *Enterprise* bridge from Commodore Stocker is a quintessential Kirk moment. This man is just *so* cool.

DEATH WISH

(VOY)
Original Airdate 2/19/96
Teleplay by Michael Piller
Story by Shawn Piller
Directed by James L. Conway

When the crew frees Q2 (Gerrit Graham), who is intent on committing suicide, from imprisonment inside a comet, Q (John de Lancie) appears on the ship, prompting Q2 to request asylum, which forces Janeway to convene a hearing to determine whether she will grant his wish.

ALTMAN (**): A missed opportunity. Though creative in bringing Q to the Delta Quadrant, the episode suffers under the weight of its lofty goals in examining the morality of assisted suicide. Frankly, it would have been much more interesting if it was our Q who had the death wish rather than being put in the unenviable position of having to urge against his suicide. There are problems in abundance, however. Q's banter with Janeway is a bit on the chauvinistic side, and a scene in which Sir Isaac Newton, Will Riker (in a pointless bit of stunt casting) and Maury Ginsberg (the man without whom Woodstock would have never happened) are assembled for the hearings is just plain loony. One of the more intriguing aspects of the episode is its depiction of the Q Continuum, which, though appropriately surreal, seemed a little overbaked.

GROSS (***): "Death Wish" manages to address both sides of the assisted suicide issue, but it doesn't offer a concrete solution on either side (how could it?). The strength of the episode comes from the conflict between the Qs, both the humorous and the dramatic, and the instant on-screen chemistry between real-life friends Kate Mulgrew and John de Lancie. The cameo by Jonathan Frakes may be stunt casting, but who cares? It's a fun moment, although the ideal *Enterprise* example for Q would have been Captain Picard. Q's tempting Janeway with returning *Voyager* to Earth is obvious (all it would take is a snap of his fingers), but her integrity in refusing to side with him regarding Q2 no matter what he offers is admirable. We come away wanting to see more of Q on *Voyager*, and that's something we will ultimately get.

DEFECTOR, THE

(TNG)
Original Airdate 12/30/89
Written by Ronald D. Moore
Directed by Robert Scheerer

Romulan commander Tomalak (Andreas Katsulas) returns, chasing a Romulan defector, Commander Setal (James Sloyan), who warns the Federation of a Romulan incursion into the Neutral Zone, which will set the stage for a massive invasion of the Federation. Picard, wary of his story, discovers that the officer is actually the legendary Admiral Jarok, who has set a trap to capture the Enterprise.

ALTMAN (***): What could have been a triumphant epic is only a mild success due to time constraints, which reduce the scope of the story. The *Henry V* teaser is a nice, if not very subtle, prelude to the events that follow. Kenneth

Branagh did it better, but Stewart's no slouch. Lexus car pitchman James Sloyan as Admiral Jarok is sensational in the first of a series of performances for the show. (Sloyan will return as Alexander/K'Mtar in "Firstborn" and Dr. Mora Pol in *Deep Space Nine*.)

GROSS (***1/2): A classic *TNG* episode with plenty of political intrigue and characterization and a truly tense climax. Guest star James Sloyan does a wonderful turn as Admiral Jarok, and one can feel his anguish at the episode's conclusion, when he realizes that he's been duped. Speaking of the conclusion, you could practically hear the audience cheering when a group of Klingon Birds of Prey materialize around the pair of Romulan vessels in an effort to protect the *Enterprise*. Just great.

DEFIANT
(DS9)
Original Airdate 11/26/94
Written by Ronald D. Moore
Directed by Cliff Bole

Tom Riker (Jonathan Frakes) arrives on Deep Space Nine pretending to be his duplicate, Will, and steals the Defiant with Kira on board. His plan is to deliver the vessel to the Maquis, who have received word of a military buildup by the Cardassian Obsidian Order. Sisko teams up with Gul Dukat to bring Riker to justice or destroy the ship.

ALTMAN (**): A disappointing *DS9*, whose execution suffers despite a potentially engaging story line. Having Tom Riker as part of the Maquis is an inspired notion, but it's left largely unexplored in lieu of the outer space pyrotechnics, many of which are only visualized inside a Cardassian control room. The lack of some desperately needed visual effects gives the episode much more of a claustrophobic feeling than it should have. Ironically, the sparring between Sisko, Dukat and Korinas of the Obsidian Order (Tricia O'Neil of "Yesterday's Enterprise") proves far more interesting than the Riker and Kira arc on the *Defiant*. The discovery that the Obsidian Order really is arming for war isn't played for the menace that it warrants.

GROSS (**1/2): As it is wont to do, *DS9* manages to take the fabric of the *Trek* universe and fold it to its own needs, this time using Tom Riker from *TNG*'s "Second Chances," a character who easily could have been forgotten, and developing him further. There's some genuine suspense generated by Riker's stealing of the *Defiant* and his intentions for it, but much of this suspense is diminished by subpar effects that look as though they may have been created for use in an Atari (yes, I'm dating myself) video game. Character, of course, takes center stage, and there are some wonderful scenes between Sisko and Gul Dukat.

DEJA Q

(TNG)
Original Airdate 2/3/90
Written by Richard Danus
Directed by Les Landau

Q has been stripped of his powers by his disenchanted peers in the Q Continuum and deposited aboard the Enterprise *for his indiscretions, leading the ship to be pursued by a race of aliens seeking revenge against Q for his practical jokes. This puts Picard and company in the awkward position of having to save their old nemesis.*

ALTMAN (***): Q's back, and he's never been funnier. The ending, in which he materializes a Mexican mariachi band on the bridge, along with cigars and beautiful blonde bimbos for Picard and Riker, is laugh-out-loud hysterical. Less impressive is Corbin Bernsen as Q2, who goes way over the top in playing his omnipotent superbeing, seemingly channeling the spirit of Jack Nicholson. The episode also is hurt by some weak special effects. "Deja Q" is a rare and refreshing *TNG* comedy with some genuine pathos, but it's not nearly as funny as it could have been.

GROSS (****): From the instant a naked Q hits the bridge deck and announces "Red alert!" to the final moment, when his powers have been returned to him and he's accompanied by a salsa band, "Deja Q" is a laugh riot. Beneath the humor, there's a touching story of an immortal who suddenly becomes human and, for the first time, realizes just how far from humanity he really is. John de Lancie delivers another great performance, and his interactions with the crew, particularly Picard, crackle.

DESCENT, PART I

(TNG)
Original Airdate 6/21/93
Teleplay by Ron Moore
Story by Jeri Taylor
Directed by Alexander Singer

The Borg return to menace the Federation as vicious, individualistic killing machines. Data feels his first emotion — anger and subsequently pleasure — in killing one of the metamorphosed automatons and is drawn to a Borg colony, which he learns is run by his brother, Lore, who has become leader of the once mass totality.

ALTMAN (***): "Descent" is full of great moments, but as a whole it lacks the ominously fatalistic mood and searing interpersonal histrionics of its two-part Borg predecessor. Data's personal dilemma is absorbing, although the most interesting conflict is that between Picard and Admiral Necheyev, who is befuddled by Picard's decision not to annihilate the Borg during their last encounter ("I, Borg"). The final moments, in which Lore is revealed, are chillingly effective, and the teaser with Stephen Hawking is delightful, marked by an irascible star turn by *Baron Münchhausen*'s John Neville as Sir Isaac Newton. There are some fine effects, although the new Borg ship is a letdown. Director Alexander Singer uses filters to create a sufficiently creepy alien look on the surface of the unexplored planet.

GROSS (***): The Borg are back, and they are unlike any Borg we've seen before. This season-six cliff-hanger works effectively largely due to the new breed of Borg, who are vicious killing machines, as opposed to monotone automatons. Brent Spiner's Data goes through an interesting evolution, killing a Borg and finding that he actually enjoys it, which only deepens the mystery about what's going on. When he departs the *Enterprise* with a Borg, it piques the audience's curiosity further. The revelation that Lore is actually leading the Borg collective following its collapse (see "I, Borg") is a real shocker.

DESCENT, PART II

(TNG)
Original Airdate 9/20/93
Written by Rene Echevarria
Directed by Alexander Singer

In the conclusion of "Descent," Hugh is enraged at the Enterprise crew for introducing emotions into the Borg collective, which paved the way for Lore to become their leader. Despite his anger, he works with Picard to stop Lore and free Data from Lore's maniacal grip, while Dr. Crusher must outwit the malevolent automatons in space.

ALTMAN (1/2*): To call this episode abysmal is an understatement. "Descent, Part II" is not only the worst finish to a *TNG* cliff-hanger ever, but it is also gratuitously violent to boot. On the planet's surface, Geordi LaForge is brutally tortured for no apparent reason, while Dr. Crusher's outer space cat and mouse game with a Borg ship is just plain stupid, as she takes the *Enterprise* into the corona of a nearby star. I'm a science moron, and even I have a problem believing that one. It was stupid in "Suspicions," and it's even more stupid now. As for the development of the relationship between Data and Lore, except for the requisite mustache twirling from Soong's troubled child, very little new develops, and Data's slaying of his evil brother isn't imbued with the mythological import that such an act calls for.

GROSS (**): A tremendously disappointing conclusion to this two-part episode. What should have been an epic tale of the struggle between good and evil in the form of Data and Lore, as well as an exploration of the cultlike situation between the new Borg and Lore, gets incredibly short shrift. Instead, we're given a standard action/adventure story, with Data going through motions that don't seem terribly new. Too many ideas and not nearly enough money to make them a reality hampers the story.

DESTINY

(DS9)
Original Airdate 2/18/95
Written by David S. Cohen and Martin A. Winer
Directed by Les Landau

A Bajoran Vedek warns Sisko about an impending mission with the Cardassians to establish a communications buoy in the Gamma Quadrant, warning that prophecy has foreseen the destruction of the wormhole.

ALTMAN (**1/2): Although the story of Sisko and Kira examining their faith and addressing issues of secularism versus religion is dealt with in a fresh and compelling way, it is resolved in a more traditional fashion, with some indecipherable technobabble involving diverting a comet substituting for a legitimate plot resolution. Ultimately, "Destiny" could have gone further in dealing with Kira's belief in Sisko as the Emissary and Sisko's own introspection, and more political shenanigans with the two Cardassian scientists and their companion from the Obsidian Order could have been included.

GROSS (**1/2): Humor abounds as every effort to discourage the idea of a prophecy is contradicted. The nice thing is that this prophecy, rather than turning out to be a negative, ultimately has a positive effect. See also "Emissary" and "Accession."

DEVIL IN THE DARK, THE

(TOS)
Original Airdate 3/9/67
Written by Gene L. Coon
Directed by Joseph Pevney

When miners on Janus VI are murdered by a creature that can move through solid rock, the Enterprise *crew joins the hunt to stop it. Kirk and Spock then learn that the creature is actually an intelligent being called the Horta, which is protecting its young from the miners.*

ALTMAN (***1/2): Another inspired Classic *Trek* title featuring that famous moving-carpet alien, the Horta. Despite lapses in pro-

duction design, "The Devil in the Dark" works beautifully because of its skillful execution and message of understanding and tolerance, which is as relevant today as on the day the episode was filmed. Eschewing the "monster is bad" scenarios of shows such as *The Outer Limits, Star Trek* turns the tables on the audience and makes us question our fundamental values when it is revealed that the "monster" is a mother fighting for her children.

GROSS (****): Gene L. Coon proves once again why he was the perfect writer for *Star Trek*, managing to home in on the characters and the show's philosophical direction in a way that no other writer could. "The Devil in the Dark" is a beautifully crafted tale in which *we're* the bad guys, as opposed to the supposed monster. Spock's mind-meld with the Horta is a great scene. Leonard Nimoy does a brilliant job of conveying the Horta's physical pain from being wounded by a miner, as well as its emotional turmoil over being the last of its kind and the fact that its babies are being killed by Federation miners.

DEVIL'S DUE

(TNG)
Original Airdate 2/4/90
Written by Philip Lazebnik and William Douglas Lansford
Directed by Tom Benko

Reworked from an original premise for the aborted Trek TV revival in the 1970s, "Devil's Due" plays

like a 1966 Enterprise *voyage in which Kirk —
er, Picard — must argue in court that a woman,
Arda (Marta DuBois), claiming to be the devil
is really a charlatan in order to nullify a
contract she has on that world and the* Enterprise.
*Picard challenges the validity of her claim on
the world; Data serves as arbitrator in a contest
of wills that could cost Picard his soul —
or, something equally valuable, his self-
esteem.*

ALTMAN (**1/2): "Devil's Due" is
an amusing, if slightly routine,
Trek story with a number of enjoyably riotous moments contributed
by its myriad writers. Arda is sufficiently voluptuous, harking back
to the typical female protagonists
of Classic *Trek*. Even if the story is
a silly retread of "The Devil and
Daniel Webster," it's nice to see
something a little different — particularly when Arda pays an unexpected house call on Picard. Its
origins show, however; *TNG* it's
not.

GROSS (***): In this episode, Captain Picard tries to convince Judge
Data that the defendant, Arda, is
nothing more than an intergalactic con artist. Yes, he presents a
convincing argument, and there
are plenty of humorous moments,
but enough courtroom drama.
Marta DuBois makes this episode
enjoyable. She's kind of a female
Harry Mudd, and it wouldn't have
been so bad to see her make a return visit to the series. (Note: The
script began as an episode of the
aborted *Star Trek Phase II* series, in
which Captain Kirk would have
gone up against the devil in an
alien courtroom.)

DIE IS CAST, THE

(DS9)
Original Airdate 5/6/95
Written by Ronald D. Moore
Directed by David Livingston

*Garak is invited to join his mentor (and father, as
we later learn), Enabran Tain (Paul Dooley), in the
attack on the Founders, which he is happy to do.
Less pleasurable is his assignment to torture Odo
to learn anything he can about the Founders. In
the end, it is all for naught, as Tain and the Romulans learn that they have been manipulated by the
Founders and are defeated by a massive fleet of
Jem'Hadar vessels.*

ALTMAN (**): There are some
wonderful special effects sequences here, but the epic scope of
the invasion of the Gamma Quadrant plays second fiddle to Garak's
interrogation of Odo. Frankly, I
was far more interested in the interstellar machinations going on
outside the confines of Odo's cell.
Not surprisingly, Rene Auberjonois
and Andrew Robinson are both
sensational and do as much with
the material as they can. Less effective is Leland Lorser as the Romulan Lovok, who turns out to be
a Founder. Despite his shape-
changing abilities, he is never able
to transform himself into a good
actor.

GROSS (***): An episode that
strikes the perfect balance between
action and character. The turn of
events for the supposed
Cardassian/Romulan alliance is
unexpected, and the fact that
they've been manipulated by the
Founders is a terrific revelation.
The real juice of the episode comes

from the sequences between Garak and Odo, in which Rene Auberjonois manages to maintain Odo's dignity even when he's literally flaking away when Garak uses a device to hold him in solid form. Andrew Robinson's desperation to get Odo to tell him *something* so that he can allow him to shift back to his natural state is powerful in its intensity and earnestness. See also "Improbable Cause" (the previous episode).

DISASTER

(TNG)
Original Airdate 10/21/91
Teleplay by Ronald D. Moore
Story by Ron Jarvis and Philip A. Scorza
Directed by Gabrielle Beaumont

While Picard is taking the three young winners of a science contest on a tour of the ship, the Enterprise is struck by a natural phenomenon that causes power failures throughout the vessel. Communication is cut off, forcing Worf to deliver Keiko O'Brien's baby in Ten-Forward, while Troi takes command as the senior officer on the bridge. Meanwhile, Riker and Data try to reach engineering to restore power.

ALTMAN (***): Ron Moore skillfully recycles one of the oldest plots in the book into one of the fifth season's best episodes. Despite its tired origins (read: *"The Poseidon Adventure* meets *Battlestar Galactica*'s 'Fire in Space' "), "Disaster" has everything going for it but George Kennedy. Fortunately, it allows for some wonderful character conflict between the returning En-

sign Ro and Troi and Worf, who has a delightfully memorable moment delivering Keiko O'Brien's baby. (It's a comedic tour de force for Michael Dorn.) Equally memorable is Patrick Stewart's star turn with a bunch of crybaby kids stranded in the turbo-lift, culminating in a wonderfully whimsical coda.

GROSS (**1/2): "There's no evidence that anyone's alive in the drive section." "There's no evidence that there isn't!" "Irwin Allen Meets *Star Trek*" as the *Enterprise* is immobilized, with each section of the ship losing contact with the others. Who's alive? Who's dead? What's the next move? These are the questions that everyone is trying to answer as they fight for survival. It is interesting to see Troi in the same command position she coached Geordi LaForge through during season one's "The Arsenal of Freedom." While Ensign Ro comes across bitchier than necessary, Picard shows true character growth in terms of his dealing with children (compared to the man we met five years earlier). Worf provides some pleasant comic relief as he assists in the delivery of Keiko O'Brien's baby. And Riker, working with Data's disconnected head — who thinks up this stuff, anyway?

DISTANT VOICES

(DS9)
Original Airdate 4/15/95
Teleplay by Ira Steven Behr and Robert Hewitt Wolfe
Story by Joe Menosky
Directed by Alexander Singer

After an alien attack, Bashir lies comatose and dying. To survive, he must access different aspects of his subconscious mind, which are personified in the form of other crew members.

ALTMAN (*1/2): A disappointing *DS9* that, despite some fine acting from Alexander Siddig, is saddled with a lame premise and some poorly realized old-age makeup for the doctor. Ultimately, I just didn't buy the show's conceit, and the reflections of his subconscious mind are unexciting. It reeks of being a high-concept Joe Menosky story and is far more suited to *TNG* or *Voyager* than *DS9*, which has avoided this kind of muddled, technobabble-ridden storytelling.

GROSS (**): A tour de force performance by Alexander Siddig, who ages throughout the episode in what is probably the best old-age makeup ever seen on *Star Trek*. The actor actually is capable of making you feel as though he's getting older. It's interesting to see all the familiar faces acting out of character as they assume different facets of Bashir's mind. The plot is intriguing, though somewhat incomprehensible. It may take a couple of viewings to truly get this one.

DOOMSDAY MACHINE, THE

(TOS)
Original Airdate 10/20/67
Written by Norman Spinrad
Directed by Marc Daniels

The Enterprise *investigates the destruction of several star systems and finds what's left of the USS* Constellation, *with its commander, Commodore Matt Decker (William Windom), the only one left on board. Decker relates a terrifying tale of a doomsday machine that devours entire planets, just as Spock notifies them that the planet killer has set its sights on the* Enterprise.

ALTMAN (****): The *Star Trek* credo: Never wear red, look both ways before you cross the street and never beam down to the third planet! This is the definitive "*Enterprise* in peril" story, in which the *Constellation* gets munched on by the proverbial planet killer. Sol Kaplan's score, with its pulsating percussion, is classic — the kind of thing the subsequent *Trek* series haven't done. It's nail-biting drama of the highest order, with an energetic performance by Windom as the tortured Matt ("there was, but not anymore") Decker.

GROSS (****): Easily the best "*Enterprise* in battle" episode of the original series, with Windom's riveting performance as Decker and Kirk's desperate attempts to save his ship and destroy the alien device using what's left of the *Constellation*. There's wonderful character conflict when Decker uses his rank to assume command of the *Enterprise* while Kirk is on the *Constellation*. The Ahab-like Decker is determined to destroy his white whale, even if it takes the starship to do so. But Kirk later points out, "Not with my ship you don't!" Decker's ultimate sacrifice redeems the commodore for allowing his crew to die, while also revealing a possible way to destroy the device. Some suspense is generated as the doomsday machine approaches the *Constellation* and Spock tries desperately to beam Kirk out of there before it's too late. The intercutting between starships is a wonder of editing, punctuated by William Shatner's perfectly timed comments ("Mr. Spock, this would be a good time to turn on the transporter"). See also *Star Trek: The Motion Picture* (Will is Matt Decker's son).

DRAMATIS PERSONAE

(DS9)
Original Airdate 5/31/93
Written by Joe Menosky
Directed by Cliff Bole

The telepathic energy of a destroyed species in the Gamma Quadrant takes over the crew of DS9, forcing them to reenact the Shakespearean power struggle that destroyed their world.

ALTMAN (*1/2): The idea of an alien mind probe taking over isn't new, but the concept of its manifestation creating a literal power play aboard the station makes it a captivating conceit. Regrettably, the "Mirror, Mirror"–like dynamics of the feuding factions play out far too tamely and are hurt by a number of surprisingly weak performances, lacking the spit and vinegar of the political show-

downs in the Classic *Trek* episode. Ultimately, the episode is devoid of passion, functioning simply as a tame bottle show, when it has the potential to be far more compelling, with some genuine conflict.

GROSS (*1/2): Listen closely. Hear that munching sound? That's the sound made by actors chewing the scenery, and there's a lot of that going on in this episode. That wouldn't be so bad if the story line causing them to munch wasn't such old hat. There are some fun moments here, but all in all this episode isn't a first-season highlight.

DREADNOUGHT

(VOY)
Original Airdate 2/12/96
Written by Gary Holland
Directed by LeVar Burton

A Cardassian superweapon, reprogrammed by B'Elanna Torres in the Alpha Quadrant, wreaks havoc in the Delta Quadrant, imperiling an alien world as well as the Voyager *itself.*

ALTMAN (**1/2): Simple but skillfully executed, "Dreadnought" is a high-concept retread of "The Ultimate Computer" and "The Doomsday Machine." There are some nice character moments involving B'Elanna Torres's guilt over unleashing the destructive force in the Delta Quadrant. Janeway's relationship with the threatened alien world is another high point. But there's just no intellectual juice to the denouement. The crew resolves its dilemma by simply tinkering aboard the missile, making a potentially engaging *Voyager* premise another missed opportunity.

GROSS (***): An episode that works on several fronts, first as an action/adventure story, as all of *Voyager*'s attempts to stop the weapon prove fruitless, and then as a character study, as Torres's past as a Maquis catches up with her and may ultimately result in her death. A bit anticlimactic, but an effective entry.

DRUMHEAD, THE

(TNG)
Original Airdate 4/29/91
Written by Jeri Taylor
Directed by Jonathan Frakes

A Klingon is caught on board the Enterprise spying for the Romulans, resulting in Admiral Satie (Jean Simmons) coming on board to get to the heart of a suspected espionage ring. A witch-hunt for his collaborator ensues, which leads all the way back to Picard.

ALTMAN (***): The *Trek* team has paid endless lip service to *TNG*'s allegorical content, but rarely have we seen an episode that has so carefully straddled the line between entertainment and social commentary. The performances by Patrick Stewart and *Dark Shadows*' Jean Simmons as Satie are terrific, as is Jonathan Frakes's direction in this budget-saving bottle show. Ron Jones's evocative score and Jeri Taylor's savvy script, which intricately weaves in several strands of *Trek* narrative from a number of episodes, contribute to making

Trek's fantasy world a credible realm in which fundamental human rights are trampled due to fear, suspicion and paranoia. To see how far *TNG* has come, compare this episode to the first-season "Coming of Age."

GROSS (****): One of *TNG*'s best allegories, highlighted by a series of great performances, particularly Patrick Stewart's and guest star Jean Simmons's. The beauty of this episode lies in the way Admiral Satie starts off as a highly respected Starfleet official who has a job to do. As the episode unfolds, she slowly unravels her true agenda, and an absolutely frightening situation ensues. Her confrontations with Picard crackle, and her driving home of the point that the captain, as Locutus of Borg, was responsible for the deaths of more than eleven thousand people is one hell of a below-the-belt punch. Director Jonathan Frakes never allows the proceedings to get boring. This episode is a highlight of the fourth season and the entire series.

DUET

(DS9)
Original Airdate 6/14/93
Teleplay by Peter Allan Fields
Story by Lisa Rich and Jeanne Carrigan-Fauci
Directed by James L. Conway

Kira believes that a Cardassian who comes to DS9 is a war criminal named Gul Darhe'el, the commandant of a Cardassian prison labor camp.

ALTMAN (***1/2): Like *TNG*'s "The Drumhead," "Duet" proves that a little money can go a long way. As good as Nana Visitor is in the penultimate episode of the season, Harris Yulin is nothing short of a revelation as Marritza, the Cardassian prisoner who may or may not be the perpetrator of heinous crimes against the Bajoran people. Although the episode's Holocaust allegory is a little too on the nose, the crisp writing by Peter Allan Fields, along with vibrant direction from Jim Conway and a moving coda, makes the story one of the first year's highlights. The characters — and the show — are at their best.

GROSS (****): "Duet" represents the best type of bottle show that can be produced. Peter Allan Fields has written what is probably his finest script, and director James Conway has done his share in bringing the episode to riveting life. Naturally, though, it is the performances of Nana Visitor and guest star Harris Yulin that hit home. Their scenes together are electric, capturing Kira's fury and Marritza's initial arrogance and ultimately pitiable qualities. Above all, "Duet" proves that you don't need high concepts, heavy doses of science-fiction plot lines or encyclopedias of technobabble to make a great episode. Two people in a room can do it — if you give them the right script.

E

ELAAN OF TROYIUS
(TOS)
Original Airdate
12/20/68
Written and directed
by John Meredyth Lucas

While transporting the Dolman of Elaas to her wedding on Troyius, Kirk must tame the wild spirit of the impetuous Dolman (France Nuyen), whose tears can enslave a man, through love, for life. Meanwhile, one of her party is a Klingon spy, who is seeking to sabotage the Enterprise *and the mission.*

ALTMAN (**): A thinly veiled version of *The Taming of the Shrew*, the episode is largely carried on the shoulders of William Shatner, who manages to make the proceedings watchable as he tries to tame the wild Dolman and later overcome the effect of her love tears. He is ultimately cured of his affliction by his love of the *Enterprise*. (What would Freud have to say about *that?*) The espionage plot is the most interesting part of the story, and France Nuyen is sufficiently bratty and beautiful as the pampered princess. The episode is worth comparing to *TNG*'s "The Perfect Mate," which has a similar plot.

GROSS (*1/2): What a bitch! Beyond that, there isn't much about this episode to discuss, although the theme of Kirk's love for the *Enterprise* being stronger than anything else is getting tiresome. It worked in "The Paradise Syndrome," but it feels repetitive here.

ELEMENTARY, DEAR DATA

(TNG)
Original Airdate 12/3/88
Written by Brian Alan Lane
Directed by Rob Bowman

Realizing Data's familiarity with the canon of Arthur Conan Doyle hardly challenges Data's deductive capacities, Geordi LaForge attempts to create a worthwhile opponent in a Sherlock Holmes re-creation in the holodeck. As a result, LaForge inadvertently gives life to the powerful Professor Moriarty (Daniel Davis), who takes control of the Enterprise *and kidnaps Pulaski.*

ALTMAN (**): An overrated episode that recycles the trappings of the first season's "The Big Goodbye" without bringing anything new to the proceedings. The episode boasts impressive production values and costume designs, but its often striking visuals can't compensate for a weak and ill-conceived story line, in which the holodeck creates the fictional character of Moriarty, who nearly destroys the ship. Again, the show ends with an unsatisfying speech by Picard rather than something more ingenious to resolve the plot.

GROSS (***): The look of this episode (on an episodic budget) is just wonderful. It's also a lot of fun watching Brent Spiner as Data as Sherlock Holmes, particularly the android's shifting back and forth from Data to Holmes as he explains the reasoning for a deduction he has made. There's great interplay between Spiner and

LeVar Burton, who undertakes the role of Watson, and Daniel Davis is properly sinister as Professor Moriarty. A great deal of imagination makes this a terrific episode, marred by the lack of an explanation for how Moriarty gains control of the *Enterprise*. Although everyone involved deserves a great deal of credit, one has to wonder why that damn holodeck hasn't been shut down yet.

ELOGIUM

(VOY)
Original Airdate 9/18/95
Teleplay by Kenneth Biller and Jeri Taylor
Story by Jimmy Diggs and Steven J. Kay
Directed by Winrich Kolbe

"A swarm of space-dwelling life-forms" (as Janeway scientifically terms this episode's hokey space anomaly) is the catalyst for Kes's "elogium" cycle, which will lead to pregnancy, and she must decide whether to have a baby at such a young age.

ALTMAN (**): Conceptually, "Elogium" has the potential to be one of *Voyager*'s most provocative allegories, but it has little more resonance than a bad after-school special in examining the dilemma Kes faces when she must decide whether to have a baby. She and Neelix, a seemingly asexual and alien couple, must make a very important decision, which they approach in an all too human and pedantic manner. By the end of the episode, Kes has made her decision without even consulting Neelix and, for all intents and purposes, had an abortion — although this decision is reduced to a brief epilogue. Therein lies what should have been the meat of the episode, but instead we deal with the usual Sturm and Drang involving the latest in a long line of misunderstood life-forms, a cosmic dwelling band of intergalactic sperm, to which we react passively. I was expecting Woody Allen to show up at any minute.

GROSS (**): This is an attempt to explore the limited life span of Kes and what that encompasses in terms of procreating the species, but there's no real emotional connection for the audience, and the lack of content concerning the issue of abortion, as discussed above, is unfortunate. But, hey, the space whales are kind of neat.

with apathy, although I did like the Spalding Gray–like performance by Jeffrey Alan Chandler as an ailing alien reluctant to pass to the next emanation despite his family's unbridled enthusiasm over his demise.

GROSS (***): *Voyager* takes on some of the bigger issues, and Harry Kim's experience provides a fascinating journey for the audience. The idea of our universe being an afterlife for the people of another dimension is brilliant, and there are some interesting discussions of the afterlife and the nature of death. This show is trying to deal with real issues, and there's nothing wrong with that. A standout episode for Garrett Wang and his on-screen alter ego.

EMANATIONS

(VOY)
Original Airdate 3/13/95
Written by Brannon Braga
Directed by David Livingston

A race that sends its dying beings into the Voyager's *dimension, believing it is the afterlife, receives a rude awakening when Harry Kim inadvertently shows up, debunking their beliefs.*

ALTMAN (**): A great premise is sabotaged by some lightweight existential angst. David Livingston takes a stab at imbuing the alien milieu with some mystery by using skewed camera angles, but the English-speaking people with funny foreheads aren't different enough from the usual suspects to engender much interest. The whole episode left me shrugging

EMERGENCE

(TNG)
Original Airdate 5/9/94
Written by Brannon Braga and Joe Menosky
Directed by Cliff Bole

"Emergence" is a grade-B "Phantasms" in which the Enterprise *gains self-awareness and the starship itself offers clues as to how to save the ship through its holodeck anomalies.*

ALTMAN (*1/2): Writer Brannon Braga's concepts for *TNG* are often original and thought provoking, and even when his shows are less than stellar, there's usually a semblance of wit and intelligence. Unfortunately, "Emergence," Braga's attempt to indulge his fascination with surreal imagery and symbolism, is none of those things. The substantial production resources marshaled to re-create the Orient Express and the use of Paramount's New York Street back lot are wasted here in service of a premise that fails to pay off.

GROSS (*): One of the worst episodes of *TNG*, complete with a malfunctioning holodeck (anybody keeping count of the number of times this has happened?) and a premise that doesn't make any sense. The *Enterprise* gaining consciousness on its own? Was this an episode of the animated series? I have had enough of these machines that decide they've had enough of servitude and strike out on their own. Good production values, though.

EMISSARY

(DS9)
Original Airdate 1/4/93
Written by Michael Piller
Story by Rick Berman and Michael Piller
Directed by David Carson

This telefilm brings Commander Benjamin Sisko (Avery Brooks) to Deep Space Nine to administer the Bajoran space station vacated by the Cardassians. In this adventure, he meets with his new crew and has an encounter with the Wormhole Aliens, who inform him that he is Bajor's Emissary.

ALTMAN (***1/2): Substituting top-heavy New Age mumbo jumbo for the familiar technobabble, Piller aims for the cerebral resonance of the best moments of "The Cage," but "Emissary" is not always successful in that regard. Its first hour is top-notch *Trek*, establishing the premise of the new series and introducing an intriguing

array of new characters, sparked by a powerful and enticing teaser. The film's second hour is considerably less involving, as it becomes mired in Sisko's metaphysical journey into his "pagh." The opener suffers from the same problems that plagued *TNG*'s "Encounter at Farpoint," with an impressive first hour and disappointing second half. "Emissary" works best while exploring the decks of DS9 and secular humanism, but it becomes muddled once Sisko sets out on his spiritual journey. Despite a few missteps, the production values are outstanding, with the exception of a disappointing main title sequence and theme. Kudos to Michael Piller, who manages to translate his affinity for baseball into an ingenious means of explaining linear existence to the befuddled aliens inhabiting the wormhole.

GROSS (***1/2): Now *this* is a pilot. Whereas *TNG*'s "Encounter at Farpoint" clearly demonstrated the somewhat desperate attempts of its creators to match the success of the original series, *Deep Space Nine* effortlessly (almost too much so) manages to establish its own distinct identity as part of — yet apart from — the previous series. This is akin to *TNG*, which had the entire *Star Trek* legend to live up to. Ultimately, it created its own history, in the minds of many even surpassing its progenitor. Insofar as *Deep Space Nine* is concerned, the Michael Piller/Rick Berman story line immediately draws us into this new *Trek* environment, and as each subsequent character is introduced, we are given very distinct examples of the conflict that exists between them. Aided by David Carson's direction, we get the same sense of disorientation that greets the characters as they come to grips with how their lives are changing. A highlight occurs in an early scene between Sisko and Picard. When Sisko mentions the fact that his wife was killed at Wolf 359, the implication is clear. Yet Picard offers no apologies and doesn't even address the issue, although Patrick Stewart's facial expressions reveal much about the character's guilt as he relives the Locutus/Borg affair in a split second. All in all, *DS9* is off to a hell of a start.

EMISSARY, THE

(TNG)
Original Airdate 6/24/89
Written by Richard Manning and Hans Beimler
Based on an unpublished story by Thomas H. Calder
Directed by Cliff Bole

A ship full of Klingons, who believe they are still at war with the Federation, is released from cryogenic freeze. As a result, the Enterprise, *joined by Klingon ambassador K'Ehleyr (Suzi Plakson), Worf's former lover, is dispatched to persuade the Klingon ship not to resume its path of glory.*

ALTMAN (**): Suzi Plakson, who first made an impression as Lieutenant Selar in "The Schizoid Man," steals "The Emissary" with her spit-and-vinegar performance. Another great premise falters in execution, with a predictable anticlimax. The sparks between Worf and

K'Ehleyr are genuine, but it's too long before the Klingons rise and shine from cryo-stasis, looking for battle to come to them. A cat and mouse game with the *Enterprise* (à la "Balance of Terror") could have been far more interesting than the lethargic drama that ensues.

GROSS (***): Suzi Plakson is great as the half-human/half-Klingon K'Ehleyr, doing her best to knock a little of the pompousness out of the Klingon culture. Admittedly the amount of time devoted to her relationship with Worf is disproportionate in relation to that given to the reawakening Klingons, but overall it works. The ending could have been a little more elaborate and taken on the intensity of the situation between the *Enterprise* and the war-seeking Klingons. See also "Reunion."

EMPATH, THE

(TOS)
Original Airdate 12/6/68
Written by Joyce Muskat
Directed by John Erman

While attempting to rescue a research party observing the star Minara, which is about to go nova, Kirk, Spock and McCoy are abducted by the Vians, a telepathic species that begins using the three in a series of experiments. A mute humanoid woman with empathic powers looks on and is the only one who can save McCoy after he is brutally tortured.

ALTMAN (***1/2): I really hated this episode when I was a kid. It wasn't until I grew up (in body, not in mind, mind you) that I realized what a spectacularly mature episode it is. Even though the

Vians are second-rate Talosians in their physical appearance, "The Empath" is one of *Star Trek*'s most ingenious episodes, making great use of limited resources and mining the rich emotional depth of the Kirk/Spock/McCoy troika with nothing more than an empty stage, some truly wrenching torture sequences and a stunning musical score. Kathryn Hayes is superb as the mute Gem, who sacrifices herself for McCoy and wins her civilization a new lease on life.

GROSS (**1/2): After reading Mr. Altman's review, I felt I had no choice but to go back to this episode to see if my impressions may have been mistaken. I, too, hated it as a child. Now that I'm an adult, it does play considerably better, attempting to deal with mature themes and doing a lot with a low budget. Still, portions of the episode seem like a mime opera (if you can figure that one out) with exaggerated movements by the actors. One thing I can't quite figure out: Gem is so uncultured in feelings of humanity, but she can put on all that makeup, including considerable blue highlight around her eyes, all by her lonesome. Impressive.

ENCOUNTER AT FARPOINT

(TNG)
Original Airdate 9/26/87
Written by D. C. Fontana and Gene Roddenberry
Directed by Corey Allen

The maiden voyage of the starship Enterprise *NCC-1701-D begins when Captain Jean-Luc Picard sets out to investigate the mysterious and somewhat miraculous Farpoint Station. En route, the ship is boarded by the all-powerful Q, who feels that humankind has ventured far enough into space and places Picard and his crew on trial for crimes against humanity, reserving judgment until Picard has solved the mystery of Farpoint.*

ALTMAN (**): In this two-hour premiere that borrows a number of its themes from Classic *Trek,* Gene Roddenberry manages to prove one thing beyond a shadow of a doubt: *Star Trek* can live again. Like Frankenstein raising his monster, Roddenberry is able to summon lightning yet again to reenergize his franchise, which, though boasting numerous Trekkian clichés (including a literal replay of the Decker/Ilia meeting in *Star Trek: The Motion Picture*), still works thanks to the redoubtable presence of John de Lancie's Q (a character strongly reminiscent of Trelane from "The Squire of Gothos"). DeForest Kelley's cameo is pure joy, although Roddenberry's postulation of the postatomic courts of the twenty-first century is one of *Trek*'s less optimistic visions of the future. The pilot may do little more than get the franchise back on its feet, but that's really all it had to do and it does it competently.

GROSS (***): The premiere of *TNG* works in spite of itself, thanks primarily to John de Lancie's performance as Q. On paper, the character is little more than a retread of Trelane from the original series' "The Squire of Gothos," but in de Lancie's more than capable hands, Q comes to life and provides a great deal of humor. The Farpoint scenario is a bit tame, although its use of the classic "looks are deceiving" theme harks back well to the original. One complaint is the wholesale plagiarizing of Roddenberry's script for *Star Trek: The Motion Picture*, most notably the Riker/Troi relationship, which is based on the film's Decker/Ilia romance. The cast, particularly Patrick Stewart, shows great promise right from the get-go, although Denise Crosby's histrionics as Tasha Yar and Marina Sirtis's constipated look as Troi senses powerful emotions from an alien are a bit much. Look for a cameo by DeForest Kelley as an elderly Dr. "Bones" McCoy. An enjoyable first effort with spectacular effects. See also "Hide & Q," "Q Who," "Deja Q," "True Q," "Tapestry," "All Good Things," "Q-Less" and "Death Wish."

ENEMY, THE

(TNG)
Original Airdate 11/4/89
Written by David Kemper and Michael Piller
Directed by David Carson

Geordi LaForge is lost on an Away Team mission on a hostile planet, where the Enterprise *detected a downed Romulan shuttle. He encounters a wounded Romulan Centurion, Bochra (John Snyder), who takes him prisoner. Meanwhile, in sick bay, Dr. Crusher attempts to revive a dying Romulan who can be saved only by a blood transfusion from Worf.*

ALTMAN (***): The best Romulan episode of the series, featuring some stunning directorial work by

David Carson, who went on to direct *Star Trek VII: Generations*. The best aspect of the episode is Worf's refusal to give blood to a dying Romulan, despite an epistle from Picard. This act helps define Worf's character better than any other in the history of *TNG*. The episode introduces the always endearing Andreas Katsulas as Commander Tamalok. He later went on to portray G'kar in *Babylon 5*.

GROSS (***1/2): The planetside and shipboard stories work perfectly in sync. Down below, in a story arc that echoes the classic film *The Defiant Ones*, LeVar Burton is terrific as Geordi LaForge, who struggles to stay alive aided only by a Romulan. On the *Enterprise*, Worf announces that he will allow another Romulan to die rather than give him blood. One assumes that when Picard gently asks him to do the right thing, he will. It's quite a stunner when the lieutenant sticks to his phasers.

ENEMY WITHIN, THE

(TOS)
Original Airdate 10/6/66
Written by Richard Matheson
Directed by Leo Penn

The transporter malfunctions due to contamination from magnetic ore, and as a result two separate Kirks — one good, one evil — are created. Kirk's decision-making abilities are impaired, and Scotty must fix the transporter before Sulu and a landing party die on the freezing planet's surface, then reintegrate the captain.

ALTMAN (***): William Shatner gets to emote wildly (albeit quite effectively) as the two Kirks. Watching the evil Kirk cause trouble throughout the ship is quite entertaining, and the ultimate reuniting of the two Kirks is moving. The climax in engineering proves you don't need to have advanced split-screen motion-control techniques to make doppelgänger conflict exciting, as the two play a game of cat and mouse on the engineering deck. One has to wonder why the *Enterprise* never dispatched a shuttlecraft to rescue the poor Mr. Sulu, stranded on the planet's surface.

GROSS (****): Once again, William Shatner excels as Kirk, presenting two very different portrayals of the captain. One, an aggressive social bore, drinks Saurian Brandy from a bottle, forces himself on Yeoman Rand and is a bit over-the-top (his proclaiming "I want to live!" is a classic example). The other is more introspective, trying to deal with losing control of the ability to command. Richard Matheson's script is brilliant, successfully demonstrating that some of our more negative attributes are an integral part of who we are and are absolutely necessary to our being. With the exception of the Sulu issue (raised above), there's hardly a wrong step made. Leonard Nimoy's Spock finally begins locking onto the pattern of a being without emotion as he coldly explains to McCoy what has happened to Kirk and what they are witnessing in terms of the makeup of human beings. No more shouting across the bridge for this guy.

ENSIGN RO

(TNG)
Original Airdate 10/7/91
Written by Rick Berman and Michael Piller
Directed by Les Landau

After a terrorist attack on a Federation colony on Solarion Four, the Enterprise *receives a message from a man claiming to represent Bajor, who, he says, is responsible for the attack. Immediately afterward, Starfleet admiral Kennelly (Cliff Potts) dispatches the incarcerated Ensign Ro (Michelle Forbes) to assist Picard, but the admiral's agenda is very different from Picard's, as he is conspiring with the Cardassians to discredit the Bajorans.*

ALTMAN (*1/2):** "Ensign Ro" is a standout *TNG* episode with some attractive location lensing. It also introduces the wonderful and sexy Michelle Forbes as the tempestuous Ensign Ro and the Bajoran/Cardassian conflict, whose backstory will serve as the basis for *Deep Space Nine* a year later. There's some sinister political intrigue and a great Guinan scene in which Whoopi Goldberg gets to do more than just pour drinks and steal Troi's patients. All in all, a terrific episode.

GROSS (***): This episode scores on a number of levels, beginning with the fact that it's an allegory, and a highly effective one at that. Put in the Palestinians, the IRA — whomever you choose — and the tale can still be told, proving that when it works, *Star Trek* can handle the big issues better than just about any show. Beyond that, Michelle Forbes is a welcome addition to the cast as Ensign Ro. Like Diana Muldaur's Dr. Pulaski in the second season, Ro is meant to add a bit of spice and internal conflict to the ensemble. Unlike Muldaur, however, Forbes is able to pull it off in such a way that it looks as if everyone is being cruel to her, rather than the other way around. In fact, it's downright startling — pleasantly so — to see just how rude the crew can be, particularly Riker. Additionally, in the form of Kennelly, there's finally a bad seed in Starfleet, who allows his personal prejudice to govern his thinking. See also "Conundrum," "Power Play," "Cause & Effect," "The Next Phase," "Rascals" and "Preemptive Strike."

who are among the best of *TNG*'s alien creations and are used to brilliant effect in the episode.

GROSS (***): A nice showcase episode for Brent Spiner, whose Data can't understand why these people are so reluctant to evacuate their world. Obviously, logic is not enough (Spock, are you listening?). Patrick Stewart also shines brightly as Picard, desperately seeking an excuse to stall the Sheliak. His final solution — a legal loophole that will take years to resolve — and the aliens' reaction to it are quite enjoyable and humorous.

ENSIGNS OF COMMAND, THE

(TNG)
Original Airdate 9/30/89
Written by Melinda Snodgrass
Directed by Cliff Bole

Data is given his first command assignment on a planet whose human colonists are endangered by the impending arrival of the Sheliak, who have a legal claim to the world and plan to annihilate the people when they arrive. To convince the apathetic colonists to leave, Data must impress the danger upon them.

ALTMAN (***) This episode marked a turning point at the beginning of the third season, as a series of consistently entertaining episodes followed. Melinda Snodgrass's story has its flaws, but the characters and the dilemma are a refreshing change of pace. Data's dilemma is particularly compelling as he flounders in his attempt to take command of the situation. Most impressive are the Sheliak,

ENTERPRISE INCIDENT, THE

(TOS)
Original Airdate 9/27/68
Written by D. C. Fontana
Directed by John Meredyth Lucas

Apparently suffering from a nervous breakdown, Kirk sends the Enterprise deep into the Neutral Zone, where it is captured by Romulan warships. Spock reveals to the Romulans that he believes Kirk has gone insane, but in truth they are both working under cover for the Federation in an attempt to steal the Romulans' cloaking device, which allows their ships to appear invisible to sensors.

ALTMAN (***1/2): Intergalactic intrigue abounds in this marvelous and suspenseful episode, which boasts an appropriately over-the-top performance by William Shatner as the high-strung, insanely paranoid starship captain (though it's still more subdued than most of his talk show appearances). Joanne Linville turns in a lovely performance as the ill-fated Romulan commander who falls for Mr. Spock. Some of the flak Kirk takes from McCoy after being transformed into a Romulan Centurion is priceless.

GROSS (**1/2): *Star Trek* does *Mission: Impossible* in this fairly effective spy adventure. Much of the episode works, particularly William Shatner's portrayal of an insane Kirk and a Romulan commander. It's difficult to believe that Spock can seduce the female commander so easily, because he's out of character and she's completely oblivious to what's going on. The huge cloaking device also looks kind of strange being carried all over the Romulan vessel. This episode does raise one question: After all these years, why does the Federation *still* not have a cloaking device? See also "The Pegasus."

EQUILIBRIUM

(DS9)
Original Airdate 10/22/94
Written by Rene Echevarria
Story by Christopher Teague
Directed by Cliff Bole

Dax begins experiencing hallucinations involving a mysterious figure in a mask and returns to the Trill homeworld with Sisko and Bashir in tow in an attempt to investigate what she learns is a suppressed memory, which the Trill authorities would like to keep suppressed.

ALTMAN (*1/2): An intriguing idea is badly executed in addressing the nature of identity and Dax's wrestling with the secret memory of a former host who was a deranged killer. There are some

good notions here, but ultimately the pedestrian manner in which they're dealt with sinks the episode. The Trill homeworld, shot in Huntington Gardens, California, is hardly original. Dax's nightmares aren't nearly as effectively surreal as they could be. As a mystery show, the entire affair plays strangely flat despite the presence of one of *DS9*'s best writers, Rene Echevarria.

GROSS (**1/2): A fairly successful attempt to explore the character of Dax, as well as the nature of the host/symbiont relationship. The idea of a suppressed personality that is a killer is terrific, adding another facet to the character's fascinating backstory. The imagery is interesting, particularly the enigmatic figure in a mask, but the mystery just isn't mysterious enough. A middle-of-the-road show.

ERRAND OF MERCY

(TOS)
Original Airdate 3/23/67
Written by Gene L. Coon
Directed by John Newland

The Enterprise arrives at the neutral planet Organia on the eve of a war between the Federation and the Klingon Empire. Kirk attempts to recruit the seemingly apathetic Organians to accept Federation help in fending off the Klingons, but the Organians show far more concern for Kirk and Spock, who have been put in jeopardy when the Klingon invasion force arrives and the two Starfleet officers must go under cover as local merchants while attempting to sabotage the Klingon force led by Commander Kor (John Colicos).

ALTMAN (***1/2): John Colicos is great as the merciless Kor. (He was equally sensational as the treacherous Baltar in *Battlestar Galactica*.) There's some superb scope here as Kirk and Spock go on their quest to hobble the Klingon invasion force (Spock is riotous when quoting the odds), as well as a classic Gene Coon catch-22 moment as Kirk argues for the right to wage war with the Organians, revealed to be superpowerful alien beings who put a stop to the war. "It would have been glorious," growls Kor. Guest star John Abbot is perfectly cast as the Organian leader Ayelbourne.

GROSS (****): Not that anyone is keeping tabs on such things, but Gene L. Coon brings us the Klingons *and* the Organian Peace Treaty in one episode. That in itself could have been enough, but he also manages to put Kirk and Spock in the heart of the action, bringing them face-to-face with a new enemy quite unlike any they have encountered before. The Klingons, as personified by John Colicos's Kor, are a powerful and ruthless enemy to whom war and battle are second nature, a fact accentuated by the deaths — off camera — of one hundred Organians for each hour that Kirk and Spock aren't handed over to the Klingons. The scenes between Colicos and William Shatner are terrific, with a powerful undercurrent of tension. Leonard Nimoy is at his best and driest as Spock. The backdrop of the story — the mounting Federation and Klingon forces approaching each other,

about to start an intergalactic war — is highly effective and believable, without us seeing a single ship from either side. The climax, in which Kirk is outraged that the Organians are interfering with the Federation's right to wage war, is classic and a real eye-opener for the character.

ETHICS

(TNG)
Original Airdate 3/2/93
Teleplay by Ronald D. Moore
Story by Sara Charno and Stuart Charno
Directed by Chip Chalmers

Worf is seriously injured when a support beam breaks and causes a heavy container to fall on him. He awakens in sick bay and learns that he is paralyzed from the waist down. Only the experimental technique of a neurogeneticist named Dr. Russell (Caroline Kava) can save him, but it also could kill him.

ALTMAN (**): Several strong performances and some well-written dialogue by Klingon expert Ron Moore help elevate "Ethics" above its tired *Dr. Kildare* origins, even though the relationships between Worf, his son and Riker, whom he wants to kill him, are the most interesting aspect of the show. The medical ethics questions are lightweight *ER*, and Caroline Kava as the demonic Dr. Russell disappoints. Ultimately, "Ethics" is wildly melodramatic, with a contrived and manipulative ending in which Worf dies and is resurrected following the hand-wringing over his demise.

GROSS (**): The acting is fine, particularly by Michael Dorn, but the approach really does feel like *Dr. Kildare* projected into the future. The way Worf mopes around and all the speeches about how he has to be there for his son, Alexander, add to the fifth-season feeling that we are watching a twenty-fourth-century soap opera. And that hokey ending in which Worf dies only to come back a moment or two later — puhlease!

GROSS (**): Some depth is given to Wesley Crusher via the parallels between him and Dr. Stubbs (and a possible direction for the young man to go in the future), but the whole nanite situation is nothing to speak of. Some truly amusing moments are provided when Wesley's mother, Beverly, returns to the *Enterprise,* replacing the departing Pulaski, and Wesley seems annoyed to have her back. Hey, who wouldn't be?

EVOLUTION

(TNG)
Original Airdate 9/23/89
Written by Michael Piller
Story by Michael Piller and Michael Wagner
Directed by Winrich Kolbe

A science experiment goes wildly awry when Wesley Crusher accidentally releases intelligent microorganisms called "nanites" into the ship's computer system. The accident jeopardizes an important scientific mission under the auspices of Dr. Paul Stubbs (Ken Jenkins), an obsessed scientist who will stop at nothing to proceed with his career-saving experiments.

ALTMAN (*1/2): Despite some enjoyable light character moments, the drama is negated by the silly sci-fi premise. Wesley Crusher is the catalyst for some more starship stupidity. Although Ken Jenkins gives a nice supporting turn as a disappointing Daystrom-like boy wonder, the infestation of the computer and the resulting havoc just aren't that interesting. "Evolution" also marks the return of Dr. Beverly Crusher to duty.

EX POST FACTO

(VOY)
Original Airdate 2/27/95
Teleplay by Evan Carlos Somers and Michael Piller
Story by Evan Carlos Somers
Directed by LeVar Burton

Every eleven hours, Tom Paris must relive the crime of murdering an alien scientist as punishment for the deed, while Tuvok desperately tries to exonerate him, launching a personal investigation into the crime.

ALTMAN (**1/2): For all intents and purposes, the derivative premise of the show predates *TNG*'s "A Matter of Perspective" (an episode to which it bears a striking similarity) and even "Wolf in the Fold," taking its cues from James Cain's *The Postman Always Rings Twice.* Unfortunately, the noirish conceit just doesn't work on *Voyager.* (Let's face it, it rarely works on any *Trek* show. Only *DS9* has been successful in sustaining a noir premise with "Necessary Evil.") In this show, some of Robin McKee's Lana Turner–esque lines are downright laughable (particularly an exchange about the perils of smoking and her ludicrous line, "I had to have a professional cleaning crew come to remove the bloodstains"). Tuvok's Hercule Poirot–like investigation also taxes one's credulity and passes from homage into plagiarism as he assembles the suspects at the scene of the murder. (And those mindmelds just aren't the same without that funky Classic *Trek* strumming harpsichord.) Using a Tribble to uncover an alien operative may have worked in a comedic episode of the original series, but having the dog reveal the murderer this time around is just plain dumb. Productionwise, the alien planet looks like something somebody let loose at Z Gallery would create.

GROSS (*): The notion of Tom Paris's torture is a brilliant creation, but the rest of the episode is repetitive of voyages past, seeming more like a Bogart detective thriller than an episode of *Star Trek*. This supposed alien planet is so Earth-like that it totally diminishes the show. They're smoking cigarettes, for crying out loud!

EHPLORERS

(DS9)
Original Airdate 5/13/95
Teleplay by Rene Echevarria
Story by Hilary J. Bader
Directed by Cliff Bole

Trying to see how much truth there is in a Bajoran myth, Sisko constructs an ancient space vessel with solar sails so that he and his son, Jake, can re-create a legendary journey from Bajoran history.

ALTMAN (***1/2): An original and engaging episode that tells two equally appealing stories. The quiet moments between Sisko and Jake are genuine and emotional. It may not be *Field of Dreams,* but it's good father/son stuff to be sure. The entire solar-sail concept is intriguing science fiction and well realized. Equally compelling is Bashir's concern over meeting the woman who beat him out as valedictorian of his graduating medical class. The scene in which O'Brien and Bashir indulge in a night of drunken revelry is notable, as is the valedictorian's ennui over serving on a starship, which the show's writers use to remind us of how much more exciting life on Deep Space Nine is. They may be right.

GROSS (****): Only *Deep Space Nine* could successfully take an episode that is little more than a father/son vacation with some bumps along the way and make it into something so enjoyable. The chemistry between Avery Brooks and Cirroc Lofton has always been strong, but never to the extent that it is here. Sisko also learns that his son is not interested in entering Starfleet Academy, instead wanting to be a writer, but Jake is worried about his father being left alone. Marc Alaimo as Gul Dukat has a nice moment, lending the Siskos a welcome hand in their quest. An episode that works on the level of honest emotions between two flesh-and-blood human beings.

EYE OF THE BEHOLDER

(TAS)
Original Airdate 1/5/74
Written by David P. Harmon
Directed by Hal Sutherland

While searching for the survivors of a missing starship, Kirk, Spock and McCoy are captured by the sluglike race of Lactra VII and put in cages as exhibits in an alien zoo.

ALTMAN (**1/2): Surprisingly, the concept of having the *Enterprise* crew incarcerated in an intergalactic zoo is not completely awful thanks to some deft writing by David Harmon, but the visualization of the superintelligent aliens as pink versions of the Snuffalupagas from *Sesame Street* helps blunt the impact of the episode. Although the landing party battling myriad creatures on the planet's surface is far too Saturday morning for me, the final resolution, in which the crew is freed after the creatures learn that humans are intelligent, does pack some punch.

GROSS (**): This remake of "The Cage" (albeit a softer, more cuddly version) successfully conveys the *Star Trek* philosophy and is an OK episode, but it's nothing to write logs about.

EYE OF THE BEHOLDER, THE

(TNG)
Original Airdate 2/28/94
Teleplay by Rene Echevarria
Story by Brannon Braga
Directed by Cliff Bole

During an investigation into an officer's suicide, Troi is overwhelmed by psychic images dating back

to the ship's construction eight years earlier. Before you can say "psychic residual trace, hyperkeritosis in the plasma injectors," Troi finds herself in a tempestuous affair with Worf, jealously eyeing his interest in a younger and equally attractive ensign.

ALTMAN (**): Despite its melodramatic theatrics and inane psychobabble, "The Eye of the Beholder" is enjoyable *Trek* camp, or, better yet, "Melrose Trek." The episode clearly exists only to explore the unlikely Worf/Troi pairing first addressed in "Parallels," and the show's coda, which makes a halfhearted attempt to explain what has happened, is a ludicrous conceit. Despite my better instincts, I found myself enjoying "The Eye of the Beholder." Jonathan Frakes is particularly amusing in a brief scene with Worf in Ten-Forward. It seems as though the trend during the sixth season of *TNG* was that they could break the Roddenberry rules as long as they did so in a dream sequence.

GROSS (*1/2): OK, it's an investigation of a suicide that turns into a murder mystery that turns into a . . . what? Soap opera? Did I beam into the wrong show? Beam me outta here!

EYE OF THE NEEDLE

(VOY)
Original Airdate 2/20/95
Teleplay by Bill Dial and Jeri Taylor
Story by Hilary J. Bader
Directed by Winrich Kolbe

The Voyager *crew communicates with the Alpha Quadrant through a miniature wormhole, only to* find that they've reached a Romulan ship twenty years in the past.

ALTMAN (***): Although the premise is inherently interesting and the episode is marked by a solid Romulan performance by Vaughn Armstrong, the major plot twists are handled less adeptly than they could have been. The fact that the *Voyager* has reached a Romulan ship in the Alpha Quadrant is too quickly revealed. The twist that the Romulan ship is decades in the past is a great revelation, but unfortunately it's discovered through tech talk rather than character, which is a mistake. A B story involving Kes entreating the crew to treat the doctor as a human and not a piece of computer hardware is not all that inventive but is ultimately satisfying thanks to the pleasant rapport between Lien and Picardo. On the whole, a good premise that is executed adequately but is ripe with unrealized potential.

GROSS (***1/2): One of the most effective episodes of *Voyager*, which is fascinating to watch thanks to the interaction between Captain Janeway and the Romulan captain, Telek. Watching their mistrust turn into respect and then admiration is extremely satisfying, and the revelation that this Romulan exists in the past is a real shocker worthy of Rod Serling. The idea of getting *this* close to home and having it snatched away at the last moment is not the contrived cheat that so many similar opportunities come across as. An early-series triumph.

F

FACE OF THE ENEMY
(TNG)
Original Airdate 2/8/93
Written by Naren Shankar
Story by Rene Echevarria
Directed by Gabrielle Beaumont

In an atypical Star Trek *adventure, Troi awakens aboard a Romulan warbird and finds that she has been transformed into a Romulan officer, Major Rakal, a member of the feared Tal Shiar. She is responsible for helping several important Romulan dignitaries defect to the Federation.*

ALTMAN (***): "Face of the Enemy" is a terrific and original installment (though evoking memories of "A Matter of Honor," in which Riker spends most of the time aboard a Klingon warship). The episode is unpredictable and exciting, thanks to a strong performance by Marina Sirtis as a member of the Tal Shiar, the Gestapo-like Romulan secret police. What keeps this conceptually challenging episode from being a classic is its disappointing production values. The production design for the Romulan ship looks like an art deco museum. In addition, despite another dynamic performance by Carolyn Seymour as Toreth, the Romulan commander (she also plays a Romulan commander in the second season's "Contagion" and a scientist in "First Contact"), the Federation's primary antagonists come across as far too human. The show does give us an all too rare glimpse inside the Romulan Empire, but by lifting their enigmatic veil, the writers reduce the Romulans to praetors in prosthetics.

GROSS (***): A true tour de force for Marina Sirtis, whose Deanna Troi has to pull off the masquerade of being a member of the Romulan Tal Shiar. She is more than up to the task. Tying in nicely with the events of season five's "Unification," "Face of the Enemy" is an effective espionage adventure that brings the audience a bit deeper into the Romulans' world, which has remained vastly underexplored in comparison to the Klingons'. In some ways, the episode is reminiscent of the series *Wiseguy,* in which the lead undercover cop is this close to being exposed for what he is but manages, at the last possible second, to avert suspicion. This happens to Troi several times. A terrific show.

FACES

(VOY)
Original Airdate 5/8/95
Teleplay by Kenneth Biller
Story by Jonathan Glassner
Directed by Winrich Kolbe

In the latest Trek incarnation of "The Enemy Within," B'Elanna Torres's human and Klingon halves are wrenched asunder by the Vidiians in an attempt to cure their Phage condition.

ALTMAN (***): Roxann Biggs-Dawson has proved to be one of the most consistently interesting actors on *Voyager,* and in "Faces" she is particularly adept at portraying her troubled human half. In playing the Klingon side, she's slightly less emotive than William Shatner as Kirk's campy evil twin, but only slightly. She takes her bellicose Klingon a little over the top, seemingly basing her portrayal too closely on Lursa and B'Etor. Otherwise, the show does almost everything right. The cold teaser gets us into the action right away. There are also some nice character moments between Tom Paris and Torres, and the Vidiians prove to be *Voyager's* most interesting new alien adversaries, particularly in a gruesome Grand Guignol moment, where a misguided alien scientist shows up wearing the face of one of the captured *Voyager* crew. Creepy but cool.

GROSS (****): The Phage aliens return, and their impact is just as powerful as it was on their first appearance, although one is left wondering whether writer Kenneth Biller has been spending too much time with Brannon Braga. On the surface it seems that "Faces" is merely a remake of "The Enemy Within," but the writers manage to explore the character of B'Elanna Torres by allowing her human and Klingon halves to interact and actually work together. There is something morbidly touching about Torres's keeper wanting to impress her by wearing the face of one of her comrades so that his looks will be more palatable to her. Maybe he caught a satellite transmission of *The Silence of the Lambs* or something. Once again, director Winrich Kolbe proves why he's so suitable for *Trek,* and Roxann Biggs-Dawson proves herself to be one of the show's most versatile actresses.

FACETS

(DS9)
Original Airdate 6/17/95
Written by Rene Echevarria
Directed by Cliff Bole

Dax engages in a Trill ceremony that will allow her to meet her previous hosts. This is accomplished when a guardian from her homeworld comes to the station, and Dax chooses her closest friends to embody these hosts. Things heat up when Sisko is taken over by Duran, the psychotic, and get worse when Curzon enters Odo's mind and doesn't want to go back.

ALTMAN: I haven't watched this episode, and I'm not going to lie to you and tell you that I did. But I'm sure it's fine; it sounds cool. You can find out my opinion if we ever get to revise this book. If it's on, give me a call and I'll let you know what I think.

GROSS (**): An interesting attempt to personify the various personalities coexisting inside Dax by putting them in series regulars' bodies. The story is too close to the many "alien possession" stories that *Star Trek* has done over the years, particularly in terms of "I like this body; I don't think I want to give it back."

FAMILY

(TNG)
Original Airdate 10/1/90
Written by Ronald D. Moore
Based in part on a premise by Susanne Lambdin and Bryan Stewart
Directed by Les Landau

While the Enterprise *is refurbished in space dock, Worf's adoptive human parents, Sergei and Helena (Theodore Bikel and Georgia Brown), visit the ship; Wesley Crusher is given a recording made for him by his late father, Jack (Doug Wert); and Captain Picard returns to Earth to visit his jealous brother Robert (Jeremy Kemp) in France, where the captain is driven to undergo a painful catharsis purging the bitter memories of his Borg experience.*

ALTMAN (****): "Family" perfectly illustrates the type of risks *TNG* took in its fourth season and is atypical *Trek* in every respect. Taking place on Earth (and mostly on location), the episode is a character-driven piece featuring superb performances by an exceptional guest cast that includes Jeremy Kemp, Theodore Bikel and Samantha Eggar. At times moving and other times hysterical, only the Wesley Crusher subplot involving a holodeck re-creation of his father falls flat. The ending, in which Picard's nephew watches the *Enterprise* leave orbit and dreams of his future as a starship captain (*Star Trek: The Next, Next Generation*?), is both powerful and evocative (though somewhat negated by his death in *Star Trek VII: Generations*). This is as good as *TNG* gets.

GROSS (***1/2): Although the idea of continuing themes was generally deemed syndication unfriendly, it works like a charm in "Family," which picks up where "Best of Both Worlds" leaves off. We are witnessing the emotional ramifications of the Borg on Picard and his need for a bit of emotional security. Patrick Stewart is outstanding, and the sense of continuity between episodes is wonderful. Regarding Wesley Crusher, in the early days of the series, the death of Jack Crusher was an important dramatic element. Unfortunately, here it lacks the emotional punch that such a meeting between son and long-dead father should have, although it does tug at the heartstrings a bit. The subplot involving Worf and his parents is both interesting and humorous. (Note: Picard's feeling of family is elaborated on in *Star Trek VII: Generations*.)

FAMILY BUSINESS

(DS9)
Original Airdate 5/20/95
Written by Ira Steven Behr and Robert Hewitt Wolfe
Directed by Rene Auberjonois

Quark and Rom head back to the Ferengi homeworld when they learn that their mother, Ishka (Andrea Martin), has violated Ferengi law by making a profit.

ALTMAN (**1/2): What amounted to a lascivious throwaway line about the Ferengi not clothing their women in *TNG*'s "The Last Outpost" has been developed into a huge mythology, mostly courtesy of *DS9*, and boy is it shticky. Yes, "Family Business" is cute, and

Armin Shimerman, Max Grodenchik and Andrea Martin do turn in solid performances. But it really isn't funny enough to be a pure comedy, nor allegorical enough to work on a metaphorical level. There are some nice moments between the two brothers and Mom, in which they talk about their father being a failure in business, but the Ferengi profit obsession is becoming a little old. A B story in which Jake tries to play matchmaker for his dad is a one-gag throwaway (the woman likes baseball) introducing the character of Kasidy Yates (Penny Johnson), who will play a more prominent role in the episodes to come.

GROSS (**1/2): The Ferengi get all warm and cuddly. This is an effective episode exploring the familial relationships between Quark, Rom and their mother. However, a visit to the Ferengi homeworld is not as interesting as a Ferengi story taking place on DS9. Jake's setup of Sisko with Kasidy Yates is effective, successfully laying the groundwork for future episodes.

FASCINATION

(DS9)
Original Airdate 12/13/94
Teleplay by Philip Lazebnik
Story by Ira Steven Behr and James Crocker
Directed by Avery Brooks

It's "Love Potion Deep Space Nine" when the arrival of Lwaxana Troi, whose hormones are always on overdrive, triggers a mysterious virus that results in passionate responses in all the crew members, who start pairing off with each other.

ALTMAN (*1/2): An abysmal episode in which the crew falls all over each other making goo-goo eyes. There's actually comic gold to be mined in the concept of the crew being afflicted with an insatiable lust that heightens some long-simmering passions, but "Fascination" takes the easy way out by creating such unlikely pairings as Jake and Major Kira. "The Naked Time" (TOS) showed us that exploiting the characters' inner desires can make for great drama, and the animated series' "Mudd's Passion" did this far better than here. Lwaxana Troi as the catalyst reflects the sheer nonsense of it all. Will you still respect me in the morning? Not if you liked this episode.

GROSS (**1/2): As always, the return of Lwaxana Troi means trouble, this time triggering passionate couplings of various people. What sounds on the surface to be a goofy alien disease story turns out to be an effective episode, thanks to earnest performances and a healthy amount of humor. Particularly strong is the look at the strained marriage of Miles and Keiko O'Brien, the only married couple in the various incarnations of *Trek*. There are also some nice moments between Odo and Lwaxana, who senses the shape-shifter's unrequited love for Kira and lets him know that she's there for him if he ever gets tired of waiting, all of which is surprisingly touching. A great bit of humor comes from Vedek Bareil, who feels that Sisko is standing between him and Dax and comes out swinging. An exasperated Sisko effortlessly blocks his blows before Dax herself steps in and dispatches the Vedek. Nice production values, giving the impression that the station is actually going through a Bajoran festival of sorts.

FINAL MISSION

(TNG)
Original Airdate 11/19/91
Teleplay by Kasey Arnold-Ince and Jeri Taylor
Story by Kasey Arnold-Ince
Directed by Corey Allen

Wil Wheaton's swan song to Star Trek, in which a shuttlecraft carrying Picard and Wesley Crusher to a conference crash-lands on a desert planet. When they attempt to gather water from a shielded fountain, Picard is critically wounded, and Crusher must take charge. The shuttle captain, Dirgo (Space 1999's Nick Tate), persists in his attempts to raid the water spring and is killed by the system's defensive mechanism. Crusher must rely on his wits to figure out a way to obtain some water before Picard dies.

ALTMAN (**1/2): A somewhat clichéd story is redeemed by some strong writing, in which Picard and Wesley Crusher share their feelings for each other, and some magnificent location work, in which Picard trots across the desert sand in search of shelter. All that's missing is a Maurice Jarre score. The silly B story, in which the *Enterprise* must escort a garbage scow through an asteroid field, doesn't work, and Dirgo, the slovenly and unkempt shuttle captain, is killed off too early, not giving Crusher the chance to prove his leadership ability.

GROSS (**1/2): Unlike Tasha Yar, Wesley Crusher is at least given a fitting farewell episode (although Denise Crosby was given a second chance in "Yesterday's Enterprise"), and that is the highlight of "Final Mission." In his attempts to help the captain, Crusher's monologue allows us to learn a little more of the boy's feelings for this father figure. The rest of the episode is mediocre.

FIRST CONTACT

(TNG)
Original Airdate 2/18/91
Teleplay by David Russell Bailey, David Bischoff and Joe Menosky
Story by Marc Scott Zicree
Directed by Cliff Bole

The Enterprise *must make "first contact" with an alien world on the verge of obtaining warp technology. When Riker is injured on the planet, Picard must accelerate his plans to retrieve his wounded first officer or risk violating the Prime Directive. Ultimately, the minister of the planet rejects the Federation's overtures, realizing that by embracing other cultures in the galaxy, he will jeopardize his homeworld, where the citizens are not ready to accept that they are not the center of the universe.*

ALTMAN (***1/2): Told from the point of view of the alien culture, "First Contact" is an impressive episode showcasing *TNG* at its best and most ambitious, even alluding to the origins of the original Klingon/Federation conflict. Wonderful performances by *Max Headroom*'s George Coe (Durkin), Carolyn Seymour (Mirasta Yale) and Michael Ensign (Krola) support the intriguing and original

script, as does a show-stealing cameo by *Cheers*' Bebe Neuwirth as one of the aliens who "has always wanted to have sex with an alien" and beds Riker in exchange for her help in arranging an escape attempt from a hospital ward.

GROSS (***1/2): The perfect complement to season three's "Who Watches the Watchers?" This is what *Star Trek* is all about — seeking out new lives. We've seen the *Enterprise* of the first two series interacting with various societies that are about to join or have recently joined the Federation, but this is the first time we see how it all comes about. There are fantastic performances all around, Cliff Bole's direction is first-rate and the script is literate, humorous and meaty. A real joy.

FIRST DUTY, THE

(TNG)
Original Airdate 3/30/92
Written by Ronald D. Moore and Naren Shankar
Directed by Paul Lynch

While en route to the Starfleet Academy, where Picard is scheduled to deliver the commencement address, the crew learns of a devastating in-flight accident involving Wesley Crusher and his squadron, who they suspect are involved in a cover-up of the incident.

ALTMAN (***1/2): "The First Duty" is a character-based Earthbound story driven by dynamic performances by Patrick Stewart and the returning Wil Wheaton. Ray Walston enchants as the wizened Starfleet Academy groundskeeper Boothby. Everything about "The First Duty" works, including Wesley Crusher's relationship with his fellow students. Dan Curry's matte work is exceptional, and Ed Lauter as the dead cadet's father is quite moving. Crusher finally pays the price for his annoying insolence and narcissism and is deservedly humbled for it.

GROSS (****): Wil Wheaton gives his best performance as Wesley Crusher in "The First Duty," an intelligent, thoughtful and dramatic look at facing up to your mistakes, no matter how dramatic the consequences. The scene between Crusher and Picard, in which the captain confronts Crusher with the truth, crackles. Picard recounts his relationship with the young man over the past five years, leaving Crusher to decide for himself whether he will step forward with the truth. Picard's disappointment is tangible, and it touches Crusher deeply. The performances are great, and director Paul Lynch has done an outstanding job of maintaining the pace and energy throughout.

FIRSTBORN

(TNG)
Original Airdate 4/25/94
Teleplay by Rene Echevarria
Story by Brian Kalbfeld
Directed by Jonathan West

Worf's son, Alexander, comes back as K'Mtar (James Sloyan) to try to prevent Worf's death, which the crew suspects may be the work of old nemeses Lursa and B'Etor from the house of Duras.

ALTMAN (**): A potentially compelling premise goes unrealized in an episode that is little more than a talky family affair. James Sloyan, who is wonderful in "The Alternate" on *DS9*, stars as K'Mtar and gives an equally engaging performance as the powerful Klingon warrior. Unfortunately, we never for a minute believe he's actually Alexander as a grown-up, as we learn in the story's climactic twist. The episode unfolds fairly routinely, and the quest for Lursa and B'Etor proves a pointless red herring, except to remind us that these busty baddies are still around for the next movie. Like "Unification," which did little more than set up *Star Trek VI: The Undiscovered Country*, "Firstborn" is little more than a minor footnote in *TNG* lore, serving as the prelude to *Star Trek VII: Generations*.

GROSS (**): "Be true to yourself" is the message of this fairly successful episode that presents a possible life for a Klingon who refuses to be a warrior. Good performances by Michael Dorn, James Sloyan and Brian Bonsall highlight the episode. See also "Reunion," "Redemption," "Past Prologue" and *Star Trek VII: Generations*.

FISTFUL OF DATA, A

(TNG)
Original Airdate 11/9/92
Teleplay by Robert Hewitt Wolfe and Brannon Braga
Story by Robert Hewitt Wolfe
Directed by Patrick Stewart

When the holodeck malfunctions in a western town setting, Worf, Alexander and Troi find themselves facing off against the specter of many gunmen as duplicates of Data take over the computer-generated town, turning what was supposed to be a simple fantasy programmed by Alexander into a most dangerous game indeed.

ALTMAN (***): For a series whose high-concept titles fail to show the near poetic imagination of "City on the Edge of Forever" and "Requiem for Methuselah" with such mundane appellations as "The Hunted" and "The Vengeance Factor," the moniker "A Fistful of Datas" earns this episode a three-star accolade simply for its title. Although the premise strains credulity, even for *Star Trek*, director Patrick Stewart delivers a winning episode with his assured mastery over the western iconography. Infrequent diversions down the road of lightweight, high-concept plot lines such as this are welcome on occasion, and Michael Dorn and Brent Spiner (in his enjoyably devious multiple roles) seem to relish this atypical *Trek*. But the true delight is Marina Sirtis, who steals the show as the mysterious stranger Durango.

GROSS (***): By this point in *TNG* history (sixth season), I'd grown pretty tired of malfunctioning holodeck stories, but "A Fistful of Datas" works like gangbusters. Taking on all the conventions of a traditional western and turning them on their ear, the episode is, quite simply, a lot of fun. Data's intrusion into the fantasy is logical (he's tied into the ship's main computer at the time) and carries

with it a real threat. Michael Dorn's Worf undergoes an interesting transformation, from a father going through this program in an effort to please his son to someone truly enjoying himself to the warrior who has to protect those around him from overwhelming odds. Once more, Brent Spiner seems to be having a wonderful time. Some salt with that scenery? Look for the great final moment when the *Enterprise* "rides" off into the sunset.

FOR THE CAUSE
(DS9)
Original Airdate 5/4/96
Teleplay by Ronald D. Moore
Story by Mark Gehred-O'Connell
Directed by James L. Conway

Putting the paranoia about shape-shifters aside, the crew has suspicions of a different kind when they think that Sisko's love, Kasidy Yates (Penny Johnson), as well as DS9 crewman Eddington (Kenneth Marshall), may be part of the Maquis, former Starfleet officers protesting the Cardassian demilitarized zone.

ALTMAN (***): Although the Maquis almost seem superfluous in the wake of the collapse of the Cardassian Empire after the Klingon invasion, the writers prove that there's still some juice in their presence on the show. Whatever emotional beats were missing from Cal Hudson's betrayal of Sisko in the second season's "The Maquis" are made up for here by Kasidy Yates's rejection of Sisko's Federation values. Much to its credit, the episode doesn't take the easy way out and is all the better for it. There's a wonderful speech by Commander Eddington, also revealed to be a Maquis, in which he takes the Federation to task for becoming too complacent and sacrificing the well-being of its own people for peace — comparing their assimilating nature to that of the Borg. It's a powerful moment that seems to reflect the writers' own reservations with the *Star Trek* universe, which often proves uncomfortably limiting for them. Nonetheless, Sisko delivers a stinging rebuttal, with an ire and venom seldom seen on the show, which no one but Avery Brooks (or William Shatner) could have pulled off. Good stuff.

GROSS (***): The return of the Maquis and some personal stakes for Sisko, who is truly torn between his feelings for Kasidy Yates and his responsibilities to Starfleet. Surprisingly, the episode does not have the clichéd happy ending. Yates is guilty of the charges against her, and crewman Eddington (Kenneth Marshall) also is found to be a member of the Maquis. In this episode, the human elements really work, primarily the actions of Avery Brooks, whether it's smelling Kasidy's pillow after she's left his quarters or trying to open up his heart to Jake and not being able to do so in a coherent manner. Not the type of show you'd find on the other *Trek* spin-offs. See also "Family Business."

FOR THE WORLD IS HOLLOW AND I HAVE TOUCHED THE SKY

(TOS)
Original Airdate 11/8/68
Written by Rik Vollaerts
Directed by Tony Leader

The Enterprise attempts to save the population of an artificial asteroid, Yonada, built by the ancient Fabrini, which is on course to destroy a solar system. McCoy, who is diagnosed with an incurable disease, decides to stay with the civilization's leader, Natira (Kate Woodville).

ALTMAN (**): Another third-season stinker in which McCoy's sudden illness is a plot contrivance of the worst kind. The *Starlost*-like plot of a civilization that doesn't realize it's living inside a ship is sort of a neat idea, but we really don't see any of the scope that such a story demands. The Oracle is yet another in a long line of advanced civilization throwbacks that we've seen time and again, and I don't buy the romance between McCoy and Natira for a second.

GROSS (**1/2): The third season of the original *Star Trek* seems to alternate between a lead character falling in love and getting an incurable disease that's cured by episode's end. In this case, Rik Vollaerts has managed to combine both. DeForest Kelley gives an earnest performance as the "dying" McCoy, and there's a nice bit of chemistry between him and guest star Kate Woodville (Natira). Additionally, the notion of an asteroid actually being a traveling spaceship is intriguing, though hardly original to the genre. Outside of that, this show has a lot of tired elements, such as Kirk and Spock desperately looking for the controls to change the course of this asteroid/ship and yet another society ruled by a computer.

FORCE OF NATURE

(TNG)
Original Airdate 11/15/93
Written by Naren Shankar
Directed by Robert Lederman

A dull and plodding would-be technothriller in which two alien scientists attempt to warn the Enterprise *crew about the dangers of warp drive to the fabric of subspace in their sector while the* Enterprise *is engaged in a rescue mission to find a missing ship.*

ALTMAN (*): The most egregious sin this show commits is its preaching about the environmental consequences of warp speed, a thinly veiled allegory for the effect of carbon monoxide pollution on Earth's ozone layer. The message is heavy-handed, and the show's coda — in which a straight-faced Patrick Stewart quietly ponders the dangers of warp speed, leading LaForge to reply stoically, "We still have time to make it better" — is laughably simplistic. Although there are some attempts to break up the monotony of the show's tech talk, even the recurring gag of Data training his cat is taken to a ponderous extreme, considering the cat's abnormal behavior doesn't relate to the show's plot. One of the more effective Ferengi characterizations is briefly introduced, then dropped abruptly,

making this a pointless exercise in unwarranted polemic.

GROSS (*1/2): A real groaner that was designed to be an environmental allegory but falls flat. The sheer stupidity of the premise is exacerbated by the fact that the implications of the episode are forgotten weeks later. I tend to enjoy issue-oriented shows, but this is a total misconception.

FORSAKEN, THE

(DS9)
Original Airdate 5/24/93
Teleplay by Don Carlos Dunaway and Michael Piller
Story by Jim Trombetta
Directed by Les Landau

A hidden computer program causes havoc on the station and traps Lwaxana Troi and Odo in a turbo-lift as Odo begins to change back into his natural gelatinous form.

ALTMAN (**1/2): The pathos involving a dissolving Odo and Lwaxana Troi is effectively realized. Piller's and Dunaway's script also is laden with several other strong character-driven exchanges between Troi and her would-be paramour, as well as a pleasantly offbeat C story involving Bashir's tour of the station for a coterie of insufferable visiting Federation ambassadors. Less palatable is the computer virus MacGuffin, although Colm Meaney's earnest acting almost makes the story line credible. One gnawing flaw is the fact that both *TNG* and *DS9* have yet to get the Vulcans right, no matter how hard they've tried. Jack

Shearer as Vulcan ambassador Vadosia is just dreadful.

GROSS (***1/2): Let's handle the story lines in reverse. The C story is humorous. The computer virus B story, a rather clichéd MacGuffin, leads to a wonderful A story. Never having been much of a fan of Lwaxana Troi (although that was dispelled in her last few visits to the *Enterprise* during seasons five and six), it's delightful to see her in such fine form. Trapping her and Odo in the turbo-lift seems like the most contrived method of creating a bottle show imaginable, yet the writing, as well as Les Landau's intimate direction, brings these characters to life in new and unexpected ways. Each gradually strips away the facades they normally wear so proudly and reveal their inner selves. A real highlight is Rene Auberjonois's quiet attempt to resist the transformation into his base self and Majel Barrett's gentle assurance that she will take care of him.

FRAME OF MIND

(TNG)
Original Airdate 5/2/93
Written by Brannon Braga
Directed by Jim Conway

Riker finds himself propelled between a life aboard the Enterprise *and that as an inmate of an alien mental asylum while acting for Dr. Crusher in a play, "Frame of Mind." Unable to discern reality from fantasy, Riker believes that he really is insane and that the* Enterprise *is a figment of his imagination.*

ALTMAN (***1/2): Beginning in the midst of an eerie and dissonant teaser, Brannon Braga crafts a dark and brooding episode. "Frame of Mind" is riveting for its first several acts, propelled by a powerful performance by Jonathan Frakes, startling direction by Jim Conway, starkly effective production design and an appropriately atonal score. Defying convention and formula, "Frame of Mind" has a dark intensity unmatched by any other *TNG* episode. Unfortunately, its brilliant script suffers from an unsatisfying conventional resolution, which dilutes the overall impact of the Kafka-esque nightmare and ultimately ends as "Future Imperfect" revisited.

GROSS (****): What is real, and what is fantasy? Those are the questions raised by Brannon Braga's incredibly disorienting teleplay, in which Riker tries to determine which is which. In one of the most satisfying episodes of the sixth season, Braga, Jonathan Frakes and director Jim Conway manage to make the audience truly understand how thin the line between reality and fantasy could be for any of us. After a while, we begin to question, at least to some degree, which reality is Riker's. A terrific episode.

FRIDAY'S CHILD

(TOS)
Original Airdate 12/1/67
Written by D. C. Fontana
Directed by Joseph Pevney

The Federation and the Klingons vie for an alliance with the people of Capella IV, which is no easy task for Kirk and the Enterprise. *The Klingon commander, Kras (Tige Andrews), backstabs them and at-*

tempts to manipulate the Capellans at every turn, while McCoy tries to save the child of Eleen (Julie Newmar), the wife of the planet's former ruler.

ALTMAN (**1/2): The best thing about "Friday's Child" is how cool the Capellans' weapons are. Although Tige Andrews won't go down in history as one of the great Klingons, watching the *Enterprise* landing party deal with the honor-bound warrior race, as well as Scotty's own dilemmas in answering a phantom distress call, is entertaining. There's some great location filming, and the action culminates in a grand finale, as Kras gets what he deserves, with the usual terrific Spock/McCoy banter. Julie Newmar is enjoyable as always, but I prefer her scratching her claws on Batman's cowl rather than nursing babies.

GROSS (**1/2): This episode features political machinations by the Klingons as they try to gain a foothold on an alien planet in accordance with the Organian Peace Treaty. Naturally, this puts them in conflict with Kirk and the *Enterprise*. The standout in the episode is Julie Newmar, who is so bitchy as Eleen that she'd give Joan Collins a run for her money. "Friday's Child" succeeds in its establishment of an alien culture and its mores. Admittedly, their clothes look like bad Halloween costumes, but production values were never a highlight of the original series. Lots of fun is garnered in the antagonistic relationship between McCoy and Eleen and in the birth of her son. This provides a terrific tag on the bridge of the *Enterprise*,

where Kirk and McCoy discuss the child, Leonard James Akeer. With a cocked eyebrow, Spock responds, "I believe the two of you are going to be insufferable for at least a month." Great stuff.

FUTURE IMPERFECT
(TNG)
Original Airdate 11/12/90
Written by J. Larry Carroll and David Bennett Carren
Directed by Les Landau

After beaming down to a mysterious planet, Riker awakens in sick bay sixteen years later. He has a son, and peace negotiations are continuing in earnest with the Romulans. What Riker fears could be a Romulan plot to discover the secret location of Outpost 23 actually turns out to be the fantasy of a lonely alien boy.

ALTMAN (***1/2): The excellent premise is well executed by director Les Landau. The scenes between Riker and his "son" are delightful, and the episode's double switch, in which Riker thinks he is in a Romulan holodeck, only to find out that it's all an illusion, makes for a splendidly clever twist. The episode also features one of the series' best teasers and the return of Minuet (Carolyn McCormick), who serves as the catalyst for Riker's realization that he is being duped.

GROSS (***): The premise of the episode is fairly old hat, seeming as if it could have been lifted from an episode of *Mission: Impossible*. Indeed, even the short-lived *V* did a variation on the idea. This episode is saved by Jonathan

Frakes's performance and the double-twist ending, which would have made Rod Serling proud. The return of Minuet is brilliant. A surprisingly effective episode despite the setup. See also "11001001."

GALAXY'S CHILD

(TNG)
Original Airdate 3/11/91
Teleplay by Maurice Hurley
Story by Thomas Kartozian
Directed by Winrich Kolbe

The Enterprise accidentally kills a pregnant space creature, whose offspring attaches itself to the ship's hull. Returning is Leah Brahms (Susan Gibney), first introduced in the third-season "Booby Trap" as a hologram who helps Geordi LaForge navigate the ship away from a minefield. This time she beams aboard the Enterprise *in the flesh. LaForge courts her, only to discover that the fetching scientist is married. Together, they save the space baby attached to the hull.*

ALTMAN (***): The real gem of this episode is the return of Leah Brahms (Susan Gibney), one of the *Enterprise*'s engine designers, whom Geordi LaForge re-created in the holodeck in "Booby Trap." LaForge now meets her for the first time, and she turns out to be nothing like he imagined (which

was mostly written by an uncredited Jeri Taylor). After he tries to wine and dine her, he discovers that she's married. The space baby story, which boasts some impressive special effects, is less satisfying and far more routine.

GROSS (***): It's my belief that in the annals of *Trek* history Maurice Hurley will be fondly remembered for the contribution he made to *TNG*. "Galaxy's Child" demonstrates yet again that he understands Gene Roddenberry's universe as well as Rick Berman or Michael Piller. The LaForge/Brahms story is great, and the revelation that she's married is a real slap in the face to LaForge, who has created a relationship with this woman in his mind based on their holographic interactions. The infant alien story works remarkably well, primarily due to Patrick Stewart's performance. You can feel his profound sadness when the *Enterprise* accidentally kills the mother and his determination to do whatever is possible to help the offspring. This is the *Star Trek* philosophy at its best: respect for all life-forms. A job well done.

GALILEO SEVEN, THE

(TOS)
Original Airdate 1/5/67
Written by Oliver Crawford and S. Bar David
Directed by Robert Gist

While en route to deliver medical supplies to Makus III, the Enterprise pauses to examine a quasar formation, and the shuttlecraft crash-lands on the surface of Taurus II, with its deadly primitive inhab-

itants. Meanwhile, the Enterprise crew desperately attempts to locate the lost shuttlecraft before they have to leave for their rendezvous.

ALTMAN (***1/2): Spock struggles with the duties of command in a superbly imaginative episode. Everything from the production design of the shuttlecraft to the towering primitive creatures that endanger the crashed ship are extremely well conceived. Spock's realization that he must leap beyond logic after encountering nothing but bitter hostility from his crew, who have grown to accept their impending deaths, is wonderful, as is his desperate solution resulting in their rescue. There's semitragic pathos as McCoy says with a sigh, "So ends your first command, Mr. Spock." In a way, you almost wish they hadn't survived, giving "Bones" the chance to gloat. Some have compared the episode to *The Flight of the Phoenix*, but that film didn't have Mr. Spock and McCoy at each other's throats.

GROSS (**1/2): The problem with this episode is that the Spock character, no matter how dire the situation, just isn't as interesting without Kirk to bounce lines off of. (As *Star Trek VII: Generations* proved, the same can't be said of Kirk, who's interesting to watch no matter whom he's interacting with.) As a result, it's difficult to get thoroughly involved in the story, although it's commendable that Spock actually grows as a character, accepting the fact that luck can occasionally be as effective as logic. Check out the crea-

ture they encounter on the planet's surface; it looks like an extra from *Lost in Space*.

GAMBIT, PART I

(TNG)
Original Airdate 10/11/94
Teleplay by Naren Shankar
Story by Chris Hatton and Naren Shankar
Directed by Peter Lauritson

Riker is abducted by mercenaries who he believes are responsible for killing the captain. Then he comes face-to-face with Picard, who is pretending to be a smuggler of rare artifacts.

ALTMAN (***): Although it's as pulpy as the most campy episode of *Buck Rogers* (I would expect nothing less with the starring guest role being played by veteran genre baddie Richard Lynch), "Gambit" is a fun, action-packed change of pace for the series. It boasts the requisite interpersonal conflict of the season in its opening moments — Riker and Troi arguing over how to handle the captain's demise — and its mercenary milieu is a refreshing variance from the claustrophobic confines of the *Enterprise*. Also notable is another cold comic book–like teaser in which the crew attempts to unravel the captain's disappearance by posing under cover at an alien bar. *Star Trek III: The Search for Spock*'s Robin Curtis is particularly adept in her role as the villainous Tallera, a Vulcan isolationist.

GROSS (***): A rollicking episode that comes out of nowhere and shakes up the *Star Trek* formula a bit. Patrick Stewart is a riot as the constantly sneering and snarling pirate Galen (named after the captain's mentor, no doubt), and guest star Richard Lynch does his patently evil shtick as Baran, the leader of this impressed group of mercenaries. Former Saavik Robin Curtis does an impressive turn as a Vulcan isolationist who is more than she appears to be. Director Peter Lauritson never lets us forget that we're supposed to be having fun with the episode.

GAMBIT, PART II

(TNG)
Original Airdate 10/18/94
Teleplay by Ronald D. Moore
Story by Naren Shanker
Directed by Alexander Singer

The search of the pirates leads to an ancient Vulcan artifact that can turn thoughts into reality and is perceived as the ultimate weapon. When Robin Curtis's Vulcan character, Tallera, reveals her desire to have the device so as to conquer the universe, she is horrified to learn that it is ineffective against nonaggressive personalities. In essence, it's useless.

ALTMAN (**1/2): While part II is not nearly as inventive or fun as part I, "Gambit" concludes with a punchy finale, despite its faux *Raiders of the Lost Ark* resolution. Its preachy "love, peace and understanding" mysticbabble made me yearn for some good old-fashioned technobabble. However,

James Worthy's performance as an imposing Klingon, a spicy confrontation between Worf and Data and a particularly lively ending in the vein of Classic *Trek* all work to good effect. Writer Ron Moore also mines the "Data in command" B story for all it's worth. Alas, the poor Vulcans, whose culture was so skillfully drawn in the original series, are yet again butchered by some insidious plot contrivance involving Vulcan isolationism.

GROSS (***): Jonathan Frakes joins the party as Riker's search for Picard leads him to the pirates, who manage to capture him and believe they have been able to turn him against both the *Enterprise* and the Federation. While reaching the destination isn't nearly as much fun as getting there, the Vulcan weapon and Tallera's attempts to control the galaxy with it are certainly effective. The weapon's ineffectiveness against those with nonaggressive intentions captures Gene Roddenberry's take on *Trek*, while simultaneously giving us insight into why the Vulcans shed their emotions in the first place. Overall, "Gambit" is one of *TNG*'s most satisfying two-parters. One complaint is the absolutely nutty scene between Data and Worf, a confrontation that quickly turns into this exchange: "I hope I have not ruined our friendship, Mr. Worf." "No, Commander, it is I who have endangered our friendship." Why don't they hug and get it over with already?

GAME, THE

(TNG)
Original Airdate 10/28/91
Written by Brannon Braga
Story by Susan Sackett and Fred Bronson
Directed by Corey Allen

During a romantic respite on Risa, Riker's lady friend, Etana (Katherine Moffat), gives him an electronic mind game that he takes back to the ship. The game secretly subverts the crew in an attempt to co-opt the Enterprise *and the Federation. Only Wesley Crusher and his new girlfriend, Ensign Lefler (Ashley Judd), can stop the infiltration of the alien game.*

ALTMAN (***): Although the returning Wesley Crusher does save the ship again, the episode's much too ridiculous to be taken seriously. Bordering on high camp, it's one of the most offbeat and entertaining *TNG* installments. It's basically *Invasion of the Body Snatchers* for the Nintendo generation, but it works well on that level. It's not art, but it has enough action, humor and romance to satisfy. Actress Ashley Judd (*Heat, Ruby in Paradise*) as Robin Lefler is intoxicating, showing a lot more affinity for Crusher than the fans have.

GROSS (***): But can we have it in the stores by Christmas? Seemingly a tribute to some of the genre classics of the 1950s, "The Game" is a shipboard show that really works. Beginning with some truly wonderful quiet moments between the characters, the episode becomes more serious as the game's influence is felt throughout the *Enterprise*. Director Corey Allen conveys a true *Body Snatchers* feeling, as Wesley Crusher is the lone nonparticipant and *everyone* wants him to join. This particular method of mind control is highly original and one that every Sega-obsessed kid (or at least their parents) can probably relate to. It's nice to have Wil Wheaton back but disturbing to see how quickly the writers slip into the "Crusher saves the ship" formula. You have to wonder how the *Enterprise* survived without him.

GAMESTERS OF TRISKELION, THE

(TOS)
Original Airdate 1/5/68
Written by Margaret Armen
Directed by Gene Nelson

Kirk, Chekov and Uhura are kidnapped by the beings of the planet Triskelion and forced to partake in gladiator games that a race of advanced alien gamesters have designed to amuse themselves.

ALTMAN (***): The S&M episode, in which the leather-clad crew combats alien warriors for the amusement of their captors — cool, multicolored brain beings that thrive on sport. It's not the most cerebral episode, but it sure is fun. Kirk's tutorial on kissing to Angelique Pettyjohn's Shana is a classic William Shatner moment. In addition, the many action scenes are exceptionally choreographed. John Ruskin is menacing as the alien slave master, Galt, though not nearly as cleverly conceived as the Triskelion game masters themselves. It's better than going to Vegas.

GROSS (*1/2): *Star Trek* does S&M as Kirk, Uhura and Chekov run around in leather collars, testosterone pumping all over the place. One of the worst episodes of the second season, this is extremely contrived and not very satisfying — except, perhaps, for guest star Angelique Pettyjohn and her infamous silver outfit. Kind of reminds me of "The Cage" on steroids.

GENESIS

(TNG)
Original Airdate 3/21/94
Written by Brannon Braga
Directed by Gates McFadden

It's "Starship of the Apes" when Barclay gets the flu and Dr. Crusher inadvertently triggers a genetic virus in an attempt to cure him. The virus then begins transforming the crew into primitive creatures.

ALTMAN (***): "Genesis" could have been campy fun if it wasn't so obsessed with trying to justify its silly premise with its pervasive technobabble. There are some spooky moments, but it's hard to take the show seriously with the actors, under oodles of prosthetics, running around the ship as devolved primates. By the time Picard starts gingerly spraying pheromones to attract a metamorphosed Worf-monster, the episode is completely laughable. As long as you're willing to discard logic and accept the episode on its own goofy terms, it's also enjoyably loony.

GROSS (**1/2): One of those disturbing episodes of *TNG*, with some of the most bizarre images you've ever seen this side of the Alpha Quadrant. Troi as an amphibian? Worf as a creature let loose on the ship? Hey, you won't find that kind of stuff anywhere else on the tube!

HALF A LIFE

(TNG)
Original Airdate 5/6/91
Written by Peter Allan Fields
Directed by Les Landau

Lwaxana Troi falls in love with an alien scientist, Timicin (David Ogden Stiers), who is supposed to kill himself on his sixtieth birthday in accordance with the rules and rituals of his planet's culture.

ALTMAN (***): A wonderfully realized episode that features one of Majel Barrett's best performances as Lwaxana Troi. There's the expected humor content of the annual Lwaxana outing ("I'm a woman dressing for a man, something you might try now and again, dear daughter"), but the episode also is a poignant and thought-provoking allegory looking at the place of the elderly in society. It's not a particularly enlightening viewpoint, but it's a testament to the ability of *Trek* to use metaphor in telling intelligent science-fiction stories. It's by far the best of the Lwaxana episodes and features a strong supporting performance by *M*A*S*H*'s David Ogden Stiers as Timicin.

GROSS (***): In my review of "Haven," I compare Lwaxana Troi to a dentist's drill, and by the time I saw "Menage A Troi," I wished that someone would beam her into open space. What can I say? In "Half a Life," Majel Barrett is splendid as Lwaxana, thanks primarily to a sensitive and rather touching script by Peter Allan Fields that successfully tackles the question of aging in our society. David Ogden Stiers is always a welcome presence on any show, and his portrayal of Timicin truly showcases a man in turmoil as he must choose between the customs of his society and his personal happiness. All the regulars are fine, although they take a backseat to Barrett and Stiers. Definitely a pleasant surprise. See also "Haven," "Manhunt," "Menage A Troi," "Cost of Living," "Dark Page," "The Forsaken" and "The Muse."

HARD TIME

(DS9)
Original Airdate 4/15/96
Teleplay by Robert Hewitt Wolfe
Story by Daniel Keys Moran and Lynn Barker
Directed by Alexander Singer

In the dark, twisted flip side of "The Inner Light," O'Brien suffers from the false memories of a twenty-year prison sentence as he uncomfortably tries to readjust to life aboard the station in this remarkably realized high-concept sci-fi psychodrama.

ALTMAN (***1/2): Unlike the *Voyager* episode "Ex Post Facto," in which Tom Paris is implanted with the memories of a murder victim as punishment, "Hard Time" uses its creative sci-fi conceit to relate a compelling human drama in which O'Brien must wrestle with the demons of a twenty-year prison term that never really happened. Although using E'Chem, played effectively by Craig Wasson, as an illusionary manifestation of his guilt doesn't quite work, Alexander Singer's direction, a surprisingly powerful score by Dennis McCarthy and a searing performance by Colm Meaney make this another *DS9* triumph.

GROSS (****): Essentially the flip side of *TNG*'s "The Inner Light." Whereas that episode celebrated life, "Hard Time" takes a closer look at the darker aspects of a man's soul. An extremely atmospheric episode that manages to segue effortlessly from the station to O'Brien's holding cell and back again without being jolting. It's unsettling to watch Colm Meaney's O'Brien, an officer with a fair amount of self-control, losing it again and again, and seeing him use his survival skills, picked up while he was in "prison," is fascinating. A nice supporting turn by Alexander Siddig, as Dr. Bashir desperately tries to help his best friend. See also "Ex Post Facto."

HAVEN

(TNG)
Original Airdate 11/28/87
Written by Tracy Torme
Story by Lan O'Kun
Directed by Richard Compton

Troi's mother, Lwaxana (Majel Barrett), beams aboard to put into motion her daughter's prearranged marriage to Wyatt Miller (Rob Knepper), which comes as much of a surprise to the counselor as it does to the rest of the crew. Meanwhile, a Tarellian plague ship enters orbit around the planet Haven, on which the woman from Wyatt's mysterious dreams resides.

ALTMAN (**1/2): A former *Trek* classic that ages poorly. The introduction of the campy Lwaxana Troi is as amusing as ever, but the subplot involving a plague-stricken ship is a disappointing adjunct to an otherwise delightful episode. Writer Tracy Torme labels the farce a disappointment, and, in retrospect, he's probably right. The highlight is *The Addams Family*'s Carel Struycken as Troi's valet, Mr. Homn, and a prewedding dinner reception that goes wildly awry.

GROSS (**1/2): A good character episode for Deanna Troi, providing some lighter moments, but the overall show is a mixed bag. Majel Barrett's Lwaxana Troi grinds on you after a while, kind of like a dentist's drill (though, it should be pointed out, she does get better with subsequent appearances). The plague ship idea is intriguing on its own, but its connection to the main story line seems tenuous at best. Interesting casting note: Wyatt Miller's father is played by

Robert Ellenstein, who also portrayed the Federation president in *Star Trek IV: The Voyage Home.*

HEART OF GLORY

(TNG)
Original Airdate 3/19/88
Written by Maurice Hurley
Story by Michael Michaelian
Directed by Rob Bowman

A trio of Klingons are rescued from a damaged freighter within the Romulan Neutral Zone. One of them dies, but the other two are fugitives from the Klingon Empire. They try to convince Worf to help them take over the Enterprise and begin a crusade of vengeance across the galaxy.

ALTMAN (***): The first show proving that *TNG* could do no wrong when it came to the Klingons. It's an exciting, action-packed, well-written story that unfolds quickly under director Rob Bowman's able hand. The early scenes in which the crew oohs and ahhs over the transmission coming from Geordi LaForge's VISOR is less palatable, however. Better Klingon stories are yet to come.

GROSS (***1/2): One of Gene Roddenberry's biggest complaints about the original show's Klingons was that they were merely the villains of the week, and he wanted them to be expanded to a three-dimensional level. For this reason alone, "Heart of Glory" must have been a dream come true. The first in *TNG*'s numerous Klingon-oriented stories, this is a truly kick-ass episode, and the Klingons have never been better. Besides a terrific action/adventure approach, we are given new insights into the Klingon people and a powerfully dramatic story line for Michael Dorn's Worf, as he is torn between two cultures. We learn that when a Klingon dies, those around him bellow heavenward as a warning to those above that a Klingon warrior is about to join them. Just great.

HEART OF STONE

(DS9)
Original Airdate 2/22/95
Written by Ira Steven Behr and Robert Hewitt Wolfe
Directed by Alexander Singer

In an effort to get Odo to admit his love for Kira, the Founders take the form of Kira and try to convince Odo that she is going to die. Nog tries to convince Sisko to sponsor his application to the Starfleet Academy.

ALTMAN (**): The story involving Odo and Kira drowns in a melodramatic sea of pathos, ending with a rather predictable and unsatisfying climax. The Nog B story works remarkably well, however, spearheaded by a terrific performance by the always entertaining Aron Eisenberg. It's unfortunate that the Odo/Kira relationship, which held the promise of such ripe drama, is squandered on such an inane premise.

GROSS (***1/2): *Deep Space Nine* has managed to do more with bottle shows than any other *Trek* series. This episode in particular is a great opportunity for Rene Auberjonois to explore Odo's feelings for Kira. He thinks that he is going to

lose her and finds it within himself to verbalize the feelings he's never dared speak before. To learn that he's been used by the Founders is truly heartbreaking. This is incredibly powerful characterization. The B story involving Nog's being embarrassed about his people and wanting to join the Starfleet Academy is totally unexpected but a wonderful character conceit.

HERO WORSHIP

(TNG)
Original Airdate 1/27/92
Teleplay by Joe Menosky
Story by Hilary J. Bader
Directed by Patrick Stewart

The Enterprise *investigates the disappearance of the* Vico, *a research vessel lost inside a Black Cluster. They find that the sole survivor is a young boy named Timothy (Joshua Harris), who secretly blames himself for what happened to the ship and believes the* Enterprise *will meet the same fate.*

ALTMAN (***): A charming show about a youth who embraces Data as a father figure after his family is killed. There is some particularly strong dialogue from Joe Menosky, who has always serviced Data better than any of the other characters. Surprisingly, "Hero Worship" also features a compelling B story involving the *Enterprise*'s investigation of the mysterious and eerie Black Cluster. The MacGuffin in which the *Enterprise* suspects that the *Vico* was attacked by alien aggressors provides an engrossing mystery to underscore the human drama involving Timothy and Data.

GROSS (**1/2): As in *TNG's* fifth-season episode "New Ground," you cannot fault the performances in "Hero Worship." Joshua Harris is extremely touching as Timothy, and Data is surprisingly compassionate in this little boy's dilemma, but it just feels like more suds. The Black Cluster element works well, but it's not enough to detract from the "invasion of the kids" that began en masse in the fifth season. Patrick Stewart handles the situation well, bringing some vitality to the story line.

HEROES AND DEMONS

(VOY)
Original Airdate 4/24/95
Written by Naren Shankar
Directed by Les Landau

When the Voyager's *holodeck is taken over by an alien being that transforms living creatures — including Kim, Tuvok and Chakotay — into pure energy, the ship's holographic doctor must overcome his system's limitations and enter the medieval holodeck milieu to do battle with the alien and restore everyone to normal.*

ALTMAN (***): It's easy to forgive the insipid premise of "Heroes and Demons," given Robert Picardo's tour de force performance as the doctor, temporarily taking the nom de plume Lord Schweizer when he is forced to do battle with Grendel in a holodeck re-creation of *Beowulf.* While transpiring in the holodeck, "Heroes and Demons" works as well as any previous holodeck adventure in

TNG — the kind of adventure that Classic *Trek* used to have occur on planets. Although it occasionally gives me the feeling of being trapped at a Renaissance fair, this episode is a delightful romp during its *Beowulf* sequences. The show falters only when it treads the familiar turf of inadvertently trapping this week's energy creature, a "photonic being that lives in the proto-star."

GROSS (***): I was ready to hate this show based on the fact that it was another misadventure in the holodeck, but the production values are quite splendid, and Robert Picardo makes it all very palatable. When this series began, it's unlikely that anyone knew what they were getting with this actor. The notion of our people accidentally trapping an alien being — enough already!

HIDE & Q

(TNG)
Original Airdate 11/21/87
Written by C. J. Holland and Gene Roddenberry
Story by C. J. Holland
Directed by Cliff Bole

Intrigued by the Enterprise *crew based on the events of "Encounter at Farpoint," Q (John de Lancie) wants to study the human species more closely. To this end, he decides to bestow omnipotence on Riker, who must then learn to cope with his godlike abilities.*

ALTMAN (**): The episode is conceptually intriguing in its first two acts as John de Lancie toys with the crew, but it turns silly when Riker's temptation completely transforms his character and he begins to bestow the crew's secret desires. It's too hard to accept the last temptation of Riker, as he is undone by the corrupting influence of absolute power. It's a less competently done take on Gary Mitchell's transformation into a deity in the original series' "Where No Man Has Gone Before," which was handled with far greater subtlety.

GROSS (**): Power corrupts, and absolute power corrupts absolutely. The retreads continue, this time coming from the 1965 pilot episode "Where No Man Has Gone Before." Kirk and Gary Mitchell handled the "power corrupts" theme much more effectively than the actors do here. De Lancie is great in his first reprisal of the Q character, but even his performance isn't enough to save this episode. Adding insult to injury is the fact that the episode's ending, in which an agitated Q is sucked back to his Continuum despite protests to the contrary, is an exact steal from the similar climax to the original series' "Charlie X." See also "Encounter at Farpoint," "Deja Q," Q-pid," "Q Who," "True Q," "Tapestry," "All Good Things," "Q-Less" and "Death Wish."

HIGH GROUND, THE

(TNG)
Original Airdate 1/27/90
Written by Melinda Snodgrass
Directed by Gabrielle Beaumont

Dr. Crusher is kidnapped by a band of terrorists who are demanding independence for their terri-

tory and believe the Federation has allied itself with the government. Crusher attempts to save the life of the terrorist leader, Kyril Finn (Richard Cox), who is suffering from the tissue degeneration caused by their method of instantaneous teleportation.

ALTMAN (**1/2): The show tries too hard for social relevance and mistakenly tackles the Irish issue, rather than simply being content as an engaging action yarn. One of the episode's best scenes is a terrorist attack on the *Enterprise,* during which the rebels teleport aboard in an attempt to destroy it. The attack culminates in the usually stoic Picard slugging one of the invaders when he attempts to disable the helm control. Assisted by a pulsating Ron Jones score, this scene makes the episode palatable even as Gates McFadden struggles through some sloppy and pedestrian writing on the planet's surface.

GROSS (**): One of the weakest shows of the third season, "The High Ground" is an allegory that goes wrong. Gates McFadden tries to hold her own, but it's not enough to save the show. The terrorists' method of transport is intriguing, but the show just hammers you over the head with its message.

HIPPOCRATIC OATH

(DS9)
Original Airdate 10/16/95
Teleplay by Lisa Klink
Story by Nicolas Corea and Lisa Klink
Directed by Rene Auberjonois

While conducting a biological survey in the Gamma Quadrant, O'Brien and Bashir are stranded on a planet with Jem'Hadar soldiers, who recruit Bashir (at phaserpoint, of course) to help free them from the addiction to "the white," the substance provided by the Founders to ensure their loyalty.

ALTMAN (***): There's always been magic in the O'Brien/Bashir dynamic, but it's probably never been exploited better than in "Hippocratic Oath" by freshman writer Lisa Klink. The episode has been compared unfavorably to "I, Borg," which I believe is unfair. The conflict between Bashir and O'Brien — who pursue separate agendas, almost sinking them both — is far more legitimate than the contrived and credulity-stretching actions of Picard, who refuses to destroy the Borg in that less than stellar *TNG* installment. Though not the best episode of the season, "Hippocratic Oath" sets up a thoughtful dilemma and resolves it in a way that more than holds my interest.

GROSS (***): Probably the only time that a Starfleet medical officer on one of these series has taken on a task and ultimately failed at it, making him more human as a result. Alexander Siddig is outstanding as Bashir, desperately trying to find an addiction cure for the Jem'Hadar, and the sequences between him and Colm Meaney's Chief O'Brien are a joy to watch, particularly as these friends pull rank, disobey direct orders and come into heated conflict with each other. By episode's end, their friendship has been frayed, which both men acknowledge, but not broken. Although the look of the

Jem'Hadar is not as strong as it will eventually become, some fascinating background is provided, particularly regarding their feelings for the Founders as gods who barely acknowledge the existence of their chief defenders.

HOLLOW PURSUITS

(TNG)
Original Airdate 5/5/90
Written by Sally Caves
Directed by Cliff Bole

Barclay (Dwight Schultz), an introverted crew member, retreats to the relative safety of the holodeck to spend his life in a fantasy world he creates for himself. When he misses an important staff meeting, Geordi LaForge invades his holodeck world and discovers a re-creation of The Three Musketeers, *in which the characters are based on the senior staff, including Troi as the goddess of empathy and Riker as a fearful knave.*

ALTMAN (***): A wake-up call for Trekkies who need to get a life. Dwight Schultz gives a savvy performance as the bumbling Lieutenant Barclay, who finally eschews his fantasy world for reality. Although the ending, in which he saves the ship and proves his value to the crew, should be retired to cliché heaven, the show is truly inspired, with Marina Sirtis particularly amusing as the goddess of empathy. Not surprisingly, Barclay's fantasy world proves that the holodeck is nothing more than a twenty-fourth-century 1-900 number, as he uses it to indulge his private desires. One has to wonder what the implications are when LaForge barges in on Barclay's holodeck world without knocking (or the twenty-fourth-century equivalent), but this violation of privacy is never tackled by the holier-than-thou crew.

GROSS (***): An episode quite different from the typical *TNG* fare, and that's precisely why it works. It's a lot of fun from beginning to end, with Dwight Schultz being one of the series' best "discoveries" since John de Lancie first took on the role of Q. It's nice to see that the holodeck is used in such a spirit of fun (in the re-creation of *The Three Musketeers*) and nicer still that for once it doesn't malfunction and put either the ship or the crew members in danger.

HOME SOIL

(TNG)
Original Airdate 2/20/88
Written by Robert Sabaroff
Story by Karl Guers, Ralph Sanchez and Robert Sabaroff
Directed by Corey Allen

The Enterprise *arrives to give medical exams to the terraforming scientists of Velara III, just as one of them is killed by an errant laser weapon that almost kills Data as well. It turns out that the terraformers have disturbed a previously undiscovered life-form, which quickly takes control of the* Enterprise, *dismissing humans as "ugly sacks of mostly water."*

ALTMAN (1/2*): A dreadful retread of the original series' "The Devil in the Dark," in which cheesy, glowing crystals have supplanted the Horta as the misunderstood alien life-form of the week, which is responsible for killing the

terraformers. The story is further sabotaged by substandard production values, a ridiculously inane plot and some uninspired direction by Corey Allen. A stinker.

GROSS (*): They did it better in the 1960s with "The Devil in the Dark." A poor episode in every respect, and it's becoming increasingly tiresome to have these self-important aliens putting us down. OK, we're savages; we're barbarians. Accept it already, and let's move on.

HOMECOMING, THE

(DS9)
Original Airdate 9/27/93
Teleplay by Ira Steven Behr
Story by Jeri Taylor and Ira Steven Behr
Directed by Winrich Kolbe

When Quark gives Kira information that proves a Bajoran resistance fighter named Li Nalas (Richard Beymer) is alive on a Cardassian prison colony, she and O'Brien take a runabout to execute a rescue, while an anti-Federation movement known as the Circle begins to wreak havoc on the station.

ALTMAN (***): A knockout second-season opener with lively direction by Winrich Kolbe, in which Kira leads a rescue mission to free a legendary Bajoran resistance fighter from a Cardassian prison camp. *Twin Peaks'* Richard Beymer plays the character's many subtle nuances with dignified elegance, and the episode combines well-executed fisticuffs with some memorably spicy dialogue. The kickoff for a fabulous three-part series of episodes.

GROSS (****): The second season of *DS9* begins with a terrific three-parter that gives the series a shot in the arm and lets the audience know that this show isn't taking any prisoners! Interestingly, what might have been perceived as a limitation in terms of the show's emphasis on Bajor and the spiritual nature of its people is actually proving to be a major strength. Director Winrich Kolbe generates genuine suspense during Kira and O'Brien's rescue mission, and there's some real poignancy when Jaro tells the major that she is to be reassigned to Bajor. See also "The Circle" and "The Siege."

HOMEFRONT

(DS9)
Original Airdate 1/1/96
Written by Ira Steven Behr and Robert Hewitt Wolfe
Directed by David Livingston

Sisko is promoted to head of Starfleet security when the Federation suspects Dominion infiltration of the highest echelons of government, as life back home begins to take a sinister turn.

ALTMAN (***): The most disturbing aspect of "Homefront" is its attempt to emulate other franchises by touching on both the dark, conspiracy-ridden Earth problems of *Babylon 5* and the paranoia of *The X-Files*. Frankly, neither seems particularly well suited to the *Star Trek* franchise, although *DS9* makes a noble attempt. Although some of the conflicts between Sisko and his father seem contrived and the people of Earth are too quick to relinquish their hard-earned freedom, there are some really nice moments with Jake, Nog and the elder Sisko, played well by Brock Peters.

GROSS (***): Picking up thematic threads from "The Adversary" and "The Way of the Warrior," this episode manages to heighten the paranoia that became more prominent in *DS9*'s third season. The performances are universally good, from Avery Brooks to Cirroc Lofton and Rene Auberjonois, who is in the difficult position of being a changeling working with the Federation in their battle against the Dominion. Brock Peters (Admiral Cartwright in *Star Trek IV: The Voyage Home* and *Star Trek VI: The Undiscovered Country*) adds some emotional heat as Sisko's father, and Robert Foxworth brings forth the proper authority in the somewhat enigmatic role of Admiral Leyton, whose motives seem to be in the right place in terms of wanting to increase Earth's security against changelings. What's most interesting about this episode is how easy it is, despite some initial resistance, to increase a government/military presence in the name of security. Even Sisko thinks this is a good idea! The final image of armed Starfleet personnel patrolling the streets is extremely disturbing. The story concludes in "Paradise Lost."

HOMEWARD

(TNG)
Original Airdate 1/17/94
Teleplay by Naren Shankar
Story by Spike Steingasser
Directed by Alexander Singer

Worf's foster brother, Nikolai (Paul Sorvino), violates the Prime Directive by attempting to save the remnants of a dying race by secretly using the holodeck to transport an alien village, which will keep them from learning the truth about their world.

ALTMAN (**): An unsatisfying concoction of tried-and-true *Trek* — everything from "Friday's Child" to "For the World Is Hollow and I Have Touched the Sky" and "Who Watches the Watchers?" Just add water and stir. The holodeck gag of duplicating the terrain of an alien culture so that they don't know they've left their own planet is interesting, but the show's "ticking clock," a malfunctioning holodeck program, seems completely indiscriminate and an obvious plot contrivance. Paul Sorvino delivers a subtle and strong performance, but the producers seem to be skirting Worf's Jewish heritage, established in "Family," which could have been the source of much more humor, as opposed to the relatively standard approach to the strained but loving brotherly relationship that "Homeward" takes. By the way, don't you think Worf would have introduced his son, Alexander, to his brother? Just because Brian Bonsall was off shooting a movie is no reason to make such an obvious faux pas.

GROSS (**): The relationship between Dorn and Sorvino works nicely, but this episode is a pastiche of a variety of past shows, leaving an unsatisfying aftertaste. I would also like to gain some understanding as to how people are able to do things such as beaming an entire colony into the holodeck without anyone on the *Enterprise* knowing, either before or as it's happening. Starfleet security is making me kind of nervous.

HOST, THE

(TNG)
Original Airdate 5/13/91
Written by Michael Horvath
Directed by Marvin V. Rush

Dr. Crusher falls in love with a Federation ambassador, the Trill Odan (Franc Luz), who is being ferried aboard the Enterprise *to negotiate a planetary dispute. When Odan is injured, the crew discovers a parasitic creature inside his body, which is the real ambassador.*

ALTMAN (***): Gates McFadden shines in this remarkably ambitious episode, which sports a novel science-fiction premise that serves as the catalyst for real human drama, full of pathos and humor. The issues raised, albeit delicately, about gay rights are as daring as this show has ever been in addressing a contemporary social issue. It cops out at the end, however, when Crusher rebuffs Odan, who gets transplanted into the body of a woman, Kareel (Nicole Orth-Pallavicini), even though Crusher was clearly in love with the entity regardless of its form. "Perhaps someday our ability to love won't be so limited," suggests Crusher in the story's affecting conclusion. Jonathan Frakes turns in a subtle and sly performance when he becomes temporary host for the alien ambassador, echoing the nuances of Luz's performance.

GROSS (***1/2): Easily one of Gates McFadden's best performances as Dr. Beverly Crusher. This is one romance that you can believe in, and the actress does a fine job of gradually falling in love with Odan again after he has been transplanted into Riker's body but finding it too frustrating to love the ambassador when it transfers to Kareel. The final moments of the episode are extremely touching, when Crusher forces herself to back away from Odan — not because he's suddenly in the body of a woman, but because she doesn't know how long it will be before the ambassador will move to yet another body, and she cannot get used to the changes. The fact that she isn't turned off by Odan in Kareel's body is an example of the *Star Trek* philosophy at work.

HOUSE OF QUARK, THE

(DS9)
Original Airdate 10/15/94
Teleplay by Ronald D. Moore
Story by Tom Benko
Directed by Les Landau

After Quark accidentally kills a drunken Klingon in the bar, he starts bragging about his fighting prowess, which leads to his being forced to marry the widow of the Klingon he killed. Suddenly he is trapped in a bitter feud between a pair of Klingon houses and finds himself in a battle to the death.

ALTMAN (***): A delightfully wry and lightweight episode in which Quark devises a novel solution to extricate himself from a potentially deadly situation. The relationship between Grilka (Mary Kay Adams) and Quark is charming, and Ron Moore puts a nice comedic spin on the usually dour Klingon proceedings.

GROSS (***): Although it's not clear how they've done it, the producers of *DS9* have made the Ferengi in general, and Quark in particular, palatable to the viewer. This is an outstanding episode, in which Armin Shimerman is able to bring new shadings to Quark, who is always in character whether he's taking credit for killing a Klingon who actually slipped and killed himself or taking part in a supposed battle to the death. Writer Ron Moore has come up with a solution to the battle that keeps Quark alive while not insulting the viewer's intelligence. The Klingons maintain their honor, and, most important, Quark's character remains true to form. A surprisingly effective show.

HOW SHARPER THAN A SERPENT'S TOOTH

(TAS)
Original Airdate 10/5/74
Written by Russell Bates and David Wise
Directed by Bill Reed

The Enterprise *encounters the Mayan god Kulkukan, who captures members of the landing party and demands that they worship him as a* god, just as the people of Earth did thousands of years earlier.

ALTMAN (**1/2): The episode is wildly derivative of "Who Mourns for Adonis?" in which the god Apollo wishes to reclaim his human worshipers. In this case, it's the Mayan god Kulkukan who has come in search of his children (prompting Spock to say, "Vulcan was visited by aliens; they left much wiser"). Unfortunately, the idea works about as well here as it did in the live-action show. Ultimately, Kirk makes a compelling case for the maturity of the human species, and this so-called kid-vid fare ends with the captain quoting Shakespeare, from which the episode takes its name ("How sharper than a serpent's tooth it is / To have a thankless child"). Kid-vid, indeed.

GROSS (*1/2): Kulkukan would have been an interesting character to explore had Apollo not beaten him to the punch. Check out the live-action version instead.

HUNTED, THE

(TNG)
Original Airdate 1/6/90
Written by Robin Bernheim
Directed by Cliff Bole

Genetically altered veterans of a war on Angosia 3 have been consigned to exile on a prison colony. When rogue soldier Roga Danar (Jeff McCarthy) is captured and flees the Enterprise, *he attempts to enlist his fellow officers in a coup against the government, which is petitioning to join the Federation.*

ALTMAN (**): A heavy-handed allegory of the plight of the Vietnam veteran falters in an abbreviated ending forced by budget trimming during shooting, as well as some poor direction. Despite some nice action moments and character dynamics between Data and Troi, this episode just never takes off.

GROSS (**1/2): The basic premise of "The Hunted" is long overdue, but by making Roga Danar into a combination of Superman and Rambo, the writers also make him unbelievable. The one scene that comes to mind is when he is able to disrupt a transporter beam through sheer will. Sorry, guys, this just doesn't wash. Still, the theme and level of action/adventure, as well as the notion of Picard being against a planet's entrance into the Federation due to its policies, make this a worthwhile episode.

I, BORG

(TNG)
Original Airdate 5/18/92
Written by Rene Echevarria
Directed by Robert Lederman

Picard sends an Away Team to investigate the wreckage of a small craft and finds that the only survivor is a young Borg (Jonathan Del Arco). Once the Borg is on board the Enterprise, *Geordi LaForge and Dr. Beverly Crusher begin working* with him to teach him independence from the Collective, and Picard rebuffs a plan to use the young Borg to destroy the Collective.

ALTMAN (***): Philosophically, "I, Borg" is remarkable in that it is able to give the so-called enemy a human face. Unfortunately, the Borg don't need a human face. This story would have worked marvelously with any villain, and by making it a Borg, the writers negate the power of the Borg as *TNG*'s primary antagonist, which provides the essential dichotomy of the show. This is an astoundingly rich and well-written installment with a strong message, and yet it's a mistake. Despite its inherent strengths, the Borg are too effective as villains to be given the "talking heads" treatment. Uncredited writer Jeri Taylor provides some great character moments, particularly between Picard and Guinan, but overall "I, Borg" disappoints by reducing the Borg's malevolence to the mundane.

GROSS (***): This one's a real coin toss. On the one hand, it's a beautifully crafted tale of overcoming personal prejudice, but on the other it dilutes a kick-ass villain who had been portrayed as a continuing threat. Now, no matter what they do, the Borg will be seen as human beings forced by the Collective to do evil. Coming off the fifth season, when the crystalline entity became a misunderstood friend and even the Romulans (some of them) were starting to become nice guys, this is a major blow. Why does *everything* have to work out perfectly in the future? Surely there has to be room for a bit of grittiness and darkness.

I, MUDD

(TOS)
Original Airdate 11/3/67
Written by Stephen Kandel
Directed by Marc Daniels

The Enterprise *is forced to an uncharted planet by an android minion of Harry Mudd's (Roger C. Carmel). There, the android population is set on taking over the* Enterprise *and tempering the illogic of humans throughout the galaxy. Kirk then embarks on a plan of outwitting the androids with bizarre behavior.*

ALTMAN (***1/2): Probably the most intelligent of *Trek*'s comedy troika (along with "The Trouble with Tribbles" and "A Piece of the Action"). Although it begins like a routine action/adventure story, with Kirk losing control of the ship to a bunch of androids, the story soon devolves into cerebral absurdity, as Mudd loses control of the androids and is enlisted by Kirk to engage in a series of increasingly surreal plots to overcome their computerized captors. Some of the bits involving Scotty's death from too much happiness and Kirk's attempts to outwit the logical automatons, enlisting the help of Spock, are wildly funny. Equally memorable is Mudd's haranguing, shrewish wife, Stella.

GROSS (**1/2): Whereas the humor in "The Trouble with Tribbles" is more subtle and character based, it's way over the top in "I, Mudd." As a result, despite some very funny scenes, it isn't as successful an episode. Harry Mudd is played completely for laughs, unlike in "Mudd's Women," where his humor always has an undercurrent of danger. The androids' desire to spread their kind throughout the galaxy is a repeat of Dr. Korby's plans in "What Are Little Girls Made Of?" It is amusing to watch Kirk once again talk a machine into destroying itself.

though the story line involving his father does get a bit soapy at times. To their credit, Jonathan Frakes and guest star Mitchell Ryan manage to exude a sense of genuine hostility toward each other. On the Worf front, this Age of Ascension business seems a bit forced and too similar to Spock's need to experience pon farr in the "Amok Time" episode of the original series.

ICARUS FACTOR, THE

(TNG)
Original Airdate 4/22/89
Written by David Assael and Robert L. McCullough
Directed by Robert Iscove

Riker is offered his own command by his estranged father, Kyle (Mitchell Ryan). Meanwhile, Worf begins acting strangely and must undergo the Klingon Age of Ascension ritual.

ALTMAN (**): Two totally disparate stories are incorporated ineptly, with some decidedly soap operatic moments. The visit from Riker's father is pretty standard sudser stuff, culminating in a bizarre ambu-jetsu match in the ship's gym as the two Rikers work out their problems in a scene that's straight out of *Battlestar Galactica*. Meanwhile, Worf's Age of Ascension is another wacko Klingon ritual, akin to an otherworldly bar mitzvah, with electric cattle prods substituting for the haftarah. It's a little too "Amok Time" for me.

GROSS (**): A good opportunity to explore the Riker character, al-

IDENTITY CRISIS

(TNG)
Original Airdate 5/25/91
Teleplay by Brannon Braga
Story by Timothy DeHaas
Directed by Winrich Kolbe

The crew of an Away Team mission Geordi LaForge was on five years earlier while serving on the USS Victory are all disappearing. Then he finds out that his friend and colleague, Susanna Leitjen (Maryann Plunkett), is metamorphosing into an alien creature and he's next. As he begins to unravel the mystery with the use of a holodeck re-creation of the mission, he also begins his startling transformation. Only with the help of Leitjen is the Away Team able to return LaForge to the ship before his transformation is complete.

ALTMAN (***): An interesting premise that benefits from some impressive direction by Winrich Kolbe. The ultraviolet lighting technique used in making "Identity Crisis" serves the episode well. LeVar Burton is particularly good as he desperately tries to unravel the secret of his transformation before he is metamorphosed. Ultimately, though, accepting the fact that LaForge could be turned human again after undergoing such a substantial transformation is a stretch.

GROSS (***): For some reason, this episode is reminiscent of the movie *D.O.A.* Maybe it's because that film deals with a poisoned man who has forty-eight hours to find his murderers. The clock is ticking, and there's a fair amount of suspense as LaForge tries to solve the mystery before it's too late. The effects and cinematography are great.

IF WISHES WERE HORSES

(DS9)
Original Airdate 5/17/93
Teleplay by Neil McCue Crawford, William Crawford and Michael Piller
Story by Neil McCue Crawford and William Crawford
Directed by Rob Legato

The crew's imagination gives life to their innermost fantasies, resulting in an all too real threat to the station — only to find out that the enigmatic visions are aliens visiting the station to learn more about humans and their pesky dreams.

ALTMAN (**): An overcooked stew of every *Trek* cliché imaginable. Riddled with technobabble, "If Wishes Were Horses" makes the wise decision to derive its illusions from its characters, which is what provides the episode's emotional juice. Bashir's fantasies involving Dax are a comedic triumph, and Terry Farrell is particularly adept at playing the lighter moments. The scenes between Sisko and baseball player Buck Bokai (Keone Young) have a surprising degree of emo-

tional resonance, although I am dubious of Piller's postulation that baseball's future is in jeopardy. What could have been a charming and emotionally revealing episode suffers from the misstep of saddling the show with a menacing jeopardy plot.

GROSS (**): Earnest performances save this episode from being a complete disaster, but the whole premise reeks of *Trek*s past. There are some good moments, particularly those within the Dax/Bashir/Dax triangle, but not enough.

IMAGINARY FRIEND

(TNG)
Original Airdate 5/4/92
Teleplay by Edithe Swensen and Brannon Braga
Story by Ronald Wilkerson, Jean Matthias and Richard Fliegel
Directed by Gabrielle Beaumont

Clara Sutter (Noley Thornton), the imaginary friend of the daughter of one of the crew members, becomes a frightening reality when she threatens to destroy the ship.

ALTMAN (*1/2): If you missed *TNG*'s first season, here's a primer. "Imaginary Friend" boasts an array of *TNG* clichés too numerous to count: a youngster in angst, cosmic strings jeopardizing the ship, a muddled B story, Troi's "I feel good, you feel good" counseling and an impassioned speech by Picard at the end that saves the ship and the day. The kids aren't bad, but it just isn't *Star Trek;* it's more *Space: 1999.* We're exploring the enigma of the week while some glowing alien space bug turns human and threatens the ship, really just misunderstanding humans. Let's retire this one with the "The Devil in the Dark" rip-offs and amnesia and split-personality shows.

GROSS (*1/2): Between season five's "Disaster," "Hero Worship," "Cost of Living" and "Imaginary Friend," it seems as if the producers are desperately trying to remind us that there are families on board the *Enterprise*. Perhaps they are prepping audiences for a new sitcom featuring those wild and wacky *Enterprise* kids. Although the children are fine in "Imaginary Friend," the story is so weak that you have to wonder why they pursued this one in the first place. We've seen enough evil children in the genre and on this show. Do we really need any more?

IMMUNITY SYNDROME, THE

(TOS)
Original Airdate 1/19/68
Written by Robert Sabaroff
Directed by Joseph Pevney

A giant creature surrounded by a mysterious zone of darkness has destroyed the Gamma 7A star system, and the USS Intrepid is discovered to be a giant amoeba that is about to reproduce.

ALTMAN (***1/2): The original space anomaly episode, which provided the template for the seemingly endless spate of strange space beasties and clouds to come. And it's still the best. Sure, the idea of an interstellar amoeba is kind of goofy, but it's really just the MacGuffin for some of the

most dramatic character moments the series has to offer, including Kirk's reluctant decision to send Spock off on an apparent suicide mission to destroy the spawning star killer. When Spock tells McCoy, "You should have wished me luck," it's one of the most wrenching scenes ever, and the deep friendship between the two has never been more apparent.

GROSS (***1/2): He reacts to a great disturbance in the force, as though a million voices cried out and were silenced. Sounds like Obi-Wan Kenobi in *Star Wars,* but replace the inhabitants of Alderaan with a starship filled with Vulcans, and you've got Spock during an early scene in "The Immunity Syndrome," which obviously had an impact on George Lucas. As noted in the previous review, the space anomaly is not all that interesting, but the sheer quantity of character moments is amazing. Early in the episode, when McCoy seems uncharacteristically unmoved by the death of the *Intrepid*'s crew, Spock notes pointedly, "For someone who often criticizes the coldness of the Vulcan heart, it is surprising how little warmth there is in yours." More significant, and proof that you can have character banter in the middle of a heated moment, is a scene toward the end when Kirk is desperately trying to rescue Spock from certain death, despite the Vulcan's protests. "Shut up, Spock," snaps McCoy. "We're rescuing you." Spock cocks an eyebrow and replies, "Yes, sir, *Captain* McCoy." Just wonderful.

IMPROBABLE CAUSE

(DS9)
Original Airdate 4/29/95
Teleplay by Rene Echevarria
Story by Robert Lederman and David R. Long
Directed by Avery Brooks

When Garak's shop explodes, Odo begins an investigation to determine who is trying to kill the tailor and why. Eventually, the evidence suggests that Garak blew up his own shop in an attempt to rejoin his onetime mentor, Enabran Tain (Paul Dooley), the head of the Cardassian Obsidian Order, who is about to launch an invasion of the Gamma Quadrant in conjunction with the Romulans so as to destroy the Founders.

ALTMAN (***): Any episode that has both Andrew Robinson as Garak and Paul Dooley as Enabran Tain is worth watching, and "Improbable Cause" is no exception, setting up the epic events that are to follow as the Alpha Quadrant fleets charge into the Gamma Quadrant to take care of the Dominion once and for all — or so they think. "Improbable Cause" has a neat little mystery at its core, but it's a little too pat, and the wrap-up in "The Die Is Cast" is a definite *Deep Space Nine* disappointment.

GROSS (***): Odo and Garak do not come into contact with each other very often, so that dynamic is interesting from the moment a suspicious Odo begins investigating the explosion in the tailor shop. It's wonderful watching how Garak seems to be constantly answering questions while raising numerous others. It's also fascinating to see Garak's change in attitude — the sense of superiority he shows — when he is back in his old element with Tain and the excitement he's feeling when he has the opportunity to recapture something of his old life. The announcement of the Cardassian-Romulan alliance is a surprising bit of business, whetting the appetite for "The Die Is Cast."

IN THE HANDS OF THE PROPHETS

(DS9)
Original Airdate 6/21/93
Written by Robert Hewitt Wolfe
Directed by David Livingston

Vedek Winn (Louise Fletcher), vying to become Kai, rallies the Bajoran occupants of the station against Keiko O'Brien's secular teachings, and an assassination attempt is made on Commander Sisko.

ALTMAN (***1/2): Ironically, this episode achieves a level of sophistication and social relevance that the original show prided itself on but rarely achieved, except in the broadest of terms. Avery Brooks finally breaks out of his laconic stupor and displays some passion in a speech that is as good as his "A Man Alone" pontificating was bad. Louise Fletcher brings weight and legitimacy to the role of Vedek Winn, and David Livingston's slow-motion assassination sequence and the final shot of the first season in ops are both executed with finesse.

GROSS (***): Although it took nearly the entire first season, *DS9* finally connects back with the pilot in terms of dealing with Bajoran spirituality and the political struggles erupting on Bajor. An underlying tension surrounds the episode, beginning with the moment Louise Fletcher appears as Vedek Winn and continuing right through the suspenseful attempted assassination of Vedek Bareil. Even during the closing scene between Sisko and Kira, where they discuss all that has been accomplished thus far and their hopes for the future, there is a sense that no one is sure just how volatile the situation on Bajor will ultimately become. All of this helps to establish a feeling that this is a real world, in which problems are not dealt with completely in a one-hour episode and the things we do today will have an impact on tomorrow.

IN THEORY

(TNG)
Original Airdate 6/3/91
Written by Joe Menosky and Ronald D. Moore
Directed by Patrick Stewart

The long-anticipated Data love story is finally consummated. An Enterprise *cadet named Jenna (Michele Scarabelli), on the rebound from a bad relationship, falls for the didactic Data, a stoic android devoid of emotion.*

ALTMAN (**): That should be enough of a story for one episode, because of all the inherently exciting possibilities, but as we've seen time and again, an inane sci-fi B story is added to the mix. The *Enterprise* passes through a phasing nebula in which parts of the ship are dematerializing in and out of existence, and Picard must navigate the ship to safety. The dynamics of Data's relationship with Jenna are far more interesting and compelling than the "Tholian Web" rehash occurring outside the ship's walls. Yet the characterization of Data still seems inconsistent, as the endearing android has handled love relationships far more adeptly in the past ("The Ensigns of Command") and shown the ability to adjust to emotional situations, for good ("The Offspring") or ill ("The Most Toys"). Brent Spiner is superb as always and contributes a particularly strong performance as the android, befuddled by the advances of his colleague, seeks advice from many of his peers (most amusingly Picard and the ever-lascivious Number One), only to end up quoting old movies and alienating his new girlfriend. Less impressive is Patrick Stewart's maiden voyage as director. Despite eliciting fine performances from the cast, Stewart does not illustrate a particularly impressive visual technique, except for the creative final shot.

GROSS (**): From the moment this episode begins, you know that Data is not going to be able to feel love for Jenna, which means that the show really has nowhere to go. Admittedly, there's quite a bit of humor as Data tries to simulate a lovers' quarrel, and there is some chemistry between Brent Spiner and Michele Scarabelli (Susan Francisco in *Alien Nation*), but it's not enough to make this a first-rate episode. Patrick Stewart definitely deserves another shot at the director's chair (which he will get).

INDISCRETION

(DS9)
Original Airdate 10/23/95
Teleplay by Nicolas Corea
Story by Toni Marberry and Jack Trevino
Directed by LeVar Burton

Gul Dukat (Marc Alaimo) and Kira go in search of a missing Cardassian ship, the Ravanok, which is carrying Bajoran prisoners of war. Kira learns that Dukat has ulterior motives when he reveals that he has a half-Bajoran/half-Cardassian daughter who is on board the ship.

ALTMAN (***1/2): Nice location shooting by director LeVar Burton helps contribute scope to this striking episode, which boasts exceptional character drama both on and off the space station, while at the same time injecting some kinetic action sequences. Dukat and Kira's relationship is nicely addressed, and there's a superb B story in which Sisko grapples with Kasidy Yates's decision to take quarters on DS9. Sisko's less than enthusiastic response prompts an interesting dilemma for him, which no previous *Trek* captain has ever had to deal with. The moments in which he seeks the advice of Bashir and Dax, as well as Jake contributing his two cents' worth, are priceless.

GROSS (***): Gul Dukat continues his transformation from ruthless Cardassian to a soldier serving his country — at heart, a human being with a wife and family like everyone else. This series' devotion to character continues, as the relationship between Dukat and Kira evolves from bitter enemies to a duo working together to being on opposite sides of the fence when Kira learns that Dukat plans on killing his half-Bajoran daughter if she's still alive. At episode's end, it's extremely moving when Dukat embraces his daughter, no matter what the consequences back home. Meanwhile, back at the station, Sisko's relationship with Kasidy Yates (Penny Johnson) moves a step closer to commitment. There's real chemistry between Avery Brooks and Johnson as the commander tries to figure out what he wants from the relationship.

INFINITE VULCAN, THE

(TAS)
Original Airdate 10/23/73
Written by Walter Koenig
Directed by Hal Sutherland

The Enterprise *discovers a giant being who is actually a clone of Dr. Starros Keniclius (voice of James Doohan), a scientist who practiced during Earth's Eugenics Wars. Keniclius plans to clone a giant Spock so that the duplicate Vulcan can serve as a galactic peacemaker, despite the fact that it will result in the death of the original Spock.*

ALTMAN (**): Written by Walter Koenig, "The Infinite Vulcan" is a rather dopey animated outing, with its giant Keniclius and oversize Spock. There are a few moments of inspiration, including some neat Escher-like visuals among the stock shots and a reference to the Eugenics Wars, which prompted Keniclius's research into creating a master race of interstellar police officers. But ultimately the story is too reminiscent of

"Spock's Brain." Not exactly the prototype for great *Trek* now, is it?

GROSS (*1/2): One of the episodes of the animated series that points dangerously to how the show could degenerate. Although the tie-in to the Eugenics Wars is welcome, a giant Spock is the kind of thing you'd expect (and, indeed, did see a variation of) in an episode of *Lost in Space*. See also "Space Seed."

INHERITANCE

(TNG)
Original Airdate 11/22/93
Teleplay by Dan Koeppel and Rene Echevarria
Story by Dan Koeppel
Directed by Robert Scheerer

Data is surprised to encounter a scientist exploring seismic activity on Atrea who claims to be his mother, Juliana (Fionnula Flanagan), the wife of the late Dr. Noonian Soong. Data is reluctant to believe her, until an accident reveals that she also is an android.

ALTMAN (***): Fortunately, the show's ludicrous B story, involving the planetary disaster of the week, is reduced to a few insignificant scenes, allowing writer Rene Echevarria to concentrate on the relationship between Data and his mother. Fionnula Flanagan is exceptional as Juliana, and although the film's final gag, involving her secretly being an android, doesn't come as a big surprise, it allows Data to confront a vexing dilemma. The use of the Lal backstory is effective and emotionally satisfying.

GROSS (***): Data gets a mommy in this often touching story that plays so successfully due to the acting skills of Brent Spiner and guest star Fionnula Flanagan, as well as the sensitive teleplay and direction. Particularly interesting is Data's dealing with his suspicions that this woman is not who she claims to be. He's driven more by curiosity than emotion, but when he finds out the truth about Juliana, he has the compassion to let her live out the rest of her life believing that she's a human being. See also "Datalore" and "Brothers."

INITIATIONS

(VOY)
Original Airdate 9/4/95
Written by Kenneth Biller
Directed by Winrich Kolbe

Chakotay is attacked by a young Kazon-Ogla warrior named Kar (Aron Eisenberg), who is intent on earning his stripes in battle but is defeated by the Voyager's first officer. When the two are seized by the Kazon, Chakotay is taken prisoner, and Kar is disowned for failing in his mission.

ALTMAN (**): The episode begins routinely with yet another race beginning with K obsessed with honor and ritual. This seems to surprise Chakotay, despite his lineage as a Native American, many tribes of which were equally obsessed with such things. Even more kooky is Chakotay lecturing the boy about what it took for him to earn his stripes as a Starfleet officer. Excuse me, but isn't he a traitor? So much for the Maquis backstory. Although the episode owes a debt to *TNG*'s "Suddenly Human" and even "Final Mission," in which Picard and Wesley Crusher bond while stranded on a desert planet, I do credit writer Ken Biller with surprising me with a coda in which Kar finally redeems his lost honor by killing the Kazon leader. However, the goofy Indian mysticism is as tiresome as Neelix, whose shtick is ceaselessly grating.

GROSS (**1/2): Certainly an admirable attempt to explore Chakotay's background, although the whole notion of Indian mysticism is a little bit difficult to grasp. The often adversarial relationship between him and the young Kazon, Kar, is fairly effective, as are some of the Kazon traditions. Kar's saving himself by killing his superior is a surprising turn of events. One glaring problem is the casting of Aron Eisenberg as Kar. Since he's often seen and heard as *DS9*'s Nog, it's disconcerting to see him in a different role.

INNER LIGHT, THE

(TNG)
Original Airdate 6/1/92
Teleplay by Morgan Gendel and Peter Allan Fields
Story by Morgan Gendel
Directed by Peter Lauritson

Picard is rendered unconscious by an alien space probe and experiences an entire lifetime on another world while remaining comatose aboard the Enterprise *for twenty-five minutes.*

ALTMAN (***): "The Inner Light" boasts one of the most spectacular and interesting high-concept science-fiction premises ever explored on the show. Unfortunately, despite solid tech credits from Michael Westmore's standout makeup, solid guest performances and Richard James's expansive production design, "The Inner Light" never really shines. The audience doesn't become as intimately involved in Picard's new life as it should because of time constraints, and, even more important, the implications of Picard's reawakening aboard the *Enterprise* after experiencing fifty years of another life are never exploited for their ripe dramatic potential. Patrick Stewart carries the day, making as much out of the inventive idea as he can.

GROSS (****): One hell of a science-fiction concept. The very notion of experiencing another lifetime in the course of twenty-five minutes is enough to boggle the imagination, and Patrick Stewart effortlessly conveys the passage of time and his acceptance of this life he never knew he lived. There are only two problems with the episode. First, how would Picard respond to finding himself back on the *Enterprise* after so many "years" away from it? Second, what was the aliens' basic motive for pulling him away in the first place? Picard is told that he was brought to this other world to keep the memory of their existence alive — certainly a noble enough cause — but wouldn't it have made more sense for those

INNOCENCE

(VOY)
Original Airdate 4/8/96
Teleplay by Lisa Klink
Story by Anthony Williams
Directed by James L. Conway

A marooned Tuvok cares for a trio of Drayan children who are terrified of a creature that they fear will claim their lives at night. He then discovers that these children are actually at the end of their lives and have come to the moon to die.

ALTMAN (***): A wonderful vehicle for Tuvok. Lisa Klink's teleplay is subtle and sentimental without being maudlin. Tiffany Taubman as Tressa gives a particularly affecting performance, and the episode effectively breaks the *Trek* curse, in which episodes involving children are traditionally among the worst. There are also some nice moments when the captain first makes contact with the Drayans. Although the Drayans' mores seem a little too human, the episode works nonetheless.

GROSS (***1/2): At the outset, I expected this to be a remake of the original series' "And the Children Shall Lead." Instead, this episode gives Tuvok an opportunity to shine, illuminating not only a bit of the character's family background but also the Vulcans' general approach toward children. The revelation, at episode's end, that this race ages backward sounds, on the surface, like the kind of plot that would have been used in the animated series, but it plays much more realistically than that. Good performances and the Drayans' intriguing notion of their own circle of life root the show in reality. An interesting alien culture, and the type of people *Voyager* should encounter more often.

INTERFACE

(TNG)
Original Airdate 10/4/93
Written by Joe Menosky
Directed by Robert Wiemer

Geordi LaForge is hooked up to a new virtual reality probe, and while investigating the wreckage of a ship, he discovers his mother, Captain Silva LaForge (Madge Sinclair), on board after word arrives from his father (played by Ben Vereen) that she has disappeared. Despite Picard's warnings, LaForge continues his experiments to save what he believes is his mother from death.

ALTMAN (*1/2): Unfortunately, the only reality about "Interface" is that it's a virtual turkey, except that writer Joe Menosky is so good with character nuances that he is able to make the episode palatable solely on the basis of the show's dialogue, including a particularly well-written Data and LaForge. Moments such as Riker trying to console LaForge about the death of his mother and Data's advice to him keep the episode from being a high-concept disaster. Robert Wiemer's direction is serviceable, and cameos by LeVar Burton's *Roots* costars Ben Vereen and Madge Sinclair are nice bits of stunt casting. Best of all is the genuine character conflict that's allowed to germinate, thanks to the show's being in its final season. Not only is LaForge hostile to his crew mates, but a scene in which he refuses to tolerate Troi's Dr. Feel-good act also brings a smile to my face.

GROSS (**1/2): As season two's "The Icarus Factor" and season four's "Family" are for Riker and Picard, respectively, "Interface" is an attempt to explore familial relationships for Geordi LaForge. LaForge's determination to save his mother is admirable, but the episode is marred by too much technobabble. There's a nice emotional core, but it's difficult to find with all the discussions of probes and warp funnels. The reunion of LeVar Burton with his *Roots* costars is a nice touch.

INVASIVE PROCEDURES

(DS9)
Original Airdate 10/18/93
Teleplay by John Whelpley and Robert Hewitt Wolfe
Story by John Whelpley
Directed by Les Landau

Dax's worst nightmare comes true when a group of people, led by the timid Verad (John Glover), board DS9 after it has been virtually evacuated due to an approaching plasma storm. Verad is a Trill who was rejected as a symbiont host and is determined to fulfill his destiny by stealing the symbiont from within Dax.

ALTMAN (**): Sometimes a little mystery goes a long way, as "Invasive Procedures" proves when it turns the enigmatic Trill symbiosis into a rather mundane thriller convention. The ultimate bottle show, the episode takes place almost exclusively in ops as a Trill named Verad (John Glover) plots to steal the symbiont Dax. Despite some well-staged fight scenes and competent directing by Les Landau, who manages to prevent the confined quarters from feeling claustrophobic, "Invasive Procedures" doesn't work because the premise is never fully realized. In addition, two Klingon guest performances are absolutely dreadful. Otherwise, the *DS9* ensemble all turn in strong, multidimensional performances — although Quark never gets his comeuppance, and the show ends with a sappy and unemotionally engaging coda that falls flat when Dax says she remembers everything that has transpired. As a rape allegory, the episode is a total failure. As an entertaining diversion, it succeeds somewhat better.

GROSS (***1/2): Like season one's "Duet," this episode proves that when *Star Trek* hits its mark with a bottle show, it can't be touched. This wonderful story line provides a wealth of information on Trills — not so much on the physical aspects of a symbiont and host, but rather on a purely emotional level. To this end, the episode is helped immeasurably by Terry Farrell and guest star John Glover. In what is probably Farrell's best performance to date, she makes the audience feel her loss when the symbiont is removed. For his part, Glover brings forth two distinct personalities for Verad prior to and after the operation. The scene between him and Sisko after the symbiont has been implanted is wonderful.

INVESTIGATIONS
(VOY)
Original Airdate 3/13/96
Teleplay by Jeri Taylor
Story by Jeff Schnaufer and Ed Bond
Directed by Les Landau

After the increasingly insubordinate Tom Paris leaves the ship, the Maquis kidnap him from the Talaxians as part of their plan to capture Voyager.

ALTMAN (**): The episode begins unpromisingly with a witless prologue in which Neelix decides to inaugurate an intership news broadcast. When he learns that there may be a traitor on board, he turns into Woodward and Bernstein, regaling those around him with stories of journalistic ethics (I didn't realize they had the First Amendment on Talaxia). Frankly, why would you want to tell an espionage story through the eyes of your comic relief? There are some amusing diversions, including Neelix's attempt to recruit the doctor to be part of his broadcast ("I'm a doctor, not a performer"). Halfway through, "Investigations" turns into a middling episode of

The Rockford Files. The misguided traitor arc is resolved with little subtlety. And doesn't it seem ludicrous that at any point a person would be left alone in engineering?

GROSS (**): In an effort to give Neelix something to do, the writers give him his own news show to be broadcast throughout the ship. Neelix, with his investigative skills, uncovers the fact that Paris has been kidnapped by the Kazon, and we learn that he is not such a bad guy after all — he was just attempting to find the real spy on *Voyager*. All the buildup in previous episodes leads to this? Bummer, man. And why such a fascination with the Kazon? Their continuing presence hurt *Voyager* far more than it helped it in the show's second season.

IS THERE NO TRUTH IN BEAUTY?
(TOS)
Original Airdate 10/18/68
Written by Jean Lisette Aroeste
Directed by Ralph Senensky

The Enterprise transports the Medusan ambassador, who represents a race of energy patterns so horrifying that one look can drive a human insane. The Medusan is escorted by Dr. Miranda Jones (Diana Muldaur) and Marvick (David Frankham), who is driven insane and transports the Enterprise to the ends of the universe.

ALTMAN (***): A kooky third-season episode that, despite its hokey premise, is filled with neat set pieces. Diana Muldaur's Dr. Miranda Jones is the biggest *Star Trek* bitch you'll ever meet. She's so jealous of Spock that she even allows him to inadvertently sacrifice his sanity to protect her position. But what's really great about this episode is Ralph Senensky's direction. He shoots all his insane characters' points of view using a long wide-angle lens that gives the scenes a distinctive, off-kilter look. In addition, the special effects for the strange trip the *Enterprise* takes out of the galaxy are gorgeous.

GROSS (**1/2): Chewing the scenery time again, as half the cast goes insane. A *very* strange concept that is fairly successful, although it does feature another of those "aliens take over a human body" stories (albeit for only part of the episode). Guest star Diana Muldaur does a nice turn as Dr. Miranda Jones, and the fact that she's blind is indeed a surprise. A pretty dopey episode that works in spite of itself.

JEM'HADAR, THE
(DS9)
Original Airdate 6/13/94
Written by Ira Steven Behr
Directed by Kim Friedman

On a camping trip to the Gamma Quadrant, Sisko, Jake, Nog and Quark encounter the Jem'Hadar,

soldiers of the Dominion who rule that area of space. Meanwhile, the USS Odyssey, a galaxy-class starship, is destroyed in an attack.

ALTMAN (***): "The Jem'Hadar" (originally titled "The Dominion") is an uneasy mix of broad comedy (Quark trying to use the monitors for selling merchandise, including Vulcan IDIC pins), soapbox polemic (Quark and Sisko feuding over human disdain for the Ferengi) and ominous foreboding (the introduction of the Dominion). The episode amounts to little more than a concoction of "Captain's Holiday" and "Best of Both Worlds" when Sisko and son, along with Quark and Nog, come across the Dominion's foot soldiers in the Gamma Quadrant. Although the show takes much too long to get going, the episode culminates in some first-rate pyrotechnics as the *Odyssey* goes up in smoke.

GROSS (***): Despite the fact that there is much about this episode that suggests "Q Who" and "Best of Both Worlds," it works because it establishes a new Federation enemy with the ability to kick some galactic ass. Already we can tell that our people are going to have their backs shoved against the wall by these aliens, and their ensuing response is something to watch for. In a way, the Jem'Hadar represent what the Borg should have been in "Descent" but weren't. Great special effects.

JETREL

(VOY)
Original Airdate 5/15/95
Teleplay by Jack Klein, Karen Klein and Kenneth Biller
Story by Jim Thornton and Scott Nimerfro
Directed by Kim Friedman

A war criminal named Ma'bor Jetrel (James Sloyan), who designed a weapon called the Metreon Cascade that obliterated a Talaxian colony, comes aboard the Voyager *warning that Neelix has a fatal disease only he can cure while he also wrestles with his guilty conscience.*

ALTMAN (***): An intriguing story in which Neelix must face his inner demons, as well as the one who destroyed his family, Dr. Jetrel, played ably by the ever-reliable James Sloyan. Unfortunately, the Oppenheimer allegory is laid on a little too thick. Another problem is the fact that *Voyager* continues to traverse the Delta Quadrant as if it was their neighborhood rather than the alien and mysterious environment it should be. They casually visit Talaxia when they're supposedly heading back in the direction of the Alpha Quadrant. Fortunately, Ethan Phillips shines in his first chance to add some needed depth to a formerly lightweight character. Favorite line: As B'Elanna Torres beams aboard a strange energy particle from the destroyed planet's atmosphere, placing it in a magnetic chamber, she tells a concerned Dr. Jetrel, "Don't worry, we do this all the time." Yeah, tell me about it.

GROSS (**1/2): An episode that stands on the considerable acting talents of Ethan Phillips and guest star James Sloyan and manages to add some background to the character of Neelix, making him more than just the show's comic relief. Addressing Hiroshima is important, to be sure, but there seems to be little room for allegory in this story that grabs the viewer by the shoulders and screams out its message.

JIHAD

(TAS)
Original Airdate 1/13/74
Written by Stephen Kandel
Directed by Hal Sutherland

Kirk and Spock are among the beings recruited by the Vendala to take part in a mission to recover the stolen soul of Alar, the leader of the Skorr, a warrior race that has turned to peaceful benevolence. If the soul is not recovered, the Skorr will wage a jihad (holy war) across the galaxy.

ALTMAN (**1/2): Of all the animated episodes, this probably most resembles traditional Saturday morning fare — though with *Trek*'s traditionally heady bent. The alien "Magnificent Seven" (give or take a few) are all bizarre alien amalgamations, and the myriad exploding volcanoes and other perils are the stuff of serials. Still, some of the banter between Kirk and the huntress Laura, who flirts with Kirk and talks with a moll-like Brooklyn accent, is amusing, and the basic plot is vintage *Trek*. Even the null gravity combat is clever, paving the way for a similar scene twenty years later in *Star Trek VIII: First Contact.*

GROSS (***): If *Mission: Impossible* were remade as a sci-fi show, this episode would give you a pretty good idea of what the series would be like. Definitely atypical *Trek*, it works for precisely that reason. It's interesting to watch Kirk, chosen to lead due to his superb command abilities, head up this group of disparate beings. A lot of fun to watch.

JOURNEY TO BABEL

(TOS)
Original Airdate 11/17/67
Written by D. C. Fontana
Directed by Joseph Pevney

The Enterprise *serves as a transport for various alien races en route to the planet Babel for an important diplomatic conference. When the Tellarite ambassador, Gav (John Wheeler), is murdered on board, suspicion is directed toward Spock's father, Ambassador Sarek (Mark Lenard).*

ALTMAN (****): A triumph of diplomatic skulduggery, filled with classic *Star Trek* moments, including Spock and father Sarek's incessant bickering and McCoy's final rebuff of them both ("I finally got the last word"). Kirk's battle with an Andorian and his stubborn determination to remain on the bridge despite his injuries when Spock refuses to give up command is exceptional writing. Even the murder and subsequent mystery about who is trying to sabotage the diplomatic conference is brilliantly conceived. The guest performances are all top-notch, including Jane Wyatt as Spock's put-upon mother and William O'Connell and Reggie Nalder as Andorians (sort of).

GROSS (****): One highlight of the episode is seeing a variety of alien creatures (obviously where the episode's budget went), which may have had some influence on the cantina scene in *Star Wars*. The meat of the show is the relationship — or lack thereof between Spock and his parents. This episode defines Spock as a character in terms of his background, and there's absolutely no mention of a brother named Sybok! Check out the scene where an injured Kirk returns to duty so that Spock can be with his stricken father. As soon as Spock leaves the bridge, an agonized Kirk takes off as well. Great show.

JOURNEY'S END

(TNG)
Original Airdate 3/28/94
Written by Ronald D. Moore
Directed by Corey Allen

Wesley Crusher transcends this plane of existence to join the Traveller in exploring the cosmos during Picard's attempt to dislodge a Federation colony of Native Americans from the demilitarized zone with Cardassia, thanks to a new treaty that redraws the line of demarcation.

ALTMAN (**): Although "Journey's End" has some genuinely fine moments, it is ultimately undone by its ludicrous reliance on spirituality over science fiction. As long as the show is dealing with the fascinating political jockeying between the Federation, Cardassia and a band of Indians, it is quite effective. Unfortunately, Wesley Crusher's story is given short shrift. The idea of his not wanting to follow in his father's footsteps is intriguing, but Wil Wheaton's performance is shrill and annoying. The ultimate resolution of Crusher's mystical awakening into a V'ger-like metamorphosis is completely unsatisfying and an unwelcome intrusion of New Age nonsense into a secularly grounded series.

GROSS (**1/2): Where did this fascination for Indian mysticism and spirituality come from? It obviously does not jell well with the realm of *Trek,* as evidenced by the frequent vision quests of *Voyager*'s Chakotay. Still, the political arena as represented here works, as does Wesley Crusher's change of heart regarding Starfleet, though that does seem a bit abrupt given what we've seen of the character in the past. Those ideas just don't seem to come together with Indian mysticism. The return of the Traveller (Eric Menyuk) serves as a nice bracketing for the Crusher character. See also "Where No One Has Gone Before" and "Remember Me."

JUSTICE

(TNG)
Original Airdate 11/7/87
Written by Worley Thorne
Story by Ralph Willis (John D. F. Black) and Worley Thorne
Directed by James L. Conway

The Enterprise *takes shore leave on Rubicum III, but when Wesley Crusher accidentally violates one of the Edo's laws, he is sentenced to death. Intent on preventing this, Picard tries to rescue Crusher when the Edo's god, a giant vessel in orbit, intercedes, demanding that the* Enterprise *leave orbit.*

ALTMAN (*1/2): There's a really interesting story at the heart of "Justice," in which the writers postulate a world that enforces criminal justice by having a death penalty for even the most minor infractions. Unfortunately, Gene Roddenberry indulges his predilection for god fetishes by adding a judgmental deity to the mix, negating the power of the show's allegory. It then becomes simply a lightweight retread of "The Apple," whose only redeeming feature is the multitude of scantily clad women that cavort across the Edo planet. (The male cast members loved it, too, as Jonathan Frakes and Michael Dorn confided to me during one of my many set visits covering the show.) Picard's speech, in which he exhorts the alien being not to kill Wesley Crusher, is excruciatingly awful. Only William Shatner can get away with those kind of diatribes.

GROSS (**): The basic premise behind this episode is wonderful (a world without crime because the penalty for *all* transgressions is death), but the execution leaves much to be desired. Once again, Roddenberry's libido has made sex an overriding theme, which wouldn't be bad if it served some purpose. Add to this the umpteenth god-machine that the *Enterprise* has come up against and some truly silly moments (such as Crusher explaining to an Edo woman, "There are some games I don't play yet" and "We're with Starfleet; we don't lie"), and you have a truly awful episode.

LAST OUTPOST, THE

(TNG)
Original Airdate 10/17/87
Teleplay by Herbert J. Wright
Story by Richard Krzemien
Directed by Richard Colla

The Enterprise *pursues a Ferengi marauder, which has stolen a T-9 energy converter from a Federation outpost, and tracks the marauder to a mysterious planet, which holds both ships in stasis. With their power rapidly draining, the* Enterprise *crew beams down to the surface and finds the last sentry of the long-lost T'Kon Empire.*

ALTMAN (**): Enter: The Ferengi. Exit: The Ferengi. Mistaking the Ferengi for villains rather than comic foils was a huge error made early in *TNG*'s inception. Ultimately, "The Last Outpost" is one big, inferior rip-off of "Arena," the Classic *Trek* in which Kirk was tested by the Metrons. There's a certain mythic quality to the show's premise, in which the *Enterprise*'s survival hinges on Riker's being able to provide the right answer for the Portal's riddle in what amounts to the Cliffs Notes version of Sun Tzu's *Art of War*. The most interesting thing here is the guardian of an ancient empire, who is awakened to learn he is rendered irrelevant by the death of his civilization, but this is barely touched on. The production values also are fairly weak.

GROSS (***): OK, OK, the episode is once again influenced by the original series, particularly "Errand of Mercy" and "Arena," and the meeting between humans and the Ferengi is anticlimactic, but "The Last Outpost" also is a lot of fun. There's mystery, some action, a certain amount of philosophy and something pleasantly dopey in the idea of the Portal being asleep while his empire was obliterated. A guilty pleasure.

LEARNING CURVE

(VOY)
Original Airdate 5/22/95
Written by Ron Wilkerson and Jean Louise Matthias
Directed by David Livingston

Tuvok is assigned to run a boot camp for several Maquis officers who are having trouble adapting to life aboard a Federation starship. Complicating matters is the requisite B jeopardy story in which the Enterprise*'s bioneural computer gel packs become infected with a virus.*

ALTMAN (**1/2): Ultimately, "Learning Curve" plays like a lightweight version of the same writers' "Lower Decks," the exceptional *TNG* episode focusing on four *Enterprise* cadets. That was more effective because there was more tension inherent in the espionage story and we knew the cadets' *Enterprise* superiors a lot better at the time, so the off-concept approach was more of a novelty. This show is another nice step in Tuvok's development, particularly in a strong scene between Neelix and the Vulcan. Each of the four Maquis officers are well drawn and interesting, especially a loquacious Bolian. David Livingston's direction is effective as always, particularly his use of a finite number of sets in creating a larger sense of space on board the vessel during the *Officer and a Gentleman* training scenes. The worst offense of the episode is a "cheesy" tech catalyst in which the cheese in Neelix's galley literally holds the clue to the virus. Ugh!

GROSS (***): A significant episode for Tim Russ's Tuvok, who learns that logic cannot be applied to every situation and that he must look upon his crewmen as individuals. Some very humorous moments and an interesting look at how these Maquis officers pull themselves together and truly become part of the crew. The ship's circuitry getting ill is fairly bizarre, but what other show (with the exception of *The X-Files*) could take on a plot like this?

LEGACY

(TNG)
Original Airdate 10/29/90
Written by Joe Menosky
Directed by Robert Scheerer

The legacy of Tasha Yar continues to haunt the En-terprise crew when they come upon Tasha's sister, Ishara (Beth Toussaint), on the late Tasha's war-ring homeworld, where a Federation ship's emergency shuttle has crashed. Offering to assist the Away Team in rescuing their stranded comrades, Ishara hides a secret agenda that will allow her to disable the defenses of her clan's enemies and lead an offensive strike against them.

ALTMAN (***): The producers are still trying to make up for "Skin of Evil," it seems. "Legacy" is an action-packed episode featuring a strong guest performance by Beth Toussaint as Tasha's sister, Ishara. Some of the contemporary gang allegory falls flat (*Colors* it's not), but Ishara's betrayal of the crew is poignant and well played, particularly the ambiguities in her character as Data bids her farewell and she beams back down to her planet in the episode's coda.

GROSS (***): Wonderful manipulation and intrigue highlight this episode, which gives us a taste of what Tasha Yar's upbringing must have been like. But coming so soon after the return of Data's brother, Lore, it's a bit tiring to meet yet another family member. Nonetheless, Ishara Yar is an interesting character. (By the way, note how similar actress Beth Toussaint looks to Linda Hamilton.)

LESSONS

(TNG)
Original Airdate 4/5/93
Written by Ronald Wilkerson and Jean Louise Matthias
Directed by Robert Wiemer

Picard becomes romantically involved with Nella Daren (Wendy Hughes), the new chief of the Stellar Sciences Department on board, with whom he shares a love of music. Unfortunately, he may be forced to assign her to a mission in which her life will be at stake.

ALTMAN (***1/2): A potentially mundane and maudlin hour avoids all the potential pitfalls, thanks to some extraordinary character drama courtesy of un-credited story editor Rene Echevarria, which broadens the character of Picard and provides the most satisfying romantic entanglement ever depicted on the show. "Lessons" wisely downplays its fiery jeopardy coda, choosing instead to focus on the developing relationship between Picard and Daren, in which Picard must grapple with showing favoritism to his amamorta. Wendy Hughes is sensational and has great chemistry with Patrick Stewart, who finally seems comfortable exposing vulnerability in Picard. The scenes in which he discusses his experiences from "The Inner Light" broaden his character and provide a satisfying cap to some unresolved issues from that intriguing episode. Robert Wiemer's direction is ambitious and quite striking, although some shaky Steadicam work is jarring.

GROSS (**1/2): An interesting episode that drives home the explanation for why most starship captains are consumed by love for their vessels rather than a good woman. Some lovely character moments (particularly Picard's discussing his experiences from "The Inner Light") and a difficult choice for Picard to make when it comes

time for Daren to take part in a dangerous assignment.

LET THAT BE YOUR LAST BATTLEFIELD

(TOS)
Original Airdate 1/10/69
Written by Oliver Crawford
Story by Lee Cronin (Gene L. Coon)
Directed by Jud Taylor

The Enterprise *finds itself in the midst of a chase by an alien law enforcement officer named Bele (Frank Gorshin), who is chasing Lokai (Lou Antonio). Each man's face is black on one side and white on the other, and on their planet racial prejudice has destroyed both civilizations.*

ALTMAN (**): Heavy-handed polemic of the worst kind. "Let That Be Your Last Battlefield" is the episode pundits turn to when they talk about *Star Trek*'s progressive social allegory, but it's probably the worst example. It's not only obvious, but it's also stupid. There's an awful scene of the assembled crew enraptured by Lokai's sermon about race. Fortunately, there are some redeeming elements, including the suspenseful self-destruct scene (co-opted for *Star Trek III: The Search for Spock*) and Bele and Lokai's climactic chase through the ship, only to beam down to the surface of their homeworld to find it destroyed due to racial hatred and ignorance. I could think of worse messages.

GROSS (**): Run, run, run. Talk, talk. Run, run, run. Talk, talk. Run, run, run. The end. That's basically what happens in this black/white relations allegory that requires viewing with a shock helmet in preparation for the bludgeoning impact of the episode's message. Guest star Frank Gorshin (*Batman*'s the Riddler) is engaging as Bele, but the episode is sabotaged by its obviousness. Great line, though, when Kirk and Spock question Bele as to why he is pursuing Lokai: "Don't you see — he's white on the wrong side!"

LIAISONS

(TNG)
Original Airdate 9/28/94
Teleplay by Jeanne Carrigan-Fauci and Lisa Rich
Story by Roger Eschabacher and Jaq Greenspon
Directed by Cliff Bole

Troi, Worf and Picard find themselves manipulated by the Lyaaran ambassadors when they agree to take part in a cultural exchange program. Picard becomes stranded on a planet and encounters the mysterious lone inhabitant, Anna (Barbara Williams), who takes him prisoner.

ALTMAN (**): A taxing *Misery* retake is lightened up by some agreeable humor involving three alien ambassadors who are sent to experience the human emotions of aggression, pleasure and intimacy. Although Picard's tenure in the care of a troubled young woman, Anna (Barbara Williams), is far too derivative (where's Kathy Bates when you need her?) and ultimately predictable, the exploits of the remaining two ambassadors as they cause chaos aboard the *Enterprise* are mildly amusing.

GROSS (**1/2): Some very amusing and other just plain weird moments highlight this episode, which features earnest performances by guest stars Eric Pierpoint (*Alien Nation*), Paul Eiding and Michael Harris as the Lyaaran ambassadors. Troi's forever snacking companion is easily the most humorous, and there are plenty of laughs to be had from Worf's attempts to control his temper as he is constantly provoked. Picard's being trapped on the planet's surface and his companion's (transformed, unbeknownst to him) efforts to experience love with him are rather touching. Picard doesn't seem the least bit turned off by the fact that the woman trying to seduce him turns out to be a man. Ah, that twenty-fourth-century tolerance!

LIFE SUPPORT

(DS9)
Original Airdate 2/4/95
Teleplay by Ronald D. Moore
Story by Christian Ford and Roger Soffer
Directed by Reza Badiyi

Vedek Bareil (Philip Anglim) is injured in a shuttle accident, and Dr. Bashir must try an experimental drug to keep him alive through vital negotiations with the Cardassians.

ALTMAN (**): Many of you will remember *TNG*'s "Ethics," an unfathomable, dull medical drama in which Worf copes with paralysis. Like that episode, this show dwells on medical minutiae, which ultimately amount to very little. This time, however, Ron Moore gets to kill the character in question, hardly a surprise. The biggest problems are that we're not emotionally invested enough in

Bareil's character (a cold fish from day one) and the show's vital negotiation, a peace treaty between Bajor and Cardassia (the very foundation of *DS9*'s mythology), shouldn't have been relegated to being a catalyst for this story, but instead should be an episode in and of itself. The most interesting aspect of the story are the political underpinnings of the feud between Vedek Winn and Bashir, which get short shrift. Once again, Nog and Jake provide the fodder for a thoroughly agreeable B story about a double date that goes terribly awry. Despite all the emoting and angst, however, "Life Support" is ultimately much ado about nothing.

GROSS (**1/2): Yet another episode that works through characters to explore an issue, this time the notion of medical devices keeping a body alive beyond the point of its readiness to stop living. Although Nana Visitor does a nice job of conveying Kira's pain over losing her lover, Bareil was never that interesting to begin with, so the audience doesn't really feel his loss. There is something morbidly fascinating about watching his body collapse further, with Bashir reluctantly coming up with yet another device to keep him moving through negotiation of the peace treaty. When Bashir reaches the point where he says, "That's it," you recognize the next step would have been the creation of something inhuman. The main problem with the show is its lack of focus — should it be the relationship between Bareil and Kira or the question of medical ethics that Bashir faces?

LIFESIGNS
(VOY)
Original Airdate 2/25/96
Written by Kenneth Biller
Directed by Cliff Bole

The doctor falls in love with a Vidiian Phage victim, Dr. Danara Pel (Susan Diol), whom he has transferred into a holodeck body while he attempts to cure her.

ALTMAN (***): Unfortunately, despite the brilliant premise, the show wallows in clichés and pedestrian dialogue. The episode doesn't go far enough with its romantic relationship and is further hindered by the untenable B story involving Paris's insubordination and Raphael Sbarge's treacheries on board. There's a delightful reference to Dr. McCoy, and Susan Diol turns in a solid performance as the stricken Vidiian woman. To their credit, the writer drops a debate about whether B'Elanna Torres will help the Vidiian, which has echoes of *TNG*'s "The Enemy," before it becomes too derivative. There's a moving coda reflecting the nature of their doomed relationship and the doctor's amusing courting of the woman in a 1957 Chevy on Mars. Unfortunately, Kes summarizes my feelings about this episode when she notes, "There's nothing sadder than a missed opportunity."

GROSS (***): A nice opportunity for Robert Picardo's doctor to shine, allowing the character to take yet another step toward "humanity" as he discovers amorous feelings. There's a real Cinderella feeling to this story, in which the dying Danara Pel is allowed to feel some joy in her life before the Phage takes it all away. There's a beautiful scene in the holodeck, where the doctor re-creates a classic automobile and a romantic atmosphere. Writer Kenneth Biller and director Cliff Bole present a very sensitive and touching episode. In addition, the insubordination by Tom Paris is obviously leading somewhere.

LIGHTS OF ZETAR, THE

(TOS)
Original Airdate 1/31/69
Written by Jeremy Tarcher and Shari Lewis
Directed by Herb Kenwith

Scotty's new lady love, Lieutenant Mira Romaine (Jan Shutan) is possessed by the lights of Zetar, a cloudlike being that is actually the collective existence of a now-dead race.

ALTMAN (*1/2): Another third-season clunker, although I must admit that the mysterious cloud always scared me as a kid, particularly when Romaine starts to speak in the voice of the Zetarians. Once again, though, Scotty's relationship with his engines proves to be far more interesting than his occasional dalliance with women. Still, like all Classic *Trek*, the episode has some good moments, and Mira's precognitive vision of the destruction of the Memory Alpha Research Outpost is somewhat chilling.

GROSS (*1/2): Scotty forsakes his engines for a woman, and she turns out to be the receptacle of an alien consciousness. Damn. In many ways, this is a remake of "Return to Tomorrow." James Doohan has some nice moments, but there's not much else to recommend this episode.

LITTLE GREEN MEN

(DS9)
Original Airdate 11/4/95
Teleplay by Ira Steven Behr and Robert Hewitt Wolfe
Story by Toni Marberry and Jack Trevino
Directed by James L. Conway

While transporting Nog to Earth for his induction into the Starfleet Academy, a ship also ferrying Quark and Rom is sent spiraling back in time, and the three Ferengi are taken prisoner in Roswell, New Mexico, in 1947.

ALTMAN (***1/2): A brilliantly inventive high-concept comedy that is beautifully told and solidly executed by director James Conway. There are some nice flourishes, including a long-overdue explanation of why it seems that every race in the universe speaks English. Strong supporting performances, homages to classic 1950s science fiction and a nod to the vision of Gene Roddenberry are all thrown in the mix to make "Little Green Men" the most enjoyable Ferengi romp yet. (The only thing missing is having the zealous scientist turn out to be Gene Roddenberry himself.)

GROSS (****): *Deep Space Nine*'s answer to "The Trouble with Tribbles" is one of the funniest episodes of *Trek* ever produced. In this parody of the alien invasion movies of the 1950s, it's wild to watch 1940s military types interacting with Quark, Rom and Nog, and it's absolutely hysterical when the universal translators fail and both groups attempt to communicate by mugging, signing and tapping heads (you have to see it to understand), each believing that the other has the intelligence of monkeys. Later, when the translator is fixed, only Quark will try to profit from the situation, offering information on future technology in exchange for gold. Rene Auberjonois has some amusing moments as a stowaway Odo, who finds himself surrounded by idiots on the left (twentieth-century humans) and idiots on the right (the Ferengi). (Note: Charles Napier, portraying Denning, guest starred on the original series as a space hippie in "The Way to Eden.")

LONELY AMONG US

(TNG)
Original Airdate 10/31/87
Written by D. C. Fontana
Story by Michael Halperin
Directed by Cliff Bole

The Enterprise *is transporting Selay and Andican delegates to a peace conference, when the ship passes through a cloud and inadvertently catches a living entity in its wake. The entity then begins to take over the crew members.*

ALTMAN (1/2*): The B story is a tired retread of "Journey to Babel," with its feuding alien ambassadors. Unfortunately, the A story is even worse, as Picard chooses to vacate the ship and explore the galaxy with the gaseous child-cloud. This is among the worst episodes *TNG* has to offer.

GROSS (**): The only positive thing about ripping off the original series in this first-season *TNG* episode is that the writer, D. C. Fontana, is the same in both instances. This time she takes "Journey to Babel" and brings it into the twenty-fourth century (in terms of the *Enterprise* serving as a transport for battling diplomats), although the conclusion — in which one ambassador eats the other — is supposed to provide some morbid amusement but instead falls flat. The cloud entity idea is old hat, but the concept of Picard wanting to become one with the cosmos is intriguing.

LORELEI SIGNAL, THE

(TAS)
Original Airdate 9/29/73
Written by Margaret Armen
Directed by Hal Sutherland

Kirk, Spock and McCoy are led to the Taurean star system by a mysterious signal. There, they are captured by a race of female aliens who intend to use the men's life force to sustain their own immortal existence.

ALTMAN (***): It's *"Star Trek: Baywatch"* when the female inhabitants of a planet lure the *Enterprise* with their Siren-like calls. Although its by-the-numbers formula is more akin to *Super Friends* than *Star Trek*, "The Lorelei Signal" has its moments. Most notable is Uhura's strong presence when she takes command of the ship after the male crew members fall under the spell of the coterie of blonde babes. There's a moment of bizarre surrealism when Scotty is heard humming a Scottish hymn as the *Enterprise* slowly orbits the planet. Moments like this keep the show interesting despite its formulaic story.

GROSS (**): Sad to say, this animated episode looks at the notion of a society of dominant women with more finesse than the live-action *TNG* entry, "Angel One."

LOSS, THE

(TNG)
Original Airdate 12/31/90
Teleplay by Hilary J. Bader, Alan J. Adler and Vanessa Greene
Story by Hilary J. Bader
Directed by Chip Chalmers

Troi loses her empathic powers due to a cloud of two-dimensional creatures, which are leading the Enterprise *into a deadly cosmic-string fragment. Faced with being human, she announces her desire to resign as ship's counselor, and despite the crew's sympathy, she turns curt and hostile as she drowns in her own self-pity. Only when the creatures are freed from the ship's perimeter does Troi regain her powers and ask to resume her regular duties.*

ALTMAN (**1/2): A flawed but at times engaging episode, in which the personal story of Troi's depression over being rendered powerless is a fascinating vehicle for Marina Sirtis. The story suffers, however, by being coupled with an inane MacGuffin and an overdose of

technobabble ("The energy we wanted to transfer to the nacelles was absorbed by the graviton wave instead. It set up a torrential wave that rebounded back to the ship . . .") involving creatures that are all too familiar. We've seen the floating-cloud syndrome one too many times in *TNG*. It's also hard to believe that in Gene Roddenberry's rose-colored *Trek* universe, where everyone always gets along, Troi turns into the superbitch of the universe. Marina Sirtis does Joan Crawford. No more wire hangers!

GROSS (**): Do Betazoids suffer from PMS? Judging by Deanna Troi's attitude throughout this episode, they do. The idea of Troi losing her powers is interesting, but there's so much whining and bitching going on that you start to lose sympathy for her. There really is no lesson to be learned here, because it isn't until her powers are returned at episode's end that she seems genuinely happy again. Add to this the latest cloud entity, and you've got a rather disappointing episode.

LOUD AS A WHISPER

(TNG)
Original Airdate 1/7/89
Written by Jacqueline Zambrano
Directed by Larry Shaw

A deaf-mute negotiator named Riva (Howie Seago), who telepathically shares his thoughts through a chorus of interpreters, is sent to negotiate peace on a feuding planet. When his chorus is killed during an ambush, he is forced to learn to communicate by using sign language and is coun-

seled by Troi, who helps him overcome his handicap and successfully negotiate the treaty.

ALTMAN (*1/2): Another potentially intriguing idea is poorly realized. The heavy-handed social commentary diminishes the dramatic impact of the story of the negotiator struggling with his handicap. Troi is given more than her usual "I feel [fill in the blank]" dialogue for a change. "Our job is not to police the galaxy," Riker tells Picard, an observation that is indicative of the complete lack of subtlety in this episode.

GROSS (**): The notion of a diplomat operating with a chorus of interpreters is a fascinating one, and guest star Howie Seago carries the role off nicely. In turn, he provides Marina Sirtis's Deanna Troi with some interesting material to play off of. There are some bright moments, but overall this is a fairly average episode.

LOWER DECKS

(TNG)
Original Airdate 2/7/94
Teleplay by Rene Echevarria
Story by Ronald Wilkerson and Jean Louise Matthias
Directed by Gabrielle Beaumont

A refreshingly original and moving episode in which we get to see life aboard the Enterprise *for several young cadets who become involved with a secret mission to return a Cardassian spy across enemy lines.*

ALTMAN (****): The show wisely eschews the geopolitical posturing involved in its B story to explore the compelling character dynam-

ics between its junior officers. Structurally, the show echoes "Data's Day" but manages to avoid its missteps by focusing on an engaging cast of characters. The highlight of the show is an amusing montage combining a poker game among the senior staff with a game among the junior officers. The scenes have a genuine warmth, which *TNG* rarely achieved in its final season. Shannon Fill shines as Ensign Sito.

GROSS (***): Rumors abounded that the group of cadets in this episode would be the stars of a spin-off series that never came to pass. This is a terrific study of personalities under pressure and gives a wonderful sense of continuity with "The First Duty." There are several extremely powerful scenes between Patrick Stewart and Shannon Fill. In a sense, all the characters are more human than is the norm in the series.

MAGICKS OF MEGAS-TU, THE

(TAS)
Original Airdate 10/27/73
Written by Larry Brody
Directed by Hal Sutherland

When the Enterprise *is thrust into another dimension, the crew encounters a Pan-like being named*

Lucien, who, like all his people, has magical abilities. When the Megans detect the Enterprise's incursion into their space, they put Kirk and Lucien on trial for what humanity did to their people during the Salem witch trials.

ALTMAN (***): An intriguing animated episode postulating that witches on Earth were actually travelers from another dimension where magic exists. Although "The Magicks of Megas-Tu" owes a great debt to the live-action "Plato's Stepchildren," in which Kirk and company also gain superpowers, it's actually a better episode, as Kirk pleads humanity's case to the Megans. In fact, in a novel twist for children's television, the show actually has Kirk defending Lucifer himself from banishment, as the captain notes that he will not fall prey to legendary superstition. Spock says to Kirk, "This is the second time Lucifer was cast out and, thanks to you, the first time he was saved." Not quite *Power Rangers*, is it? Of course, it's not quite *The Crucible* either, but it is ambitious for Saturday morning television.

GROSS (***): One of the best animated episodes, which puts Captain Kirk in the bizarre position of having to defend a misunderstood Satan. This is some pretty heavy stuff for Saturday morning, but it's somehow appropriate that *Star Trek* is able to pull it off so successfully.

MAN ALONE, A

(DS9)
Original Airdate 1/18/93
Teleplay by Michael Piller
Story by Gerald Sanford and Michael Piller
Directed by Paul Lynch

Shortly after having a confrontation with Odo, who once arrested him, a Bajoran named Ibudan (Yom Klunts) turns up dead, making Odo the prime suspect. Only the DNA clues Bashir discovers in Ibudan's quarters may reveal the identity of the true murderer.

ALTMAN (**): *Cape Fear* it's not. What works within the familiar murder mystery trappings are the inspired character moments, particularly between Dax and Bashir, and the developing Odo and Quark relationship. Not altogether unpalatable is the B story in which Keiko O'Brien establishes a school aboard the ship. What doesn't work at all is the story's soapbox preaching regarding tolerance, in which a contrived scene of mob violence takes place in front of Odo's office. There's no dramatic justification for the violence, and Sisko's chiding has little resonance, as does the plot's denouement involving cloning, which is not entirely unexpected but completely hokey.

GROSS (**1/2): The conflict continues as Odo's sensibilities come up against Sisko's, and the question of how far one can go to enforce a personal set of laws is raised. Subplotwise, the series continues to lay the groundwork for the characters, including establishing the friendship between Jake Sisko and the Ferengi youth, Nog, and the fascinating Trill/host relationship between Dax and Sisko. However, Bashir, in his attempts to pick up Dax, is really annoying. Keiko O'Brien is given a nice turn as she attempts to find a purpose for herself and locks onto teaching. The biggest problem with the murder mystery is that you don't believe for a second that Odo is guilty. When a similar situation was raised regarding Scotty on the original series episode "Wolf in the Fold," they went a long way to raise the possibility that he was guilty. An interesting moment is when the crowd tries to corner Odo on the promenade to kill him, giving the impression of a twenty-fourth-century version of *Frankenstein*. The only thing these "villagers" are missing are their burning torches. The twist — a man killing his clone — is a fresh idea.

MAN OF THE PEOPLE

(TNG)
Original Airdate 10/5/92
Written by Frank Abatemarco
Directed by Winrich Kolbe

Lumerian ambassador Alkar (Chip Lucia) and a woman he identifies as his mother, Maylor (Susan French), beam aboard the Enterprise *to mediate a conflict. After Maylor's mysterious death, Alkar engages in a death ritual with Counselor Troi, using Troi as the receptacle for his negative emotions. As a result, Troi transforms into a jealous vamp and a rapidly aging shrew.*

ALTMAN (*1/2): An episode laced with ludicrous sci-fi stupidity that begins in the teaser, in which the Lumerian ambassador's so-called mother, Maylor (Susan French), taunts Troi and appears to be waiting for a house to fall on her in her ghastly witchlike makeup. She seems sadly out of place away from Kansas, Dorothy and Toto. The audience is never sold on the idea that an effective mediator must divest himself or herself of strong negative emotions, which negates the whole sci-fi premise. The entire episode borders on incoherence and is resolved in a final dull expository scene between Riker and Troi that explains what has transpired, violating every tenet of good drama. If not for some pleasant character moments and another solid performance by Marina Sirtis, which also boasts a healthy dose of high-camp kitsch (including Troi's transformation into a sex kitten), the episode would be a complete and unmitigated disaster.

GROSS (**1/2): An intriguing sci-fi premise, but the real highlight here is Marina Sirtis's transformation of Troi into a real vamp and tramp. Her histrionics are wild, and as her hair first starts graying, she bears an uncanny resemblance to Majel Barrett's Lwaxana Troi. Talk about having to tame a shrew. As noted above, if a mediator needed to divest himself or herself of negative emotions to get the job done, the only mediators would probably be Vulcans.

MAN TRAP, THE

(TOS)
Original Airdate 9/8/66
Written by George Clayton Johnson
Directed by Marc Daniels

The Enterprise *delivers medical supplies to planet M-113 and encounters the planet's only two inhabitants, Robert and Nancy Crater (Jeanny Bal and Alfred Ryder), who are actually manifestations of a shape-changing alien that is the last of its species and thrives on salt.*

ALTMAN (***): A really cool creature supplements the already interesting idea of a monster that is struggling to survive. In *Star Trek*, there is no black and white, just shades of gray (no pun intended), and even a horrible, murdering salt creature is capable of evoking our sympathies. There are some nice moments as Nancy Crater takes on various guises and a particularly spooky scene in which she approaches Uhura in the corridor as a suave African officer. As Uhura begins to suspect that something is wrong, the episode becomes a real nail-biter.

GROSS (***): The first televised episode of *Star Trek* probably appealed to NBC because it had a monster that the network could promote. What works so splendidly is the fact that the shapeshifter represents the last of its species, and there are some wonderful parallels made between it and the American buffalo. By far not the best episode of the first season, it is certainly representative of *Trek* as a series, particularly the philosophical argument between Spock and Kirk as to whether the salt creature should be exterminated.

MANEUVERS

(VOY)
Original Airdate 11/20/95
Written by Kenneth Biller
Directed by David Livingston

The Voyager *is attacked by the Kazon, led by the Cardassian traitor Seska (Martha Hackett). Using her "intimate" knowledge of the ship, Seska is able to disable the crew and steal a transporter module that will allow the Kazon to master Federation technology. Janeway must then pursue the Kazon ship to regain the module.*

ALTMAN (**1/2): "Maneuvers" is an action-packed and fairly captivating episode that uses the Kazon in a rather engaging way. The character conflict between Chakotay and Seska makes "Maneuvers" more than a simple shootout, allowing it to examine more mature themes. Unfortunately, Martha Hackett, who has more charisma than anyone else in the cast, is underused, although Robert Beltran gets another chance to shine as Chakotay. Regrettably, like most *Voyager* episodes, the show climaxes with some absurd technobabble that substitutes for legitimate plotting. Having B'Elanna spouting techno gobbledygook is just plain unacceptable. The episode also plays the same beats as the first season's "Prime Factors," only this time it's Chakotay (instead of Tuvok) who acts recklessly without seeking the captain's approval, further weakening her already tenuous captaincy.

GROSS (***): Some of *Voyager*'s best space battle scenes highlight this episode, which is one of the few to make effective use of the Kazon. The strength of the show is Chakotay blaming himself for the Seska situation and feeling responsible for retrieving the transporter module. He screws up again when his shuttle is captured, allowing the Kazon even more access to Federation technology. Although the *Voyager* manages to come to the rescue, there are some very powerful torture scenes along the way as the Kazon try to get vital strategic information about the starship. Most unsettling is Seska's communiqué that she has injected herself with Chakotay's DNA and is now pregnant with his child. Do you know what that means? The damn Kazon are going to be back!

MANHUNT

(TNG)
Original Airdate 6/17/89
Written by Terry Devereaux (Tracy Torme)
Directed by Rob Bowman

A sequel to "Haven" and "The Big Goodbye," in which a horny Lwaxana Troi (Majel Barrett) is on the prowl for a mate. She attempts to seduce Picard, who takes haven in the holodeck (as Dixon Hill) to hide from her amorous advances. Also aboard are a band of alien delegates intent on sabotaging an upcoming diplomatic conference.

ALTMAN (1/2*): A plodding and disappointing sequel to two of *TNG*'s first season's best episodes. "Manhunt" would be totally worthless if not for a delightful scene in which Picard attempts to

elude Lwaxana Troi by summoning Data to his quarters for some "lively after-dinner conversation."

GROSS (*): Bid a big good-bye to this mishmash. Put simply, nothing works, with the exception of a humorous moment or two. An extremely forgettable episode. See also "Haven," "The Big Goodbye," "Menage A Troi," "Half a Life," "Cost of Living," "Dark Page," "The Forsaken" and "The Muse."

MAQUIS, THE, PART I

(DS9)
Original Airdate 4/25/94
Written by James Crocker
Directed by David Livingston

Sisko and Gul Dukat (Marc Alaimo) team up to investigate terrorist activity in the demilitarized zone between Cardassia and the Federation and learn that one of Sisko's closest friends, Cal Hudson (Bernie Casey), a Starfleet attaché to the Federation colonies, is now one of the Maquis' leaders.

ALTMAN (***): Directed vigorously by David Livingston, "The Maquis, Part I" is a fascinating setup for the Maquis' backstory and is marked by a powerful performance by Marc Alaimo as Gul Dukat, one of DS9's true unsung heroes. Another welcome addition is Richard Poe as Gul Evek, who gives another strong Cardassian performance (he was last seen in *TNG*'s "Journey's End").

GROSS (***): *DS9* continues to thrive with its political story lines, and by establishing the Maquis, it begins to show the cracks in what the Federation has always stood for (one has to wonder what Gene

Roddenberry's feelings regarding these Federation renegades would be). Because of this, we're able to analyze fracturing friendships as sides are chosen. One drawback of the episode is Bernie Casey, whose Cal Hudson is emotionally flat. See also "Journey's End," "Preemptive Strike," "For the Cause" and "Caretaker."

MAQUIS, THE, PART II

(DS9)
Original Airdate 5/2/94
Written by Ira Steven Behr
Directed by Corey Allen

Sisko must do everything he can to prevent the volatile situation between Cardassia and the Maquis from exploding into a full-scale war. To this end, he tries to convince Cal Hudson to cease his attacks, forcing the two to square off against each other in space.

ALTMAN (**1/2): A less than stellar resolution to the Maquis story line, which culminates in some pointless pyrotechnics rather than exploring the issues of betrayal raised by Hudson's defection. Further sabotaging the episode is yet another dreadful Vulcan performance (a new *Trek* tradition) by Bertila Damas as Sakonna, who figures prominently in the show's B story involving Quark. Of greater note, there's a wonderful scene with Gul Dukat aboard a runabout. It's also nice having Natalija Nogulich back in her recurring role as Admiral Necheyev, the woman who provided so much angst for Picard.

GROSS (***): An effective follow-up to part I. It's nice to see Sisko and Gul Dukat working together, elevating Marc Alaimo's Dukat to something more than just a space Nazi. In fact, one gets the impression that the producers are softening up Dukat for more regular appearances on the show, though later episodes have the character take a couple of steps backward. See also "Journey's End," "Preemptive Strike," "For the Cause" and "Caretaker."

MARK OF GIDEON, THE

(TOS)
Original Airdate 1/17/69
Written by George F. Slavin and Stanley Adams
Directed by Jud Taylor

Kirk attempts to beam down to the xenophobic planet Gideon and is shocked to find himself back aboard the Enterprise, *where everyone except a mysterious woman named Odona (Sharon Acker) has disappeared. We learn that Odona is from a planet suffering from overpopulation because the citizens are disease free. We learn later that she and Kirk are actually on Gideon, which is the planet she is referring to.*

ALTMAN (**): This episode makes no sense. If there's no room on the planet, how the hell do they re-create the *Enterprise?* And second, *how* the hell do they re-create the *Enterprise?* The one thing Gideon does have going for it is a perpetually spooky ambience as Kirk and Odona cruise the empty corridors of the *Enterprise* looking for clues to their dilemma. There are also some classic moments between Spock, McCoy and Hodin

(David Hurst), the council leader on Gideon, who is trying desperately to convince them to stay away. Even Spock looks askance at him, making several acerbic remarks at the expense of politicians. In the end, the idea that a father would sacrifice his daughter so that his race could live is vintage *Star Trek* and not altogether uninteresting.

GROSS (*): In the late 1960s, overpopulation was a hot topic, and this third-season episode bludgeons the viewer to death with it. Once again, a somewhat interesting premise is done in by illogic: How could the people of Gideon have created an exact duplicate of the *Enterprise*? It makes no sense, thus nullifying the entire episode.

MASKS

(TNG)
Original Airdate 2/21/94
Written by Joe Menosky
Directed by Robert Wiemer

The Enterprise encounters an alien space probe, the archive of an ancient civilization, which possesses Data, endowing him with various personalities from among its records. Meanwhile, it begins transforming the Enterprise into an ancient city.

ALTMAN (*): Whether it was to give a fidgety Brent Spiner a chance to stretch his acting muscles before closing the barn doors or simply because a prop house was having a sale on Egyptian artifacts, "Masks" is among *TNG*'s worst and most ludicrous episodes. This is a show even Fred Freiberger (the producer of Classic *Trek*'s infa-

mous third season) would have passed on. Managing to stay afloat in this vast cosmic morass of interstellar insipidity is Brent Spiner, who dives into his "thirteen faces of Eve" role with relish (except for a dying old man, in which he sounds like a reject from a bad Woody Allen movie). Director Bob Wiemer also makes the most of what he has to work with, as does Patrick Stewart, who is able to remain earnest enough through his labyrinthine tangle of babbling inanities to warrant kudos. I am shocked that Joe Menosky perpetrated this subpar rip-off of his own "Nth Degree," unless it's some grand joke on *Trek* fans that the audience is not clued in to. Even the old, long-retired cliché of having Picard talk his way out of peril is resurrected — quite unsuccessfully, I might add.

GROSS (*): This episode was about *what?*

MASTERPIECE SOCIETY, THE

(TNG)
Original Airdate 2/10/92
Teleplay by Adam Belanoff and Michael Piller
Story by James Kahn and Adam Belanoff
Directed by Winrich Kolbe

The Enterprise encounters a biosphere colony of genetically engineered individuals that is imperiled by an approaching stellar core fragment. In an attempt to avert the disaster, the xenophobic populace must work with the Enterprise crew, which leads to Troi falling in love with the colony's leader, Aaron Conor (John Snyder), while Geordi LaForge and scientist Hannah Bates (Dey Young) work on board the Enterprise.

ALTMAN (**): Adequate at best. The idea of the utopian ethos is successfully plumbed, although the tech dilemma is not so successfully resolved. Troi's one-night stand with the colony's administrator, played by a low-key John Snyder, is completely lacking in credibility. It's hard to believe that Troi would see anything in this bore. Unfortunately, some weak casting and substandard production values help undermine what could have been a much better episode.

GROSS (***): To explore strange new worlds, remember? It's about time. The *Enterprise* goes to seek out new lives and new civilizations rather than having them come to the starship. Although "The Masterpiece Society" is far from a perfect episode, there are enough elements to make it intriguing. It's interesting to examine a genetically engineered society and explore the notion that if you remove one link, the entire chain could be on the verge of collapse. Flipping to the other perspective, as is the case in "First Contact," it's interesting to examine the reaction to aliens coming to your world. The people within the biosphere have looked at their home as the center of the universe, and in comes the *Enterprise*, which challenges their imaginations and whets their appetites for what lies beyond. The romantic entanglement of Deanna Troi and the leader of this community is probably the weakest part of the episode. One of the strongest parts is the downbeat conclusion, where

Picard wonders whether breaking the Prime Directive will ultimately be less damaging to the community than the stellar core fragment would have been. A very enjoyable episode.

MATTER OF HONOR, A

(TNG)
Original Airdate 2/4/89
Written by Burton Armus
Story by Wanda M. Haight, Gregory Amos and Burton Armus
Directed by Rob Bowman

As part of a Federation exchange program, Riker transfers to a Klingon warship and slowly begins acclimating to their alien ways, until the Klingons discover a structural breach they believe has been caused by the Enterprise. *The captain, Kargan (Christopher Collins), attacks the starship and demands Riker's allegiance in destroying his former vessel.*

ALTMAN (***): This show marked an upturn in the flagging fortunes of *TNG*'s second season. Jonathan Frakes, finally handed the substantial role he had previously been denied, gives a sensational performance. The Klingon characterizations are compelling as well, although the inclusion of an obnoxious Benzite alien who, along with Wesley Crusher, helps unravel the technomystery is less palatable. Rob Bowman's lensing is impressive.

GROSS (****): A true *Star Trek* classic unlike any episode produced before it, and a real standout effort for Jonathan Frakes, whose Will Riker is given the opportunity to be a flesh-and-blood human being rather than a Kirk wanna-be. As was the case with season one's "Heart of Glory," "A Matter of Honor" reinforces the idea that the Klingon episodes offer an inherent fascination. It's the kind of show that proved *TNG* could stand on its own within the *Star Trek* mythos, fulfilling Gene Roddenberry's ambition of making the Klingon Empire more than a race of black hats. The audience, along with Riker, comes to understand the Klingons a little better without whitewashing them in the least.

MATTER OF PERSPECTIVE, A

(TNG)
Original Airdate 2/10/90
Written by Ed Zuckerman
Directed by Cliff Bole

Riker is accused of murdering an alien scientist, Dr. Apgar (Mark Margolis), and destroying a scientific space station, thus forcing Picard to arbitrate over a holodeck re-creation of the events to establish whether there are sufficient grounds for his first officer to be extradited and put to death for his crimes.

ALTMAN (*1/2): A brilliant, *Rashomon*-like premise, in which the holodeck is used to re-create a crime from varying perspectives, is sabotaged by some weak directing by Cliff Bole and an even worse script. The episode's conclusion, in which Riker is vindicated, is so improbable and ludicrous that it's laughable. Mark Margolis is sufficiently creepy as Apgar, as is Craig Richard Nelson as Inspector Krag, but the other supporting guest cast falls flat.

GROSS (*1/2): An episode with an intriguing premise, but the execution of that premise is handled so ineptly that it leaves much to be desired. Frankly, the plot seems a little too high-concept even for *TNG*, and the episode is quite similar to the original series' "Court Martial." Incidentally, with the way these guys continue to serve as lawyers, judges and arbiters, there might have been some potential for a "Starfleet Law" spin-off. Any doubts? Read on.

MATTER OF TIME, A

(TNG)
Original Airdate 11/18/91
Written by Rick Berman
Directed by Paul Lynch

A mysterious visitor, historian Berlingoff Rasmussen (Matt Frewer), who has materialized from the future in a time pod, says he is observing the Enterprise crew on a critical mission to save an asteroid-devastated planet from environmental destruction, but he hides a more sinister secret.

ALTMAN (***): Series executive producer Rick Berman scores with a witty and well-conceived story, which boasts an outrageously over-the-top, albeit effective, guest performance by Matt Frewer as the deceitful Rasmussen. Despite the requisite overreliance on technobabble in the B story, Frewer interacts delightfully with the cast, and several vignettes involving a skeptical Troi and an enraged Picard, who attempts to persuade his visitor from the future to confess the outcome of his actions on Penthara Four, are top-notch *Trek*.

GROSS (***): From the moment he appears on-screen, you don't know what to make of Rasmussen — whether he's friend or foe. And *that* is the charm of the episode, because there's something about him you can't help but like, until he really starts giving the impression that he has a hidden agenda. Rick Berman deserves credit for coming up with an effective time-travel idea that provides Picard, in particular, with some sturdy acting moments. The audience feels the captain's anxiety over his next step regarding Penthara Four and his frustration when Rasmussen tap-dances around the question. This leads to a wonderful moment when Picard acknowledges the possible results of sparing a world destined to die, which could conceivably give birth to a monster as hideous as Hitler or Khan Singh.

MEASURE OF A MAN, THE
(TNG)
Original Airdate 2/11/88
Written by Melinda Snodgrass
Directed by Robert Scheerer

Commander Bruce Maddox (Brian Brophy), a gung-ho cybernetics expert, wants to disassemble Data to learn more about his positronic brain. Picard defends the android in court to establish his sentience, sparring with court-appointed litigator Riker.

ALTMAN (***1/2): Widely considered one of *TNG*'s best episodes, this show's only failing is a plot contrivance in which Riker must prosecute the case against Data, pitting him unrealistically against

Picard. Writer Melinda Snodgrass does a fabulous job of bringing the characters to life in this courtroom drama that's more *Caine Mutiny* than "Court Martial." Picard's manner of exonerating Data is particularly inspired, as he makes a strong case for establishing the android as a sentient being.

GROSS (****): This episode takes the axiom "I think, therefore I am" to new levels. Everyone is quite splendid, and it is probably the best Starfleet courtroom episode since "The Menagerie" in 1966. A touching Data episode that conveys the character's dilemma despite his inability to show emotion. Patrick Stewart is particularly impassioned as he defends his android science officer's right to exist. Brian Brophy's Commander Bruce Maddox, the man who wants to create an army of androids based on Data's design, is further proof of the dark underbelly of the future. See also "The Naked Now."

MELD
(VOY)
Original Airdate 2/5/96
Teleplay by Michael Piller
Story by Michael Sussman
Directed by Cliff Bole

A Maquis ensign, Suder (Brad Dourif), is found guilty of murder, prompting Tuvok to mind-meld with the officer to gain insight into the seemingly incomprehensible crime.

ALTMAN (**): The entire premise strikes me as an extremely contrived attempt to service Tuvok's underutilized character. Despite Tim Russ's fine performance, the whole affair is a pointless exercise, failing to lend any insight into violence and murder. It ultimately diminishes the Vulcan as a responsible and intelligent crew member since his mind meld seems so unjustifiable. Some lip service is paid to weighing the capital punishment issue, but I found the breakdown of Tuvok's emotional suppression abilities (due to the mind-meld, which plunges him into insanity) difficult to fathom (although I was amused by Suder's description of the process as "that Vulcan thing where you grab someone's head"). It seems like *Voyager*'s attempt to do *Seven*. The doctor proves Suder's guilt, claiming that "DNA doesn't lie." Maybe someone should have told that to the O. J. jurors.

GROSS (****): With the exception of the original series' "Wolf in the Fold," the idea of a serial killer has never been explored on *Star Trek*, which is probably why "Meld" is such a powerful episode. On a level of sheer contrast, a serial killer seems incongruous in Gene Roddenberry's utopian universe. Indeed, when it's first discovered that Suder is killing people, nobody knows what to do with him. It's only logical (no pun intended) that Tuvok be the one to try to understand him through a Vulcan mind-meld. The backwash of emotions is surprising and extremely effective as Suder becomes calmer and more contemplative, while Tuvok gradually descends into madness. Guest star Brad Dourif,

with his shark eyes, is one of the most disturbing characters we've ever met — a Jeffrey Dahmer in outer space who is unable to resist the urge to kill. Tim Russ gives the performance of his career, presenting a side of Tuvok that we've never seen before, and the raw power of that character unleashed is a frightening thing. Thankfully, no one tries to offer a technobabble explanation for random violence.

MELORA

(DS9)
Original Airdate 11/1/93
Teleplay by Evan Carlos Somers, Steven Baum, Michael Piller and James Crocker
Story by Evan Carlos Somers
Directed by Winrich Kolbe

Dr. Bashir becomes romantically involved with an Elaysian woman, Melora Pazler (Daphne Ashbrook), who is confined to a wheelchair due to the difference in gravity between the station and her home planet.

ALTMAN (***): There's some genuine emotion in the relationship between Bashir and Melora, played ably (or disably, as the case may be) by Daphne Ashbrook. Unfortunately, there's a forced attempt to link the plot with a poorly developed B story in which Quark is threatened by his ex-partner. "Melora" is plagued by a frequent problem that has typified both *DS9* and *TNG*, which is a tendency to think that a personal story can't sustain an episode without an action coda. As a result the episode's finale, in which Melora is phasered and subsequently subdues the baddie by flying into him when she disables gravity, is fairly ludicrous.

GROSS (**1/2): From a character point of view, "Melora" is a very nice episode, allowing Dr. Bashir to deal with a female without being thoroughly annoying in his inane attempts to pick her up. There's some nice emotion here, particularly Melora's realization that if she goes through with the operation, she will be giving up a big part of who she is, but it's not as strong as it should be. That may be due to the silly ending, in which the character impersonates Superman sans flowing red cape.

MENAGE A TROI

(TNG)
Original Airdate 5/19/90
Written by Fred Bronson and Susan Sackett
Directed by Robert Legato

Riker, Deanna Troi and her mother, Lwaxana (Majel Barrett), are kidnapped by a lovestruck Ferengi named Tog (Frank Corsentino), who wants the elder Troi not only for her body but also for her brain (its telepathic powers). Pursued by the Enterprise, the Ferengi is willing to release Deanna and Riker if, in return, he is allowed to marry Lwaxana.

ALTMAN (*1/2): A disappointing misfire featuring some nice locales, including a picnic on Betazed and the interior of a Ferengi vessel. The only noteworthy part is the riotous conclusion, in which Picard is forced to woo the annoying Lwaxana Troi back from the Ferengi by reciting romantic quotations from Shakespeare. Writers Susan Sackett and Fred Bronson

miss a prime opportunity to explore the dynamics of the Troi/Riker relationship, instead choosing to focus on the inane antics between the Ferengi and Lwaxana. In addition, a brief scene in which the blushing Betazoid and her mom are disrobed and imprisoned nude in accordance with Ferengi custom is not milked for nearly any of its inherent comic potential.

GROSS (**): The Ferengi, as humorously as they have been played, have begun wearing out their welcome on *TNG*. Coupled with the return, yet again, of Lwaxana Troi, this is an even worse offense.

MENAGERIE, THE

(TOS)
Original Airdates 11/17/66 and 11/24/66
Written by Gene Roddenberry
Directed by Marc Daniels

When a crippled and paralyzed Christopher Pike is beamed aboard the Enterprise, Spock commandeers the vessel to Talos IV, a world deemed off-limits by the Federation. As a result, the Vulcan is court-martialed for mutiny, and during the trial, the ship's viewscreen flashes back to footage from "The Cage," which details Pike's connection with the Talosians. It is Spock's hope that Pike will find some happiness among that alien race.

ALTMAN (****): *Trek*'s first two-parter is Gene Roddenberry's best screenwriting effort for the show and features a powerful performance by Jeffrey Hunter. For a medium that had given us *My Mother the Car, Captain Video* and *The Beverly Hillbillies*, the achievement of "The Menagerie" is no small feat. In addition, the way Roddenberry cleverly incorporates the unaired *Trek* pilot footage into the show is sheer genius. The bookends, with Spock kidnapping Captain Pike aboard the *Enterprise,* are riveting. In part II, there are some extraordinary moments between Kirk and Spock and between Pike and his captors. Ultimately, the revelation that Spock is bringing his former captain to Talos IV to end his suffering and reunite him with Vina (Susan Oliver) is moving and further strengthens the character of Spock and his loyalty to those he serves. Kirk's final words with the Talosian captor are a fitting coda for a sensational two-parter. Guest star Oliver is a seductive presence as Vina.

GROSS (****): Besides having created the series in the first place, this episode is Gene Roddenberry's crowning achievement with *Star Trek.* What might have been a simple clip show with the barest excuses for using scenes from "The Cage" ("Gee, Mr. Spock, what was it like to serve with Captain Pike?") soars as Roddenberry creates an original story that's every bit as intriguing and powerful as his earlier effort. It's stunning to see Spock essentially betray Kirk for someone else and interesting to study Kirk's understated response to it. The court-martial sequences are quite stirring, and for the first time I was truly wondering whether Spock would get out of this situation. Check out Leonard Nimoy's passionate Spock and the depth he brings to the character's feelings

toward Pike. It's truly something to witness. See also "The Cage."

MERIDIAN

(DS9)
Original Airdate 11/19/94
Teleplay by Mark Gehred-O'Connell
Story by Hilary J. Bader and Evan Carlos Somers
Directed by Jonathan Frakes

Dax falls in love with Deral (Brett Cullen), one of the inhabitants of an alien world that becomes corporeal in our dimension for only short periods of time. Before he departs, she decides to leave with him, but it nearly costs her her life and the lives of the aliens, as she cannot exist on their dimensional plane.

ALTMAN (no stars): High-concept idiocy at its worst: *Deep Space Nine* does *Brigadoon!* What were the writers thinking? The ludicrous story hinges on an even more inane contrivance — that we will accept Dax falling in love with Deral, played with little charisma by Brett Cullen. I didn't buy that for a minute, nor do I believe that she is willing to give up Starfleet for a life with this clown. The only thing the show has going for it is some nice direction from Jonathan Frakes.

GROSS (**): An old-fashioned, goofy sci-fi premise is sabotaged by a low budget. The notion of a planet and its people becoming corporeal for only a short period of time is interesting, but we just can't get a true sense of what it would be like. Some moderate suspense is generated by Dax's threatening the planet's shift back to its own space, but this turn of events is predictable. As hard as Terry Farrell tries, the love story just doesn't ring true, and everyone knows that Dax is not going away with this planet or this guy.

METAMORPHOSIS

(TOS)
Original Airdate 11/10/67
Written by Gene L. Coon
Directed by Ralph Senensky

Kirk, Spock and McCoy are transporting Federation commissioner Nancy Hedford (Elinor Donahue) when their shuttlecraft is captured by an energy cloud that brings them to Gamma Canaris N. There they encounter Zefram Cochrane (Glenn Corbett), the creator of warp drive.

ALTMAN (***): An enchanting *Trek* romance that is touching despite its occasional sexist lapses. The episode also features some classic Kirk moments. Best line: McCoy screaming at the alien Companion, "You're killing them!" as William Shatner and Leonard Nimoy pantomime asphyxiation. Glenn Corbett is great as Zefram Cochrane and far more noble than James Cromwell's take on Cochrane in *Star Trek VIII: First Contact.*

GROSS (****): Only the pen of Gene L. Coon could bring us a *Star Trek* episode that spends so much time discussing the nature of love and compassion for a cloud entity. This is one of the most sensitive episodes the series ever produced, with fully rounded character arcs for the regulars as well as guest stars Glenn Corbett as Zefram Cochrane and Elinor Donahue as Nancy Hedford. William Shatner is

at his best, underplaying his passionate attempts to make the Companion understand what true love is. Kudos to director Ralph Senensky, who takes an obviously limited budget and gets quite a bang for his buck. See also *Star Trek VIII: First Contact.*

MIND'S EYE, THE

(TNG)
Original Airdate 5/27/91
Written by Rene Echevarria
Directed by David Livingston

In this twenty-fourth-century retelling of The Manchurian Candidate, *Geordi LaForge is cast in the role originally played by Laurence Harvey, and Data assumes the role played by Frank Sinatra. The Romulans brainwash LaForge to assassinate a Klingon governor in an attempt to undermine the alliance between the Federation and the Empire. Larry Dobkin plays a Klingon traitor named Kell, based on the role played by Angela Lansbury in the film.*

ALTMAN (**): A potentially riveting story is undermined by a weak by-the-numbers ending in which Data unravels the Romulan plot and the pieces of the disturbing puzzle fall too easily into place. David Livingston's freshman outing as director is accomplished, however, and he contributes some of the episode's eeriest and most unsettling moments aboard the Romulan warbird, where the vicious Centurion Taibak (John Fleck) reprograms LaForge into a killing machine, as well as some well-executed VISOR point-of-view shots.

GROSS (***): It's obvious that the plot is similar to that of *The*

Manchurian Candidate, but it is so well executed that it really doesn't matter. Director David Livingston keeps things moving along nicely, and LeVar Burton does well as the brainwashed Geordi LaForge. The most annoying aspect of the episode is the attempt to keep Tasha Yar's descendant hidden in the shadows so as to hide her identity from the audience. This nonsense went out in the 1960s with such films as the James Bond thrillers, wherein Bond came up against Ernst Stavro Blofeld, who was unseen in two films before we finally met the guy with the cat in *You Only Live Twice.*

MIRI

(TOS)
Original Airdate 10/27/66
Written by Adrian Spies
Directed by Vincent McEveety

On an Earth-like planet, a landing party discovers a group of 300-year-old children who have a disease that prolongs youth. When they reach adolescence — no matter how long it takes — the disease triggers madness and then death. The landing party becomes infected and is trapped there until McCoy can devise a cure. In the meantime, a young woman named Miri (Kim Darby) develops a crush on Kirk and is threatened by Yeoman Rand.

ALTMAN (**): A routine viral thriller that is distinguished only by Kirk's relationship with Miri, played well by Kim Darby. It's also Grace Lee Whitney's best performance as Yeoman Rand, and her horror at watching the disease begin to infect her is a great analogy for what any human being feels as

his or her looks begin to wither with age. The first show ensuring that viewers should be wary of any *Star Trek* involving kids.

GROSS (***): An episode that alternates between being touching and being frightening by dealing, in its own allegorical way, with the nature of becoming an adult and leaving childhood behind. Thankfully, real-life adulthood isn't quite as frightening as "Miri" makes it out to be. The power of this show comes mostly from guest star Kim Darby, a young woman about to enter adolescence who develops unrequited feelings for Kirk. When she realizes that he has feelings for Yeoman Rand, she executes a plan that could be deadly, and her change in character is startling. A great deal of the credit for this episode belongs to director Vincent McEveety, who could have gone for every *Bad Seed* cliché in the book. Instead, he manages to capture the intensely frightening image of a group of psychotic children with death on their minds. The so-called bonk-bonk scene, where they pummel Kirk, is surprisingly effective. Not one of *Star Trek*'s best episodes, but a lot more impressive than anything else in the genre airing on TV at the time.

MIRROR, MIRROR

(TOS)
Original Airdate 10/6/67
Written by Jerome Bixby
Directed by Marc Daniels

During an ion storm, Kirk, McCoy, Scotty and Uhura are transported to a parallel universe, where the Enterprise crew members are savages and the Federation rules the galaxy with an iron fist. Unless Scotty can devise a way to return home in a few hours, they will be trapped in the mirror universe forever.

ALTMAN (****): Jerome Bixby's marvelous and inventive story about the *Enterprise* landing party finding itself in an alternate universe is unforgettable. It's well shot, deliciously overacted (particularly when we get to see the mirror counterparts in our universe as Spock looks on bemusedly) and exceptionally written. Barbara Luna's Marlena Moreau is a memorable femme fatale, and the finale, as Kirk beams back home, is powerful, its memory unblemished by subsequent *Trek* forays into the mirror universe.

GROSS (****): Now *this* is a trip through the looking glass. The flip sides of the regular *Trek* characters' personalities are really something. In particular, Leonard Nimoy's bearded Spock is a sight to behold. He is logical at all times, but now ruthless in a way we've never seen before. It's a joy watching Kirk, McCoy, Scotty and Uhura try to acclimate to a universe where they metaphorically find themselves serving on what could be a warship belonging to the Klingon Empire. Check out Kirk's coolness under fire, immediately covering up his confusion until he is able to figure things out and always maintaining a sense of command. And who else but Kirk could have a hand in the fall of an empire? There are some quibbles, particularly the dopey notion that our he-

roes would appear in this dimension wearing their counterparts' uniforms, but who cares? See also "Crossover," "Through the Looking Glass" and "Shattered Mirror."

MORE TRIBBLES, MORE TROUBLES

(TAS)
Original Airdate 10/6/73
Written by David Gerrold
Directed by Hal Sutherland

The Enterprise *rescues Cyrano Jones (voice of Stanley Adams) from the Klingons. The crew then learns that Jones has stolen a glomer, a genetically engineered Tribble predator, and the Klingons, led by Captain Koloth (voice of James Doohan), will stop at nothing to get it back.*

ALTMAN (**1/2): This animated sequel to "The Trouble with Tribbles" pales in comparison to the fifth-season *DS9* episode "Trials and Tribblations," but despite the typically clunky animation and sometimes sophomoric humor, it has much to recommend it. Stanley Adams returns as the voice of Cyrano Jones and provides most of the comic hijinks. Unfortunately, William Shatner walks through his role and butchers several pronunciations, most notably the ubiquitous quatrotriticale. Ultimately, the episode replays too many of the same beats of the original to stand effectively on its own, and William Campbell is desperately missed as the voice of Koloth.

GROSS (**1/2): The problem with this episode is that it's like the majority of sequels — basically a thinly veiled remake of the original. Writer David Gerrold manages some nice character humor, but the Klingons come across as too cuddly to be considered dangerous, and the Tribble jokes are a little tired. It's great that Stanley Adams was able to reprise his role as Cyrano Jones, though. See also "The Trouble with Tribbles" and "Trials and Tribblations."

MOST TOYS, THE

(TNG)
Original Airdate 5/12/90
Written by Shari Goodhartz
Directed by Timothy Bond

Data is abducted by an alien, Kivas Fajo (Saul Rubinek), who collects rare and valuable items and intends to turn Data into a piece in his museum. Meanwhile, the Enterprise *crew is deceived into believing he has perished in a shuttlecraft explosion.*

ALTMAN (*1/2): Yet another member of the bridge crew is abducted, but at least the handwringing over Data's perceived demise is handled adeptly. *True Romance*'s Saul Rubinek gives a hammy and over-the-top performance, and the shocking and surprisingly lousy production values torpedo an already overstuffed episode. Only the story's provocative coda, in which Data learns that sometimes it's necessary to kill, is of note. It's a step forward in the evolution of the character and a fascinating issue for *Star Trek* to address. Unfortunately, the dialogue subsequent to Data's return to the *Enterprise* is botched. The character's growth and a well-

placed baseball card are the only elements that elevate this above your average episode of *Buck Rogers*.

GROSS (***): Saul Rubinek's Kivas Fajo is another in *Trek*'s long line of whining adult children given access to great power, and if it weren't for Brent Spiner, this episode would be a disaster. Spiner, and his unique handle on Data, makes this an infinitely interesting character study. His final lesson is a bold step for the series to take.

MOVE ALONG HOME

(DS9)
Original Airdate 3/15/93
Teleplay by Frederick Rappaport, Lisa Rich and Jeanne Carrigan-Fauci
Story by Michael Piller
Directed by David Carson

Aliens from the Gamma Quadrant bring aboard a mysterious game that turns deadly for Sisko, Kira, Bashir and Dax when they become the innocent pawns in Quark's quest for financial gain.

ALTMAN (*1/2): If not for David Carson's atmospheric direction and another sturdy performance by Armin Shimerman, "Move Along Home" would be a new low for the series. Its plot seems more suited to *Lost in Space* than *Deep Space Nine*. Again, more unsavory visitors from the Gamma Quadrant imperil the senior staff. Although Michael Piller provides the requisite wit in the teaser, along with some amusing exchanges bordering on the surreal throughout the game, the show, originally called "Sore Losers," is just that —

a loser bordering more on fantasy than science fiction.

GROSS (**): Using characters as living game pieces (Q's favorite pastime) is fine, but the episode falters in its presentation of the game itself. There simply wasn't enough money in the budget to make the threats our heroes endure real. To make matters worse, at one point they have to play hopscotch to proceed to the next level. Puhlease! Interesting character moment: Quark's agony over having to make a decision that could result in the deaths of his comrades. Gee, never knew the guy had it in him.

MUDD'S PASSION

(TAS)
Original Airdate 11/10/93
Written by Stephen Kandel
Directed by Hal Sutherland

Kirk rescues Harry Mudd (voice of Roger C. Carmel) from a group of miners whom the redoubtable con man is trying to swindle with a faux love potion. Once on board the Enterprise, *Mudd convinces Nurse Chapel to try the elixir on Spock, who falls madly in love with her. Soon afterward, the potion infects almost everyone on board.*

ALTMAN (***): Harry Mudd makes a welcome return in the animated series, hawking a love potion to the unsuspecting. Once on board the *Enterprise*, chaos ensues when Nurse Chapel attempts to ensnare the logical, unemotional Mr. Spock. Although the episode ends with the crew battling dinosaur creatures, what makes "Mudd's

Passion" such a hoot are its sophisticated wit and humor. It's far more entertaining than *DS9*'s "Fascination," in which the crew begins falling in love with each other due to the empathic influence of Lwaxana Troi. Roger C. Carmel is in top form once again as the inscrutable Harry Mudd. Lines such as the lovelorn McCoy's bragging while wooing a woman that he's saved the life of virtually every command officer on the ship — adding, "If the *Enterprise* had a heart, I'd save her, too" — make this episode a high point for the often overlooked animated series.

GROSS (***): Unlike many of the other episodes in the animated series, which seem content to rehash the live-action elements, "Mudd's Passion" expands on the original series, bringing back a familiar character and taking the story in a new direction. It offers plenty of humor and, particularly for Kirk, some dangerous situations. Kudos to writer Stephen Kandel for so successfully bringing the character of Harry Mudd back to life. See also "Mudd's Women," "I, Mudd" and "Fascination."

MUDD'S WOMEN

(TOS)
Original Airdate 10/13/66
Teleplay by Stephen Kandel
Story by Gene Roddenberry
Directed by Harvey Hart

The Enterprise *beams aboard interstellar con man Harry Mudd (Roger C. Carmel) and the beautiful women he has brought along as his cargo. In a*

desperate search for dilithium crystals to restoke the engine depleted by their rescue, Kirk takes the ship to the Rigel Mining Colony, where the miners demand the women in payment for their crystals. We then discover that the women's beauty has been achieved artificially.

ALTMAN (***): An inventive story that muses on the issues of natural beauty and our culture's obsession with physical appearance. All this is incorporated into a yummy yarn featuring Roger C. Carmel as the rakish Harry Mudd, one of the series' most enjoyable recurring characters. Director Harvey Hart effectively evokes the inhospitable Rigel milieu, and despite some over-the-top lasciviousness by the male crew members toward the women, it's a solid episode. (After all, it's not as if these men haven't seen a pretty face before.)

GROSS (***1/2): The introduction of Roger C. Carmel's Harcourt Fenton (aka Harry) Mudd, a character who manages to be both amusing and a genuine threat to the *Enterprise*. Harry is the quintessential con man, who could sell just about anything to anyone. The episode also provides some interesting bits of character development for Kirk, who for one of the few times in the series, blunders badly and spends the rest of the episode trying to make up for it (see also "Tomorrow Is Yesterday"). Scotty warns him that the *Enterprise* can't stand the strain of locking tractor beams on Harry's ship, but Kirk does so anyway, and the starship is knocked nearly out of commission. This episode is obviously dealing with drug abuse and

prostitution — a fact that went completely over the heads of the NBC yahoos in the 1960s. What a shock. See also "I, Mudd" and "Mudd's Passion."

MUSE, THE

(DS9)
Original Airdate 4/29/96
Teleplay by Rene Echevarria
Story by Majel Barrett Roddenberry and Rene Echevarria
Directed by David Livingston

Lwaxana Troi (Majel Barrett) returns to the station, now pregnant and married, while a mysterious stranger, Onaya (Meg Foster), literally sucks the creative juices out of Jake.

ALTMAN (**): "The Muse" is not a total disaster despite it's questionable story concepts. It reminds me of those really goofy, but momentarily enjoyable, episodes that occasionally pop up in the original *Trek*'s third season. It's actually a tribute to *DS9* that when it's bad, it's not completely unwatchable. In fact, Rene Echevarria does as much with the loopy stories as he can. Meg Foster gives a reliably droll, sinister performance, imbuing her character (Onaya) with as much menace as she can muster in a story that seems like a bad *Buck Rogers* retread (remember "Space Vampire"?). As for the show's latest attempt to appease Mrs. Roddenberry with her annual acting gig, at least it is better than "Fascination."

GROSS (**1/2): Surprisingly, the aspect of this episode that works the best is Odo's coming to grips with his feelings for Lwaxana Troi. The notion of the so-called Muse is intriguing, but there is no explanation of where this being came from and what it's truly about. For *Trek* to succeed, it usually has to provide a logical background for any alien that it features — living up to the Gene Roddenberry adage that no being is all good or all evil. By the by, Meg Foster's eyes have creeped me out for years, and they do so here as well. See also "Haven," "Manhunt," "Menage A Troi," "Half a Life," "Cost of Living," "Dark Page" and "The Forsaken."

NAGUS, THE

(DS9)
Original Airdate 3/22/92
Written by Ira Steven Behr
Directed by David Livingston

The royal Ferengi Nagus Zek arrives at DS9 to divvy up shares in the business opportunities awaiting them in the Gamma Quadrant. He fakes his death to test his son's worthiness, bestowing his crown, as part of the ruse, upon Quark, who then becomes the object of several assassination attempts — including one by his own brother, Rom.

ALTMAN (**): "The Nagus" features some strong directing by David Livingston in his first *DS9* outing, witty writing by Ira Steven Behr and a fun performance by the always lively Wallace Shawn, who is brilliantly cast as the aged Ferengi royal. The pint-size playwright/actor is best known for his acting turns in *My Dinner with André* (with André Gregory), *The Princess Bride* and, of course, Woody Allen's *Manhattan* (as Diane Keaton's irresistible ex). The B story involving Nog and Sisko's son, Jake, is enjoyable corn, though probably a little too mundane for a science-fiction show. This is another fine vehicle for Quark, to the detriment of the rest of the ensemble.

GROSS (***): An episode about the Ferengi that's actually thoroughly enjoyable. Considering how absolutely annoying that race was when first introduced on *TNG*, it's nice to see how they've evolved from comic relief to fleshed-out human beings (well, sort of human). Wallace Shawn, perhaps best known as the Sicilian in *The Princess Bride*, steals the show as the Nagus, a sleazy little toad of a Ferengi. Armin Shimerman carries things nicely as Quark is temporarily elevated in status (although one wouldn't want to see a zany spin-off featuring the character). The B story of Jake secretly trying to teach Nog how to read works surprisingly well. See also "Rules of Acquisition" and "Prophet Motive."

NAKED NOW, THE

(TNG)

Original Airdate 10/3/87
Written by Michael Bingham
Story by John D. F. Black
Directed by Paul Lynch

The Enterprise *is sent to investigate the status of the SS Tsilkovsky, which was examining a collapsing star when all communication was lost. An Away Team learns that the entire crew is dead and that they had been gripped by madness. The same virus spreads to the* Enterprise, *stripping the crew of its inhibitions.*

ALTMAN (*1/2): It never ceases to amaze me that the *Trek* ensemble numbers this among their favorite episodes. It's an insipid retread of the original *Trek's* "The Naked Time," featuring liberal doses of sexual innuendo and pure idiocy. Some of the character moments are amusing, but the "ship in peril" plot is sheer stupidity, filled with contradictions and quantum leaps in logic. The exploration of character that a premise such as this seems to offer goes sadly unrealized. Only a fully functional Data's liaison with a horny Tasha Yar has any resonance, playing an integral part in "The Measure of a Man." "The Naked Now" was a deeply disturbing kickoff for the one-hour episodes, boding badly for what was to come.

GROSS (*1/2): Probably the biggest question that comes to mind is *why?* To allow the second installment of *TNG* to be a remake of an original series episode was poor creative judgment. What could have been in Gene Roddenberry's mind? His idea may have been to delve into the characters, but the episode's preoccupation with sex and chief Tasha Yar are the only things delved into. Great special effects, lousy drama. See also "The Naked Time."

NAKED TIME, THE

(TOS)

Original Airdate 9/29/66
Written by John D. F. Black
Directed by Marc Daniels

An Enterprise *landing party contracts a disease that is brought back aboard the starship and starts to spread, stripping the crew of its inhibitions. As a result, they live out their fantasies or confront their worst nightmares, all of which might result in the demise of the starship itself.*

ALTMAN (***): The best of the alien virus episodes, in which the crew falls prey to their suppressed emotions. It's a great way to learn more about what makes these characters tick, as Spock's logic gives way to emotion, Captain Kirk panics over losing command and Sulu brandishes a rapier down the corridors of the *Enterprise*. Listening to Lieutenant Riley sing "I'll Take You Home Again, Kathleen" never ceases to send me into hysterics. It all culminates in a suspenseful climax as the crew attempts to break away from Psi 2000 before being destroyed.

GROSS (***): An early, fascinating exploration of the *Star Trek* characters via a space virus. Sulu gets to run around the corridors of the *Enterprise* with a sword — the one sequence that seems to epitomize Sulu in the original series and the only one that actor George Takei can truly hold on to as his own. Plenty of laughs are provided by Bruce Hyde's Lieutenant Riley, who fancies himself something of a starship captain and is nearly responsible for the destruction of the *Enterprise*. We also come to understand that Nurse Chapel (Majel Barrett) loves Mr. Spock and that the internal war between logic and emotion is always being waged within the Vulcan. Seeing him break down is *very* moving. Kirk, of course, defines the relationship between a captain and his starship as one in which he must constantly give and the ship constantly takes; a private life is impossible. It's interesting that Kirk's losing control is enough to snap Spock out of his own self-pity. Far superior to *The Next Generation* remake, "The Naked Now."

NECESSARY EVIL

(DS9)
Original Airdate 11/15/93
Written by Peter Allan Fields
Directed by James L. Conway

Odo investigates a five-year-old murder of a Bajoran named Vaatrick, who had been a member of the Bajoran slave force held by the Cardassians. The more Odo digs, however, the more likely it seems that Kira was involved in the murder.

ALTMAN (***1/2): This is the first *Trek* murder mystery that comes close to being rewarding, mostly because of its visually stunning, noirish look, courtesy of director Jim Conway and director of photography Marvin Rush. The episode, which relies on numerous flashbacks to the pre-Federation station, excels as dramatic television, balancing a malevolent tone with a dark, brooding look wholly distinguishable from the mise-en-scène of the station post-UFP. Although the mystery itself isn't particularly inspired, the bleakness of DS9's Cardassian occupation is, as are some sparkling character moments involving Rom and Kira. "Necessary Evil" also provides another fascinating look into the enigmatic character of Odo.

GROSS (****): Flashbacks are usually an annoying storytelling device, but "Necessary Evil" is the exception to the rule. This is an innovative and intriguing look into the past, with Odo's attempts at unraveling a murder case taking him (and us) back to DS9's earlier days, when the station was occupied by Cardassians. It's a fascinating exercise, as we're given a firsthand look at the kind of life the Bajorans led on the station (particularly after we've heard so much about it), made even more intriguing by the grittier look of the flashback sequences. The highlight of the show is the tarnished relationship between Odo and Kira, proving once again that it all comes down to character. Kudos to both Rene Auberjonois and Nana Visitor for pulling this off so effectively.

NEUTRAL ZONE, THE

(TNG)

Original Airdate 5/14/88
Teleplay by Maurice Hurley
Story by Deborah McIntyre and Mona Glee
Directed by James L. Conway

The Enterprise *comes across a vessel containing a group of Earthlings in suspended animation who must be acclimated to life in the twenty-fourth century. This story serves as a backdrop to the series' first confrontation with the Romulans.*

ALTMAN (**): The entire episode, a semicomic retread of "Space Seed," serves as a prelude to a tense showdown that never occurs. Having planted the seed of the reemergence of the Romulans as a force to be reckoned with in "Angel One," these Classic *Trek* baddies finally reappear with a new ship and an attitude to match in the show's — and the first season's — climactic final minutes. Setting the stage for an encounter to come, the Romulans concede that they are concerned about the destruction of their outposts along the Neutral Zone, warning ominously that they have been diverted by internal problems but that they are back. The threat is never addressed, however, as the second season virtually ignores the showdown in the Neutral Zone.

GROSS (**): They did it better with Khan. These twentieth-century arrivals make me wonder how the species ever made it to the *Star Trek* era. Still, there are enough amusing moments to keep things moving, and the true highlight (albeit an anticlimactic one) is the return of the Romulans, a villain race that the series desperately needed to shake things up. There are some silly mistakes, which were probably due to the imminent Writers Guild strike in 1988, such as Data and Worf beaming over to the cryogenic ship, with Data *then* informing the *Enterprise* that the atmosphere is suitable for life. Good thing for Worf, huh? See also "Q Who."

NEW GROUND

(TNG)

Original Airdate 1/6/92
Written by Grant Rosenberg
Directed by Robert Scheerer

Worf's mother brings his son, Alexander, back to the Enterprise *when she realizes that she and her husband can no longer give the youngster what he needs. Meanwhile, an experiment with a new warp field Solitan wave goes awry, jeopardizing the ship.*

ALTMAN (**): "New Ground" treads a lot of old ground. There's nothing particularly offensive about the episode; it's just not all that interesting. Worf's difficulties acclimating to fatherhood are handled adeptly despite occasional lapses into soapy melodrama. Unfortunately, the show suffers from another in a long line of pathetic B stories, resulting in a trivial anticlimax in which Worf must rescue his son. The scene in the classroom with Alexander's pets is absurd.

GROSS (**): There is wonderful chemistry between Michael Dorn's Worf and Brian Bonsall's Alexander, and the two really do come across as father and son. That having been said, "New Ground" is something of a disappointment, playing like a prime-time soap opera, as opposed to the most popular science-fiction series ever on television. I'm really happy that these two guys are making the effort to work out their differences, but *who cares?* It just isn't the kind of story that should carry an episode of *TNG*. The B story involving the Solitan wave is so mundane that you can't help focusing your attention back on the A story. Is that winning by default?

NEXT PHASE, THE

(TNG)
Original Airdate 5/11/92
Written by Ronald D. Moore
Directed by David Carson

Ensign Ro and Geordi LaForge seem to be killed in an explosion aboard a disabled Romulan warbird but are actually "phased" into another dimension, where they encounter an evil Romulan Centurion. The duo have to convince the Enterprise *crew that they're not dead before the ship is destroyed by a Romulan trap.*

ALTMAN (***): Like "The Game," "The Next Phase" doesn't offer any deep messages, philosophical debates or probing insight into the human condition. In fact, it doesn't even boast any cheap sophomoric gags inherent in LaForge's and Ro's sudden invisibility (no stumbling into Troi's quarters while she's taking a shower, thankfully). But it's a thor-

oughly agreeable effort and a great chance to pair the perpetually underused LaForge with Ro. Both actors shine, and Ro watching Riker eulogize her is a highlight. Less effective is Marvin Rush's mise-en-scène aboard the Romulan warbird. The ship looks like a bad set, lacking the ominous ambience required here.

GROSS (***): An OK episode with some spectacular effects and nice performances all around. This new Romulan weapon is interesting and certainly capable of serving as an adequate MacGuffin to get the plot started, but the real charm comes from Ro and LaForge as they try to determine whether they are actually dead and they watch as their *Enterprise* crew mates plan memorial services for them. The real highlight is the *Ghost*-like effects. An episode worth checking out.

NIGHT TERRORS

(TNG)
Original Airdate 3/18/91
Written by Pamela Douglas and Jeri Taylor
Directed by Les Landau

Trapped in a Tykin's rift, the Enterprise *crew members suffer sleep deprivation and start imagining their worst nightmares.*

ALTMAN (1/2*): What would a season of *Star Trek* be without one really dreadful episode? "Night Terrors" is the fourth season's "Spock's Brain," filled with horrors as the crew imagines their most terrifying nightmares. Potentially interesting, right? Wrong. Snakes in the bed, corpses rising from morgue tables and, most ludicrous of all, the turbo-lift collapsing on Picard aren't scary; they're stupid. A good story, in which an alien vessel also caught in the Tykin's rift (a space anomaly) is trying to communicate with Troi, gets lost in this sloppy mess. The scenes of Troi flying in her dreams are laughable. You won't believe a woman can fly. "Scary stuff boys and girls . . ." Hardly.

GROSS (*1/2): "The Naked Again." This episode is a disaster, recycling material from "The Naked Now" and offering little that is fresh. Picard's turbo-lift nightmare, coupled with the one he had in "Where No One Has Gone Before," leads me to believe that he should be using a Jeffries tube to get around. As far as Troi flying — can you read my mind?

NON SEQUITUR

(VOY)
Original Airdate 9/25/95
Written by Brannon Braga
Directed by David Livingston

Harry Kim is shocked to awaken in twenty-fourth-century San Francisco, where he works as a design specialist in Starfleet engineering. Reunited with his fiancée, Libby (Jennifer Gatti), he accesses his service records and learns that he was never a crew member aboard the Voyager. *Kim is approached by Cosimo, an alien being who takes the shape of a local store owner and explains that a temporal anomaly in the space continuum has led him here. If Kim doesn't set things right, Tom Paris will be condemned to life as a convicted traitor, living as a paranoid, paroled drunk in Marseilles. Unfortunately, this leads Starfleet to believe that Kim may be a spy for the Maquis.*

ALTMAN (***): "Non Sequitur" is one of the liveliest and most enjoyable episodes of *Voyager* to date, although it bogs down in insufferable technobabble, which substitutes for legitimate drama and the suspense in the show's final act. (The MacGuffin that prompts the intriguing scenario boils down to a race of beings who "exist in a temporal inversion fold in the space time matrix." Ugh.) That's a shame because this is one of the best episodes for both Garrett Wang and Robert Duncan McNeill, who gets to shine in a moment of Han Solo bravado. Jennifer Gatti also performs admirably as Kim's fiancée, Libby, although one can't help but wonder why Kim never makes an attempt to contact his parents, for whom he's been pining away for two seasons. David Livingston's direction, including judicious use of the studio back lot, helps elevate the episode's action. Even the score is more bombastically effective than the usual new *Trek* outings. Unfortunately, the episode tips its hand early in the teaser, when we hear Janeway's voice piercing Kim's temporally distorted world. This is a bad call, rendering the entire milieu less surprising and foreshadowing later developments.

GROSS (***1/2): A wonderful mystery, as Garrett Wang's Harry Kim attempts to unravel what has happened to him, at the same time encountering people whom he knows — some of whom know him, and others (such as Tom Paris) who don't. Kim's mounting paranoia as he tries to prove his claims is sustained nicely by director David Livingston. Also effective are Kim's pleas to Tom Paris, who comes away from the experience so entranced by the idea of an alternate, more heroic life he never had that he decides to help Kim. The most grating part of the episode is the alien's explanation for what's happened to Kim — essentially just an "oops."

NTH DEGREE, THE

(TNG)
Original Airdate 4/1/91
Written by Joe Menosky
Directed by Robert Legato

Barclay (from "Hollow Pursuits") returns and has his intellect enhanced by aliens attempting to bring the Enterprise to the center of the universe to say hi.

ALTMAN (**1/2): Although "The Nth Degree" works only sporadically and is nowhere near as good as Barclay's first outing on the show, it is helped by Robert Legato's impressive incorporation of state-of-the-art visuals and a strong return performance by Dwight Schultz as Barclay. A teaser in which he performs in *Cyrano de Bergerac* (Gérard Depardieu he's not) and some subsequent scenes in which he becomes more assertive thanks to his alien gift (flirting with Troi and engaging in a physics discussion with Albert Einstein in the holodeck) are all right on. Ultimately, however, the resolution is unsatisfying and all too familiar.

GROSS (***): The return of Dwight Schultz's Barclay gives every indication of another Q in the making in terms of a character whose sporadic appearances are most welcome. (Barclay even makes a surprising cameo in *Star Trek VIII: First Contact*.) "The Nth Degree" offers quite a departure from "Hollow Pursuits" in that Barclay doesn't need the holodeck to live out his fantasies. Granted, aliens do influence him this time, but at least he's moving toward functioning in the real world. Interestingly, the plot line bears some striking similarities to *The Twilight Zone*'s "Mr. Dingle, the Strong," in which Burgess Meredith is endowed with great strength by a pair of alien beings. See also "Hollow Pursuits," "Realm of Fear," "Ship in a Bottle" and *Star Trek VIII: First Contact*.

O

OBSESSION

(TOS)
Original Airdate 12/15/67
Written by Art Wallace
Directed by Ralph Senensky

Kirk becomes obsessed when he has the opportunity to battle a gaseous creature that feeds on human blood cells and that he faced previously as a lieutenant. Half of the crew of the USS Farragut perished during that earlier battle, and Kirk has blamed himself ever since because he hesitated in firing his phaser at the entity.

ALTMAN (***): A great Kirk episode in which the captain becomes obsessed with destroying the creature he thinks he let go years before. William Shatner is great as the Ahab-like captain, and there are some fine emotional fireworks between the characters as they clash over his fixation on destroying the creature. It's nice to see Kirk lose control for a change. The creature's methodology for murder also is fairly gruesome.

GROSS (***): A tour de force performance for William Shatner as he presents a side of Kirk that we've never really seen before — an obsessive commander willing to risk everything to rectify a personal wrong. Some real suspense is generated in the battle with the creature, and Kirk is redeemed when he learns that he could have done nothing in the past that would have made any difference.

OFFSPRING, THE

(TNG)
Original Airdate 3/10/90
Written by Rene Echevarria
Directed by Jonathan Frakes

Data creates a daughter for himself (Lal, played by Hallie Todd). Although hoping to tutor his new and improved cyborg in humanity, his plans are upset when Starfleet admiral Haftel (Nicolas Coster) announces his plans to take Lal back to Starfleet headquarters with him for study. Picard is persuaded to defend Data, who is reluctant to give up his daughter.

ALTMAN (***): Despite being reminiscent of "The Measure of a Man," "The Offspring" succeeds on its own terms, primarily due to a dynamic performance by Hallie Todd as Lal, Data's android offspring. Jonathan Frakes handles his directorial duties with aplomb and contributes an amusing bit in which the sexual predator Riker is embraced by Lal, much to his bemusement. This leads Data to query, "What are your intentions toward my daughter?" A hysterical moment, which soon gives way to pathos as Lal's life span comes to an end.

GROSS (**1/2): Though paling a bit in comparison to "The Measure of a Man," "The Offspring" nonetheless adds some depth to familiar themes because Data is now fighting for his daughter rather than himself, that paternal feeling bringing him a step closer to humanity. As always, Brent Spiner is able to handle a wide variety of emotional issues in his own unique unemotional manner, while still being able to convey the character's needs to the audience. Hallie Todd does a nice turn as Lal, and Jonathan Frakes demonstrates a sure directorial hand.

OMEGA GLORY, THE

(TOS)
Original Airdate 3/1/68
Written by Gene Roddenberry
Directed by Vincent McEveety

Yet another renegade Federation captain, this time Ronald Tracey (Morgan Woodward), interferes with a frontier society and alters its progression.

ALTMAN (*1/2): A truly painful episode. It begins promisingly with an eerie scene in space aboard the USS *Exeter* and the landing party's subsequent contact with the Asiatic Kohms, now led by renegade Captain Tracey, played with insane malevolence by Morgan Woodward. Shortly thereafter, "The Omega Glory" becomes completely nonsensical, as the rebel Yangs display an American flag as part of their sacred ceremony and begin reading from the U.S. Constitution, getting a little help from Kirk. Ultimately, we learn that the Kohms represent the communists and the Yangs represent the Yankees. It makes me cringe every time.

GROSS (*1/2): Starfleet captain Ronald Tracey has broken the Prime Directive on yet another alien world, and the *Enterprise* crew must try to set things right. The entire episode is redundant of things we've seen in the past, with the Khoms and Yangs thinly veiled versions of the communists and Americans. Kirk's reading of a document bearing an amazing resemblance to the U.S. Constitution is hilarious in its blustery self-importance. This script was one of those vying to become the second *Trek* pilot. Thankfully, somebody chose "Where No Man Has Gone Before" instead, or this book would be a pamphlet.

ONCE UPON A PLANET

(TAS)
Original Airdate 11/3/73
Written by Len Jenson and Chuck Menville
Directed by Hal Sutherland

This sequel to the live-action show's "Shore Leave" has the Enterprise *crew return to the planet where any wish can come true. Once again, things go terribly wrong, as the Keeper has died and no one is in charge of the equipment.*

ALTMAN (**1/2): Although the episode begins promisingly, paying homage to the original "Shore Leave," it sputters midway through in a morass of kid-vid clichés, only to redeem itself with Kirk convincing the planetary computer that it could benefit from its contact with humans. Never before has "Shore Leave" seemed more like the precursor to *Westworld* than in this episode, which boasts some major animation glitches, including one that shows Sulu on the bridge at the same time he is fighting for his life with McCoy on the planet's surface.

GROSS (*): This is pretty much a remake of the live-action show "Shore Leave." Rather disappointing. See also "Shore Leave."

ONE OF OUR PLANETS IS MISSING

(TAS)
Original Airdate 9/23/73
Written by Marc Daniels
Directed by Hal Sutherland

An energy cloud that consumes planets that lie in its wake is threatening the population of

Mantilles, and the Enterprise must devise a way to combat this threat before it's too late. Only after the starship is pulled inside the cloud does Spock come to the conclusion that it is actually an intelligent creature that can be reasoned with.

ALTMAN (***): Providing a precursor to *Star Trek: The Motion Picture* and the seemingly endless space anomaly episodes that characterized *TNG* and *Voyager*, "One of Our Planets Is Missing" is one of the most interesting of this type of shows (although it clearly owes a debt to "The Immunity Syndrome"). The animation competently conveys the size and scope of the marauding cloud, which endangers a Federation world governed by none other than Governor Bob Wesley. (Yes, it's the Bob Wesley who was a commodore in "The Ultimate Computer." Cool continuity!) Ultimately, Spock's mind-meld with the cloud is both logical and satisfying, and Kirk and Spock's wrestling with the need to protect life-forms is intelligent and provocative. Kirk even references "A Taste of Armageddon" when he talks about the decision "not to kill today."

GROSS (***1/2): A highly satisfying animated episode that nicely encapsulates the *Star Trek* philosophy. Kudos to writer Marc Daniels, whose experience directing the original show obviously paid off — he actually paid attention to the material. One of the best the animated spin-off has to offer.

11001001

(TNG)
Original Airdate 1/20/88
Written by Maurice Hurley and Robert Lewin
Directed by Paul Lynch

The Enterprise stops off at a starbase for repairs, which are initiated by a species of computer-interdependent creatures called the Binars. While the repairs are being done, Riker becomes infatuated with a "woman" in the holodeck named Minuet. Unbeknownst to Picard or Riker, this is all a diversion by the Binars to commandeer the ship in the hopes that they can reactivate their homeworld's main computer, which has been damaged by sunspot activity.

ALTMAN (***1/2): One of the few first-season episodes that continues to hold up today. A standout that boasts a dynamite sci-fi premise and superb visual effects. The Binars are a unique *TNG* creation, and the sultry Carolyn McCormick is wonderful as Minuet, Riker's holodeck honey, who diverts his attention from the hijacking of the *Enterprise*. It's a character-driven piece with little action, but great dialogue that provides a fascinating musing on the nature of reality and fantasy.

GROSS (***1/2): A classic *Trek* that features a truly imaginative story line. The Binars are one of the most original races created for the series, and their plan to steal the *Enterprise* so as to reactive their homeworld is brilliant. The episode is highlighted by feature-quality special effects and an opportunity to explore some of the characters, particularly Riker, in more depth. Jonathan Frakes makes you believe that the commander has fallen in love with Minuet, and you feel his pain when he is unable to retrieve the program at episode's end. The show also subtly raises one of the drawbacks of the holodeck — creating an environment so vivid that it can become more pleasurable than reality. Note: Carolyn McCormick, who plays Minuet, went on to a recurring role in *Law & Order,* and Gene Dynarski (Orvil Quinteros), appeared in the "Mudd's Women" episode of the original series as an interstellar miner.

OPERATION ANNIHILATE

(TOS)
Original Airdate 4/13/67
Written by Stephen W. Carabatsos
Directed by Herschel Daugherty

On the planet Deneva, the Enterprise crew investigates the death of a colony, including Kirk's brother. Further investigation leads them to amoeba-like creatures about the size of large rodents, which take over a "host's" nervous system.

ALTMAN (***): Although the death of Kirk's brother is a throwaway, there's some great drama in the crew's investigation of the mysterious deaths caused by the strange flying parasites. Leonard Nimoy is particularly good as Spock suffering under the onslaught of alien mind control. There are some nice quiet moments between McCoy and the Vulcan, as well as a more suspense-

ful menace on the planet, where danger lurks in the darkness.

GROSS (**): An episode that suffers from particularly goofy special effects (these creatures look like pancakes with tails) and the immersion of Spock into soap opera histrionics, first when he goes insane and then when he goes blind, leading McCoy to ponder the fact that he made a mistake ("Damn it, Jim, it's my fault Spock's blind!"). But this situation is miraculously rectified by a hidden Vulcan eyelid that, for some reason, Spock forgets to mention until the end of the episode.

OUR MAN BASHIR

(DS9)
Original Airdate 11/25/95
Teleplay by Ronald D. Moore
Story by Robert Gillan
Directed by Winrich Kolbe

Garak intrudes on Bashir's holosuite program, where he finds the doctor relaxing as a suave secret agent working for England in 1964. Bashir is upset over the intrusion, but soon both he and Garak have their hands full when Sisko and the senior staff are stored by the computer in the holosuite buffers when they are beamed away from an exploding shuttlecraft. As a result, they take the form of the various characters in Bashir's 007-inspired adventure.

ALTMAN (***1/2): One of the most inventive and enjoyable romps in the history of *Star Trek* compares favorably with such classics as "The Trouble with Tribbles" and "A Piece of the Action," in which Bashir's 007 fantasy turns deadly. Mimicking the structure of a James Bond adventure, "Our Man Bashir" is written with a rapier-like wit and even includes a clever caper for the villainous Dr. Noah (Sisko), bent on world domination by plunging Earth into a watery grave. Only Julian Bashir's secret agent man can save the world. Some may take issue with the hokeyness of the premise, but this holodeck adventure holds together well with precious little technobabble, despite the techno-MacGuffin. It's a loving homage by Ron Moore to the spy thrillers of the 1960s, and it's clear that the cast is reveling in the loosely controlled anarchy of their doppelgängers, with Avery Brooks and Nana Visitor chewing the scenery with particular relish. I just love this episode.

GROSS (****): A totally unexpected and fully realized tribute to the early James Bond films of the 1960s that represents the best use of a malfunctioning holodeck since "The Big Goodbye" and "A Fistful of Datas." Alexander Siddig is wonderful as the Connery-esque spy, interacting with all the icons from those 007 films, including Kira as KGB agent Colonel Anastasia and Dax as a beautiful scientist working for Sisko's Dr. Noah, the supervillain who wants to melt the polar ice caps. There's a real sense of danger as the holosuite's protective sensors are off-line and anyone can die. There's also a sense of danger and humor in a debate between Bashir and Garak, who refuses to continue the adventure no matter what it means to the other officers — until Bashir nearly takes

his ear off with a bullet. The music is John Barry inspired, the production values are extraordinary and director Winrich Kolbe captures the flavor of those early Ian Fleming thrillers. Kudos to writers Ron Moore and Robert Gillan for pulling this one off.

OUTCAST, THE

(TNG)
Original Airdate 3/16/92
Written by Jeri Taylor
Directed by Robert Scheerer

While working with Soren, a member of an androgynous alien race known as the J'naii, Riker begins to fall in love with her, despite a prohibition by the planet's leaders against relationships with other races that have gender. Any violation of this law will have dire consequences for the perpetrator.

ALTMAN (***): Despite similarities in tone to "The Host" (which is probably more effective and certainly subtler), "The Outcast" works as both science fiction and a strong but obvious allegory of sexual tolerance. *Star Trek* should be commended for tackling the issue, although it is a bit of a cop-out that Melinda Cullea's Soren is so decidedly female. Writer Jeri Taylor's dialogue crackles with genuine wit, and there's a touching scene between Riker and Picard, as well as a loyal Worf coming to Riker's aid when they attempt a rescue, only to learn that Soren has been turned into Frances Farmer.

GROSS (***): Besides scoring for its strong allegory, "The Outcast" is successful in taking its time to develop the relationship between

Riker and Soren to the point where you believe they're actually falling for each other. The episode doesn't provide any solutions to society's intolerance toward the gay community, but Soren's final speech brings their argument to the forefront, and that's an important step in the right direction.

OUTRAGEOUS OKONA, THE

(TNG)
Original Airdate 12/10/88
Teleplay by Burton Armus
Story by Les Menchen, Lance Dickson and David Landsburg
Directed by Robert Becker

The Enterprise *picks up a space rogue named Okona (William O. Campbell), who is sought by two feuding races for supposed crimes. Meanwhile, the Comic (Joe Piscopo) and barmaid Guinan (Whoopi Goldberg) give Data a lesson in humor.*

ALTMAN (*1/2): More pulp science fiction than *Star Trek*, "The Outrageous Okona" offers up the most clichéd and hackneyed story of a space scoundrel imaginable. *The Rocketeer*'s William Campbell is a bore as the supposedly rakish rogue, and comedian Joe Piscopo comes across like nails on a blackboard as he attempts to help Data come to terms with his own identity.

GROSS (*): The Okona story line is mildly interesting, but the B story of Data trying to understand humor falls flat, particularly in terms of the "assistance" provided by Joe Piscopo. If you were trying to learn comedy, is *this* the guy you'd turn to?

PARADISE

(DS9)
Original Airdate 2/14/94
Teleplay by Jeff King, Richard Manning and Hans Beimler
Story by Jim Trombetta and James Crocker
Directed by Corey Allen

Sisko and O'Brien find themselves trapped on a planet led by Alixus, a well-known proponent of life without technology. It's a lifestyle she insists on imposing on the duo whether they like it or not.

ALTMAN (***1/2): A far more intriguing look at the dynamics of cult leadership than the relatively ponderous *TNG* entry "Descent, Part II," in which O'Brien and Sisko crash-land on a world that is deprived of technological devices to do a strange tech field. O'Brien and Sisko work well together, and the story itself is intriguing as the downed landing party begins to discover that their benevolent benefactors live in a perversely agrarian society under the unnatural rule of Alixus (Gail Strickland). Avery Brooks turns in a strong performance, although I must admit to wanting to see the humanist Starfleet commander take a slug at Alixus over their failure to communicate in this "Cool Hand Sisko" installment.

GROSS (***): *Trek* works best when exploring issues, and in "Paradise" that issue is cultism. It's fascinating to watch the seemingly benign society's subtle yet forceful efforts to get Sisko and O'Brien to conform to their wishes. Real praise should go to guest star Gail Strickland, whose Alixus has the same ability as Louise Fletcher's Vedek Winn to be nice to you to your face while stabbing you in the back.

PARADISE LOST

(DS9)

Original Airdate 1/6/96

Teleplay by Ira Steven Behr and Robert Hewitt Wolfe

Story by Ronald D. Moore

Directed by Reza Badiyi

Sabotage of Earth's power grid plunges the planet into a nightmare of catastrophic proportions, prompting Starfleet to mobilize its forces against a possible changeling attack. Initiating blood tests, Sisko discovers that Earth is not going to be invaded by the Dominion but is being manipulated by the traitorous Admiral Leyton and his unwitting accomplice, Commander Benteen, who are terrified of the Dominion. They will do anything to increase Earth's vigilance, even if it means sacrificing personal freedom.

ALTMAN (***1/2): "Paradise Lost" has taken some raps as being a padded attempt to fill out a two-parter, but I think it's much stronger than its predecessor ("Homefront"), boasting a nice *Seven Days in May* ambience, while also providing Sisko with the chance to be a strong action hero. There's also some effective space battle action, but the fireworks between Robert Foxworth's driven Admiral Leyton and Avery Brooks's compelling Sisko are the real action here. Whereas "Homefront" seems like a spiritual successor to *TNG*'s "Conspiracy" without its sense of mounting tension, "Paradise Lost" delivers, particularly in a scene between Sisko and one of the few actual changelings on Earth that has taken the shape of O'Brien. This scene perfectly encapsulates the sense of paranoia provoked by the changelings (shades of *The Twilight Zone*'s "Monsters Are Due on Maple Street"). It's unquestionably one of the best episodes of the fourth season.

GROSS (***1/2): The strength of this episode lies in Sisko's conversion from a believer in the cause to a proponent of the truth. Avery Brooks's growing outrage as he uncovers the truth is extremely powerful, and the confrontations between him and Robert Foxworth are electric in their intensity. There are some similarities to *TNG*'s fourth-season episode "The Drumhead," but that doesn't diminish the impact of "Paradise Lost." As Sisko points out to Gowron in "The Way of the Warrior," giving in to the paranoia that the Dominion is trying to spread is the best way to ensure their success in vanquishing the Federation and the Empire. Look for an off-kilter scene between Sisko and a changeling that looks like O'Brien and seems to be enjoying the man-made panic on Earth. This is the conclusion to the previous episode, "Homefront."

PARADISE SYNDROME, THE

(TOS)
Original Airdate 10/4/68
Written by Margaret Armen
Directed by Jud Taylor

When a planet is threatened by an asteroid, a landing party beams down to try to evacuate the people. An accident gives Kirk amnesia, and he is eventually found by a tribe of Indians, who look upon him as a god. Referring to himself as Kirok, he takes a bride and is ultimately the victim of the changing mood of the crowd, who realize that he is merely mortal.

ALTMAN (**): Captain Kirk dances with wolves when he gets amnesia and thinks he's a Native American god on a distant planet. Even though the premise is a stretch, there's some real emotional heat between William Shatner and Sabrina Scharff as his bride, Miramanee. When Kirk is pelted with rocks and the planet comes closer to destruction, there's some genuinely moving drama, particularly as Kirk tenderly watches Miramanee die. Great location photography and a beautiful score make the dopey premise tenable.

GROSS (**1/2): An interesting opportunity to see Kirk stripped of the responsibilities of command (so he steps into godhood instead, no rest for the weary) and embracing the simpler things in life — in particular a normal, loving relationship with a woman without his starship competing for his attention. The ending, in which he and Miramanee are stoned with (obviously) Styrofoam rocks, has unusually tragic results in terms of the series: Miramanee dies with

Kirk's unborn child. A highlight of the episode is the moment when Spock attempts a Vulcan mind-meld to restore Kirk's memory and the captain is determined to hold on to his identity as Kirok as long as he can. One of the few good third-season episodes.

PARALLAX

(VOY)
Original Airdate 1/23/95
Teleplay by Brannon Braga
Story by Jim Trombetta
Directed by Kim Friedman

Voyager encounters a quantum singularity after receiving a signal from another vessel that seems to be in jeopardy. The crew's attempts to rescue this ship fail, and they eventually learn that it is actually the Voyager *that is trapped in this strange time-space anomaly. In the B story, there is a debate over who should be the ship's chief engineer: Janeway wants a Starfleet officer, and Chakotay believes that his Maquis engineer, B'Elanna Torres, would be better suited for the role.*

ALTMAN (**1/2): A surprisingly effective technoromp, in which the *Voyager* becomes trapped in a quantum singularity. The episode avoids the traditional pitfalls of such stories by embracing character issues with gusto, while also presenting its technobabble in plain language — and even making fun of it in one amusing exchange between Janeway and a befuddled Paris. What really elevates the show is its wit and intelligence in tackling the simmering conflict between Maquis and Federation officers. A gag involving a shrinking doctor doesn't quite work, but the show succeeds marvelously in further defining the series ensemble in an effective and satisfying way.

GROSS (★★★): The trapped, second starship *Voyager* is a conceit that differs greatly from the typical anomaly encountered in space, but the real meat of this episode is in the relationships, particularly in choosing a chief engineer. The conflict between the Maquis and Starfleet is still very evident in this early episode, and it's both fascinating and believable to watch the relationship between Roxann Biggs-Dawson's B'Elanna Torres and Kate Mulgrew's Captain Janeway begin antagonistically but gradually become one of mutual trust and affection.

PARALLELS

(TNG)
Original Airdate 11/29/93
Written by Brannon Braga
Directed by Robert Wiemer

Returning home from a bat'telh tournament, Worf finds himself experiencing several alternate realities aboard the Enterprise, *including one in which he is married to Counselor Troi. After Data learns that a flaw in Geordi LaForge's visor has expanded a rift in realities, an attempt is made to return Worf to his own reality. En route, he is led to an infinite number of converging universes.*

ALTMAN (★★★): Mired in enough ludicrous technobabble to fill a physics tome, "Parallels" is an interesting idea that doesn't achieve its full potential. One of the show's most profound failings is its slow buildup, which leads to an intriguing intersection of parallel realities involving an infinite number of *Enterprise*s. Unfortunately, this neat gag is squandered as a quick coda for an episode that instead dwells on Worf's incredulity as the reality he knows breaks down. The show eschews a compelling science-fiction story for soap opera dramatics aboard the *Enterprise*, as Worf discovers that he is married to Counselor Troi ("As the Worf Turns"?). The most annoying problem is the blatant similarities to "Future Imperfect," "Yesterday's Enterprise" and even Braga's own "Frame of Mind." Had the converging quantum realities been explored in more depth, along with Riker's feelings about facing a Captain Picard he knows died four years before, rather than the more simplistic and emotionally unrewarding Worf and Troi married twist, "Parallels" could have been a classic rather than the derivative and mildly rewarding episode that it is.

GROSS (★★1/2): A character trapped outside the space-time continuum is pretty repetitive throughout the course of *TNG*. Some mild interest in Worf's predicament is generated, but as noted above, the most intriguing element of the episode is the glance into alternate *Enterprise*s, one in which a frantic Riker pronounces that the Borg have conquered the Federation, and another in which Riker is captain, having lost Picard several years earlier. The episode does open the door for a romance between Worf and Troi, although this being the last season of *TNG*, it is never brought to fruition.

PARTURITION

(VOY)
Original Airdate 10/9/95
Written by Tom Szollosi
Directed by Jonathan Frakes

Tom Paris begins to develop an interest in Kes, which stirs up violent jealousy in Neelix, who instigates a mess hall fight with the cocky pilot. Afterward, Janeway sends the two on a shuttle mission to a planet where they hope to find food for the ship. When a storm forces the ship to land on the treacherous planet, the crew takes shelter in a cave, where they find an embryonic pod that produces a baby hatchling. They agree to care for the baby until its parent arrives to take it home.

ALTMAN (**): A contrived and rather uninspired episode in which Neelix and Paris are trapped on an inhospitable alien world. *Voyager* resolves one of its more interesting story arcs, involving Neelix's jealousy toward Paris over his interest in Kes, in a less than stellar way. Just because Neelix is the cook, what makes him an expert on alien agriculture? What do those other two-hundred-odd crew members do, anyway? Finding an alien baby (which looks like Muppet Baby Gonzo by way of *Space Precinct*), Paris and Neelix play house and resolve their differences in some clumsily scripted scenes. *Voyager* moralism is invoked as Neelix refuses to abandon the baby until it's accepted by its mother (a concept handled in a far superior way in the penultimate

episode of *Space: Above & Beyond*). All I can say is when the original *Star Trek* did its baby episode, it involved Klingons, flying killer triangles and Captain Kirk kicking ass, not injecting an alien hatchling with methane gas to keep it alive. Ah, the good old days.

GROSS (*1/2): Just when Neelix was becoming a more appealing character, this episode comes along and makes him petty and the kind of overbearing boyfriend that an Earth woman would have dumped in a second. Forcing him and Paris into a confined situation where they have to work together is a tired contrivance that serves the purpose, but not very creatively.

PASSENGER, THE

(DS9)
Original Airdate 2/22/93
Written by Morgan Gendel, Robert Hewitt Wolfe and Michael Piller
Directed by Paul Lynch

An alien murderer named Vantika seems to die on DS9, but in actuality he has managed to transfer his consciousness from body to body, ending up in Bashir. His goal is to receive a large quantity of deuridium, a drug that is noted for prolonging life in his species. Dax plays an important role in stopping him.

ALTMAN (**): Despite its title, which makes it sound like Italian neorealist cinema, "The Passenger" is a rather tame genre piece. Although it's a concoction of tried-and-true science-fiction clichés, the writers wisely choose to explore the character dynamics between Odo and a Starfleet security officer who the constable feels is encroaching on his turf. That part of the story works, although, like much of early *DS9*, the conflict sometimes seems forced. What doesn't work is the episode's conclusion, another all too familiar wrap-up in which technobabble substitutes for drama in resolving the plot. Quark and his rogues' gallery of mercenaries is effective, but the implications of his first blatantly illegal profiteering are never really explored.

GROSS (**): A nice addition to the series (though dropped after one additional appearance) is a Starfleet security officer who immediately comes into conflict with Odo. The main plot — a killer gaining immortality by transferring his consciousness from one body to another — is mildly interesting, but there's a certain lack of urgency to everything that takes place. "The Passenger" never really comes to life, and the technobabble-filled (and seemingly illogical) conclusion really mars the episode. Still, Alexander Siddig has a great time chewing the scenery once his body is taken over.

PAST PROLOGUE

(DS9)
Original Airdate 1/11/93
Written by Katharyn Powers
Directed by Winrich Kolbe

Kira is reunited with former Bajoran underground rebel Tahna (Jeffrey Nordling), who is not ready to give up his days as a warrior. Tahna is soon to receive a bomb from the Klingon Duras sisters, which he will use to close the wormhole, thus removing Bajor from the influence of the Federation and the Cardassians. Kira finds herself torn between her past and the present.

ALTMAN (**): Certainly indicative of the show's more passionate approach to character interaction are two terrific scenes: one between Odo and Kira and the other in which Sisko rebukes Kira after she disputes his actions with a Starfleet admiral. The real highlight is the relationship between a Cardassian spy, Garak, played sensationally for the first time by *Dirty Harry*'s Andrew Robinson, and Alexander Siddig as Bashir, who brings a manic enthusiasm to the role. This relationship instills the episode with a vibrancy that's lacking in the espionage story, although Lursa and B'Etor Duras (and their wonderful Bob Blackman–designed costumes) are welcome additions. See also "Reunion," "Redemption," "Firstborn" and *Star Trek VII: Generations*.

GROSS (**1/2): A fairly strong episode that continues to establish conflict between the characters, particularly Sisko and Kira, when she goes over his head after deciding that she doesn't like his handling of the situation. When Sisko tells her that if she goes over his head again, he'll have *her* head on a platter, you believe it. The political aspect of the story line — a warrior refusing to end his struggle and willing to kill anyone in the name of his cause — is effective and initiates the development of

Kira's character from a Bajoran freedom fighter to someone who has to begin living by the rules. Andrew Robinson has a great time as Cardassian tailor Garak, but Alexander Siddig is really annoying as a completely naive Dr. Bashir.

PAST TENSE, PART I

(DS9)
Original Airdate 1/7/95
Teleplay by Robert Hewitt Wolfe
Story by Ira Steven Behr and Robert Hewitt Wolfe
Directed by Reza Badiyi

A transporter malfunction sends Sisko, Bashir and Dax back in time to San Francisco, circa 2024, where the homeless are imprisoned in areas known as Sanctuary Districts. The trio arrives at a precipitous moment in history: A series of events, sparked by anti-Sanctuary leader Gabriel Bell, that will define humanity's future has just begun. Bell is killed while trying to save Sisko and Bashir in a brawl, and Sisko must take Bell's place in history.

ALTMAN (***1/2): "Past Tense" is an effective, well-plotted thriller featuring a surprisingly good use of the studio back lot. But it also indulges in some unbearable diatribes regarding homelessness, and its naive, technobabble-ridden view of temporal mechanics prevents it from being in the same category as "City on the Edge of Forever," an episode to which it bears a striking resemblance. (In fact, according to Bashir, Starfleet even has a temporal displacement policy, since it has become such a frequent occurrence. It's a reflection of the post–Classic *Trek* shows, in which time travel is no longer something special but instead merely a plot contrivance.) The film's soapbox polemic is an even more heinous affront than Tasha Yar's infamous "Just Say No" speech in *TNG*'s first-season episode "Symbiosis."

GROSS (***1/2): With the homeless not far from anyone's front door, "Past Tense" is one of the most *necessary* episodes of *Star Trek* ever produced. Most powerful is that the notion of Sanctuary Districts does not seem that far removed from today; indeed, these districts seem like a distinct possibility. Unusual for *Trek* is the death of a historic figure such as Gabriel Bell. This is the first time that a Federation officer has been forced to step into history to make sure that the future takes its proper course. There are two things that hurt this episode. First, having the transporter malfunction in such a way as to project people back in time stretches one's credulity. Second, Avery Brooks's initial understated reaction to everything gives the impression of someone who wishes he were elsewhere. It's unbelievable that after the transporter mishap, Sisko turns to Bashir and says, in a complete monotone, "Doctor, we've traveled three hundred years back in time." So, wanna catch a flick? Do Chinese? These are quibbles, but they take away from the overall impact.

PAST TENSE, PART II

(DS9)

Original Airdate 1/14/95
Teleplay by Robert Hewitt Wolfe
Story by Ira Steven Behr and Robert Hewitt Wolfe
Directed by Jonathan Frakes

Sisko, pretending to be Gabriel Bell, must defuse a hostage crisis in a Sanctuary District to prevent time from being changed, while Kira and O'Brien hopelessly try to find the commander before the future is irreparably altered.

ALTMAN (***): It would be easy to criticize the second part of "Past Tense" for being too confined to the interior of an office, which is clearly the result of budget exigencies. However, this may be one of the most successful conclusions to a *Trek* two-parter since "The Menagerie." Rene Echevarria's (uncredited) writing lacks the heavy-handedness (for the most part) of the first installment, and there's some crisp direction by Jonathan Frakes. Unfortunately, the episode may have the silliest and most inept moment in the entire thirty-year history of *Star Trek*: Kira and O'Brien, searching for the missing Away Team, find themselves on a street corner in the 1960s during the Summer of Love and encounter a couple of beatniks who are blaring Jimi Hendrix from their van. It's the most offensive portrayal of the counterculture since *Forrest Gump* and surpasses even "The Way to Eden" on the stupidity meter.

GROSS (***): Some of the impact of part II is diminished by the fact that much of the episode is a hostage situation set in a single room, playing like any number of similar situations we've seen before. Still, Avery Brooks comes alive as Sisko turned Gabriel Bell, trying to open people's eyes to the reality of what is happening in the Sanctuary Districts. Kira and O'Brien's search through time is kind of pointless, designed to provide some levity to the heavy drama, but their encounters with people in a couple of time periods (all obviously shot on the Paramount back lot) fall flat. A nice change in attitude occurs in Sanctuary District cop Vin (Dick Miller), who finally comes around to seeing the other side when Sisko/Bell takes a bullet meant for him. The homeless issue is something that needed to be discussed, and *Star Trek* was the best forum in which to do so. There's a cute coda in which Starfleet history books have a photo of Sisko accompanying a biography of Bell (which will be revisited, albeit briefly, in the *DS9* episode "Little Green Men").

PATTERNS OF FORCE

(TOS)

Original Airdate 2/16/68
Written by John Meredyth Lucas
Directed by Vincent McEveety

The Enterprise *arrives at Ekos, a planet controlled by Nazis. The Nazis are led (in name only) by Federation historian John Gill (David Brian), who believes that the efficiency of Hitler's regime, if handled with a conscience, will work.*

ALTMAN (★★★): *Schindler's List* it's not. What some dismiss as a hokey idea, berating it as "Nazi Planet," is actually a fairly entertaining story. The potentially offensive plot actually has a potent message about racism, although it lays on the metaphor a little thick. Fortunately, there are some great action moments as Spock and Kirk infiltrate the bastion of the Nazi government, and David Brian gives a solid performance as the misguided Professor Gill, who learns, in true George Santayana form, that those who forget the past are condemned to repeat it.

GROSS (★★★): Although the notion of societies growing parallel to ours became tiresome in the original series, "Patterns of Force" manages to raise the controversial issue of whether the underlying notion behind the Nazi movement — that of a country using all its resources toward a goal — could be a controlled and ultimately positive thing. As this episode proves, it cannot, as power once again corrupts. Some amusing banter between Kirk and Spock, particularly the look Kirk gives his first officer when he puts on a Gestapo uniform and Spock comments, "You should make a very convincing Nazi, Captain." By this point in the series, thanks to Gene L. Coon's contribution, it had been decided that the show was about Kirk, Spock and McCoy, and those relationships, even in the midst of the action, always manage to be showcased.

PEAK PERFORMANCE

(TNG)
Original Airdate 7/8/89
Written by David Kemper
Directed by Robert Scheerer

As a result of his confrontation with the Borg, Picard consents to a war games drill in which Riker takes command of a Starfleet frigate. Riker includes Worf and Wesley Crusher as part of his team to fend off the Enterprise *in mock battle. During the engagement, and while the* Enterprise's *weapons systems are deactivated, the Ferengi attack.*

ALTMAN (★★★): A solid space action/adventure story showcasing the Ferengi to maximum advantage. The exciting battle scenes are coupled with some delightful character moments, including Worf building a model ship in his cabin and Data's bout with insecurity. Unfortunately, Wesley Crusher gets to save the ship yet again, but Data and Worf have their chances to shine as well. Genre vet Roy Brocksmith as alien strategist Sirna Kolrami is a pompous delight.

GROSS (★★★): A wonderful opportunity to explore many of the show's characters as we see them pitted against each other in war games. An interesting intellectual battle between Picard and Riker in command of their respective vessels highlights the show. Some nice continuity to "Q Who" is provided, and some genuine suspense is generated during the war games, as well as in the battle against the Ferengi.

PEGASUS, THE

(TNG)
Original Airdate 1/10/94
Written by Ronald D. Moore
Directed by LeVar Burton

The Enterprise *goes in search of a missing starship that vanished twelve years earlier while conducting a mysterious experiment. The ship had been captured by Admiral Pressman, who has taken command of the mission. His former first officer, Riker, is torn between his loyalty to Pressman and his loyalty to Picard, as the experiment involved an illegal phasing cloaking device.*

ALTMAN (***1/2): An episode that is absolutely riveting for its first half hour but suffers from a less than engaging wrap-up. By now it appears that every admiral in Starfleet is completely unhinged, although you couldn't ask for a better performance than that given by Terry O'Quinn as Admiral Pressman. "The Pegasus" addresses some long-overdue questions regarding cloaking technology, and it boasts the most interstellar scope since "Relics," as the *Enterprise* navigates the confines of an asteroid field. It also features a memorably spicy confrontation between Picard and Riker, and we learn more about why Picard picked Riker as his first officer.

GROSS (****): This episode crackles, and all that energy comes from characterization and character confrontation. First-rate performances by Jonathan Frakes, Patrick Stewart and guest star Terry O'Quinn. The effects are spectacular, and there are some wonderful confrontations with a smug Romu-

lan commander. One of the last episodes of the series and an absolute winner.

PEN PALS

(TNG)
Original Airdate 4/29/89
Written by Melinda Snodgrass
Directed by Winrich Kolbe

Data receives a distress call from an alien girl (Nikki Cox) on a planet in the throes of geographic turmoil and responds to her communiqué despite the Prime Directive. Wesley Crusher, given his first command assignment, in this case of a geographic survey team studying the phenomenon, must face the dilemma of whether to save the planet and restore its tectonic balance or allow it to be destroyed naturally.

ALTMAN (***): One of *TNG*'s most thoughtful explorations of the Prime Directive. From the opening teaser, in which the holodeck is well utilized as Picard indulges in some equestrian action, "Pen Pals" is a low-key, well-written, intelligent installment. The highlight is a spirited debate about the Prime Directive, for which Data's response to the child's plea for help serves as a catalyst.

GROSS (***): One of the more interesting aspects of the Data character is that he longs to be human, and as *TNG* goes on, he takes small steps toward that goal. "Pen Pals" is representative of this, as he essentially ignores — for the first time in his career — the Prime Directive by responding to this child in danger, who touches more humanity in the android than in his human counterparts. A terrific second-season episode and one that appeals to the child in all of us who yearn to be touched by beings from the stars.

for the better good is nothing new, and the story line bears some resemblance to the original series' "Elaan of Troyius."

PERFECT MATE, THE

(TNG)
Original Airdate 4/27/92
Teleplay by Reuben Leder and Michael Piller
Story by Rene Echevarria and Reuben Leder
Directed by Cliff Bole

A beautiful, empathic mesomorph, Kamala (Famke Janssen), who is intended to serve as a peace offering to end a centuries-old war, is freed from stasis and seduces Picard.

ALTMAN (***): It may not be politically correct, but "Perfect Mate" is still a fanciful *TNG* installment featuring some wonderful writing by Michael Piller and Rene Echevarria. *GoldenEye*'s sensuous Famke Janssen more than holds her own with Patrick Stewart. The writers mine comic gold when Janssen's mesomorph goes into Ten-Forward, causing a near riot with her irresistibly attractive charms. The Ferengi also provide some genuine wit in an episode with a depressing coda.

GROSS (**1/2): An episode that works effectively enough and has a nice quotient of humor (thank you, Ferengi). The story does not provide anything original, however, with the exception of the mesomorph itself. Patrick Stewart and Famke Janssen (*GoldenEye*'s Xenia Onnatop) work wonderfully together, but the notion of someone sacrificing his or her true love

PERSISTENCE OF VISION

(VOY)
Original Airdate 10/16/95
Written by Jeri Taylor
Directed by James L. Conway

As the crew prepares for a first encounter with the Bothan species, a psionic field puts them into a delusional state and brings their deepest thoughts to the surface. During the ordeal, characters in Janeway's Victorian holonovel program become real, and her beloved Mark, the man she left behind on Earth, appears to her. Paris faces off with his disparaging father; Tuvok is reunited with his wife, T'Pel; and Torres is seduced by Chakotay. The ship is effectively disabled, so it's up to an unaffected Kes and the doctor to block the mysterious field.

ALTMAN (*1/2): A truly dreadful episode that seems designed around budget exigencies. The show begins with Janeway's holodeck fantasy, in which she seems obsessed with being in a Merchant Ivory film. The characters begin manifesting themselves as illusions all over the ship. Unfortunately, this is an old *Trek* technique, combining the holodeck misadventures of countless episodes with the horrors of others, such as "Schisms." It's a Brannon Braga wet dream. The biggest problem, other than the pointlessness of this exercise, is that the telepathic illusions don't lend any insight into the characters who experience them, with the only possible exception being B'Elanna Torres's vision of a torrid affair with Chakotay. Although a certain dark ambience pervades the episode, thanks to James Conway's direction, it is ultimately vacuous, contributing little to the *Trek* mythos and totally failing to entertain.

GROSS (*): If there's one *Star Trek* cliché that's more prevalent than a disease spreading across the ship or an alien presence leaping from body to body, it's the notion of crew members having their deepest thoughts revealed. Seldom are those thoughts very interesting, and this episode is no exception. Definitely a budget saver.

PHAGE

(VOY)
Original Airdate 2/6/95
Teleplay by Skye Dent and Brannon Braga
Story by Tim DeHaas
Directed by Winrich Kolbe

As the crew searches for Voyager *power sources, they come across a planet seemingly filled with dilithium crystals. They eventually learn that the planet is really a base for an alien race that must steal body organs to fight the Phage, a disease that eats away at their bodies and destroys their organs. The aliens, the Vidiians, steal the lungs of Neelix, who is kept alive via holographic lungs supplied in sick bay. He can never move, or those lungs will malfunction. Ultimately, he is saved by Kes's donation of one of her lungs.*

ALTMAN (**1/2): A rather grotesque premise is handled adeptly by writers Skye Dent and Brannon Braga, although it's a misstep to make the race so sympathetic rather than the natural baddies they promised to be. The episode starts out like gangbusters, although it begins to falter at midpoint as the *Voyager* finds itself inside an asteroid, losing power and in another technonightmare while seeking the alien ship. The scenes are reminiscent of *TNG*'s "The Pegasus," without that episode's intensity or sense of foreboding. Ultimately, the situation is resolved too easily, and the denouement, in which Kes volunteers her lung to save Neelix, is somewhat unrewarding. The show is marked by some welcome levity, mostly courtesy of the doctor and Neelix.

GROSS (****): Undoubtedly two of the greatest inventions the writers of *Voyager* have devised are the Vidiians and the Phage. Admittedly grotesque in appearance, these beings, suffering from a debilitating AIDS-like disease, nonetheless garner our sympathies, despite their ruthless means of replacing organs. This episode also features one of Kate Mulgrew's best moments as Janeway, when she confronts the leader of the Vadiians. Both horrified by what they do to other living creatures and sympathetic to their plight, she lays down the law: Any attack on her people will be met with deadly force. And you absolutely believe her! Just a tremendous achievement on all fronts, from acting and writing to direction and makeup.

PHANTASMS

(TNG)
Original Airdate 10/25/93
Written by Brannon Braga
Directed by Patrick Stewart

When Data begins experiencing some frightening nightmares, including one in which he is disassembled by miners, he realizes that these images may hold the clue to a parasitic invasion of the ship that could result in the crew members' deaths.

ALTMAN (***): Brannon Braga indulges his fascination with dream imagery in a surreal and sometimes downright scary episode in which Data's nightmares hold the clue to a parasitic invasion of the ship. Although the logic of the show's premise sometimes proves elusive, including the dumb tech talk of how the creatures have manifested their presence in Data's subconscious, Braga crafts some startling imagery. Equally deserving of kudos is Patrick Stewart, whose assured direction is unsettling and spooky. It's not only his best directorial effort, but it's also the first time *Trek* has successfully created a nightmarish milieu (although the *Psycho* scene of Data stabbing Troi with a knife is so derivative that the only thing missing is a Bernard Herrmann score). Sigmund Freud, used largely for comic effect, probably goes a little too far in servicing Braga's anti-psychological sentiments, but "Phantasms" is a wildly off-concept show that could have been done only in the series' final season. There are some interesting parallels to Classic *Trek*'s "Operation Annihi-

late" and it's fascinating to compare that show's action/adventure plot to the more cerebral musings of *TNG*'s take on the parasitic/vampiric invasion theme.

GROSS (***1/2): Counselor Troi as a living birthday cake being cut into pieces by hungry crewmen? Dr. Crusher sucking a red substance through a straw inserted in Riker's skull? Yep, it can only be the work of Brannon Braga. (Why hasn't *The X-Files* snapped this guy up?) *Trek*'s darkest writer struts his stuff to great effect in this surreal exploration of Data's inner mind and his attempts to get to the bottom of his nightmares. There are a number of frightening moments in this Patrick Stewart–directed effort, not the least of which is when Data, a vacant look on his face, begins cutting into the real Troi with a knife, just as he did in his dream. Unsettling, but splendid.

PIECE OF THE ACTION, A

(TOS)
Original Airdate 1/12/68
Written by David P. Harmon
Directed by James Komack

A century after the crew of the USS Horizon *visited Sigma Iotia, the* Enterprise *arrives to examine the level of "contamination." What the crew finds is a society based entirely on a book detailing the mob wars of Chicago in the 1920s, prompting Kirk to take on the persona of a mob boss so as to reunite the planet and undo the damage of the* Horizon's *visit.*

ALTMAN (****): The best of *Trek*'s comedy episodes gives William

Shatner and Leonard Nimoy a chance to shine in their respective roles as mobsters. Kirk's creation of the card game "fizzbin" to extricate himself from the incarceration of Bela Oxmyx is inspired writing, and the guest performances, ranging from Anthony Caruso's Oxmyx to Vic Tayback's Krako, are superb. "A Piece of the Action" is nothing short of a laugh riot, which all comes out of a legitimate story with myriad memorable bits and quotable lines.

GROSS (***1/2): Probably the funniest part of "A Piece of the Action" is watching Kirk and Spock trying to comprehend just what kind of people these barbarians are and then trying to fit into that culture. You haven't lived until you've seen Spock trying to pass himself off as a gangster. Shatner and Nimoy are obviously enjoying the hell out of themselves, trying to walk the walk and talk the talk, but managing to stay in character — particularly Spock, who always seems to be a step out of place. The new incarnations of *Trek* should take a look over their shoulder to see that it's OK to have some laughs in the future.

pirates, who steal its cargo. Kirk must recover the cure before time runs out.

ALTMAN (**): There are some notable animation glitches in this episode, including a scene in which the background alternates between the bridge and sick bay (McCoy does the same), but these aren't as glaring as the story missteps. The plot is business as usual, revolving around Orion pirates who commandeer the cargo of a Federation freighter that is carrying a lifesaving drug for Mr. Spock, leading Kirk to duke it out with the Orion captain on an explosive asteroid. *Trek* comic vet and writer Howard Weinstein, then a wet-behind-the-ears college student, contributes some clever dialogue, including McCoy's frustrated crack over treating Spock in sick bay: "That's the last time I waste my bedside manner on a Vulcan."

GROSS (***): Kudos to writer Howard Weinstein for creating a race of pirates and managing to capture the flavor of the live-action series so successfully. Lots of fun interplay between the famous *Trek* troika. See also "Journey to Babel."

PIRATES OF ORION, THE

(TAS)
Original Airdate 9/7/74
Written by Howard Weinstein
Directed by Hal Sutherland

When Spock contracts a strain of choriocytosis, Kirk has three days to rendezvous with the SS Huron, a vessel equipped with the antidote for this disease. En route, however, the Huron is attacked by Orion

PLATO'S STEPCHILDREN

(TOS)
Original Airdate 11/22/68
Written by Meyer Dolinsky
Directed by David Alexander

Responding to a distress signal, a landing party finds itself amongst a race of people who have based their society on ancient Rome. The difference is that they have developed extraordinary teleki-

netic abilities, which they use to control their jester, a dwarf named Alexander. The Platonians eventually reveal that they want Dr. McCoy to stay behind to tend them should they get ill. When Kirk refuses to allow this, these self-proclaimed gods start trying to control them, forcing Kirk, Spock, Uhura and Nurse Chapel into some humiliating positions.

ALTMAN (**): This episode won't go down in history as one of *Star Trek*'s best, but it has received a certain amount of notoriety over featuring the first TV interracial kiss between Kirk and Uhura. The premise is extremely dopey, but it's hard to resist Kirk finally getting his revenge on the Platonians when he assumes their telepathic powers and gives them a taste of their own medicine. They definitely have it coming after some of the indignities they've subjected the *Enterprise* landing party to. Power corrupts, indeed.

GROSS (***): The power-corrupting theme and guys in togas are somewhat old hat, but the episode is morbidly fascinating in some of the images it presents. On the surface, some of the Platonians' manipulations of the crew seem kind of silly (Kirk neighing like a horse, Spock reciting children's rhymes while dancing), but they're disturbing in that these people are being forced so out of character. For all intents and purposes, the first interracial kiss (between William Shatner and Nichelle Nichols) is off-screen, and there's subtext of these aliens more or less about to force their subjects to copulate for their amusement (had they not been stopped). McCoy's

means of allowing Kirk and Spock to duplicate the powers of the Platonians is extremely contrived and stretches one's credulity, but the payoff is there as the captain gets revenge. A real standout is actor Michael Dunn, who brings pathos to the role of Alexander.

PLAYING GOD

(DS9)
Original Airdate 2/28/94
Written by Jim Trombetta and Michael Piller
Directed by David Livingston

While Dax takes Arjin, an apprehensive Trill initiate, through the wormhole, their runabout gets caught on a small amount of protoplasm in a subspace pocket. When they return to DS9, O'Brien and Dax learn that this matter is a rapidly expanding proto-universe that threatens our own.

ALTMAN (**): An appallingly inappropriate tech plot about an expanding proto-universe segues uneasily into a compelling character drama involving Dax's evaluation of a potential candidate for Trill joining. The episode boasts some of the best character development yet for Dax, with an amusing teaser and some sultry, boisterous innuendo. The writers finally avail themselves of Terry Farrell's endearing wit and charm. The problem is this all balances uneasily with a pointless jeopardy plot and the clichéd "nature of life" argument when the crew grapples with the possibility of life existing within the rapidly growing universe. Let's face it, this may have been a novel argument in 1989 with "The Measure of a

Man," but by now it's as tired as B-story jeopardy plots. As for an interesting C story involving pesky Cardassian rodents, the story line disappears after an insipid scene in which the critters pull the plug on the force field containing the explosive universe. This scene's entropy envelops an otherwise engaging hour in stupidity, as the Trill candidate navigates the universe through a wormhole, proving that the lessons of "In Theory" have not been learned.

GROSS (**): Although Dax and the Trill initiate an interesting premise involving some nice characterization, the main story about the expanding universe has the feeling of "been there, done that" without much thematic drive. Perhaps because the concept involves more discussion than action, it never pays off. Not a real highlight of the second season.

POWER PLAY

(TNG)
Original Airdate 2/24/92
Written by Rene Balcer, Herbert J. Wright and Brannon Braga
Directed by David Livingston

Troi, Data and Riker investigate the disappearance of the starship Essex, *but their shuttle crash-lands on the planet's surface. O'Brien transports through to rescue the others, but as they beam out, the spirits of the planet's exiled prisoners, which inhabit the ionosphere, possess Data, Troi and O'Brien.*

ALTMAN (**1/2): An extremely tired and cheesy sci-fi premise is recycled skillfully into an absorb-

ing and all too rare action outing aboard the *Enterprise.* Marina Sirtis, Brent Spiner and Colm Meaney get to act menacingly for an episode and give solid performances displaying their range. David Livingston's direction is impressive and moody. Jay Chattaway also provides one of his best scores for a fairly kinetic action hour. The presence of Ensign Ro is, as always, more than welcome.

GROSS (**): Ho hum. OK, maybe that's a little unfair, considering that the performances are fine and David Livingston does a creditable job behind the camera, but this story is complete rehash. Variations can be found in the original series's "Return to Tomorrow" and *TNG*'s "Lonely Among Us," "Skin of Evil" and "The Schizoid Man," as well as *Star Trek V: The Final Frontier.* It's understandable that the series is forced to do a great many bottle shows, but surely there must be more imaginative tales to tell beyond bodies being taken over by bitter little aliens.

PRACTICAL JOKER

(TAS)
Original Airdate 9/21/74
Written by Chuck Menville
Directed by Hal Sutherland

When the Enterprise *inadvertently enters Romulan territory, Kirk tries to elude Romulan warships by entering an energy field. This field turns out to be alive, taking over the ship's computer and launching one practical joke after another.*

ALTMAN (**): "Practical Joker" is not notable dramatically, but it is significant in one major respect: It is the granddaddy of all holodeck malfunction shows, a veritable subgenre in the subsequent *TNG* series. Although the holodeck is called the "rec room" in the episode, the crew is able to create any environment they choose using the computer. It then malfunctions, stranding McCoy, Uhura and Sulu in a blizzard and other inhospitable environs. Although some of the gags are humorous, by the time of the denouement, "Practical Joker" has overstayed its welcome.

GROSS (**): The idea of the *Enterprise*'s computer gaining a personality of its own is interesting, and the notion of it being that of a practical joker has an intriguing quality. But there's absolutely no attempt to explain *why* this has happened. Yes, there's an energy cloud of some kind, but the leap from that to such a personality has no credibility. As noted above, this episode introduces a holodeck on the *Enterprise* and, of course, it malfunctions, nearly killing the crew. See also "The Big Goodbye."

PREEMPTIVE STRIKE

(TNG)
Original Airdate 5/16/94
Teleplay by Rene Echevarria
Story by Naren Shankar
Directed by Patrick Stewart

Ensign Ro (Michelle Forbes) returns and is recruited by Starfleet and Captain Picard to infiltrate the Maquis. Her objective is to prevent a secret attack on a Cardassian installation. During her time under cover, she finds herself becoming attached to

the Maquis, ultimately deciding — however reluctantly — to betray Picard and join with the Maquis to protect their home against the Cardassians.

ALTMAN (***1/2): Although the failure to showcase the ensemble in the penultimate show is unfortunate, the return of Ensign Ro proves more than welcome. Michelle Forbes once again injects some well-needed spark into an episode that is sometimes overly subdued. Ro's final decision to abandon Starfleet to join the Maquis is both surprising and powerful.

GROSS (***1/2): Like "The Pegasus," this seventh-season episode thrives on character, exploring the relationship between Picard and Ro. Although she owes everything to him, she ultimately betrays the trust he has placed in her. Patrick Stewart does a wonderful job both in front of and behind the camera, and Michelle Forbes's energy as Ro is a joy to behold.

PRICE, THE

(TNG)
Original Airdate 11/11/89
Written by Hannah Louise Shearer
Directed by Robert Scheerer

The Federation negotiates with the planet Crystalia for control of what is believed to be the first stable wormhole. The Ferengi then intervene in the negotiations, hoping to place their own bid. One of the negotiators, Devinoni Ral (Matt McCoy), becomes intimately involved with Troi, who learns that he is half Betazoid, giving him a special edge during negotiating sessions.

ALTMAN (**1/2): Some strong character moments help offset this episode's many failings, including some subpar production values. The show has a surprisingly light touch, with a Ferengi DaiMon's fruitless search for chairs among the most amusing antics. Dr. Crusher and Troi engaging in a twenty-fourth-century Jane Fonda aerobics routine also is amiable. The headier philosophical discussions about the ethics of being a Betazoid are priceless. As for Matt McCoy as Troi's love interest, Devinoni Ral, he's a dud.

GROSS (**1/2): A harmless episode with the slightly crazy idea of someone actually selling a wormhole. Dramatically, there's a great confrontation between Troi and Ral regarding the ethics of using the abilities of a Betazoid to achieve one's own end. Comically, the Ferengi are so distrustful that they screw themselves while testing the wormhole. (Note: The Ferengi lost in the Delta Quadrant return in the third-season *Voyager* episode "False Profits.")

PRIME FACTORS

(VOY)
Original Airdate 3/20/95
Teleplay by Michael Perricone, Greg Elliot and Jeri Taylor
Story by David R. George III, Eric Stillwell, Michael Perricone and Greg Elliot
Directed by Les Landau

Once again, the Voyager *crew's hopes of getting home are renewed when they encounter the Sikarians, a race devoted to the pursuit of pleasure and possessing the ability to travel more than forty thousand light-years in an instant. Unfortunately, Janeway discovers that these aliens, who claim that they will help* Voyager, *are merely using the crew for their own amusement.*

ALTMAN (***): The crew is faced with an intriguing dilemma when they encounter a race that has the technology to transport them home but refuses to share it with them because of their own prime directive. Although the show's mutinous conspiracy unfolds too quickly at the end and the repercussions are too slight for all involved, this is a compelling episode. The writers have crafted an interesting alien race whose hedonistic delights are derived from literary pursuits. It's a nice spin and an inspired conceit, but I would like to have seen this aspect of their culture developed even more. Frankly, this episode begs to be a two-parter.

GROSS (**1/2): This self-involved race is particularly annoying and not the kind of people I would like to spend any time with. The real juice of the episode comes in the last act, when Tuvok, acting directly against Janeway's orders, works with Torres to steal the alien technology and install it in *Voyager*'s engine room. When it's engaged, it nearly destroys the starship. When Janeway pulls Tuvok into her ready room, the look of betrayal on her face and in her voice, as well as Tuvok's shaky response, is something to watch. Imagine your best friend in the world going behind your back, and you have some idea of the dynamic here.

PRIVATE LITTLE WAR, A

(TOS)
Original Airdate 2/2/68
Written by Gene Roddenberry
Story by Judd Crucis
Directed by Marc Daniels

Arriving on a primitive planet, Kirk and the landing party learn that the Klingons have interfered with the natural evolution of the inhabitants, so Kirk decides to provide firearms to the hill people and his old friend Tyree (Michael Witney) to maintain a balance of power on the planet.

ALTMAN (***): A heavy-handed Vietnam allegory, "A Private Little War" is one of the more embarrassing polemics *Trek* provided in the mid-1960s, particularly in its spirited argument for maintaining a balance of power, drawing parallels to the brush wars of the late twentieth century. However, there's still much to recommend this episode, including an impassioned philosophical argument between McCoy and Kirk, Spock being gunned down with a flintlock and what is probably the first orgasm ever shown on television, in which Knutu woman Nona writhes in ecstasy over Kirk as she heals him from the bite of a cheesy-looking white-horned man in a suit, better known to the inhabitants of the world as a Mugatu.

GROSS (**1/2): Gene Roddenberry hits the audience over the head with this Vietnam allegory, but it still manages to work, particularly in the debates between the characters. One explosive sequence between Kirk and McCoy is shocking in its intensity and carries the

same resonance today as it did thirty years ago. It proves that (are you listening, crew of the *Enterprise E*?) friends can have some pretty nasty fights and still remain friends. Conflict can be a beautiful thing.

PROFIT AND LOSS

(DS9)
Original Airdate 3/21/94
Written by Flip Kobler and Cindy Marcus
Directed by Robert Wiemer

Quark's former lover, a Cardassian named Natima, arrives at the station, where Garak accuses her of being a terrorist. Natima says that she is leading an underground movement that is fighting the military government so as to establish a nonviolent future for Cardassia.

ALTMAN (**): Although he's no Rick Blaine, barkeep Quark finds himself reunited with a Cardassian lost love who's fighting to change the political landscape of her homeworld. "Profit and Loss" is an enjoyable romp, despite some hackneyed writing and subpar performances (particularly Mary Crosby as Natima), because of the irresistible lure of a no-lose premise. The show's almost *Casablanca* note for note. Unfortunately, most of the dialogue doesn't come close to capturing the spirit of that movie classic. Andrew Robinson as Garak is always welcome and provides the episode with some well-needed spark.

GROSS (*1/2): There's a real credibility problem here, as the supposed relationship between Natima and Quark is simply unbelievable.

The political aspect of the story line works primarily because of the always wonderful Andrew Robinson as Garak. The episode's core, however, rings false.

PROGRESS

(DS9)
Original Airdate 5/9/93
Written by Peter Allan Fields
Directed by Les Landau

A Bajoran farmer named Mullibok (Brian Keith) refuses to vacate his farm on a Bajoran moon that has been evacuated so that Bajor can harness the moon's natural energy for the benefit of its citizenry. Kira bonds with Mullibok and is reluctant to force him out, until Sisko points out that she now represents something more to the people of Bajor than just a freedom fighter.

ALTMAN (***): Peter Fields's passionate script is superbly written, and it's easy to empathize with Kira's dilemma. Brian Keith gives a moving performance as Mullibok, and his sarcastic retorts are stinging. The Jake and Nog B story involving their first business venture is surprisingly engaging. Unfortunately, the episode's ambiguous conclusion is less satisfying, and Kira's torching of the farmer's abode brings up several troubling moral questions that the episode fails to address. The character drama finally ignites on *Deep Space Nine,* although those who enjoy *Star Trek* for its science-fiction rather than philosophical content are bound to be sorely disappointed by the show.

GROSS (***1/2): In the process of trying to complete a mission, Kira

touches a part of herself that has been missing for most of her life. After meeting Mullibok, Kira gradually embraces an idyllic lifestyle so unlike her own as a resistance fighter and later first officer of DS9. Here is a simpler life, untouched by the realities of war. The interaction between Brian Keith and Nana Visitor is wonderful, and the major's internal conflict is realistic. Kira's ultimate decision to force Mullibok to come with her is an honest one, going directly against the typical Hollywood coda, which would have had her find a way for him to stay behind.

PROJECTIONS

(VOY)
Original Airdate 9/11/95
Written by Brannon Braga
Directed by Jonathan Frakes

The doctor discovers that Voyager has been attacked by the Kazon and that most of the crew has abandoned ship. He learns from a holographic Lieutenant Barclay (TNG's Dwight Schultz) that he is actually Dr. Lewis Zimmerman, the holoengineer who created his programming, and that unless he destroys the starship, he will die and be unable to leave his holodeck illusion.

ALTMAN (**1/2): Robert Picardo's sheer charisma helps elevate an episode that, though admittedly boasting a few moments of inventiveness in which the doctor's normal state of reality is confused, is undermined by the derivative nature of its premise. The entire episode seems to spring from a five-minute scene in *Total Recall,* in which Arnold Schwarzenegger is convinced that he's experiencing a paranoid embolism inside a recall illusion on Mars. The theme of the doctor examining the question of what is reality has been explored ad nauseam on the various *Trek*s. Although there's a nice double tag of surreal horror (in the Brannon Braga tradition), ultimately the resolution is unsatisfying and unsurprising. Equally unpalatable is an absurd scene in which Neelix fends off a Kazon with a frying pan. I don't care if this is holodeck illusion or not; it's just stupid.

GROSS (**): The question of what's real and what isn't has been explored way too often on *Trek* (including Brannon Braga's own "Frame of Mind"), and there isn't a good enough reason given for its being explored yet again. There are some nice moments for Robert Picardo and guest star Dwight Schultz, and a real dilemma is raised for the doctor, but this just isn't a very riveting episode.

PROPHET MOTIVE

(DS9)
Original Airdate 2/25/95
Written by Ira Steven Behr and Robert Hewitt Wolfe
Directed by Rene Auberjonois

When the Nagus arrives on Deep Space Nine, Quark and Rom are horrified to learn that he has decided to turn the Ferengi Rules of Acquisition inside out and wants Quark to spread the word. Upon further investigation, Quark learns that the wormhole aliens from the pilot have found the Nagus and his philosophy distasteful and have altered his personality. Quark must convince them that what they've done is wrong before his whole world falls apart.

ALTMAN (**1/2): What could have been an amusing B story is the fodder for a one-note gag that gets repeated ad nauseam. Although "Prophet Motive" is probably the least effective of the Nagus episodes, playwright Wallace Shawn once again aces his role as Zek, a profiteer turned benefactor. Both Armin Shimerman and Max Grodenchik shine as they try to discover what has happened to the Nagus while engaging in some witty banter. Most notable is the work of freshman director Rene Auberjonois, whose polished lensing propels the plot briskly. He also deftly stages a surreal scene within the wormhole.

GROSS (***1/2): Wallace Shawn is a scream as the Nagus, his character completely altered as he announces that he is changing the Ferengi Rules of Acquisition. Quark's and Rom's reactions to this are equally funny, as they try to accept what their leader is saying but at the same time believe that he has lost his mind. The sheer gall of Quark's making demands on the Wormhole Aliens is something to watch, but you have to wonder why they'd bother talking to a Ferengi in the first place. Very funny stuff.

PROTOTYPE

(VOY)
Original Airdate 1/15/96
Written by Nicolas Corea and Kenneth Biller
Directed by Jonathan Frakes

The crew discovers a deactivated robot floating through space and beams it aboard. Torres takes it upon herself to repair the mysterious mechanical being, and when it is reactivated, they discover that the unit, a sentient artificial life-form, is called Automated Unit 3947 and that its race is facing extinction. The robot asks Torres to build a prototype so that more units can be constructed, but she must refuse because the Prime Directive bars her from interfering with alien cultures. When the unit's base-ship appears, however, it abducts her and threatens to destroy Voyager unless she creates a new prototype.

ALTMAN (**1/2): The episode begins well enough with a teaser told from the subjective point of view of the robot. In fact, the highlight of this episode is Jonathan Frakes's solid direction throughout. Unfortunately, the story degenerates into melodrama and makes some notable mistakes. Early on, there's an entire scene of B'Elanna Torres and the doctor discussing how to repair the unit. It's riddled with technobabble and does nothing to propel the plot. Once again, the writers need to heed the old maxim: Show, not tell. By the end, the episode is resting solely on the charisma of actress Roxann Biggs-Dawson, who manages to hold my interest throughout. Unfortunately, the episode climaxes anticlimactically as Janeway and Torres share a moment of bonding in Janeway's ready room. All the muted whispering left me turning up the volume.

GROSS (***): After a slow buildup, this episode kicks into gear once Torres has finished reactivating the unit and it decides that it doesn't like Janeway's decision not to allow Torres to build more units. In a scene reminiscent of "Samaritan

Snare" and the Pakleds, the danger is suddenly turned up a notch when Automated Unit 3947 takes matters into its own hands.

Q-LESS

(DS9)
Original Airdate 2/8/93
Written by Robert Hewitt Wolfe
Directed by Paul Lynch

When Vash comes to DS9, she is pursued by the smitten Q, who is up to his usual tricks.

ALTMAN (***): Haven't we seen this story before? A mysterious artifact that is actually a misunderstood life-form — we're talking off the meter on the hokeyness scale. There hasn't been an ending as insipid as this since "Encounter at Farpoint." Fortunately, the episode's predictable climax is offset by its utterly brilliant acerbic bite involving Q and Vash. Everything about this story is delightful, including Bashir's inept womanizing, which is in striking contrast to the assured seductiveness of Kirk and Riker. Q has never been more scathing or outrageous, and his verbal jousts with Sisko are unmatched by anything since Kirk fenced with Harry Mudd. The ultimate laugh riot for me is Quark's auction of "valuable" Gamma Quadrant artifacts, which are, in fact, valueless trinkets. This strikes me as a wry satire on the selling of *Star Trek,* in which the home shopping networks have marched a series of hucksters, including Michael Piller, before the cameras to sell wares to lobotomized fans. However, every time the story cuts from Q and Vash to ops, I cringe as its routine jeopardy plot unfolds.

GROSS (***): When *DS9* was announced, I got the immediate impression that there would be a barrage of crossover plots between it and *TNG* in which one part would air on the former and the other on the latter (similar to the *Six Million Dollar Man* and *Bionic Woman* series of the 1970s). Thankfully, as "Q-Less" demonstrates, this was not the case. The appearance of Vash (seen previously in *TNG*'s "Captain's Holiday" and "Q-pid") is perfectly logical, given what we know of her. And if Vash is here, it only makes sense that Q is here as well. As good as Jennifer Hetrick is as Vash, John de Lancie is better as Q, bringing some of the bite back to the character that he had in many of his earlier appearances. Whereas on the *Enterprise* he views the humans as playthings, on DS9 he couldn't care less about them. He wants Vash — and that's it! Which is not to say that he doesn't take the opportunity to have some fun with "Benjy." Because de Lancie is playing against Avery Brooks rather than Patrick

Stewart, the dynamic is very different. Unfortunately, it is not explored further. See also "Encounter at Farpoint," "Hide & Q," "Deja Q," "Q-pid," "Q Who," "True Q," "Tapestry," "All Good Things" and "Death Wish."

Q-PID

(TNG)
Original Airdate 4/22/91
Written by Ira Steven Behr
Directed by Cliff Bole

Vash (Jennifer Hetrick) joins an archaeological conference aboard the Enterprise and is reunited with Picard. Meanwhile, Q returns as a matchmaker who puts the two lovebirds and the crew of the Enterprise in a re-creation of Robin Hood to teach Picard a lesson about love.

ALTMAN (***): Like Classic *Trek*'s "Spectre of the Gun," "Q-pid" is a delightfully giddy little historical adventure — which doesn't mean it's good, just fun. Picard as Robin Hood is very credible, and there's an undeniable appeal to this set of circumstances. "Q-pid" is generally hysterical (Worf: "I am not a merry man!"), with moments bordering on brilliance. The *Prince of Thieves* story line is vividly brought to life, but it is ultimately inappropriate for a tale that should really be a comedy of manners about the staid captain fearing that his relationship with a younger and sensual woman will be exposed to his crew. Q is relegated to a supporting player, which is unfortunate since de Lancie is always such a joy and a welcome addition to any *Next Generation* episode.

GROSS (**1/2): The look of this show is incredible, particularly when you realize that everything was constructed on Paramount's Stage Sixteen. Even so, this is one of the weaker Q episodes, although John de Lancie is great. Despite providing some rousing fun, the story line seems to be jumping on the 1991 Robin Hood bandwagon. The sparks still fly between Patrick Stewart and Jennifer Hetrick, but the episode's not as magical as it could have been. Don't take it personally, Q. Y'all come back now, hear? See also "Encounter at Farpoint," "Hide & Q," "Deja Q," "Q Who," "True Q," "Tapestry," "All Good Things," "Q-Less" and "Death Wish."

Q WHO

(TNG)
Original Airdate 5/6/89
Written by Maurice Hurley
Directed by Rob Bowman

Warning of human complacency, Q transports the Enterprise *to the Delta Quadrant, where the crew encounters the cybernetic Borg for the first time.*

ALTMAN (****): One of *TNG*'s best. Q is at his most malevolent, and the Borg make a welcome debut. They are totally alien and completely deadly, without the shades of gray that will come to characterize them later. Here they are soulless automatons bent on absorbing humanity into their collective. The eerie and ominous mood that director Rob Bowman achieves is notable and perfectly

suited to Maurice Hurley's fatalistic script. What "Q Who" does so effectively is to combine the "to boldly go" ethos inherent in *Trek*'s optimistic philosophy with the dangers and mysteries of the unknown.

GROSS (****): One of the best of the Q episodes (his third appearance). John de Lancie becomes more lovable every time he appears. The dilemma he throws the *Enterprise* into this time is the perfect balance to the humor that the character provides. The Borg are relentless and the most fearsome antagonists ever created for any of the *Trek* series. Director Rob Bowman and writer Maurice Hurley keep the audience on the edge of their couches with the tension they generate as the Borg close in on the *Enterprise* before Q zaps them back to their own quadrant — though not before Picard is humbled and has to admit failure to the omnipotent prankster. Forget the Ferengi; send in the Borg! See also "The Neutral Zone," "Best of Both Worlds," "I, Borg," "Descent," *Star Trek VII: Generations* (the Borg are referred to, not seen) and *Star Trek VIII: First Contact.*

QUALITY OF LIFE, THE

(TNG)
Original Airdate 11/16/92
Written by Naren Shankar
Directed by Jonathan Frakes

Dr. Farallon (Ellen Bry), who has created a revolutionary mining method using a solar particle foun-

tain, has invented an even more miraculous tool: the exocomp, whose computerized brain allows it to learn. This leads Data to the conclusion that the mechanical device is a life-form and pits him against Riker, who wants to sacrifice the automatons to save an endangered Picard and LaForge.

ALTMAN (**1/2): What could have easily been a predictable technobabble romp by the show's science adviser, Naren Shankar, is a well-done exploration into the nature of life. Though not a new concept for the series, the story is kept lively thanks to its refreshingly light doses of scientific gobbledygook and some strong character moments among the crew, including a light, whimsical teaser. Shankar successfully anthropomorphizes the exocomps, which is no small feat considering they are little more than small, floating baseballs, and Data's violation of orders is made extremely credible thanks to a strong coda in which he explains his reasoning to Picard. Actor Jonathan Frakes aces another directorial assignment and proves we've come a long way since Nomad.

GROSS (**): An earnest performance by Brent Spiner brings some heart to the episode, but even he and Frakes's sure directorial hand cannot disguise the fact that this is pretty much a remake of "The Measure of a Man" and "The Offspring." It thinks, therefore it's alive. OK, fine. Let's move on.

QUICKENING, THE

(DS9)
Original Airdate 5/18/96
Written by Naren Shankar
Directed by Rene Auberjonois

For the first time in his career, Dr. Bashir is put to the ultimate test in his effort to save the remnants of a Gamma Quadrant alien society infected by the Jem'Hadar with a seemingly incurable disease. As far as he's come as a physician and as vast as his knowledge is, it may not be enough. Indeed, he may be making things worse.

ALTMAN (****): What begins as a routine medical thriller turns into a skillfully written, brilliantly executed and moving story of hubris and medical research gone awry. It's certainly one of the best Bashir shows, is vividly realized by some terrific location directing by Rene Auberjonois and features a touching score by composer David Bell. Former *TNG* science consultant Naren Shankar jettisons the usual technobabble and tells this story using real scientific jargon, which makes the episode that much more effective. In addition, the episode's allegorical underpinnings involving Trevean, a Dr. Kevorkian–like angel of death played by Michael Sarrazin, is anything but overbaked. Even the episode's teaser, in which Quark commandeers the station's vid channels for a commercial for his bar, is hilarious, which helps offset the tragic events that are to follow. A scene in which Bashir inadvertently sends a roomful of patients into agony, leading to Trevean killing them all and ending with

Bashir standing among the corpses, puts *ER* to shame and may be the most powerful scene in *Star Trek* history since Edith Keeler got hit by a truck in "City on the Edge of Forever."

GROSS (****): Much of what I wanted to say has been stated above, but it cannot be emphasized enough just how good Alexander Siddig is in this episode. Dr. Bashir has grown up and can stand proudly in a room with Leonard McCoy. His initial cockiness in his belief that he will find a cure (addressed by the character at one point) is followed by his devastation when he fails to do so. He exhibits a resolve few characters in the *Trek* mythos have demonstrated. Emmy time, Mr. Siddig.

R

RASCALS

(TNG)
Original Airdate 11/2/92
Written by Allison Hock
Directed by Adam Nimoy

Picard, Guinan, Ensign Ro and Keiko O'Brien are transformed into children during a shuttle accident, but they nonetheless prove vital in saving the Enterprise *from Ferengi mercenaries who attempt to* take over the starship. The cure to reverse the de-aging lies within the transporter's memory buffers.

ALTMAN (**): A ridiculous premise in which Picard, Guinan (Whoopie Goldberg), Ensign Ro (Michelle Forbes) and Keiko O'Brien (Rosalind Chao) are changed into children during a shuttle accident. What sounds like little more than a potentially uproarious *Saturday Night Live* skit (and actually was the plot of a *Trek* animated episode, "The Counter-Clock Incident") and one of the hokiest premises ever done by the show is pulled off fairly skillfully by an uncredited Ron Moore. Although the Ferengi takeover of the *Enterprise* is mistakenly used as a B story, wasting a potentially engaging action/adventure story line on a lightweight episode, a lot of "Rascals," much to my surprise, actually works. Most effective is Megan Parlen's delightful turn as the younger Ensign Ro. David Tristan Birken ("Family") also pulls off a fairly satisfying performance as the young Picard. One of the show's most delightful moments is Moore's parody of technobabble, in which Riker erroneously explains the *Enterprise*'s operations to a befuddled Ferengi.

GROSS (***): On the surface, this episode is the most absurd idea ever to grace a live-action *Trek,* but it somehow works thanks to the earnest performances of David Tristan Birken (Young Picard), Isis Jones (Young Guinan), Caroline Junko King (Young Keiko) and, particularly, Megan Parlen, who manages to convey the feeling of lost youth that Ro would have undoubtedly felt.

REALM OF FEAR

(TNG)
Original Airdate 9/28/92
Written by Brannon Braga
Directed by Cliff Bole

Resident Enterprise *Milquetoast Barclay (Dwight Schultz) is attacked by a strange creature while transporting on an Away Team mission to explore the disappearance of the crew aboard the USS Yosemite. No one believes him until he begins displaying the physical manifestations of his encounter inside the transporter beam.*

ALTMAN (*): A new low for technobabble terror. A dud thanks to some poorly visualized effects nightmares. The worst of the Barclay episodes commits the cardinal sin of being boring. A confusing story line that revolves around the transporter, using it as a metaphor for air travel, makes several theoretical leaps in logic that go against established Trekkian transporter lore. Ultimately, the show's poorly executed visuals and some over-the-top tech involving creatures in the transporter beam make the story untenable.

GROSS (**1/2): As always, Dwight Schultz is an enjoyable *TNG* guest star, bringing some welcome levity to the show. What mars this episode is the fact that the highly trained Starfleet crew simply will not let this man's comments about what he *thought* happened in the transporter be dismissed as a figment of his imagination. Someone should have gone into that beam to verify his claims. A highlight, though, is seeing the transporter in action from the inside looking out. See also "Hollow Pursuits," "The Nth Degree," "Ship in a Bottle," "Projections" and *Star Trek VIII: First Contact.*

REDEMPTION, PART I

(TNG)
Original Airdate 6/17/91
Written by Ronald D. Moore
Directed by Cliff Bole

The conclusion of the triumvirate arc dealing with Worf's Klingon dishonor, which began with "Sins of the Father" and continued with "Reunion." The Enterprise *returns to the Klingon homeworld so that Picard can fulfill his role as arbiter of the Rite of Succession and allow Gowron (Robert O'Reilly) to become ruler of the High Council. Meanwhile, Worf attempts to clear his family name.*

ALTMAN (***): Although "Redemption" answers many questions, it raises even more. It is not entirely successful in dealing with Worf's discommendation, as the restoration of his family honor seems like an afterthought, hurriedly shot before wrapping up production for the season. But "Redemption" does delve deeply into Klingon politics, and the political infighting that has typified that Empire throughout this series comes to a boil. Unfortunately, several attempts to bring nonregular viewers up to speed by offering a primer on Klingon political science is forced and results in some exceptionally stilted dialogue early on. Most of "Redemption" works despite its failings, however, particularly the exquisite exploration of the Picard/Worf dynamic, even if it misses the mark in availing itself of the Shakespearean scope involving kings, conspiring sisters and divisive civil war. Instead, the inane return of Tasha Yar's daughter, Sela, is spotlighted. While aspiring to lofty dramatic goals, and for the most part achieving them, this series has maintained a rigid internal logic and avoided the hokey sci-fi contrivances and melodrama rampant in the genre — until Sela.

GROSS (***): No "Best of Both Worlds," "Redemption" does serve as an adequate fourth-season cliffhanger. The Klingon portion of the show is excellent, proving yet again that these mini-arcs can work like gangbusters on *TNG*. The main problem with the episode is the return of Denise Crosby as Tasha Yar's Romulan daughter, Sela, which was undoubtedly greeted with more groans than applause when the episode first aired. Her lineage is, however, fascinating. Tasha Yar, saved from death thanks to the time alteration in "Yesterday's Enterprise," went back in time with the *Enterprise C*, was ultimately captured by the Romulans and gave birth to a half-Romulan daughter. What a great creative leap. Doc Brown would be proud. See also "Redemption, Part II," "Sins of the Father" and "The Way of the Warrior."

REDEMPTION, PART II

(TNG)
Original Airdate 9/23/91
Written by Ronald D. Moore
Directed by David Carson

Picard discovers that the Romulans are secretly providing aid to the Duras family, which is plotting to take over the Klingon Empire. Meanwhile, Worf joins his brother, Kurn (Tony Todd), as they try to keep the Empire together under the leadership of Gowron (Robert O'Reilly).

ALTMAN (**): Unfortunately, despite a visually arresting teaser in which Kurn narrowly escapes death during a space battle with a rebel Klingon ship and some atmospheric and impressive direction by David Carson, "Redemption, Part II" is quite unredeeming. The curse of syndication is that the show runs for only forty-three minutes and numerous subplots are crammed in, none of which are fully fleshed out, especially Data's first command. Despite the fact that his first brush with bigotry bears an uncanny resemblance to "Balance of Terror," with his command doubts echoing "The Galileo Seven," this story could have been compelling. The most intriguing elements remain the political and space opera tapestry involving the Klingon civil war, but this all gives way to soap opera with the introduction of Denise Crosby as Sela, Tasha Yar's daughter. It's an insipid sci-fi conceit that detracts from the overstuffed episode with oodles of clunky exposition and greatly diminishes the show's credibility. Sela is straight out of *All My Chil-*

dren and does the show an injustice, shattering the fourth wall. If the writers were intent on bringing Crosby back, this was not the place to do it.

GROSS (***): The machinations of Klingon politics hit their zenith and are wrapped up nicely (there are some wonderful allusions to these events in "Unification, Part I"). As always, the Empire remains a fascinating place to visit. The Sela aspect of the story works fairly well, although her military strategy — or lack thereof — leaves something to be desired. Nice performances by various *Enterprise* crew members who take command of other starships, particularly Data.

REJOINED

(DS9)
Original Airdate 10/28/95
Teleplay by Ronald D. Moore and Rene Echevarria
Story by Rene Echevarria
Directed by Avery Brooks

A visiting science team led by Dr. Lenara Kahn (Susanna Thompson) visits the station, much to the chagrin of Dax, since Kahn's symbiont was once married to Dax when the two were in previous hosts. Ignoring Sisko's suggestion that she take leave, Dax is reunited with her old love despite the fact that "reassociation" is prohibited by her people.

ALTMAN (***1/2): Despite nearly sinking in a morass of technobabble involving the construction of a communications array that will allow the station to communicate with vessels on the other side of the wormhole, "Rejoined" is a gutsy and provocative story in

which Dax, ignoring the pleas of her peers, engages in an illicit relationship with a Trill woman, Lenara Kahn (Susanna Thompson), to whom she was once married in a previous host. It's about time the show finally stops skirting the gay issue, which it dances around in "The Host" and "The Outcast," and finally has the guts to show two women kissing — and kissing. It's a terrific story in which Dax acts in some surprising ways and defies expectations in almost every scene. This is Terry Farrell's best performance, and the episode is commendable for shattering *Trek* taboos and shaking up the status quo.

GROSS (**1/2): There's real chemistry between Terry Farrell and guest star Susanna Thompson as two people who are trying to deny their feelings for each other but find that they cannot. The fact that they decide to come together is somewhat surprising, though not nearly as surprising as the moment when Dax is ready to give up her career for Kahn but Kahn is not ready to do the same. Some genuine emotions are at work here, and the show includes one of the longest kisses between two women ever aired on commercial television.

RELICS

(TNG)
Original Airdate 10/12/92
Written by Ronald D. Moore
Directed by Alexander Singer

The Enterprise *discovers Scotty (James Doohan) suspended in a transporter beam aboard a Federa-*

tion transport ship and rescues him from a seventy-five-year oblivion. Although at first he is a man out of time, he proves vital in saving the Enterprise *one* last time from destruction inside a Dyson's sphere.

ALTMAN (***1/2): In the capable hands of Ron Moore, the resurrection of Scotty is so skillfully performed that it's easy to overlook the hokeyness of his return. Even James Doohan, who chewed his way through many of the *Star Trek* movies, manages to deliver a strong performance. The nostalgia is laid down in spades (including the use of the original series' sound effects), and it's fun to see *The Next Generation* finally acknowledge its heritage (even "Unification" pulled its punches), particularly in the exceptionally well realized holodeck re-creation of the original bridge set. Moore, a longtime *Trek* fan, drops in several homages to the original series (including "By Any Other Name," "Wolf in the Fold" and "Elaan of Troyius"), and the story involving the Dyson's sphere seems little more than a MacGuffin for exploring the character drama between Scotty and Geordi LaForge, which is for the best.

GROSS (***1/2): Like McCoy and Spock before him, Scotty finally makes it to the twenty-fourth century, and his visit is the most enjoyable yet. Given more lines than he probably had in all the episodes of the original series combined, James Doohan is well up to handling the material. His references to old TV episodes are a hoot, and his feeling of being out of time

and place — particularly after earning his reputation as a "miracle worker" — is deeply felt. He's an old friend who's lost, and it's kind of sad in a way. At episode's end, a ray of hope appears as Scotty "borrows" a shuttle to take him around the universe. The most amazing aspect of the episode is the re-creation of the original *Enterprise* bridge in the holodeck for a touching scene between Scotty and Picard, who talk about their first vessels. Ron Moore's script and Alexander Singer's direction are wistful without being hokey.

REMEMBER ME

(TNG)
Original Airdate 10/22/90
Written by Lee Sheldon
Directed by Cliff Bole

Dr. Crusher becomes trapped in a parallel universe in which the crew of the Enterprise *is seemingly disappearing off the ship, while the real crew desperately tries to rescue her. The key to the dilemma turns out to be the enigmatic Traveler from season one's "Where No One Has Gone Before."*

ALTMAN (***): Wesley Crusher has gotten himself into a real bind this time, as he almost collapses a universe on his mom (as Simon Oakland said, matricide is the toughest crime of all for a son). It's an absolutely inane premise, but it is redeemed by some wonderful writing by Lee Sheldon in his one and only contribution to *Trek* before being banished to *TNG* never-never land. Filled with the technobabble that I so utterly despise, "Remember Me" is the ultimate paranoid fantasy in which everyone you know starts disappearing and no one still around remembers them. When only Picard and Dr. Crusher remain on a ship built for a thousand people, it's delightful to watch Picard's ludicrous justifications for why the *Enterprise* is now a tub for two. Starfleet budget cuts? It's *Star Trek* by way of *The Twilight Zone.*

GROSS (*1/2): Despite a pleasant *Twilight Zone* feeling, "Remember Me" is a real mess: a drama in which they throw in everything, including the kitchen sink. It's nice that Beverly Crusher is given an episode, but it's too bad it's such a mishmash. The Traveler, who serves as such a powerful presence in season one's "Where No One Has Gone Before," comes out of nowhere and, judging by this story line, should go back.

REQUIEM FOR METHUSELAH
(TOS)
Original Airdate 2/14/69
Written by Jerome Bixby
Directed by Murray Golden

While searching for a cure to a rare disease, Kirk, Spock and McCoy beam down to the surface of Holberg 917-G. There they are surprised to find a man named Flint, who turns out to be an immortal. Kirk falls in love with Flint's companion, Rayna, and is horrified to learn that she is actually an android.

ALTMAN (**1/2): An intriguing idea in which Flint (a sensational James Daly) is revealed to be many great historical figures. The love

triangle between Flint, Kirk and Rayna makes the show work, despite some of the contrivances used in the jeopardy plot involving the spreading virus on board. The show's resolution, in which Kirk, so grief stricken over the loss of Rayna, has his memory wiped by Spock, is a little difficult to fathom. If Kirk could get through Edith Keeler's death without Spock's help, Rayna should have been child's play.

GROSS (*1/2): A great title can't save this episode, which is little more than a remake of season one's "What Are Little Girls Made Of" (which wasn't that great of an episode to begin with). Kirk's falling in love with Rayna is totally unbelievable, although it does set up that wonderful conclusion in which Spock uses a mind-meld to remove Kirk's emotional pain. Great idea, Spock, but couldn't you have used that little trick a little earlier in the series? Do the names Edith Keeler and Miramanee ring a bell?

RESISTANCE
(VOY)
Original Airdate 11/27/95
Teleplay by Lisa Klink
Story by Kevin Ryan and Michael J. Friedman
Directed by Winrich Kolbe

Trying to obtain tellurium, which is needed to power the ship's warp engines, Janeway, Tuvok, Torres and Neelix transport to an Alsaurian city that is occupied by the fascist Mokra. During negotiations for the tellurium, Mokra soldiers open fire in the town square and capture Tuvok and Torres. Janeway is helped to safety by Caylem, an eccen-

tric local who believes that Janeway is his long-lost daughter. Neelix escapes and tells Chakotay that the Away Team has been incarcerated. While the Voyager crew attempts to convince the Mokra that their intentions are peaceful, Janeway, with the aid of Caylem, infiltrates the prison to free Tuvok and Torres.

ALTMAN (**1/2): The episode's planet-bound milieu is a welcome reprieve from the seemingly endless run of ship shows, but at the same time one cannot overlook the forced pathos and seemingly mindless antagonism. There's no subtext here. There are some attempts to build a character dynamic between the incarcerated Torres and Tuvok, but it plays second fiddle to Janeway's bonding with Caylem (Joel Grey, who though admittedly wonderful in the role, can't turn a sow's ear into a silk purse). The portrayal of Janeway is particularly offensive. As captain, she must display strength and resolve, but instead she becomes an emotional cripple in the service of Caylem, while also exploiting her body to sneak into the prison. This is not an appropriate way for a captain to behave. Ultimately, the episode is lethargic and not well thought out. Although it's nice to see some action for a change, it's frustrating that so much money was spent on such a pointless exercise.

GROSS (***): The emotional core of this show is made up largely of the relationship between Janeway and Caylem, who believes that he has found his daughter (in a dramatic motif similar to DS9's "Second Skin"). Janeway, unlike Kirk and Picard, and maybe even Sisko, is more in tune with the man's emotional needs and wants to help him on that level as much as she can, while still rescuing her officers. As far as using her body, when all else fails, you do what you have to do. Overall, a nice turn for Kate Mulgrew and guest star Joel Grey, and a chance to get off that damn ship!

RESOLUTIONS

(VOY)
Original Airdate 5/12/96
Written by Jeri Taylor
Directed by Alexander Singer

When Chakotay and Janeway contract a deadly virus from an insect bite on an alien planet, they are forced to remain behind, leaving Tuvok in command. As the ship travels out of communication range, Janeway tells Tuvok that he is not to contact the Vidiians, despite the fact that their sophisticated medical technology may be able to assist the crew in finding a cure for the virus. Janeway and Chakotay, realizing that they may be stranded for the rest of their lives, explore their feelings for each other in their bid to survive.

ALTMAN (***): Jeri Taylor is clearly on comfortable turf with her best teleplay of the year, in which Janeway and Chakotay are stranded on a lifeless planet after being infected with a seemingly incurable virus. Regrettably, some of the episode's strongest moments are offset by a whiny and overly emotional Kate Mulgrew. The crew's near mutiny also seems a little overbaked. Nonetheless, there are some nice moments aboard the Voyager and between Chakotay and

Janeway on the planet. There's also a nifty technobabble-free teaser that kicks off the action briskly. The use of Danara Pel ("Lifesigns") as the catalyst for resolving the story dilemma is particularly clever. Unfortunately, the episode totally skirts the sex issue, which is disappointing. The ending would have had far more punch had the two actually made love during their tenure on the planet — and who could blame them, since they thought they were going to have to spend the rest of their lives there together?

GROSS (***): Despite the audience's belief that by episode's end the duo will inevitably be rescued, "Resolutions" goes a long way toward making us believe that Janeway and Chakotay will spend the rest of their lives on the planet. This is a wonderful opportunity to get these two characters off the *Voyager* and put them in an environment where they must survive on their own without the use of the ship's technology — as well as get to know each other better. A nice tie-in to "Lifesigns," with the doctor's relationship with Danara Pel (Susan Diol) enabling *Voyager* to contact someone who can help.

RETURN OF THE ARCHONS, THE

(TOS)
Original Airdate 2/9/67
Written by Boris Sobelman
Story by Gene Roddenberry
Directed by Joseph Pevney

While checking up on the crew of the Archon, *who transported down to Beta III, the* Enterprise *learns that the people there are being controlled by a computer named Landru, who takes over their minds to make them all a part of the "body." Kirk takes it upon himself to destroy the mechanism and bring freedom back to that world's people.*

ALTMAN (***): Although it's always a little hard to buy Kirk's talking a computer to death, "The Return of the Archons" is the first episode in which he tries this little trick — and hey, he convinced me. More effective is the show's interesting take on cultism, as well as the world of Beta III it creates. The Red Hour, which kicks off an orgy of violence on the otherwise passive world, is fairly daring stuff for 1960s television and a striking sequence. The appearance of the Lawgivers is also well conceived. The guest performances are universally strong, and the show opens with a great teaser, as Sulu beams back aboard under the control of Landru.

GROSS (**): Using odd angles and extreme close-ups, director Joseph Pevney nicely conveys the periodic madness that grips the populace in exchange for the inner peace they feel most of the time. Other than that, the episode doesn't really go anywhere, though it does give Kirk an opportunity to patent his "talking a machine into committing suicide" shtick. At one point, Spock brings up the Prime Directive, but Kirk dismisses it, noting that the Prime Directive is for developing worlds and there is nothing developing here. Hey, at least he's quick with a response.

RETURN TO GRACE

(DS9)

Original Airdate 2/3/96
Teleplay by Hans Beimler
Story by Tom Benko
Directed by Jonathan West

Although he has been demoted in rank, Gul Dukat (Marc Alaimo) nonetheless believes that he can regain his former status within the Cardassian Empire by using his strategic abilities in a military situation. To accomplish this goal, he turns to Kira for help.

ALTMAN (***1/2): An episode that seems more like *Moonlighting* than *Star Trek* — but that's not a bad thing. The dialogue is vintage Howard Hawks, but the dilemma is definitely *DS9*, as Kira and Dukat are the underdogs in a confrontation with superior Klingon forces. There are space battles galore, but the superlative Marc Alaimo and Nana Visitor engaging in witty banter as they face overwhelming odds is character drama at its best.

GROSS (***): A look at the continuing evolution of the relationship between Kira and Dukat, who gain something of a mutual respect for each other as they encounter Klingons who destroyed a Bajoran colony. What really works here is the continuing arc of dramatic elements begun in "Indiscretion," particularly in terms of the impact Dukat's half-Bajoran daughter has had on his life. It's fascinating to see these once bitter enemies coming to some kind of understanding. Marc Alaimo is a real standout in his portrayal of Dukat, believing that this mission could put him back in a position of true power on Cardassia. It's fascinating watching him go from being depressed at his new assignment and the fact that his little freighter isn't worth being destroyed by the Klingons to being arrogant when weapons upgrades allow the crew to commandeer the Bird of Prey.

RETURN TO TOMORROW

(TOS)

Original Airdate 2/9/68
Written by John Kingsbridge
Directed by Ralph Senensky

Three aliens who have been without bodies for centuries, having lived in a purely mental state, ask Kirk, Spock and McCoy to "loan" them their bodies so that the trio can construct androids that will house their minds. After some reluctance, the Enterprise crew members agree to do so, but the being that takes over Spock decides that it likes being flesh and blood and wants to keep its host, no matter what.

ALTMAN (***1/2): A great teaser and an intelligent science-fiction premise help make "Return to Tomorrow" work. In addition, Leonard Nimoy is perfect as Henoch, who possesses Spock's body. He plays the alien with a mischievous glee that turns increasingly sinister. The love story between Sargon and his wife, Thalassa, is genuinely emotional, but the real powder keg here is Kirk's dynamite speech in the briefing room, when he tries to convince the assembled officers to go along with his plan to allow the alien entities to use their bodies. "Risk is our business," he says. "That's what this starship is all about. That's why we are aboard her." William Shatner could make the phone book interesting with his passionate histrionics, but here he has more than enough juicy material to work with, as he reaffirms the fundamental mission of the *Enterprise* and in turn makes the show soar.

GROSS (***): At the time this episode was first broadcast, the notion of aliens taking over the bodies of *Enterprise* crew members was fairly fresh. Now, of course, the idea has been done to death. The actors do a nice job as the entities acclimating themselves to corporeal living, and William Shatner is a riot as Kirk's alien proclaims what good shape the captain's body is in. Look for Diana Muldaur as Ann Mulhall. Muldaur would go on to play Dr. Pulaski in the second season of *The Next Generation*. See also "By Any Other Name," "The Lights of Zetar," "Turnabout Intruder," "Lonely Among Us," "The Schizoid Man," "Power Play," "The Passenger" and "Cathexis."

REUNION

(TNG)
Original Airdate 11/5/90
Written by Thomas Perry, Jo Perry, Ronald D. Moore and Brannon Braga
Directed by Jonathan Frakes

K'Ehleyr (Suzi Plakson, see "The Emissary") returns to the Enterprise, *surprising Worf by bringing his illegitimate son aboard. At the same time, K'Mpec*

(Charles Cooper), the head of the Klingon High Council, confides in Picard that he has been secretly poisoned, and the captain will have to decide whether Duras (Patrick Massett) or Gowron (Robert O'Reilly) will rule the Empire. Jockeying for power, and in an attempt to hide a dishonorable fact that could ruin him, Duras murders K'Ehleyr. Worf is not *a happy Klingon.*

ALTMAN (****): In the knockout follow-up to "Sins of the Father," Worf must face the dual dilemmas of discovering he has a son and taking vengeance on Duras, the member of the Klingon High Council who forced him into disgrace to hide the sins of his own father. Jonathan Frakes's sophomore outing as a director is impressive, as are the first-rate production values and the scene in which Worf discovers K'Ehleyr slain and takes vengeance on Duras.

GROSS (***1/2): Despite an often-stated aversion to continuing story lines, *TNG* continues to do them exceptionally well. Like "Family" and "Best of Both Worlds," "Reunion" ties into "Sins of the Father" but stands on its own as well. The amazing development of Worf continues, and the moment when he strikes back at Duras is positively stunning — and so atypical of *Star Trek*. Then again, Worf gets away with things that no other Starfleet officer has ever gotten away with. One unfortunate aspect of the episode is the loss of Suzi Plakson as K'Ehleyr. She'll be missed. See also "Sins of the Father," "Redemption" and "The Way of the Warrior."

RIGHTFUL HEIR

(TNG)

Original Airdate 5/16/93
Written by Ronald D. Moore
Directed by Winrich Kolbe

While undergoing a spiritual crisis, Worf visits a Klingon monastery on Boreth, where the image of the legendary Klingon warrior Kahless (Kevin Conway) appears to him. It is Kahless's intention to reclaim his position as leader of the Klingon Empire. Gowron (Robert O'Reilly), leader of the High Council, doubts the veracity of the resurrected prophet/messiah and challenges him to battle, leading Worf to the conclusion that Kahless is a clone.

ALTMAN (***): Typical of the sixth season's riskier and more off-concept storytelling, "Rightful Heir" boasts several intriguing elements, including some fairly profound pontificating by a sensational Kevin Conway as Kahless. The problem with Ron Moore's teleplay is that instead of attacking the evangelical zeal of the false messiah, it embraces his spirituality as a unifying force for Klingon society, giving it a moral foundation that not only violates the laws of the secular Gene Roddenberry universe but also tacitly endorses the proselytizing of the David Koreshes of the world by giving Kahless's claim to rule Klingon society validity. The cloning MacGuffin is inane, but the return of Robert O'Reilly as Gowron is always welcome, and the production design is top-notch. Interestingly, although much of the lore of Kahless is taken from dialogue that was cut

from "Birthright, Part II," Kahless actually first appeared in the original *Star Trek*'s third-season episode "The Savage Curtain." Played by actor Robert Herron, Kahless was considerably less friendly there, representing one of the most evil people in galactic history.

GROSS (***): Another attempt to expand the Klingon culture, this time moving to more spiritual matters, albeit in a subtler fashion than usual. Imagine if Jesus Christ returned to Earth, how would religious leaders — at least those who bask in the glory of their own power — react, and how quickly would they step down to make room for the Messiah? It's an interesting question that gets some earnest exploration from Gowron's point of view. See also "The Savage Curtain."

RIVALS

(DS9)

Original Airdate 1/3/94
Written by Joe Menosky
Directed by David Livingston

Quark finds his business suffering from DS9's newest gambling establishment, which is owned and operated by a con man named Martus (Chris Sarandon). While Quark tries to expose the truth about Martus, the B story has O'Brien starting to feel old when Bashir repeatedly beats him at racquetball.

ALTMAN (*1/2): Slight at best, the premise here is among the show's more ludicrous conceits. "Rivals" probably would have worked extremely well as a farce in the tradition of the original series comedies (such as "The Trouble with Tribbles" and "I, Mudd"), but at the time it was made, the producers were still deathly afraid of trying to do a real comedy for fear of its being hokey. Among the show's best sequences are those involving Bashir and O'Brien's racquetball rivalry and Quark's hysterical attempts to involve them in a charity game.

GROSS (*1/2): The fact that Chris Sarandon — a genre favorite since starring as vampire Jerry Dandridge in *Fright Night* — guest stars on *DS9* is enough to make you believe that you're in store for a terrific episode. Unfortunately, it isn't so, as the script is fairly pedestrian. Sarandon doesn't have much to do, and you don't *really* get the sense that he's a threat to Quark. What *does* work about the show is O'Brien's concerns about aging and the competition that develops between him and Bashir in their racquetball games.

ROYALE, THE
(TNG)
Original Airdate 3/25/89
Written by Keith Mills (pseudonym for Tracy Torme)
Directed by Cliff Bole

An Away Team beams down to a mysterious planet where a Las Vegas casino is vividly duplicated. They explore the bizarre gambling establishment and discover the body of a long-dead American astronaut. They also discern that they are trapped in the plot of a pulp gangster novel called The Hotel Royale, *created to entertain the lone survivor of the ancient Earth space expedition.*

ALTMAN (**1/2): In all honesty, what I once considered *TNG*'s darkest hour has undergone a critical reevaluation in my twisted mind. It's so different from any other episode and so strangely surreal that I find it curiously endearing. It's *Trek*'s Alice in Wonderland. Data brandishing a ten-gallon hat and winning $10 million in craps as a bemused Riker looks on and says, "Spread it around," may not be among *Trek*'s finest moments, but it's certainly among its funniest. Ron Jones's score and Herman Zimmerman's production design are outstanding. And even though the events in "The Royale" may seem ludicrous, the premise of Riker and company being trapped in the plot of a bad dime-store novel is pretty clever, particularly in light of the fact that the crew has been trapped in many worse scripts.

GROSS (***): Once again, the pen of Tracy Torme strikes wittily as an *Enterprise* Away Team discovers a surrealistic hotel casino in the middle of an otherwise dead world. Watching our heroes from the twenty-fourth century interacting with a variety of twentieth-century stereotypes is hysterical, as are the jabs at the gamblers who populate Las Vegas and Atlantic City. The episode loses some punch halfway through when the mystery of the Royale is discovered. Although much of the story line is a rip-off of the first *Trek* pilot, "The Cage," the difference between this show and others that have "borrowed" it is that the story is well executed here.

RULES OF ACQUISITION

(DS9)

Original Airdate 11/8/93
Written by Ira Steven Behr
Directed by David Livingston

The Nagus manipulates Quark to be his chief negotiator in the Gamma Quadrant, and all goes well as Quark is advised by a fellow Ferengi named Pel — who reveals herself to be a woman involved in business, one of the grossest of sins in the Ferengi Empire.

ALTMAN (**): The episode is a pleasant diversion, although its attempts at broad comedy don't come close to such Classic *Trek* episodes as "The Trouble with Tribbles" and "A Piece of the Action." It's a lightweight, altogether agreeable installment marked by some enjoyable guest performances (once again, Wallace Shawn aces his role as Zek) and some fun sparring by Dax and Kira and the ever affable Max Grodenchik as Rom. The idea of tulaberries being hailed as a twenty-fourth-century version of "plastics" by the Nagus is an Ira Behr-ism of great wit, although hair, makeup, costuming and, probably, writing conspire to render yet another Gamma Quadrant species wholly untenable. The first mention of the Dominion, which will become an important part of *DS9* lore, occurs in this episode.

GROSS (***): Barbra Streisand would be proud, as *Yentl* goes intergalactic. The core of this episode is the relationship between Quark and Pel, most notably that Quark, despite any feeling he might have to the contrary, truly wants a traditional Ferengi wife and as a result must reject Pel when she reveals that she's in love with him. Very true to the character and its heritage, which remains one of Quark's virtues to this day. See also "The Nagus" and "Prophet Motive."

RULES OF ENGAGEMENT

(DS9)

Original Airdate 4/13/96
Teleplay by Ronald D. Moore
Story by Bradley Thompson
Directed by LeVar Burton

When Worf accidentally has the Defiant destroy a civilian vessel that mysteriously decloaked in front of them in the midst of battle, he suddenly finds himself on trial, accused by the Klingon Empire of the honorless slaughter of innocents. Sisko defends Worf against a Klingon attorney named Ch'Pok (Ron Canada).

ALTMAN (***): There's some good direction from LeVar Burton and great writing by Ron Moore. Although I'm not sure I buy the dilemma (Worf seems to have been more than within his rights to fire on the Klingon ship), "Rules of Engagement" is one of the best budget-saving bottle shows *Trek* has ever done. Coasting on the adrenaline-charged courtroom proceedings, the episode is marked by solid performances, including that of Ron Canada playing the crafty Klingon litigator. The show's final scene, in which Sisko confronts Worf about the incident and discusses the tough lessons of command, really hits the mark.

GROSS (**1/2): Not the best of *Star Trek*'s courtroom dramas, primarily because the man accused, Worf, is barely allowed to speak. He sits in the defendant's chair and actually has very little to do but hear the case against him and, in one sequence, stupidly punch out the prosecuting attorney when he's provoked. In the end, it's nice that there's not some contrived little twist that gets Worf off the hook. Although innocents were killed, he is not held responsible. The coda, in which Sisko rips Worf a new one for his command judgment, is the highlight of the episode. Ron Canada is a real standout as Ch'Pok.

SAMARITAN SNARE

(TNG)
Original Airdate 5/13/89
Written by Robert McCullough
Directed by Les Landau

The Pakleds, an apparently dim-witted race, recruit Geordi LaForge to help fix their malfunctioning drive unit and threaten him with violence unless he stays aboard to assist them with their technological incompetence. At the same time, Wesley Crusher escorts Picard, via shuttle, for a lifesaving heart transplant. En route, Picard recounts his formative years, much to Crusher's great joy.

ALTMAN (**1/2): The Pakleds are a dandy new take on an alien race: a group of Forrest Gump clones who need LaForge to repair their stolen technology. There are echoes of the race from "Symbiosis," without the addiction allegory, but the Pakleds are a lot more interesting. Of particular note is Wesley Crusher's and Picard's conversation during a long shuttlecraft journey (which serves as the basis for the sixth season's "Tapestry"), which does much to contribute to Picard's fascinating backstory. The episode's resolution is pure *TNG* hokeyness, in which only Pulaski can perform a lifesaving operation. It would have made a lot more sense if it had been Dr. Crusher making a second-season cameo. As it is, it's a missed opportunity.

GROSS (***): Unconnected A and B stories that work on their own. From the outset of *TNG*, there was some question as to the connection between Picard and Wesley Crusher, with many expecting a father/son relationship to occur. Some texture is given to their characterizations here, and the thematic elements touched upon will be further developed as the series goes on. The Pakled part of the episode is filled with humor and a sense of menace. That these seeming morons suddenly become such a threat is a nice twist that catches the audience by surprise.

SANCTUARY

(DS9)

Original Airdate 11/29/93
Written by Frederick Rappaport
Directed by Les Landau

A scout ship with four Skrreeans aboard comes through the wormhole, and they are beamed aboard DS9. The group's leader, Haneek, says that there are three million of her people on the other side of the wormhole, all waiting to come through to find their homeland, Kentanna, which turns out to be Bajor.

ALTMAN (***): This heavy-handed allegory of the plight of immigrants in xenophobic America is well written and provocative. *DS9* weighs in with a timely story that incorporates topical anti-immigrant sentiment into a science-fiction milieu. The relationship between the Skrreean leader, Haneek (Deborah May), and Kira is deftly handled, as is the show's acknowledgment of a linguistic problem in embracing alien cultures. The episode's ending is gutsy and atypical, siding with the displaced aliens over the Bajorans and Kira, which helps disguise some of the blatant soapbox preaching earlier in the episode (including Nog and Quark essentially telling the "dirty little immigrants" to go away).

GROSS (***): Love those issue shows! A tremendously complicated issue is brought down to a human level thanks to the rapidly developed relationship between Kira and Haneek, who manage to explore both sides of the immigration problem. The irony, of course, is that when Kentanna turns out to be Bajor, Kira is forced to change her position and essentially turn against Haneek and her people. A real gut-wrencher for the major.

SAREK

(TNG)

Original Airdate 5/19/90
Written by Peter Beagle
Directed by Les Landau

An aged Sarek (Mark Lenard) is transported aboard the Enterprise to a diplomatic conference, where it is discovered that his mind is gradually deteriorating, with lapses into senility and illogic. Picard volunteers to mind-meld with Sarek to give him the time to complete the negotiations.

ALTMAN (***): Mark Lenard gives a powerful performance, but it's Patrick Stewart who truly shows his acting chops here when he mind melds with the emotionally ravaged Vulcan. Showcasing *Star Trek* at its finest, the episode effectively combines social commentary about the plight of Alzheimer's sufferers with a story line that can only be dubbed "fascinating." It's a character-driven show with strong performances all around, including supporting player Rocco Sisto as Sakkath and some subtle but well-placed references to Spock and his mother, Amanda. Only Joanna Miles as Perrin proves anything less than stunning.

GROSS (****): The producers of *TNG* have finally begun to loosen up in terms of connective material between the original series and its first spin-off. "Sarek" is a bittersweet experience. It's also a pleasure to welcome back a character from the original series, but his deteriorated mental state makes it a bit depressing as well. Patrick Stewart and Mark Lenard are wonderful together, and the emotional content is fantastic. The various fistfights inspired by Sarek's thought projections are silly, however, coming right out of the 1960 series. It is kind of nice to hear mention of Spock.

SAVAGE CURTAIN, THE

(TOS)
Original Airdate 3/7/69
Teleplay by Arthur Heinemann and Gene Roddenberry
Story by Gene Roddenberry
Directed by Herschel Daugherty

The ultimate battle between good and evil as Kirk, Spock, President Abraham Lincoln and Vulcan pioneer Surak go up against mad scientist Zora, Genghis Khan, murderer Colonel Green and the Klingon that inspired the Empire, Kahless. The mediator is a rock creature named Yarnek, who is curious as to which side will be victorious.

ALTMAN (***): Sure, the appearance of Abe Lincoln on the viewscreen seems a little goofy at first, but ultimately "The Savage Curtain" is one cool adventure show. Yarnek, the silicon rock creature that seeks to test good and evil, is indicative of the wildly imaginative design work that typifies the always inventive world of Classic *Trek*. And watching Kirk and Spock pair up with Lincoln and Surak in a battle to the death

with the most evil figures in history is great fun.

GROSS (***): Any episode of *Star Trek* that features our heroes in battle alongside Abraham Lincoln is worth checking out. The effects are goofy, particularly Yarnek, but somehow that just adds to the charm. It's also pretty cool seeing the progenitors of the Vulcan and Klingon races — Surak and Kahless, respectively. Undoubtedly, the original series is the only one that could have pulled this one off. See also "Rightful Heir."

SCHISMS

(TNG)
Original Airdate 10/19/92
Written by Brannon Braga
Directed by Robert Wiemer

Geordi LaForge's experiments with a new scanning system result in members of the crew being abducted and experimented on by an alien species in a distant realm of subspace. Riker is sent into the rupture in hopes of halting the aliens' incursion aboard the Enterprise.

ALTMAN (**): "Schisms" boasts great character moments, including a witty teaser in which Data gives a poetry reading while the sleep-deprived Riker struggles to stay awake, but the episode is yet another sci-fi high concept mired in Trekkian technobabble. Although the spookiness of the alien subspace millieu is undeniable, including an eerie scene in the holodeck, the plot is rife with faulty logic and myriad inconsistencies. Robert Wiemer's directing is first-rate, however.

GROSS (***1/2): Brannon Braga once again proves that he's the writer most able to bring the *Enterprise* to the creepiest, most unsettling parts of the galaxy. The premise of this episode is ingenious — crewmen being operated on while they're asleep — and simultaneously frightening. What little we see of the aliens themselves is intriguing, thanks to makeup maestro Michael Westmore. Watching the crew slowly unlock the mystery behind their abductions is fascinating, and using the holodeck to re-create the aliens' environment makes terrific use of this often malfunctioning device. At episode's end, we're left with the disturbing feeling that the same thing could happen again.

SCHIZOID MAN, THE

(TNG)
Original Airdate 1/21/89
Written by Tracy Torme
Directed by Les Landau

Dr. Ira Graves (W. Morgan Sheppard), a dying egomaniacal scientist, places his consciousness in Data's body to preserve his life. When the android begins acting strangely, the crew suspects that something is amiss. Joining the Away Team is the Vulcan doctor Selar, the first appearance of Suzi Plakson on the show.

ALTMAN (**): The real highlight here is the performances by W. Morgan Sheppard (*Star Trek VI: The Undiscovered Country* and *Wild at Heart*) as the dying scientist, Dr. Ira Graves, Suzi Plakson as Dr. Selar and the always reliable Brent

Spiner. Although Data's descent into evil is a bit overbaked, the possessed android's eulogy for Dr. Graves is among the funniest moments ever in *TNG* ("to love him was to know him and to know him was to love him"). The biggest problem is we're tipped off too early that Data has been taken over by Graves, and the crew looks pretty stupid when it takes them another half hour to realize it.

GROSS (***): Writer Tracy Torme once again proves to be one of the most important assets to the early *Next Generation* with this entry, which is both amusing and chilling in its look at Ira Graves, a sociopathic scientist who will use anyone to get his way — but nearly always humorously. Brent Spiner continues to prove his versatility when Data assumes Graves's persona. The eulogy is laugh-out-loud funny. The only real misstep is that Data's shift in personality is so abrupt that we're almost immediately alerted to what has happened.

SEARCH, THE, PART I

(DS9)
Original Airdate 10/1/94
Teleplay by Ronald D. Moore
Story by Ira Steven Behr and Robert Hewitt Wolfe
Directed by Kim Friedman

After a prolonged debriefing at Starfleet command, Sisko returns to DS9 with the starship Defiant, *a prototype vessel equipped with a Romulan cloaking device that is designed to combat the Borg but will be used instead to head off a potential attack by the Jem'Hadar. Sisko leads his key officers through the* wormhole to find the leaders of the Gamma Quadrant and rulers of the Dominion, the Founders. They learn that the Founders are changelings and that Odo has discovered his people at last.

ALTMAN (**): Conceptually, "The Search" does absolutely everything wrong, setting the tone for the season to come. There's nothing particularly wrong with Ron Moore's script, which is more than competent, but the premise is inherently flawed. Why would the Federation send a ship of ten people from Deep Space Nine into the Gamma Quadrant on their most important mission? Why destroy the enigmatic backstory behind Odo to service a weak cliff-hanger? Why introduce a powerful new Federation ship, only to virtually obliterate it fifteen minutes later? And why would a completely alien race on the other side of the galaxy covet gold-pressed latinum from Quark?

GROSS (***): It's still debatable whether Odo should have found the answer to his quest in the third season of the series, but at this point that's neither here nor there. Part I of "The Search" effectively brings us to the world of the Founders, giving us a little insight into what they're about and what their feelings are. Once again, Rene Auberjonois is a standout, as Odo must decide between staying with his people or returning to DS9 with his friends. The *Defiant* is one impressive ship, opening up future story possibilities that will allow DS9 to encompass the best of all *Treks* — stories taking place on the station as well as on a starship.

SEARCH, THE, PART II
(DS9)
Original Airdate 10/8/94
Teleplay by Ira Steven Behr
Story by Ira Steven Behr and Robert Hewitt Wolfe
Directed by Jonathan Frakes

Odo spends time with his people, eventually discovering that he doesn't belong with them, while Sisko heads back to DS9, where he finds that Starfleet has established a peace treaty with the Dominion and the Jem'Hadar have placed a strong military presence on the station. Not willing to be led like cattle, Sisko and company launch a counterattack, going so far as to destroy the wormhole to stop the invading forces.

ALTMAN (**): Hey, it's an illusion. That's clever, isn't it? No. We've seen it before. There's some nice action involving DS9 being taken over by the Dominion, but by the time the Bobby Ewing revelation is made that it was all a test to see how Sisko would react to such a situation, any drama is negated. A disappointing episode.

GROSS (**1/2): Although there are some exciting sequences, thanks to director Jonathan Frakes, as Sisko and his people fight back against the Jem'Hadar, the ultimate revelation that all of this has been a "program" implanted by the Founders in the minds of the DS9 crew members to see how they would respond to an invasion feels like a dramatic cheat. The episode has its moments, but the climax is a disappointment. A nice turn for Rene Auberjonois when Odo ultimately decides to return to DS9 with his comrades.

SECOND CHANCES

(TNG)
Original Airdate 5/24/93
Written by Rene Echevarria
Directed by LeVar Burton

Jonathan Frakes appears in two roles, Commander Riker and Lieutenant Riker, a duplicate created in a freak transporter accident eight years earlier. Still in love with Troi, Lieutenant Riker hopes to rekindle their relationship, while a fuming Commander Riker finds himself coming into conflict with his eager and abrasive doppelgänger.

ALTMAN (***1/2): A superb freshman directorial outing for LeVar Burton, in which he directs Jonathan Frakes in two roles. Burton's mastery over the episode's motion-control work is impressive, as is the fully realized performance he elicits from Frakes as Riker's doppelgänger. Not surprisingly, Rene Echevarria's teleplay is laced with wry humor and moving sentiment as it explores the dynamics of the Riker/Troi relationship in a fresh and original way. Echevarria wisely uses such Trekkian staples as the poker game to full effect and illustrates that the Troi/Crusher relationship is one of the most underutilized elements of the show. Marina Sirtis and Gates McFadden are terrific together. Indeed, several scenes, including the final one between the two Rikers and Troi and the respective scenes between each Riker and Troi, are standouts.

GROSS (***1/2): What could have been a hollow retread of the original series' "The Enemy Within" shows a considerable amount of humanity thanks to Jonathan Frakes's performance. He manages to create distinctive personalities for Will and Tom Riker, and it's intriguing to watch Tom's attempts to assimilate himself back into his old life while competing with the success of his other self. Additionally, his determination to win back Troi's heart is touching, although his being pulled along the career line that drew in Will is somewhat inevitable. Tom Riker will return in the *DS9* episode "Defiant."

SECOND SIGHT

(DS9)
Original Airdate 11/22/93
Written by Mark Gehred-O'Connell, Ira Steven Behr and Robert Hewitt Wolfe
Directed by Alexander Singer

For the first time since his wife died at the hands of the Borg, Sisko falls in love. Her name is Fenna (Salli Elise Richardson), and somehow she is the exact duplicate of Professor Seyetik's (Richard Kiley) wife, Nidell. Sisko learns that Nidell is a psychoprojective telepath, and Fenna is one of her "creations."

ALTMAN (**): Director Alexander Singer's freshman outing on *DS9* is impressive visually, although its romantic story between Sisko and an enigmatic alien woman is routine and seems like a desperate attempt to service a floundering character. The incomparable Richard Kiley gives a lively performance as an egocentric terraformer, but he can't redeem a pedestrian sci-fi premise or disguise the lack of a credibly developed relationship. The episode ends in a moment of grandiose visual splendor as Kiley takes his shuttle into the center of a dead sun, screaming, "Let there be light!" (recalling Slim Pickens's ride on a warhead in *Dr. Strangelove*).

GROSS (**): A middle-of-the-road episode in which the relationship between Sisko and Fenna lacks credibility. As a viewer from episode one, you want to see Sisko get on with his life and move beyond the death of his wife. Apparently, this just isn't the right time. Don't worry, Ben; Kasidy Yates is on her way.

SECOND SKIN

(DS9)
Original Airdate 10/29/94
Written by Robert Hewitt Wolfe
Directed by Les Landau

A lesson in self-awareness, this episode has Kira kidnapped by Cardassians who try to prove to her that she is actually one of them, taken from her parents by the Bajorans and turned against her own kind. In truth, her Cardassian "father" is attempting to use her to replace his real daughter, who died.

ALTMAN (***): Despite being reminiscent of *TNG*'s "Face of the Enemy," "Second Skin" is a wonderful Kira story that almost has you believing that she is, in fact, a Cardassian deep-cover operative. There are some solid performances all around, and it's another great opportunity for Nana Visitor to shine, even through the extensive Cardassian prosthetics she's forced to wear.

GROSS (***): In some respects a sequel to season one's "Duet," "Sec-

ond Skin" continues to expand Kira's understanding of her once-mortal enemies. Cardassian families, she learns, are just like any others she's encountered. Far from an action episode, this represents the kind of dramatic character story that has come to epitomize *Deep Space Nine*.

SHADES OF GRAY

(TNG)
Original Airdate 7/15/89
Written by Maurice Hurley, Hans Beimler and Richard Manning
Directed by Rob Bowman

To fight off an alien illness, Riker must think good thoughts (that is, scenes from previous shows).

ALTMAN (1/2*): In this abysmal attempt to save money, the only way Riker's life can be saved is by deluging him with memories (clips) from previous episodes. At least the clips are well chosen. For the real SF-TV connoisseur, the only thing missing is Gary Coleman (*Buck Rogers*'s "Blast for Buck," in which he starred, was virtually the same episode). It doesn't get much worse than this.

GROSS (1/2*): Clip shows are the worst kind of television commercialism (how to make the most money by spending the least). One of *Star Trek*'s most embarrassing moments.

SHADOWPLAY

(DS9)

Original Airdate 2/21/94
Written by Robert Hewitt Wolfe
Directed by Robert Scheerer

Odo and Dax land on a planet where a village's existence is threatened, as all but one of its inhabitants exists through a holographic projector that is starting to malfunction.

ALTMAN (***): Despite the show's shortcomings — including a predictable ending, a gimmicky premise and a forced conflict in defining the nature of a life-form (an all too familiar Trekkian argument) — some of the show's subtler moments are effective. Although the show's B and C stories, involving Kira and Vedek Bareil (who wants to have a religious experience in the major's bed) and Jake Sisko's decision not to join Starfleet, are throwaways, there are some genuinely satisfying character moments in all three story lines.

GROSS (***1/2): The introduction of the holodeck on *TNG* opened up a variety of storytelling possibilities, all of which are brought to their logical conclusion in "Shadowplay." As the various series have continued, we've witnessed the growth of holographic images into fully dimensional beings. In the case of "Shadowplay," those beings represent an entire colony on a planet, and the efforts of Odo and Kira to preserve their existence are extremely affecting. A highlight is the relationship between Odo and Taya, which echoes the feeling of innocence that often occurs on *TNG* when Data has the opportunity to interact with children.

SHAKAAR

(DS9)

Original Airdate 5/27/95
Written by Gordon Dawson
Directed by Jonathan West

When asked by Kai Winn, Kira agrees to go to Bajor to meet with her former leader, Shakaar (Duncan Regehr), to try and get him to cooperate in the rebuilding of Bajor. Discovering that Winn is once again attempting to manipulate people as though they were chess pieces, Kira decides to join Shakaar as a fugitive, which could lead to civil war on Bajor.

ALTMAN (***): "Shakaar" marks a welcome return to *DS9*'s exploration of the rich tapestry of the Bajoran political landscape. In addition, it boasts more scope than most of the third season's episodes, with much of its action transpiring in the hills and valleys of a Bajoran province (in actuality, Bronsan Canyon, U.S.A.). There are some fine performances across the board, most notably by guest stars Duncan Regehr, Diane Salinger and Sherman Howard as former members of Kira's resistance cell. The faux *Butch Cassidy* moments of the resistance brigade being hunted down by a Bajoran superposse are a welcome return to the *DS9* of yore. Less successful is a pointless and truly moronic B story involving O'Brien's dart competition at Quark's. He's in the zone, man; he's in the zone.

GROSS (***): Whereas even after several episodes there was not much chemistry between Kira and

Vedek Bareil, the spark between her and Shakaar is instantaneous. That's a major plus for this episode, but the most fascinating aspect of the story is Louise Fletcher's Kai Winn, who has grown more powerful than ever and is using that power to manipulate those around her. Kira once again finds herself in the position of having to decide between her beliefs and what's right for Bajor.

SHATTERED MIRROR

(DS9)
Original Airdate 4/20/96
Written by Ira Steven Behr and Hans Beimler
Directed by James L. Conway

Jennifer Sisko (Felicia M. Bell) from the mirror universe comes to Deep Space Nine and manipulates Jake and his feelings of loss for his mother to get him to follow her back to her realm. Commander Sisko has no choice but to follow them and finds himself having to help the alliance put the finishing touches on their own Defiant, which will be used against the Klingons and the area regent, Worf.

ALTMAN (*1/2): What may be the best premise yet for a mirror show is dreadfully executed and is the most disappointing misfire of the fourth season. The focus should have been on Jake's being reunited with a duplicate of his dead mother after almost a decade and the elder Sisko's lack of interest in rekindling a relationship. (After all, he was quite happy with Kasidy Yates.) This is a dilemma you could only have in a science-fiction show, a sort of genre version of Hitchcock's *Vertigo*. Instead, this story plays second

fiddle to the ridiculous pyrotechnics involving a mirror Worf and his antics on board his attack ship with a sniveling Garak. Unfortunately, the mirror universe has lost much of its mystique due to the seeming ease with which the two universes may be traversed. What could have been the ultimate bottle show is a pointless exercise in bombast. I only hope next time the writers restore some of the subtlety and perhaps bring the mirror universe crew to our milieu for a change (if only we could see Mirror Spock — we can dream, can't we?). Even the presence of the always appealing and sexy mirror Kira can't help this turkey.

GROSS (**): The emotional core of this story line takes a backseat to the newly formed resistance's attempts to fight back against the Alliance. Along the way, as the show has more of its characters in bondage and everyone seems to be speaking in innuendos, the mirror universe is somehow starting to feel more cartoonlike. Unlike its predecessors in this arc, it has lost some of its edge and, as a result, is beginning to lose its charm. See also "Mirror, Mirror," "Crossover" and "Through the Looking Glass."

SHIP IN A BOTTLE

(TNG)
Original Airdate 1/25/93
Written by Rene Echevarria
Directed by Alexander Singer

Sherlock Holmes's archnemesis Moriarty, created in the second season's "Elementary, Dear Data," is accidently released from computer stasis while Bar-

clay is performing a holodeck diagnostic. The supergenius threatens to destroy the ship unless Picard finds a way for him and his computer-generated lover, Countess Regina Bartholomew (Stephanie Beacham), to leave the holodeck.

ALTMAN (***1/2): Not since the crystalline entity's encore appearance in "Silicon Avatar" did I think there could be a less warranted sequel than the return of Moriarty. However, unlike "Silicon Avatar," "Ship in a Bottle" boasts a clever script laced with wry irony. In the episode's coda, Picard says dryly, "Who knows, our reality may be very much like theirs, and all this may be an elaborate simulation running inside a little device." Rene Echevarria has been one of the show's most consistent writers, and "Ship in a Bottle" is no exception. It boasts the strong character moments that are his franchise, and he turns what could have been a particularly ludicrous installment into one of the best episodes of the season. The script also presents Barclay in a vehicle that serves the character well, giving him just the right amount of screen time rather than focusing on him, as in the far less successful "Realm of Fear." Actor Daniel Davis is the physical incarnation of Moriarty, and Stephanie Beacham is good as Countess Regina Bartholomew. To its credit, the episode, which is heavily theoretical, is also surprisingly light on technobabble.

GROSS (***): The passion of guest star Daniel Davis (a regular on CBS's *The Nanny*) saves this episode from being yet another malfunctioning holodeck story. His plight is poignant, particularly considering that he has been trapped, and aware of the fact, for the past five years, while waiting for Picard to come up with some kind of solution to the situation. His festering resentment is similar to that felt by Khan (Ricardo Montalban) when left by Kirk on Ceti Alpha V (in the original show's "Space Seed"), where he remained until 1982's *Star Trek II: The Wrath of Khan.* Let that be a lesson: These captains shouldn't be so forgetful because their problems will jump up and bite them in the ass years later. See also "Elementary, Dear Data."

SHORE LEAVE

(TOS)
Original Airdate 12/29/66
Written by Theodore Sturgeon
Directed by Robert Sparr

An idyllic Earth-like planet grants crew members their every wish. As a result, they're meeting people from their past and living out fantasies. Things turn dangerous when these apparitions turn deadly.

ALTMAN (****): What makes "Shore Leave" such a terrific episode is its imaginative extrapolation on Disneyland long before anyone had heard of holodecks (or holodeck malfunctions, for that matter). From the show's amusing teaser involving *Alice in Wonderland* to Kirk's encounter with his old Academy nemesis, Finnegan, to Gerald Fried's excellent, lyrical score, "Shore Leave" is delightful from start to finish, combining humor, romance and action/adventure into an intoxicating mix.

GROSS (***1/2): Sure, we're given characters from *Alice in Wonderland,* Japanese fighters firing on our characters, man-eating tigers and knights in shining armor, but the real strength of this episode is Captain Kirk coming to grips with his past in the form of a woman he once loved (Ruth) and a cadet at the Starfleet Academy (Finnegan) who made his life hell. Thanks to this planet, Kirk has the opportunity to even the score, and he takes full advantage of it. The death of Dr. McCoy marks the first time one of the series regulars dies and is resurrected by episode's end, though this is one of the more effective means of doing so. The script by Theodore Sturgeon is wonderful. See also "Once Upon a Planet."

SIEGE, THE

(DS9)
Original Airdate 10/11/93
Written by Michael Piller
Directed by Winrich Kolbe

Most of DS9 is evacuated in preparation for arriving Bajoran troops. Sisko and his key officers remain in hiding on the station, and Kira and Dax seek out the evidence they need to prove that the Cardassians are behind the Bajoran revolution.

ALTMAN (**1/2): The conclusion of the second season's opening trilogy of episodes is the least effective of the troika, resolving its major plots in a fairly disappointing fashion. Even with the extensive setup, too much is left to the final hour, including Dax and Kira's attempt to prove Cardassian involvement with the Circle. They are shot down over Bajor, only to show up in the closing minutes and set things right. The invasion of DS9 is not handled with nearly as much aplomb as you would expect from veteran director Rick Kolbe, one of the series' best. Of course, if it's not on the page, it's not on the stage.

GROSS (***): One can't help but get the feeling that if any *Star Trek* series was given ten hours to handle a story line, the first nine hours would be extraordinary, but the conclusion would be anticlimactic. The conclusion of this three-part story is not all that disappointing, but it doesn't live up to the promise of its predecessors. Still, there's plenty of action here, as Sisko's core group of officers defend DS9 from Bajoran troops and uncover the behind-the-scenes manipulations of the Cardassians. High praise should be paid to the unbilled Frank Langella, who brings a dark intensity to Jaro. See also "The Homecoming" and "The Circle."

SILICON AVATAR

(TNG)
Original Airdate 10/14/91
Written by Jeri Taylor
Directed by Cliff Bole

The crystalline entity from "Datalore" makes a return visit, destroying everything in its path. Nonetheless, Captain Picard wants to reason with it — an approach that Dr. Kila Marr, whose son was killed by the creature, wants no part of.

ALTMAN (**1/2): Oh, no, the floating icicle is back? Beware! Sure it makes for a chilling and action-packed teaser, but what about the rest of the episode, which is completely lethargic? We get to relish some budget-busting effects, and then, as is par for the course, it becomes a ship show. There are some interesting nuances to Data's character, including his ability to re-create the voice and memories of Dr. Marr's young son, a colonist on Dr. Soong's homeworld. There's also a surprising and powerful coda in which Marr destroys the entity despite Picard's Pollyannaish attempt to communicate.

GROSS (*1/2): One expects Leslie Nielsen to step out of hiding to inform us that this is a *Star Trek* spoof à la *Airplane* and *The Naked Gun*. Unfortunately, that isn't so. The lengths to which this episode goes to show how tolerant Picard is of all life-forms, no matter what they've done, are absolutely ludicrous. Can every alien being that does us harm *really* be misunderstood? That's what we're asked to believe. The crystalline entity has wiped out thousands upon thousands of innocent lives, we know from "Datalore" that its intent is evil and Picard wants to communicate with it? It's difficult not to imagine how Captain Kirk and his crew would have handled the same situation:

CHEKOV: Approaching crystalline entity, Kiptain.
KIRK: Hold position, Mr. Chekov. Mr. Sulu, lock phasers on target and await my order.
SPOCK: Jim, it's attempting to communicate with us.
KIRK: I realize that, Spock. I just don't like what it has to say. Fire!

Bye-bye, crystalline entity! See also "Datalore" and "Brothers."

SINS OF THE FATHER

(TNG)
Original Airdate 3/17/90
Written by Ronald D. Moore and W. Reed Moran
Directed by Les Landau

Worf returns to the Klingon homeworld to defend his late father against charges of treason. He is prompted to do so by his younger brother, Kurn (Tony Todd), who is still alive and has transferred aboard the Enterprise as part of the Federation exchange program. Meanwhile, High Council member Duras (Patrick Massett) plots to keep the truth of his father's dishonor and Worf's father's framing a secret in hopes of one day heading the Council (thematically continued in "Reunion").

ALTMAN (***1/2): A Klingon episode about treachery, honor, dishonor, betrayal and loyalty written by Ron Moore. What more could you want? Virtually nothing. "Sins of the Father" kicks off a fascinating story arc for Worf, which explores the roots of the power structure of the Klingon Empire and introduces Tony Todd in a splendid performance as

Worf's long-lost brother. A less adept writer would have massacred yet another *Trek* family member discovery, but Moore keeps it credible, and the show's climactic moments are truly riveting and memorable. Also delightfully devious is Patrick Massett as Duras, who returns in "Reunion."

GROSS (***1/2): Once again, exploration of the Klingon Empire is one of the most intriguing elements of *TNG* and a reason to be grateful for the alliance between the Federation and the Empire. Interestingly, Worf, a last-minute addition to the show who was only a background player during the first season, becomes one of the most fully developed characters of the entire bridge crew. The political games in this episode also prove that the Klingons are not all that different from us, despite their supposed devotion to honor above all things. High praise for Tony Todd as Worf's brother, Kurn. See also "Reunion," "Redemption" and "The Way of the Warrior."

SKIN OF EVIL

(TNG)
Original Airdate 4/23/88
Written by Joseph Stefano and Hannah Louise Shearer
Directed by Joseph Scanlan

A shuttlecraft carrying Deanna Troi crashes on a previously unexplored planet. There, an Away Team is confronted by what can only be described as an oil slick, which is also a sentient being. This creature, Armus, is the personification of evil stripped off of the race that had once populated the planet. Stranded, the creature takes pleasure in torturing those it encounters, even going so far as to kill Tasha Yar on a whim.

ALTMAN (**): Tasha Yar is sent off to the *real* final frontier, and not a moment too soon. Unfortunately, this episode's production values are among the show's worst ever. There's a silly but enjoyable campy story about the outcast of an alien race that threatens Troi, but the story would have worked far more effectively without a monotonous scene in which Dr. Crusher tries desperately to resurrect the dead Tasha Yar in sick bay, breaking up the pace of the show. Armus, the evil oil slick, is not one of *TNG's* more memorable villains, but it's an ambitious attempt at something new. The ending, in which the crew bids adieu to their colleague Tasha Yar, is terrible. It's also reminiscent of Kirk's farewell to McCoy and Spock in "The Tholian Web," but not nearly as well written.

GROSS (**): The notion of sudden death is intriguing, particularly when it comes to a regular character on a TV series, but for some reason there isn't enough of an emotional payoff in Tasha Yar's death. Her holographic good-bye message also stretches one's credulity. Who would really think of making something like that? Conceptually, the creature, Armus, is great, but everything is lost in the execution. There are no two ways about it — that's a dude in a rubber suit covered in oil.

SLAVER WEAPON

(TAS)
Original Airdate 12/15/73
Written by Larry Niven
Directed by Hal Sutherland

While transporting a Slaver stasis box (created by a race that once ruled the galaxy), Spock, Sulu and Uhura are attacked by the catlike Kzin race, who wish to possess the device. Intrigue builds on intrigue as the box passes from hand to hand, until the Kzin are in receipt of it, resulting in the destruction of their people.

ALTMAN (***1/2): By far one of the best and most literate of the animated episodes. Adapted from his own story by sf scribe Larry Niven, "Slaver Weapon" introduces the Kzin as a fascinating new Federation adversary and establishes Slaver boxes as part of the *Star Trek* mythology. Although there's some surprisingly good guest voice work, the animation is subpar, and the decision to give the fearsome and formidable Kzin a pink ship somewhat negates their menace. The episode focuses exclusively on Spock, Uhura and Sulu, who make for a compelling troika.

GROSS (**1/2): The Kzin are an interesting race that a live-action show could not have afforded to bring to life. Sulu and Uhura have more to do in this episode than in any live-action show, but it suffers the same fate as "The Galileo Seven": without Kirk, Spock just isn't as interesting a character.

SONS OF MOGH, THE

(DS9)
Original Airdate 2/10/96
Written by Ronald D. Moore
Directed by David Livingston

Thanks to the fury of Gowron, Worf's family has been disgraced on the Klingon homeworld. As a result, Worf's brother, Kurn, arrives on Deep Space Nine demanding that Worf restore Kurn's honor by taking his life. Worf finds himself torn between the tradition of his people and his oath to the Federation.

ALTMAN (***1/2): Klingon scribe Ron Moore is back in top form with this riveting installment and the best Worf outing on *DS9* to date. His compelling writing provides a close sociological look at Klingon society, while also blending a seamless B story about the Klingons secretly mining the quadrant in the event of war. David Livingston keeps the proceedings lively with his usually capable directing. Although Michael Dorn gives one of his best performances ever, the true star is Tony Todd, who turns in a tour de force as Kurn, imbuing the tortured Klingon with both pathos and strength. Dax is particularly well used, sharing her insights into Klingon culture.

GROSS (***): Tony Todd, who scores so well as the older Jake Sisko in "The Visitor," returns as Worf's brother in an emotionally charged episode. Kurn's desire to end his life to preserve his honor seems to be a natural aspect of his culture and puts Worf in a quandary. The final solution, wiping Kurn's memory and thus sparing his feeling of dishonor, is surprising and effective. It's a real joy to watch Todd and Michael Dorn play off each other.

SPACE SEED
(TOS)
Original Airdate 2/16/67
Written by Gene L. Coon and Carey Wilbur
Directed by Marc Daniels

The Enterprise *comes across a derelict "sleeper ship" that contains a crew of seventy in suspended animation. Led by Khan Noonian Singh (Ricardo Montalban), these people turn out to be the result of genetic experimentation on Earth in the 1990s. Basically a race of supermen, they tried to conquer Earth. Now, aided by* Enterprise *historian Marla McGivers, Khan is taking another stab at it by commandeering the* Enterprise.

ALTMAN (***): The episode's reputation is exaggerated in the afterglow of *Star Trek II: The Wrath of Khan,* but it's still an entertaining *Trek* adventure due in large part to the efforts of guest star Ricardo Montalban, who makes an engaging presence as Khan. His insatiable interest in the *Enterprise* and a verbal fencing match with Spock and Kirk over dinner are particularly well done. I still find it hard to believe that Marla McGivers (Madeline Rhue) would sell out her shipmates for him (after all, this is a week after Carolyn Palamas almost sold out the *Enterprise* for the god Apollo), and the final torture scene rescue is a little too convenient. However, the finale, in which Khan paraphrases Milton ("'tis better to rule in hell than serve in heaven") after being sentenced to exile on Ceti Alpha V, as well as the memorable production design of the *Botany Bay* sleeper ship (exterior and interior), works splendidly.

GROSS (****): The verbal volleys between Ricardo Montalban's charismatic Khan and William Shatner's Kirk make this episode must-see TV (sorry, NBC). Both speak without revealing any sign of weakness, and their final confrontation as Khan attempts to take over the *Enterprise* is pretty much inevitable. The script by Gene L. Coon and Carey Wilbur is quite literate, even by *Star Trek* standards, from its prophetic look at genetic engineering (read a paper lately?) to discussions of Milton at the conclusion. The only annoying aspect of the episode is the final physical fight between Kirk and Khan, which is staged so poorly — particularly with engineering having, for the first and only time, a row of these obviously plastic handle thingies that enable Kirk to knock Khan out. A small quibble with such a great episode. It's fascinating to watch Kirk's decision to give Khan and his people a world to conquer in the savage Ceti Alpha V, not knowing that fifteen years later they would have to face the consequences of this decision in the feature film *The Wrath of Khan.*

SPECTRE OF THE GUN

(TOS)
Original Airdate 10/25/68
Written by Lee Cronin
Directed by Vincent McEveety

Upon ignoring a warning not to proceed into Melkotian space, Kirk, Spock, McCoy, Scotty and Chekov find themselves on a world surrealistically mirroring the Old West, where they are to take part in the famous gunfight at the O.K. Corral. They are the Clantons, and if history proceeds the way it's supposed to, they will be killed by the Earps.

ALTMAN (***): What could easily have been just a silly *Trek* attempt at doing a western works for the very reasons it shouldn't: the notable production limitations. The unformed and uncompleted sets give "Spectre of the Gun" a surreal, minimalist look, and there's a certain irresistible lure to Kirk, Spock, McCoy and Scotty strapping on their six-guns and coping with their new and unfamiliar surroundings. McCoy visiting the local druggist in search of supplies, only to find that he's in the office of "Doc" Holliday, is a great moment, as is the untraditional look realized by director Vincent McEveety and the truly killer score by *The Wild Bunch*'s Jerry Fielding. The Melkotians are formidable-looking adversaries in their brief appearances, as are Wyatt Earp and his clan, thanks to some great casting.

GROSS (***): A bizarre little episode that could have been written by Brannon Braga in an earlier life. Although there's nothing especially earthshaking about the show, its surrealistic setting is reminiscent of a stage play with breakaway sets. Something about the situation actually seems a little dangerous, although Spock performing another Vulcan mind trick to get them out of it is way too hokey. Imagine the holodeck malfunctioning and trapping these guys in a western setting in which everything was real. Wait a minute, that happened two decades later in *TNG*'s "A Fistful of Datas."

SPOCK'S BRAIN

(TOS)
Original Airdate 9/20/68
Written by Lee Cronin
Directed by Marc Daniels

The Eymorgs steal Spock's brain to use as a power source on their planet, and the race is on for the Enterprise *to retrieve it before his body dies.*

ALTMAN (*1/2): Considered one of the worst episodes ever, "Spock's Brain" is a truly outlandish *Star Trek* story. Kirk and McCoy marching behind an automated Spock, whose brain has been hijacked by a band of alien lovelies who get their smarts from a machine, is downright bizarre. But if you revel in the goofiness, it does provide some laughs, especially when Scotty feigns unconsciousness to help Kirk steal a phaser from one of the Nancy Sinatra look-alikes controlling the planet. If you have a few swills of Saurian Brandy and invite a couple of friends over to engage in a game of Mystery Science Theatre, "Spock's Brain" can have a strange, unpredictable appeal. At least it's never boring.

GROSS (*): Whereas "The Alternative Factor" has given me a headache for thirty years, "Spock's Brain" has made me nauseous for the same duration. As the first episode aired under Fred Freiberger's auspices, it was not the kind of impression you'd want to make. The episode makes absolutely no sense, and having Leonard Nimoy join the party as a lumbering, brain-dead Spock adds insult to injury. Additionally, the coda, in which Spock goes on and on and on (worse than usual), is there simply to give McCoy an opportunity to crack, "I knew I shouldn't have connected his vocal cords." Yuk, yuk, yuk. Excuse me, I need an antacid.

SQUIRE OF GOTHOS, THE
(TOS)
Original Airdate 1/12/67
Written by Paul Schneider
Directed by Don McDougall

The Enterprise *is captured by an alien being named Trelane, who is equipped with a variety of powers that enable him to manipulate the world around him. Bored, he has chosen Kirk and his crew to stay on his world to provide him with entertainment. Trelane grows furious when Kirk disrupts his plans, and he puts humanity on trial.*

ALTMAN (***1/2): William Campbell is wonderful as the impish Trelane, who tests Kirk with his increasingly immature acts. His childlike anger as Kirk rebuffs his overtures to serve as a source of entertainment — subsequently destroying the machine that channels his power, only to encounter the planet Gothos itself playing a game of cat and mouse with the ship — is great stuff. Campbell's delightful presence makes the episode work, and the final revelation, in which his parents call him in from play, is an appropriate twist that provides a satisfying coda for an intelligent yet witty *Trek* romp.

GROSS (***1/2): This one's a lot of fun thanks to the tongue-in-cheek performance of guest star William Campbell, whose Trelane behaves like a spoiled brat and ultimately turns out to be exactly that — a child alien taking on the form of a human. It's interesting to watch the landing party try to find their way out of his fun house, and things become decidedly more serious when Kirk is forced to defend humanity in a bizarre courtroom setting and then partake in a futuristic version of *The Most Dangerous Game* as he's hunted for sport. Perhaps most amazing of all is just how much of this episode Gene Roddenberry ripped off when creating the character of Q in *TNG's* "Encounter at Farpoint," in which Q puts humanity, represented by Picard, on trial.

STAR TREK: THE MOTION PICTURE

(TMS, 1979)
Written by Harold Livingston
Story by Alan Dean Foster and Gene Roddenberry
Directed by Robert Wise

Captain Kirk assumes command of the Enterprise *as Earth is threatened by an alien entity that turns out to be a* Voyager *space probe that has gained consciousness and wants to join with its creator.*

ALTMAN (***): One of the few films in the series to have a cinematic scope. It occasionally has moments of *2001*-like awe, but more often than not it's a plodding retelling of "The Changeling." The film's first twenty minutes work splendidly, as the crew is reunited and Kirk reclaims the captaincy of the *Enterprise*. Everyone looks great, and the ship has never looked better as Kirk stares at the new *Enterprise* with orgasmic delight. Jerry Goldsmith's score is a classic from start to finish. Suffering from a truncated postproduction window, it has some overlong shots as the crew stares in wonder at the V'ger cloud. But the movie is a cerebral *Star Trek* adventure that retains many of the best elements of the original series, including its ironic wit and embrace of the unknown. The footage added to the video release contributes nuance and texture while also removing some of the excessive visual effects.

GROSS (***): This film is listless when it should be bursting with energy, repetitive of voyages past when it should be pointing the way to the future. Yet despite its nearly nonexistent pace and cobbling of story ideas from such original series episodes as "The Changeling" and "The Doomsday Machine," *Star Trek: The Motion Picture* is a somewhat interesting film. From a plot point of view, the whole idea of V'ger is intriguing, if a bit incomprehensible and not just a bit of a cheat. (Who can forget Harlan Ellison's observation that a device capable of doing all that it can, *can't* wipe away a little bit of dirt from its nameplate to know that its name is actually *Voyager* and not *V'ger*?) The film also is marred by too much mugging for the camera, smiles exchanged between characters for no apparent reason, dramatic arm grabbing, a bald Persis Khambatta and possibly the worst delivery of the phrase "Oh, my God!" (uttered by William Shatner) in the history of the cinema. What works is the opening Klingon sequence as they battle and are ultimately destroyed by V'ger, the score by Jerry Goldsmith, any scenes featuring DeForest Kelley and the character arcs for Kirk and Spock.

Apparently since the end of the series, Kirk hasn't been doing much, and when he has the opportunity to assume command of the *Enterprise* again, he jumps at it — even if it means screwing over Captain Decker (the earnest Stephen Collins, who has little to do but boink V'ger at the end of the film). Kirk is a man obsessed, who is allowing his personal agenda to endanger the *Enterprise*. The problem with this arc is that it has no clear-cut resolution — Kirk simply starts lightening up, being friendlier to Decker and more mellow overall, encouraged in no small way by Dr. McCoy.

Leonard Nimoy has the real acting role, making Spock more machinelike than ever as he tries to cast off his human emotions. Ironically, it is the cold, machine logic of V'ger that ends his quest, bringing him closer to his humanity than ever before. There's a wonderful scene in sick bay, after he has mind-melded with V'ger, when Spock grips Kirk's hand tightly and says, "Jim, this simple feeling is beyond V'ger's comprehension." It's a pivotal moment for the character and an acknowledgment of the friendship the two have shared over the years. This is probably the most important Spock story ever presented in the history of *Trek*.

Academy Award–winning director Robert Wise fails to imbue this extravaganza with the energy that it needs, instead allowing his camera to linger on the numerous (and expensive) special effects for far too long, particularly during an exterior tour of the *Enterprise* that goes on for half of forever and a journey through the innards of V'ger that goes on for the other half.

Overall, the movie is somewhat disappointing, but at least it got the old gang together again and served as a lesson for future filmmakers as to what *not* to do.

STAR TREK II: THE WRATH OF KHAN
(TMS, 1982)
Written by Nicholas Meyer and Jack Sowards
Directed by Nicholas Meyer

In this sequel to the original series episode "Space Seed," Khan Noonian Singh (Ricardo Montalban) escapes from Ceti Alpha V, seeking revenge on Captain Kirk. It's a quest that ends with the death of Mr. Spock as he saves the Enterprise *one last time.*

ALTMAN (***1/2): Though not without its share of flaws, this is the tightest and most engaging of the *Trek* films, perhaps because it's the most evocative of an original series episode (which is also why it works better on TV than on the big screen). Ricardo Montalban is sensational as the film's baddie, and William Shatner has never been better in any of the films. The most egregious misstep is the "coffin on the Genesis Planet" coda, which was added for commercial rather than creative reasons. Kirstie Alley makes a fine addition as Saavik.

GROSS (****): *The Wrath of Khan* remains the best film in the series, taking the characters from the TV show and breathing new life into them. Much of this can be attributed to Nicholas Meyer, who has a real affinity for the material.

Unlike its predecessor, this film takes the aging process into consideration — Kirk is going through a midlife crisis (a theme that will be repeated in many of the films), pondering the emptiness of his life off a starship and assessing the emotional emptiness of his past.

Naturally, that past catches up to him in the form of former lover Carol Marcus and Kirk's illegitimate son, David, as well as Khan Noonian Singh, left by Kirk on Ceti Alpha V some fifteen years earlier and now desperate for revenge. The battle with Khan and the other events in this film renew Kirk's spirit, preparing him for the rest of his life.

Leonard Nimoy's Spock has obviously grown, thanks to his encounter with V'ger in the previous film. He's calmer, dryly humorous and more in touch with his emotions, as evidenced by the moment when an injured crewman is carried on the bridge and Spock closes his eyes in response to the youth's wounds. (Closing one's eyes may not sound like such a big deal, but it is for Spock.) The film's climax, in which he sacrifices himself to save the *Enterprise,* and the subsequent funeral service are among the most powerful sequences in the history of the franchise, and the final moments between Spock and Kirk are extremely moving.

High praise must be paid to the rest of the regular cast, particularly DeForest Kelley, who's the best he's ever been as McCoy, as well as to guest stars Bibi Besch and Merritt Butrick (Carol and David Marcus, respectively) and Ricardo Montalban, who effortlessly steps back into the role of Khan, conveying the character's charisma laced with madness and a thirst for vengeance. Perhaps the biggest surprise is Kirstie Alley as Vulcan/Romulan hybrid Lieutenant Saavik. The actress gives no indication of the wackier roles she has come to be known for.

Other highlights include the gorgeous new uniforms and set designs, the ILM-produced special effects (which truly come alive in the battle between the *Enterprise* and the Khan-commanded *Reliant*) and James Horner's score, which captures the proper naval flavor. The one complaint about this film — and it's a big one — is that Kirk and Khan never have a face-to-face confrontation. Despite this problem, the film is filled with action, suspense, true characterization, lots of humor and a poignancy that matches "City on the Edge of Forever." The real hero of *The Wrath of Khan* is, of course, Nicholas Meyer. People often say that he's the guy who saved *Star Trek.* It's true.

STAR TREK III: THE SEARCH FOR SPOCK

(TMS, 1984)
Written by Harve Bennett
Directed by Leonard Nimoy

When it's discovered that Spock's consciousness, or Katra, resides with McCoy, Kirk must steal the Enterprise, *proceed to the Genesis Planet to retrieve Spock's body and bring both it and McCoy to Vulcan for the refusion of the soul and body. There's only one problem: The Klingons, led by Kruge (Christopher Lloyd), stand in his way.*

ALTMAN (**1/2): One of the most uneven *Trek* films. The plot is ludicrous, serving only to resurrect Spock rather than tell an interesting story, but it does have its moments of inspiration, including the theft of the *Enterprise* and a bombastic James Horner score. The destruction of the ship is an emotional moment, although freshman director Leonard Nimoy doesn't milk as much pathos out of the scene as it warrants. There's too much camp and dumb dialogue, and the production values are among the worst in the series.

GROSS (***): Considerably more uneven than *The Wrath of Khan*, *The Search for Spock* nonetheless works because it focuses on the depth of the relationships between the main characters and looks at the lengths to which they will go to save Spock — even if it means losing their careers. The film is shallower than its predecessor, but it nonetheless delivers on a number of levels, particularly in terms of the battle with the Klingons, the destruction of the *Enterprise* (though there should have been a moment where Kirk takes one more look at the bridge) and the resurrection of Spock. The ever-impressive Christopher Lloyd is surprisingly good as a Klingon, bringing serious tension and dark humor at key moments. Robin Curtis replaces Kirstie Alley as Saavik and doesn't have the same charisma. I still haven't been able to figure out why they felt it was necessary to have the Klingons kill Kirk's son, David (Merritt Butrick).

STAR TREK IV: THE VOYAGE HOME
(TMS, 1986)
Written by Steve Meerson, Peter Krikes, Nicholas Meyer and Harve Bennett
Directed by Leonard Nimoy

The crew of the Enterprise *travels back in time to the twentieth century to retrieve a pair of humpback whales that they hope will communicate with a probe that is threatening all life on Earth three hundred years in the future.*

ALTMAN (***): An enjoyable romp with some pedestrian scenes set on Vulcan and twenty-fourth-century Earth resolving myriad plot points left open by the previous films. Fortunately, the Nicholas Meyer–scripted time-travel segments are delightful, although many of the moments are played too broadly by the cast. It's actually the subtle scenes that work best, with Kirk selling a pair of eyeglasses back in the twentieth century. (Spock: "Weren't they a gift from Dr. McCoy?" Kirk: "And they will be again. That's the beauty of it.") Unfortunately, Leonard Rosenman's score is completely inappropriate for a *Trek* film and a horrible choice by director Leonard Nimoy, whose work here far exceeds his efforts on the previous movie.

GROSS (****): Not everything in this film makes sense from a purely logical point of view, but who gives a damn? The culture clash is terrific. There are plenty of laughs and a bit of poignancy that harks back to the original series, particularly when Kirk looks at the humpback whale and says, "It's ironic that when man was killing these creatures, he was destroying his own future." Leonard Nimoy is obviously more sure of himself behind the camera, and every one of the cast members gets something substantial to do.

STAR TREK V: THE FINAL FRONTIER

(TMS, 1989)
Written by David Loughery
Story by William Shatner and David Loughery
Directed by William Shatner

Spock's half brother, Sybok (Laurence Luckinbill), commandeers the Enterprise *on his quest to travel to the center of the galaxy to meet with God.*

ALTMAN (**1/2): Director William Shatner continues to get a bad rap for a film that has a wealth of successful moments. Unfortunately, Bran Ferren's incompetent special effects sabotage the movie and have convinced most people that the film is irredeemably bad. It doesn't help that Shatner can't direct himself and gives a wildly over-the-top performance. Regrettably, the success of *Star Trek IV,* which includes a large dose of humor, forced the writers to include a lot of shtick in the fifth feature, and little of it works. What does work is Shatner's more than competent lensing, the · campfire scenes that bookend the picture and Kirk's insolent query "What does God need with a starship?" which is worth the price of admission.
GROSS (**1/2): Rotten special effects, the ridiculous notion that Spock has a half brother whom we (and Kirk) have never heard about

and some of the characters doing uncharacteristic things (Scotty knocking himself out on a beam in the *Enterprise*) diminish the impact of this film, which is far from the turkey that people have made it out to be. There are loads of character bits, most notably in the campfire scenes, when Sybok reveals McCoy's and Spock's greatest pains and when, in the same sequence, Kirk delivers the wonderful proclamation, "I don't want my pain taken away. It's what makes me who I am!" And who else but Kirk would have the gall to demand an explanation from the Almighty? William Shatner does a competent job behind the camera. Too bad the F/X don't support his vision.

STAR TREK VI: THE UNDISCOVERED COUNTRY

(TMS, 1991)
Written by Dennis Martin Flinn
Story by Leonard Nimoy, Mark Rosenthal and Lawrence Konner
Directed by Nicholas Meyer

The Berlin Wall comes down in outer space as the Federation and Klingons move closer to a peace treaty. Unfortunately, Kirk and McCoy are convicted of assassinating the Klingon chancellor, and it is up to Spock and the Enterprise *crew to prove their innocence before the assassins can strike again at an upcoming peace conference. The revelation that the conspiracy consists of members of both the Federation and the Empire does not bode well for the future.*

ALTMAN (***): Nicholas Meyer's political allegory suffers from some sloppy storytelling, including Scotty's offhand discovery of incriminating gravity boots and the subsequent revelation of the murdered assassins dead in the corridor. Meyer also strikes out with the self-indulgent incorporation of Shakespearean quotations throughout. Ultimately, however, *Star Trek VI* works because of its great character moments and a thrilling finale, which intercuts a super space battle with the action on Khitomer, leading to a memorable conclusion in which Kirk saves the Federation president's life. The video version is somewhat improved by the inclusion of three scenes excised from the theatrical release, including the revelation that the Klingon assassin is actually Colonel West, played by an uncredited Rene Auberjonois.

GROSS (***): The speed at which this film was made definitely shows in terms of its lack of story logic, but the spark between the actors is still a joy to watch. The political machinations are well handled, as is a wonderful anti-gravity sequence in a Klingon Bird of Prey, in which the chancellor is killed. Perhaps the most poignant moments in the film, which was released at the height of *TNG*'s popularity, come as Kirk and Spock wonder whether they have become obsolete. Judging by the film and the spectacular ending involving the *Enterprise* and Captain Sulu's (George Takei) *Excelsior,* they most certainly have not. Unfortunately, this was the final feature starring the complete original cast.

STAR TREK VII: GENERATIONS

(TMS, 1994)
Written by Ronald D. Moore and Brannon Braga
Story by Rick Berman, Brannon Braga and Ron D. Moore
Directed by David Carson

Captains Kirk and Picard finally come together, thanks to a space anomaly known as the Nexus, and the focal point is Dr. Tolian Soran, who is so determined to return to the Nexus that he will sacrifice millions of lives. During the action, the android Data inserts an emotion chip, which causes him no end of problems.

ALTMAN (*): A legitimate alternative to Sominex, guaranteed to put you to sleep in record time. It's difficult to call *Generations* a complete disaster, if only because the first fifteen minutes are so much fun. Unfortunately, immediately after Kirk's disappearance into the Nexus, the movie slows to a crawl. Beginning with the holodeck sequences aboard an eighteenth-century sailing ship, it is immediately apparent that the creative team hasn't a clue about making a feature film, as they service the characters rather than the plot — and barely even that. Whether it's shooting at sea for an insignificant and witless prologue, building a stellar cartography set in which six minutes of stultifying technobabble unfolds or crashing the *Enterprise* for no better reason than the writers thought it would be fun, they make all the wrong choices. By the time the film reaches its climax and Kirk and Picard battle the malevolent Soran (Malcolm McDowell), the scope of the film has diminished so much that it looks like kids playing on monkey bars. Even the crashing of the *Enterprise* looks like something out of an *Airport* movie. The only saving grace is John Alonzo's slick photography.

The film's attempts at emotional depth fall flat. Having Picard grappling with his mortality never pays off, and William Shatner's star power blows the lifeless Patrick Stewart off the screen. Only McDowell shines as the Sybok-like Soran, who is bent on returning to a Nexus we don't understand and destroying a star that will wipe out a planet of people we never meet in a movie so riddled with plot holes that it makes *Star Trek VI* look credible by comparison. Ultimately, this film is a terrible bore, which for *Star Trek* is unforgivable, never seizing on the exciting opportunities offered by having the two generations meet.

GROSS (**1/2): The real problem with this film can be discerned by comparing the first fifteen minutes to most of the rest of it. That opening sequence, featuring Kirk, Scotty and Chekov, has more interplay and warmth than all the rest of the film put together. The cast of *TNG* seems awfully formal with each other, having no sense of fun (outside of the incongruous sailing sequence).

The incomprehensible plot and its accompanying technobabble are awkwardly handled, as the filmmakers attempt to balance character with plot. For example, just as Picard finishes relating to Troi the horror that has befallen his brother and nephew and his fears of his mortality, Soran's probe is conveniently launched into the nearby sun. While Picard and Data are in Stellar Cartography (a beautiful set, by the way) and the computer takes the longest time we've ever seen a Starfleet computer take to regurgitate information, Data talks about how he wants to be shut down because he can't control his emotions. As soon as Picard snaps him to attention and Data composes himself, the computer — ta dah! — has the necessary information.

Probably the biggest disappointment is when Kirk and Picard are brought together. There's definitely a spark between these two guys — although William Shatner does blow Patrick Stewart off the screen — but they spend most of their time together in the Nexus cooking for some bimbo named Antonia. (Wouldn't Edith Keeler be the person Kirk would most want to be reunited with?) The disappointment continues on Veridian III, where Kirk dies in such an ignominious manner that the sequence can't hold a candle to Spock's death in *The Wrath of Khan*. Hey, Paramount, want to rectify the situation? Film Shatner's novel *The Return* — it would make one hell of a movie.

STAR TREK VIII: FIRST CONTACT

(TMS, 1996)
Written by Brannon Braga and Ronald D. Moore
Story by Rick Berman, Ronald D. Moore and Brannon Braga
Directed by Jonathan Frakes

The Enterprise E *pursues the Borg back to Earth's past, where they must stop the cybernetic race from preventing Zefram Cochrane's inaugural warp flight, which will result in the first contact with another species. At the same time, the Borg attempt the assimilation of the* Enterprise *itself, with the Borg Queen tempting Data to switch sides with the opportunity to have human skin grafted onto his android body.*

ALTMAN (***): *First Contact* compares well with some of the best episodes in *The Next Generation* oeuvre, even if it lacks the eerie, spooky resonance of "Q Who" and some of the drama and inventiveness of "Best of Both Worlds." *First Contact* delivers action on a grand scale, but the series' humanism is lost in the mayhem and carnage, despite lip service being paid to Zefram Cochrane's warp launch's paving the way for the *Trek* future. The film's plot is pretty derivative, taking its cues from films such as *Aliens, The Terminator* and even *Hellraiser.* The real problem with the film is its structure, in which untenable A, B and C stories are woven through the threadbare narrative. The most effective scenes are on the *Enterprise,* with Picard fending off a Borg invasion. However, the presence of Alice Krige's Borg Queen (in a strong performance) is less welcome. By giving the Borg a human face, you diminish their venality. Resistance isn't futile if you can seduce their queen and mislead her with lies and evasions. It's pretty ludicrous that this "girl" just wants to have fun with a fully functional Data, which gives the Borg an all too human persona, considering what made

them such great villains was their soulless, relentless quest for mechanical perfection. The scenes on Earth are less successful and far too slapsticky. The movie is empty and unemotional, though still exciting, with an action scene on the ship's deflector dish being a particular standout.

GROSS (***): A vast improvement over *Generations, First Contact* has a genuine, tangible threat in the form of the Borg, tremendous special effects (particularly a battle with a Borg cube ship) and some welcome interplay between the characters. There are some gaping plot holes, but the movie's pace is such that those holes don't really matter. Picard's Ahab-like arc is effective, presenting a side of him that we haven't seen before. The interaction between Data and the Borg Queen works only moderately well because it stretches one's credulity in terms of the film's climax. Director Jonathan Frakes has set out to make an action movie above all else, and he accomplishes that goal admirably. I'm ready for *Star Trek IX.*

STARSHIP DOWN

(DS9)
Original Airdate 11/11/95
Written by David Mach and John Ordover
Directed by Alexander Singer

The Defiant *hosts a secret meeting in the Gamma Quadrant between Quark and Minister Hanok of the Karemma. Sisko hopes to use the Ferengi as the intermediary in opening trade relations with* the local population, to avoid incurring Dominion hostility toward the Federation. Unfortunately, Hanok (Star Trek VIII: First Contact's James Cromwell) suspects that he is being taken for a ride by the Ferengi. Then the ship is attacked by the Jem'Hadar, sending the Defiant into the atmosphere of a gaseous planet in an attempt to protect the Karemma.

ALTMAN (**): An episode that suffers from *Crimson Tide* envy, in which the *Defiant* engages the Jem'Hadar in the atmosphere of a gaseous giant. The episode's biggest failing is its inability to sustain tension throughout (not to mention its similarity to *TNG's* "Disaster"), but there are some charming character moments, including one that seemingly resolves the Bashir and Dax arc. The episode is not nearly as enjoyable as "Balance of Terror," to which it bears more than a passing resemblance, but some competent production values and a solid performance by James Cromwell as Hanok, a representative of the Karemma, are satisfying. Unfortunately, this kind of genre pastiche tends to suffer in comparison to its source material, such as *Ice Station Zebra* and *The Enemy Below.*

GROSS (**): One of the very few real disappointments that *DS9* has offered. One gets the impression that the intention was to mirror the success of the original series' "Balance of Terror," but it's an intention that wasn't met. Hey, you can't win 'em all, and their track record is still better than most.

STARSHIP MINE

(TNG)
Original Airdate 3/29/93
Written by Morgan Gendel
Directed by Cliff Bole

During a routine bayron particle elimination sweep of the Enterprise, terrorists attempt to steal trilithium from the ship's engines. Picard, the sole remaining crew member aboard the starship, attempts to stop them from escaping with the deadly compound by pretending to be the ship's barber, Mr. Mott.

ALTMAN (**): Despite the episode's obvious origins in *Die Hard* lore, the show opens with an unconventional teaser laced with broad comedy, and it works terrifically as Picard is consistently accosted by his crew regarding the evacuation of the ship, including Worf's request to be excused from a reception at the Akaria Base. When the show falls into the standard genre contrivances, however, it starts to stumble, such as in a scene where the hero and villain literally talk over their communicators. It's tough to do *Die Hard* when, according to the rules of Gene Roddenberry's universe, Picard can't kill anyone. Despite its flaws, there are some wonderful character moments, including Data attempting to master the art of small talk with a gregarious Starfleet commander named Hutchinson (David Spielberg); Picard passing himself off as the barber, Mr. Mott; and a light, humorous coda reminiscent of the old *Star Trek.* As for the music, Ron Jones's bombastic scores are sorely missed, and one of these could have provided a well-needed boost to some of the episode's less effective fisticuffs. In reference to Data and the admiral, Riker asks Troi, "How long can two people talk about nothing?" Obviously, he's never seen *Seinfeld*.

GROSS (**): "Starship Mine" *should* have been the equivalent of "*Die Hard* on a Starship," but the script lacks a line of tension that Cliff Bole's direction cannot compensate for. Instead of an edge-of-the-seat thriller, we're given a middle-of-the-road action/adventure. More cuts during the action sequences would have enhanced this episode, but the bottom line is that a television budget simply can't support this type of show. The sequences at the reception are actually quite good and filled with humor. (Note: Trilithium, the target of the terrorists, is an energy form that plays an integral role in *Star Trek VII: Generations*.)

STATE OF FLUX

(VOY)
Original Airdate 4/10/95
Teleplay by Chris Abbott
Story by Paul Coyle
Directed by Robert Scheerer

As it continues home, Voyager intercepts a distress signal from a Kazon vessel that seems to have been damaged by Federation technology. The crew realizes that there is a traitor aboard the starship who has given technology to the Kazon. That traitor turns out to be Seska, who is also revealed to be a surgically altered Cardassian.

ALTMAN (**1/2): Although the investigation of the perpetrator is about on a par with *Star Trek VI: The Undiscovered Country* as far as the level of deduction goes, the emotional resonance and reversals of the story are striking — particularly those involving Chakotay's self-doubt and concerns about a trusted former member of his Maquis band. ("You were working for them. Seska was working for them. Was anybody working for me?" Chakotay plaintively asks Tuvok.) The serialized setup of Seska's character over several episodes is welcome preplanning, but the failure of anyone to apologize to Lieutenant Carrey after accusing him of collaborating with the Kazon is gnawing. Doesn't anyone remember the lessons of *TNG*'s "The Drumhead"?

GROSS (***): With this episode, *Voyager* shows that it has learned its lesson well from *Deep Space Nine* in terms of setting up events or character arcs over the course of several episodes, so that when a new twist is revealed, it's actually a shock. The revelation of Seska as a Cardassian spy carries much more resonance than would some nondescript officer selling out the *Voyager* to the enemy. Beyond that, her betrayal has an impact on the crew that trusted her, particularly Chakotay, who wonders aloud how he could have been fooled by both Tuvok and Seska and what kind of an officer that makes him. Great character stuff.

STORYTELLER, THE

(DS9)

Original Airdate 5/3/93
Written by Kurt Michael Bensmiller and Ira Steven Behr
Directed by David Livingston

While responding to an emergency situation with Bashir in a Bajoran village, O'Brien is inadvertently made the Storyteller, a mythic figure whose destiny is to ward off a cloudlike demon.

ALTMAN (***): Although the "evil entity" menace plays like a bad 1950s science-fiction B-movie contrivance, the juice of the episode is the Abbott and Costello banter between Chief O'Brien and Dr. Bashir. Both Colm Meaney and Siddig El Fadil are delightful, with Bashir taking devilish delight in O'Brien's *The Man Who Would Be King* predicament. The B story involving Jake's and Nog's affinity for a comely young Bajoran is surprisingly entertaining, distinguished by a moment of comic inspiration in which Nog hurls a bucket of oatmeal at the young Sisko, who thinks it's Odo in his disassembled form. David Livingston once again proves that he's one of the show's foremost directors in this logistically daunting installment, bringing both grandeur to the effects-laden scenes on Bajor and a new vitality to the scenes aboard Deep Space Nine.

GROSS (**1/2): Maybe it's me, but this episode feels strangely like "The Nagus," substituting O'Brien for Quark. Despite that, there's some fun to be had here, particularly between Bashir and O'Brien, although this isn't an outstanding episode from any point of view, with the exception of the opportunities it offers Colm Meaney and Alexander Siddig in their scenes together. There are some neat cloud effects, too.

SUB ROSA

(TNG)

Original Airdate 1/31/94
Written by Brannon Braga
Directed by Jonathan Frakes

While attending the funeral of her grandmother on a planet that was terraformed to resemble Glasgow, Scotland, Dr. Crusher experiences visions of a ghost that she learns has haunted her family for generations. Meanwhile, Geordi LaForge and Data attempt to repair the planet's weather-control grid, while Picard tries to convince Crusher to remain with Starfleet when she abruptly hands in her resignation to join the ghost, Ronin (Duncan Regehr), back on the planet. Only when Picard reveals that the ghost is an apparition created by a metaphasic energy being is Ronin's spell broken, and Crusher phasers him out of existence.

ALTMAN (*1/2): This may very well be one of the strangest episodes of *Star Trek* ever. The story, which plays like a particularly bad installment of *Dark Shadows,* is based on a ludicrous premise, and it's hard to understand how it ever intrigued the staff in the first place. Admittedly, it is amusing to watch Dr. Crusher writhe in orgasmic pleasure while delivering lines such as "He knew exactly how I liked to be touched; it was extremely arousing," which Gates McFadden, incredibly, manages to deliver with a straight face.

The ending is not only riddled with technobabble but also sadly predictable. The alien vampire plot is a hallmark of most really bad sci-fi TV shows, a low to which I never thought *TNG* would sink. The only one who acquits himself in this subpar effort is Jonathan Frakes, whose direction is appropriately ethereal — although one wonders what went through his mind when he read the stage directions for a scene in which the bridge becomes filled with fog.

GROSS (*): I still don't get this episode, which is in the vein of the original series' "Catspaw," with a healthy dose of *Star Trek V: The Final Frontier* thrown in for good measure. (Just exchange God for Ronin, and you have beings with similar agendas.) Some creepy atmosphere is generated, but this just doesn't feel like an episode of *Star Trek*. Sci-fi and gothic horror are not a good mix, particularly in this case.

SUDDENLY HUMAN

(TNG)
Original Airdate 10/15/90
Written by John Whelpley and Jeri Taylor
Directed by Gabrielle Beaumont

A human teenager, Jono (Chad Allen), is found aboard a damaged Tellerian ship and brought back to the Enterprise along with his comrades. Jono is responsive only to Picard's command authority. The captain tries to reacclimate him to human culture, but his adopted father, Endar (Sherman Howard), commander of the Tellerian fleet, demands his return. If he is not returned, Endar will declare war on the Federation. Jono, who may be in a somewhat abusive relationship with

Endar, must choose whether to stay with the Federation or go back to the Tellerians.

ALTMAN (**1/2): Jeri Taylor's deft writing helps elevate this episode above its thoroughly unintriguing and tired premise. (*Trek* is notorious for handling kid stories poorly — for example, "Miri" and "And the Children Shall Lead.") Some strong character moments, with Picard placed in the role of a surrogate father, along with several priceless comedic scenes between the boy and the captain in Picard's quarters, make "Suddenly Human" an acceptable offering.

GROSS (**): Patrick Stewart and Chad Allen have some effective scenes together, and the issue of child abuse is important to explore. Unfortunately, it is not taken to the lengths that it needs to be here, resulting in the tale's falling a bit flat. A good effort, but one that isn't quite there.

SURVIVOR, THE

(TAS)
Original Airdate 10/13/73
Written by James Schmerer
Directed by Hal Sutherland

A shape-shifter dupes the Enterprise crew into believing it's actually philanthropist Carter Winston, who has been missing for five years. Once on board, it transforms itself into Captain Kirk and takes the Enterprise into the Romulan side of the Neutral Zone, where the vessel is quickly surrounded by enemy vessels. The shifter, we learn, is actually a Romulan spy.

ALTMAN (**1/2): Ted Knight provides the voice for Carter Winston in this intriguing animated episode. Although the shape-changing alien is a familiar genre (and Trekkian) trope, the romantic twist in which the Vendorian spy betrays his Romulan masters for love is a nice surprise that would probably have worked better in a live-action show. There's some of the occasionally acerbic dialogue that frequently characterized the animated series, including a Romulan's response to Kirk's protestations of innocence over crossing the Neutral Zone: "You appear to have a propensity for trespassing in the Neutral Zone." When Kirk says it wasn't intentional, the Romulan answers, "It never is."

GROSS (***): An above-average episode, with some interesting pathos for the shape-shifter Carter Winston. It's very bizarre hearing Ted Baxter — er, Ted Knight — in an episode of *Star Trek*. This definitely has the feeling of a live-action show.

SURVIVORS, THE

(TNG)
Original Airdate 10/7/89
Written by Michael Wagner
Directed by Les Landau

When the Enterprise *finds only two survivors of an alien attack that destroyed the entire population of Rana 4, they are suspicious of the story told by Kevin Uxbridge (John Anderson). Picard eventually learns that Uxbridge is actually a shape-changing alien who assumed human form to marry an Earthling. When she was killed by the invaders, he destroyed their entire species across the universe.*

ALTMAN (****): Shot on location in Malibu, California, "The Survivors" is one of *TNG*'s least predictable and most compelling looks at an omnipotent alien race that isn't at all what we expect. It's a truly powerful and moving story with some gorgeous location photography. At its heart is a serious science-fiction premise, an intriguing mystery and absolutely riveting performances by the late John Anderson as Kevin Uxbridge and Anne Haney as his wife. Its examination of genocide, warfare and pacifism is both subtle and poignant. It also has one of Worf's best line deliveries ever: "Good tea, nice house." A winner.

GROSS (***): The first few acts manage to establish a nice sense of mystery, and in the end there is a real feeling of poignancy when all is revealed in terms of Kevin Uxbridge's true identity and what has actually taken place on this planet. The bottom line is that in many ways, the alien cannot be blamed for its actions. A bit of a similarity to the original series' "The Man Trap." An episode that scores on almost every level.

SUSPICIONS

(TNG)
Original Airdate 5/9/93
Written by Joe Menosky and Naren Shankar
Directed by Cliff Bole

Beverly Crusher is relieved of duty after investigating what she believes is the murder of a Ferengi scientist who has created a metaphasic shield designed to take a shuttle through a star's corona.

Relating the story in flashback to Guinan, Dr. Crusher is intent on solving the murder and salvaging her career.

ALTMAN (*): Several dreadful performances and a hackneyed mystery plot make "Suspicions" suspiciously bad. The show's gimmick, a film noir–type contrivance in which Beverly Crusher relates her story to Guinan in flashback, is one of the few elements that genuinely works. Unfortunately, the routine murder mystery plot, in which a scientist covets another's invention, makes the denouement in *DS9*'s "A Man Alone" look inspired by comparison. If not for some witty dialogue, the welcome presence of Whoopi Goldberg as Guinan, Crusher's drop-kicking of the alien murderer (no flowerpots) and the self-reflexive touch of naming a shuttlecraft for former *Trek* producer and all-around nice guy Robert Justman, "Suspicions" would be a complete stinker.

GROSS (**1/2): Gates McFadden does Columbo as Dr. Crusher tries to uncover the truth behind the Ferengi's death. A somewhat interesting mystery, but not terribly involving. The final fight scene between Crusher and the murderer on the *Justman* is pretty exciting, giving McFadden a rare occasion to get it on physically with a bad guy. One distracting element of the show is Peter Slutsker, the tallest damn Ferengi anyone's ever seen, and his behavior is so atypical of his race that it's hard to believe he's part of it.

SWORD OF KAHLESS, THE
(DS9)
Original Airdate 11/18/95
Teleplay by Hans Beimler
Story by Richard Danus
Directed by LeVar Burton

The Klingon Kor (John Colicos) returns to recruit Dax on a quest for the legendary Sword of Kahless. Dax convinces Kor to enlist the aid of Worf in retrieving the ceremonial weapon for the emperor, in the hope that he can use it to unite the Klingon people. Once they have begun their mission, though, Kor and Worf find themselves feuding almost as violently between themselves as with the antagonists they confront on their quest.

ALTMAN (*1/2): Unfortunately, "The Sword of Kahless" regurgitates the familiar Klingon tropes for the umpteenth time, as Worf and Kor talk endlessly about honor, while Dax referees their contentious dialogue. The action doesn't measure up to Winrich Kolbe's impressive pyrotechnics in the second season's "Blood Oath," and even though John Colicos gives another engaging performance, the teleplay is truly dismal. Particularly egregious is the conflict that develops between Kor and Worf, which almost leads to murder. I was waiting for a revelation that the Klingons were under some kind of external psionic influence from the sword to explain their uncharacteristic behavior, only to learn that this is their true nature. What could have been a quest story with Arthurian overtones turns into an intergalactic *Married . . . with Children* and has lapses in credibility big enough to fly a starship through. It's amazing that this got past the break session.

GROSS (**1/2): An intriguing episode that in some ways harks back to the original series, but there are some problems as well. First off, the lack of budget shows, as the characters spend most of the episode in some very claustrophobic-looking caves. Second, the effect this sword has on the Klingons is a bit difficult to fathom, with their almost psychotic desire to possess it seeming like something out of Tolkien rather than *Star Trek,* and we're not given a satisfactory answer as to why it is having this effect. Any suspicion of an outside influence turns out to be for naught. By episode's end, neither John Colicos nor Michael Dorn are very likable, with only Terry Farrell's humorous attempts to keep them apart moving things forward. See also "Errand of Mercy" and "Blood Oath."

SYMBIOSIS

(TNG)
Original Airdate 4/16/88
Written by Robert Lewin, Richard Manning and Hans Beimler
Directed by Win Phelps

The Enterprise *crew comes to the aid of a disabled Omaran ship and decides to provide aid, until they discover that a supposed plague cure is actually a highly addictive drug that the Omarans have been supplying to neighboring Bracca for two centuries.*

Picard finds himself embroiled in a battle between the drug suppliers and their clients, and he is torn between cutting off the supply and obeying the Prime Directive of noninterference, eventually developing a unique solution to the situation.

ALTMAN (**): An interesting idea that employs a clever sci-fi premise to tell a story about the dangers of narcotics is undone by weak casting and a silly script. This heavy-handed treatise against the evils of drug addiction has its moments, but Tasha Yar's "Just Say No" admonition to Wesley Crusher isn't one of them. Instead, it's one of the most stupid and blatantly idiotic moments of soapbox polemic that *Star Trek* has ever indulged in.

GROSS (***): It's nice to see *The Next Generation* take a contemporary issue and give it a twenty-fourth-century slant. The situation is dramatically sound, and Picard's decision to do nothing and thereby serve as the catalyst for a solution to the dilemma is ingenious. The episode doesn't end in the show's usual upbeat manner, but there's nothing wrong with that. The only real drawback is Tasha Yar's overbearing "Just Say No" speech to Wesley Crusher, which turns my stomach. (Note: Guest stars Judson Scott and Merritt Butrick both appear in the feature film *Star Trek II: The Wrath of Khan,* with Scott cast as Khan's number one and Butrick as Kirk's son, David.)

T

TAPESTRY

(TNG)
Original Airdate 2/15/93
Written by Ronald D. Moore
Directed by Les Landau

It's not such a wonderful life for Picard when Q (John de Lancie) gives him a chance to relive his rambunctious youth. As Picard lies dying in sick bay from a wound sustained on an Away Team mission, he finds himself in heaven with Q, who gives him a chance to stop the fight that led to the captain's being fitted with an artificial heart some years later.

ALTMAN (***1/2): One of the new *Trek*'s finest installments. Richly directed by Les Landau, "Tapestry" is one of the most compelling and well-realized stories ever told in *The Next Generation*. Patrick Stewart gives a magnificent turn, which is exceeded only by John de Lancie's tour de force performance. The ambiguities and role reversals in the episode provide for a wealth of contemplation even after the episode's final credits have rolled. Rather than serve as simply a mischievous miser of mirth, as he did in "Q-pid," Q remains enigmatic (atypically not part of the title, which contributes to the mystery of the episode), while at the same time proving the engaging catalyst for this ingenious *Trek* classic from the pen of Ron Moore.
GROSS (****): It doesn't get any better than this (well, hardly ever). From the opening moment, when

Q announces, "You're dead, Jean-Luc, and I'm God," until the end, when Picard has come to grips with his life, "Tapestry" is a fascinating character study featuring an opportunity to correct the perceived mistakes of one's youth and see how different a path one may have taken. In his case, Picard learns that his somewhat reckless early days at the Starfleet Academy were necessary for him to become the leader he is today. Ultimately, he learns that the way you live your life is what's important — a lesson that will be reinforced in the feature film *Star Trek VII: Generations*. Incidentally, after all that trouble he's caused in the past, it's great that Q shows that he truly does have a soft spot for Picard.

TASTE OF ARMAGEDDON, A

(TOS)
Original Airdate 2/23/67
Written by Robert Hamner and Gene L. Coon
Directed by Joseph Pevney

Ambassador Robert Fox (Gene Lyons) is on board the Enterprise to negotiate a peace treaty with the planet Eminiar VII, despite the world's apparent lack of interest in such a treaty. The Enterprise crew soon finds that they are casualties in an interplanetary war between Eminiar and its adversary, Vendikar, in which computers pinpoint the location of theoretical bombings and the inhabitants willingly walk into disintegration chambers.

ALTMAN (***1/2): Although some substandard production values sabotage an exceptional script, it's hard to overlook the innovative sci-fi concept and Kirk's bellicose posturing, in which he destroys the planet's computers, threatening to usher in a real war if the two combatants fail to agree to a peace treaty. Gene Lyons is sufficiently annoying as mealy-mouthed diplomat Robert Fox, as is David Opatoshu as Anan 879, the leader of Eminiar VII. The final speech, in which Kirk muses about the horrors of real war, is superb: "Death, destruction, disease, horror. That's what war is all about. That's what makes it a thing to be avoided."

GROSS (****): Prime Directive? What the hell is the Prime Directive? That's probably Kirk's defense for interfering with the natural development of another planet. Nonetheless, it's difficult to blame the captain, and William Shatner's performance is right on the money as he blasts this society for taking the true meaning out of war. One of the late Gene L. Coon's best scripts for the original series, this is a much more successful commentary on Vietnam than "A Private Little War." It definitely could have used an expanded budget, but money is not tantamount to ideas.

TATTOO

(VOY)
Original Airdate 11/6/95
Teleplay by Michael Piller
Story by Larry Brody
Directed by Alexander Singer

When Chakotay leads an Away Team to drill for minerals on a moon's surface, they accidentally disturb a village and encounter its defensive inhab-itants, a group with Indian origins that his North American ancestors encountered in the guise of sky spirits.

ALTMAN (*1/2): This may be one of the most misguided *Trek*s ever, with ludicrous flashbacks to Chakotay as a young boy experiencing events that parallel his experience on this bizarre alien world, which threatens not only the Away Team but also the ship itself. Writer Michael Piller seems to forget that *Star Trek* is not about mysticism and spirituality, but about science and technology. To his credit, Robert Beltran manages to retain his dignity throughout the proceedings (except during a ludicrous nude shot of the actor personified by his butt double). The episode is an absurd attempt to give Chakotay's character some ethnic color, despite the fact that it is inherently un-Trekkian at its core. The only thing that works is a mildly amusing B story in which the doctor attempts to learn empathy for his patients by creating a computer-generated virus for himself. The resolution is not a surprise, but is a welcome reprieve from the dour Indian mystic babble. Where is Kirok when you need him?

GROSS (**): Why is this an episode of *Star Trek*? Despite the fact that Robert Beltran holds his own as Chakotay, adding a bit more background to the first officer, the supposed connection between his people and these aliens stretches one's credulity. Earnest performances can't save this one.

TERRATIN INCIDENT, THE

(TAS)
Original Airdate 11/17/73
Written by Paul Schneider
Directed by Hal Sutherland

When the Enterprise *investigates a mysterious distress signal, the starship is struck by a lightning bolt. As a result, all organic matter on the vessel begins to shrink in size. Needing to do something before it's too late, Kirk and a landing party beam down to the source of the distress signal and discover a miniature city that is threatened with destruction when its planet explodes. The only way the inhabitants could elicit help was to infect the crew of the* Enterprise *with the same "disease" that affected them. The hero of the day turns out to be the* Enterprise *transporters, which are able to restore everyone to their natural size.*

ALTMAN (**): A thoroughly goofy installment of the cartoon series. Having the crew of the *Enterprise* shrink and lose the ability to work their controls is more akin to *Dr. Shrinker* than *Star Trek.* Among other faux pas, Sulu acts wildly out of character as he panics over the crew's continually diminishing size. The show's most ludicrous moment is when Nurse Chapel almost drowns in a fish tank — although if the series was canon as it should be, we would learn that the uniforms are composed of algae xenalon. By the way, I'm still not sure exactly why the Terratins shrink the *Enterprise* crew, but I'm sure there's a good reason for it.

GROSS (**1/2): What saves the dopey premise behind this episode — that of the crew shrink-

ing in size — is the fact that it's due to a miniature city's attempt to be noticed. There's just something so Trekkian about that.

THAT WHICH SURVIVES

(TOS)
Original Airdate 1/24/69
Written by John Meredyth Lucas
Story by D. C. Fontana
Directed by Herb Wallerstein

While exploring unique geological conditions on an unnamed planet, Kirk, Spock and McCoy confront the holographic image of a woman named Losira. She is actually a warning device left behind by an ancient civilization to repel their enemies, the Kalandans. Her "touch" is death, and it is up to the crew of the Enterprise *to shut down the computers that continue to generate her lethal image.*

ALTMAN (**1/2): Despite having a pretty average plot too reminiscent of many of the shows that preceded it, this episode has some genuinely spooky moments as Losira attempts to apply her death touch to the ones on whom she has set her sights. Lee Meriwether turns in a good guest performance, and the visual effect of her teleportation is nicely realized. Her presence on the *Enterprise* is equally fearsome as she attempts to disable the ship and the crew begins the hunt for the invader.

GROSS (**): Hey, Lee Meriwether's a real cutie. And hey, there's a cool effect when a landing party is beaming down and Kirk reacts to the image of Losira in the transporter room while he's in the midst of transporting. And beyond that — let's move on.

THAW, THE

(VOY)

Original Airdate 4/29/96
Teleplay by Joe Menosky
Story by Richard Gadas and Michael Piller
Directed by Marvin Rush

The Voyager *encounters automated messages from a Kohl settlement that survived an environmental calamity by going into artificial hibernation. Bringing the cryo-chambers aboard, the crew finds that the humanoids have been perfectly preserved. In an attempt to free the Kohl from their stasis, Torres and Kim enter the chambers themselves and encounter a virtual environment created by the computer controlling the Kohl pods. They are confronted by the evil Clown, who epitomizes fear, holding all the Kohl survivors hostage. He warns that Torres and Kim will never be able to leave this virtual prison.*

ALTMAN (1/2*): "The Thaw" may very well be the worst episode of *Star Trek* ever, bar none. There is not a moment in this episode that betrays any degree of competence in any area ranging from writing to cinematography to acting to directing. In a way, "The Thaw" epitomizes *Voyager*'s lack of direction and malaise in its second season. An inept teaser doesn't give any reason for the *Voyager*'s becoming involved in the situation in the first place, as the crew receives a message from a supposedly lifeless planet. There is a slight chance that the nutty premise could have worked if it had been handled with any degree of adroitness. But from the outset, the premise, which calls out for bizarreness in every arena, is handled in a completely pedestrian manner. The

setup is mundane, the camera angles and directing are uninspired and the music is lame. There's nothing remotely scary about the concept other than that the producers of the show could have found it viable. This used to be the stuff that passed as *Trek* parody; now it is passed off as *Trek* itself. If nothing else, it's nice to know that people have a new episode (other than "Spock's Brain") to kick around.

GROSS (*1/2): An episode that is almost as headache inducing as the original series' "The Alternative Factor." Quite frankly, the episode doesn't make much sense, seeming as if it's trying to be surreal for the sake of being surreal. In some ways, it feels like a retread of *TNG*'s "Skin of Evil," in that the Clown is the embodiment of all things evil and takes pleasure from tormenting those around him. A major disappointment for *Voyager*'s second season, though it does give us a Janeway who's a bit more ruthless in solving the problem — tricking the Clown into oblivion — than Picard ever would have been. Guest star Michael McKean does his best, but you're almost expecting his buddy David Lander to walk in at any minute to reunite the Lenny and Squiggy team from *Laverne and Shirley.*

THINE OWN SELF

(TNG)
Original Airdate 2/14/94
Teleplay by Ronald D. Moore
Story by Christopher Hatton
Directed by Winrich Kolbe

An amnesiac Data is stranded on an alien world after his shuttlecraft crashes while carrying dangerously radioactive material, which is adversely affecting the residents of a village. Back on the Enterprise, Troi studies for her commander's test under the tutelage of a less than understanding Riker.

ALTMAN (***1/2): Ron Moore seamlessly balances two divergent story lines involving Troi's officer's test and Data being stranded on an alien world after a power surge erases his memory. It's easy to overlook the fact that the amnesia story is one of the most overused clichés in television because of the deft way in which Moore weaves his intricate tale of a town affected by radiation poisoning, which immediately blames the "stranger," Data, for its affliction. Even twenty-five years after "The Devil in the Dark," the "we must kill that which we don't understand" story line continues to be a dependable Trekkian theme.

GROSS (***): The Troi story line is handled nicely, allowing the audience to believe that Troi truly has earned her promotion and opening up the possibility that she will be able to do more than just counsel people. There's also some unexpected character tension between her and Riker over the commander's refusal to make things easy for her. Data's story is the real meat of the episode, and Brent

Spiner is brilliant as the android who doesn't know who or what he is. It's fascinating watching him try to acclimate himself to life in this new society. Director Rick Kolbe does a nice job of turning up the tension as the townspeople start to get ill and begin suspecting that Data is responsible. There are some nice moments between Brent Spiner and child actress Kimberly Callum as the young Gia. It's also terrific watching the town teacher/scientist/doctor/sage offer the most bizarre diagnoses and prescriptions, only to be contradicted by Data.

37'S, THE

(VOY)
Original Airdate 8/28/95
Written by Jeri Taylor and Brannon Braga
Directed by James L. Conway

The Voyager encounters an ancient Earth truck floating in space, which leads the crew to a planet where they find several human bodies perfectly preserved. Among them is Amelia Earhart (Sharon Lawrence), who was abducted in 1937 along with the others. Also existing on this planet is a utopian civilization that Janeway fears may cause many of her crew members to abandon their journey home.

ALTMAN (*): Another atrocious episode. Not only is it extremely hokey, its premise ludicrous and its execution problematic at best, but the show also puts its money in all the wrong places. The writers force the contrivance of landing the ship on the planet for no other reason than they wanted the spectacle of the ship descending onto the planet — despite the fact that this fails to service the plot. The real meat of the episode should have been in the dilemma arising from Janeway's possibly losing members of her crew who wanted to stay behind in what is described as a truly gorgeous and marvelous city. This is described only in passing and never visualized on-screen.

GROSS (***): Once you get beyond the teaser, which has a floating car in space that brings back memories of the classic *Saturday Night Live* skit chronicling the cancellation of the original series, there's a lot to be admired here, particularly the relationship between Janeway and Amelia Earhart, two kindred spirits no longer separated by the centuries. There's a nice bit of chemistry between Kate Mulgrew and Sharon Lawrence, and one only wishes that these two visionaries had more time to spend together. One major complaint regarding the episode is all the talk about this glorious city that these people have built and then Janeway's log informing us, "They were right; their city was beautiful." Uh, excuse me? Nonetheless, it was a nice kickoff for the second season.

THIS SIDE OF PARADISE

(TOS)
Original Airdate 3/2/67
Teleplay by D. C. Fontana
Story by Nathan Butler and D. C. Fontana
Directed by Ralph Senensky

Checking up on a Federation colony, Kirk's crew members find themselves infected by planetary spores that remove all negative feelings, resulting in a placid society. Kirk's problems begin as the influence of the spores spreads through the ship, with everyone wanting to remain on the planet. Even Spock is affected, as he lets down his guard and expresses his love for colonist Leila Kalomi (Jill Ireland). Kirk, who is alone on the Enterprise, must snap his first officer out of it before the starship burns up in the planet's atmosphere.

ALTMAN (***1/2): A great show in which Leonard Nimoy finally gets to let loose as the spores open up a decidedly emotional side of the stoic Vulcan. Jill Ireland is entrancing, and it's fun to watch the *Enterprise* crew give way to the power of the spores. The way Kirk deals with the mutiny on board and fights against the spores' overwhelming influence is a result of great writing, retaining a sense of fun tension and romance throughout. Just don't expect to find these plants at your local florist.

GROSS (****): Using the alien spores as an in, writer Dorothy Fontana is able to reveal a bit of Spock's past in terms of a previous relationship with Leila and give us a glimpse inside his heart by stripping away his Vulcan logic and allowing him to express the passion he has kept pent up for his entire life. As he says during the episode's coda, he was happy for the first time in his life. He means it, and we feel it. The episode also conveys a genuine feeling of suspense regarding the fate of the *Enterprise*. When Kirk is affected and is about to beam down, it's fascinating to watch him take a last look around and suddenly proclaim, as only

William Shatner can, "I — can't — leave!" Then, with an orgasmic facial expression, he manages to cure himself. Realizing that strong emotions will counteract the effect of the spores, he has Spock beamed aboard and provokes him into an unrelenting fistfight that is brilliantly choreographed. That fight, and the conversation between the two characters, is one of the best scenes the two actors ever have together.

THOLIAN WEB, THE

(TOS)
Original Airdate 11/15/68
Written by Judy Burns and Chet Richards
Directed by Ralph Senensky

While exploring the remnants of the USS Defiant, *Kirk is accidentally trapped in another dimension. Most of the crew members believe that he is dead, although they continue to see his apparition. Meanwhile, Spock works on trying to retrieve him when the* Defiant *enters our dimension for a short period of time. Add the Tholians, who don't want the* Enterprise *in their territory, to the mix, and you have a true dilemma for Spock and the crew.*

ALTMAN (***1/2): A wildly imaginative and unsettling show that is distinguished by some spectacular effects in which the Tholians try to destroy the *Enterprise* using their infamous web. The crew's growing distress caused by interphase, along with the desperate attempt to rescue Kirk, is adeptly handled with moody aplomb. The highlight, however, is the scene in which the perpetually sparring Spock and McCoy go to Kirk's quarters and watch

a tape recorded by the captain in the event of his death, putting a quick end to their war of words.

GROSS (***): There's a lot that's hokey about this episode, particularly Kirk's appearing to be a ghost. Anyone who sees him should know that he's not a ghost — he's wearing an environmental suit, for God's sake! Despite that kind of silliness, the idea of Spock and McCoy taking the first steps toward working together without Kirk as a buffer between them works well. Their respect, and even friendship, for each other comes to the surface during this time of crisis, aided in no small way by a computer log "message" that Kirk had the foresight to record. Great moment: The instant the Tholian deadline passes, they begin firing on the *Enterprise*. Spock's reaction? "The renowned Tholian punctuality."

THRESHOLD

(VOY)
Original Airdate 1/29/96
Teleplay by Brannon Braga
Story by Michael DeLuca
Directed by Alexander Singer

Lieutenant Paris takes on the responsibility of breaking the warp barrier, becoming the first person in modern Star Trek to make a transwarp flight. Soon after his shuttle returns from warp ten, however, Paris begins undergoing a startling metamorphosis. As his cell membranes begin to degrade, he dies. Hours after he is pronounced dead by the doctor, he is discovered breathing, and his body begins to mutate, transforming into a half-human/half-amphibian being that is intent on mating with Captain Janeway.

ALTMAN (**): As absurd as the premise is, I must admit that I find a certain amount of goofy fun in "Threshold," which, while taxing one's credulity, always manages to keep my interest and is never boring. Like some of the worst of the original series' third-season episodes, which have equally insipid premises, this episode entertains. The episode is less indulgent than some of Brannon Braga's other offbeat concepts, and the story is executed about as well as something this ridiculous could be. There's a really nice moment when the doctor and Kes watch all hell break loose in engineering on a monitor screen, unable to see what's happening beyond the scope of their monitor. Though clearly dictated by budget exigencies, this is still creative storytelling. Admittedly, the ending is downright wacky, but it's much livelier than most of *Voyager's* second season. In a way, the atmosphere is slightly reminiscent of *TNG's* "Genesis" (the crew is transformed into primates) and the original series' "Where No Man Has Gone Before" (though not nearly as good), in which Gary Mitchell evolves into a highly advanced superbeing that threatens the ship.

GROSS (**): One of the strangest episodes of *Voyager's* second season, with Tom Paris's transwarp journey reminding me of Keir Dullea's star trip in Stanley Kubrick's *2001*. What's most interesting about the episode is the shift in Paris's attitude, and it's a credit to Robert Duncan McNeill that he's able to pull it off. Paris's emotional arc goes from enthusiasm over being the first person to travel at transwarp to fear over what's happening to him, resentment at Janeway's allowing him to take the flight in the first place and, finally, arrogance when he feels that he's achieving a greatness no other human being could possibly understand. Visually, this is a truly bizarre, but effective, episode.

THROUGH THE LOOKING GLASS

(DS9)
Original Airdate 4/22/95
Written by Ira Steven Behr and Robert Hewitt Wolfe
Directed by Winrich Kolbe

O'Brien from the mirror universe arrives on Deep Space Nine and convinces Sisko to come back to help save the rebellion by taking the place of his recently murdered counterpart. Their mission: to rescue his dead wife, Jennifer Sisko (who died in this universe), before she is forced to develop a weapon to be used by the Bajoran/Cardassian alliance.

ALTMAN (***1/2): With moments of delightful high camp right out of *Buck Rogers* (the overplayed lesbian scenes with Kira and a man who looks uncomfortably like Tiger Man), in which Nana Visitor vamps in true Pamela Hemsley tradition, "Through the Looking Glass" is tightly plotted and engaging. Its linear story is intriguingly realized and at moments achieves a *Star Wars*–like effectiveness. It's not without flaws, mostly due to compressing an epic story line into one episode, as well as not milking the reunion of Sisko and Jennifer for all the pathos it's worth. Avery Brooks shines, and Terry Farrell, Max Grodenchik and Alexander Siddig rise to the occasion in small but effective cameos.

GROSS (***): An effective follow-up to "Crossover," moving the mirror universe closer to a space opera than the original series episode that spawned it. In many ways, it is like a classic Errol Flynn adventure, eschewing allegories or examinations of polar opposites of the regular characters and simply allowing this ensemble to take on what are essentially new roles in an epic pirate adventure in space. The episode is a lot of fun, and it doesn't have anything more than that in mind. Director Rick Kolbe seems the perfect choice for this type of adventure. See also "Mirror, Mirror," "Crossover" and "Shattered Mirror."

TIME AND AGAIN

(VOY)
Original Airdate 1/30/95
Teleplay by Michael Piller and David Kemper
Story by David Kemper
Directed by Les Landau

The Voyager's sensors pick up a shock wave in space generated by an explosion on a nearby planet. An Away Team beams down to investigate the situation, only to discover that all life-forms have been wiped out. Shortly thereafter, subspace fractures transport Janeway and Paris back to a time shortly before the explosion, and they discover that they are responsible for what happened.

ALTMAN (**): A thinly veiled allegory of the nuclear power debates of today. To be honest, I vacillated a number of times while watching this episode for the first time. At first I was charmed by the banter between Harry Kim and Tom Paris, then revolted by the outrageous and indecipherable technobabble, intrigued by Janeway's and Paris's plight and finally exasperated by the thoroughly unsatisfying wrap-up. Playing like a second-rate "Cause & Effect," this episode is a good example of what happens when the writers tackle a half-baked notion without taking the time to craft a logical resolution. Although the situation itself is interesting enough, embellished by some good photography by Marvin Rush and welcome location shooting, the resolution of the story line, in which the crew members find themselves revisiting the planet whose destruction they caused, is as infuriating as the show's lack of narrative logic. If the crew members discover the destroyed planet and learn that they are responsible, how could they have caused the accident in the first place?

GROSS (**): Hang on a second while I bang my head against the wall a couple of more times. Nope, I still don't understand how the heck *Voyager* caused this disaster prior to even arriving on the planet, and I don't think any distortion in the space-time continuum is going to explain it. Another problem with this episode is the fact that these aliens don't seem very alien at all. Not a highlight of the first season.

TIME SQUARED

(TNG)
Original Airdate 4/1/89
Written by Maurice Hurley
Directed by Joseph Scanlan

The Enterprise *rescues a disabled shuttlecraft and finds an incoherent Captain Picard aboard. Reviewing the ship's logs, the crew discovers that the shuttle was sent back in time to warn them of the* Enterprise's *impending demise in a deadly space anomaly. Now Picard and his people must determine exactly what to do.*

ALTMAN (**): What could have been a *Trek* classic is undone by ambiguity, illogic and a lack of narrative cohesiveness. The premise is superb and unsettling, as Picard goes back in time to warn of the *Enterprise's* imminent demise, but the strange time anomaly responsible for bringing about these mysterious events is never explained. In addition, Picard's indecisive behavior is totally out of character, which is a shame because the premise is good. Had writer Maurice Hurley been able to use the story as a prelude to the events of "Q Who" as he intended, perhaps the episode would have packed a lot more punch.

GROSS (*1/2): An intriguing premise is sent into disarray by a lack of dramatic focus and enough illogic to make the average Vulcan chuck his cookies. The *Enterprise* can survive destruction by a space vortex by piloting the ship *into* that vortex? Oh, yeah, that works. Patrick Stewart, as always, manages to make everything believable from a character point of view, but that's not enough. Pretty much a mess.

TIME TRAP

(TAS)
Original Airdate 11/24/73
Written by Joyce Perry
Directed by Hal Sutherland

The Enterprise *gets trapped in the Delta Triangle, an intergalactic version of the Bermuda Triangle, which has become something of a graveyard for vessels that have disappeared over the centuries. Kirk and the crew are shocked to discover that the descendants of the crews of these various vessels are still alive and have formed something of a government under the umbrella title the Elysian Council. Escape from the triangle is deemed impossible until Kirk and the Klingon Kor (from "Errand of Mercy") realize that they have to work together to discover the key to this elusive puzzle.*

ALTMAN (***): Although the "Bermuda Triangle of space" aspect is a fairly routine fantasy chestnut, the resulting cooperation between the Klingons and the *Enterprise* is adeptly done. The decision to depict a number of existing Federation races representing the many lost ships, including the Andorians, Tellarites, Vulcans, Orions and even the plant creatures from "The Infinite Vulcan," is a nice touch. Overreliance on Nichelle Nichols and James Doohan for voice work (particularly Doohan, rather than John Colicos, as Commander Kor) is less effective.

GROSS (**1/2): A very Trekkian episode that is highlighted from a UN-like conference room, with representatives from a variety of

Trek aliens working together peacefully (which in some ways predates *TNG*'s "Birthright, Part II," in which Romulans and Klingons live and work together in peace). This is a very positive message, and Kirk working alongside Kor adds to it — until the Klingons predictably attempt to sabotage the *Enterprise*.

TIME'S ARROW, PART I

(TNG)
Original Airdate 6/15/92
Written by Joe Menosky and Michael Piller
Directed by Les Landau

Data's head is discovered in a cave on Earth, which prompts the Enterprise crew to lead an investigation into Earth's past, where they discover aliens abducting humans from the nineteenth century to the future. They also meet Guinan.

ALTMAN (**): When Data's head is unearthed in a cave, along with other remnants from five hundred years ago, the *Enterprise* goes in search of extraterrestrials in a disappointing cliff-hanger. The headless imagery is ironic, since this is a totally by-the-numbers, mindless episode. It misses the mark, despite opening promisingly with the discovery of Data's head and the crew tap-dancing around the issue of Data's impending demise. The episode is so full of redundant technobabble that it begins to sound like Lewis Carroll substituting for meaningful character bits, deep-sixing a promising premise. Whoopie Goldberg is a disappointment, playing a Victorian era Guinan far too anachronistically. She sounds as if she's from the

Bronx rather than turn-of-the-century San Francisco. In the end, "Time's Arrow" is a poor man's version of "City on the Edge of Forever," with a dash of *The Young Indiana Jones Chronicles'* kiddy predilection for featuring historical characters thrown in for good measure. Hey, look, it's Jack London and Mark Twain! The fun of time travel is squandered on a silly premise, with nearly the entire senior staff sauntering back in time, surrounded by a bunch of Roger Corman–type aliens in the show's less than punchy cliff-hanger.

GROSS (**): As the final credits roll on this fifth-season cliff-hanger, one can't help but be disappointed. Both "Best of Both Worlds" and "Redemption" — even "Unification, Part I" — keep you wondering what the next step might be. But "Time's Arrow" elicits only a confused "Huh?" Although the opening gives the impression that a great mystery is about to unfold, the road to solving it goes from interesting to confusing to annoying. *TNG* has done some great episodes involving time travel. This isn't one of them.

TIME'S ARROW, PART II

(TNG)
Original Airdate 9/21/92
Written by Jeri Taylor
Directed by Les Landau

The Away Team enters the temporal distortion on Devida Two and finds itself in the nineteenth century, hoping to rescue Data and put an end to the murders by alien life-forms on Earth. While they attempt to return to the twenty-fourth century,

Samuel Clemens (Jerry Hardin) is inadvertently transported to the future and the starship.

ALTMAN (**1/2): Though superior to the first installment, a rarity for a *TNG* cliff-hanger, and boasting above-average special effects and period costume and production design, "Time's Arrow, Part II" is still muddled by technobabble and a story in which the menace is never clearly defined, squandering a potentially intriguing time-travel scenario. Not surprisingly, Jeri Taylor improves on part I by injecting some pleasant character drama, including an extremely amusing scene in which Picard attempts to persuade the landlady at his boardinghouse that the Away Team is a troupe of actors performing *A Midsummer Night's Dream*. Also of note is Jerry Hardin's scenery-chewing guest turn as Samuel Clemens. The episode's conclusion reverts back to the past, rather than wrapping up the Picard/Guinan story arc, which proves jarring and emotionally unrewarding.

GROSS (**1/2): You have to give the writers a lot of credit: It's obvious that they tried to create a time-travel yarn with plenty of twists and turns. But this one is so convoluted that you walk away from it needing an aspirin rather than being creatively satisfied. Jerry Hardin does a credible job as Samuel Clemens, but after a while the character starts to grate. And why, no matter what the situation, would they let this guy see *anything* once he makes it to the twenty-fourth century?

TIMESCAPE

(TNG)
Original Airdate 6/14/93
Written by Brannon Braga
Directed by Adam Nimoy

Returning to the Enterprise via a runabout, Picard, LaForge, Troi and Data find the ship trapped in time in the middle of a battle with a Romulan warbird. Leading an investigation aboard the ships in stasis, Picard realizes that they must reverse time if they have any hope of saving the Enterprise and Dr. Crusher, who has been wounded by a disrupter blast.

ALTMAN (**1/2): Although it hits many of the same beats (and is just as ludicrous) as "The Next Phase," which is more fun, "Timescape" begins promisingly with some genuinely amiable character interplay that fizzles in the last two acts. Brannon Braga postulates an intriguing science-fiction dilemma that is handled far more adeptly than the first season's time debacle, "We'll Always Have Paris," or even Classic *Trek*'s "Wink of an Eye" (in which Kirk is sped up in time and everyone else on the ship appears to be immobile). The episode stumbles, however, when it comes time to explain the phenomenon and solve the tech. Sophomore director Adam Nimoy acquits himself nicely throughout.

GROSS (**1/2): An episode that could easily have been an episode of *The Twilight Zone,* highlighted by great special effects that somehow manage to overshadow the story itself. Still, it's intriguing to see a time-travel story told on a smaller scale than one in which the entire galaxy is at stake.

TIN MAN

(TNG)
Original Airdate 4/29/90
Written by Dennis Putnam Bailey and David Bischoff
Directed by Robert Scheerer

A telepathic Betazoid, Tam Elbrun (Harry Groener), is assigned to the Enterprise *to communicate with a new life-form, a living space vessel dubbed "Tin Man." Complications arise with the intervention of two Romulan warships intent on keeping the life-form from falling into Federation hands.*

ALTMAN (**): *Star Trek: The Motion Picture* meets "Encounter at Farpoint" in this familiar story recounting myriad tried-and-true *Trek* themes. A fine score by Jay Chattaway helps this derivative story, which features a fine guest performance by Harry Groener as the egotistical Betazoid negotiator, Tam Elbrun. The Romulans play too small a role in the proceedings and could have offered a great deal more menace.

GROSS (**): One thing we learn from this episode is that Deanna Troi is just about the only Betazoid who is not spoiled, self-centered, manipulative and just plain insensitive to those around her. Data has a nice moment when Tam Elbrun looks at one of his paintings hidden under a cover and Data gives him a look conveying that he'd like the Betazoid to respect his privacy. How positively — human. The rest of the story is deriv-

ative of *Star Trek: The Motion Picture* and "Encounter at Farpoint," as well as *Star Trek V: The Final Frontier.* Everyone tries his or her best, but it just doesn't jell.

TO THE DEATH

(DS9)
Original Airdate 5/11/96
Written by Ira Steven Behr and Robert Hewitt Wolfe
Directed by LeVar Burton

A strange alliance forms when Sisko leads a team of his officers and some Jem'Hadar soldiers in an effort to stop Jem'Hadar renegades from strengthening their power base.

ALTMAN (***1/2): This action-packed episode ends with a scene of extraordinary carnage as the crew combats the Jem'Hadar renegades, but what lies at its heart is far more compelling. There's some remarkable dialogue in which Sisko spars with the Jem'Hadar leader, played powerfully by Clarence Williams III. There are also some witty exchanges between various characters, and Worf has never been used to better effect. He works superbly in providing a counterpoint to the jingoistic bravado of the Jem'Hadar soldiers and delivers the episode's best line in assuring Sisko that if the Jem'Hadar leader kills him, "he will not live to boast about it." I was pleased to see the obscure second-season *TNG* episode "Contagion" used to provide the backstory for the Iconian gateway, which is well realized by Herman

Zimmerman and his team of art directors.

GROSS (***1/2): As with the best of *Trek*, no matter what the series, action is supported by strong characterization and dialogue, and this episode has it all. LeVar Burton manages to generate a constant sense of tension during the tentative alliance between Starfleet and the Jem'Hadar (these actors turned directors certainly are a surprise on *Trek*). Most important, the audience learns that there are some chinks in the armor of the Jem'Hadar and that the Founders may not be so invincible as they seem to think. See also "Contagion."

TOMORROW IS YESTERDAY

(TOS)
Original Airdate 1/26/67
Written by D. C. Fontana
Directed by Michael O'Herlihy

After an encounter with a black hole, the Enterprise is hurled back in time to the twentieth century and Earth orbit. The starship is photographed by Air Force captain Christopher (Roger Perry), who is flying his jet when the ship momentarily enters the atmosphere. Kirk has the jet placed in the ship's tractor beam, but it proves too frail and breaks up. Christopher is brought aboard before the fatal moment, and Kirk has to figure out how to return him without threatening the course of history.

ALTMAN (***): *The X-Files* meets *Star Trek*. Having the *Enterprise* thrown back in time and mistaken for a UFO is a great, juicy premise, and everything but the clunky special effects and convoluted tempo-ral mechanics works like gangbusters, especially the teaser, which is one of the best ever. When Captain Christopher finds himself beamed aboard the *Enterprise*, it's far more adeptly handled than Alfre Woodard's presence in *Star Trek VIII: First Contact.* (Christopher's shock at seeing Mr. Spock is repeated beat for beat when Woodard's Lily first sees Worf.) Kirk's attempt to retrieve incriminating footage of the *Enterprise* leads to some great moments on twentieth-century Earth. The glitch that has the main computer flirting with the crew members in a decidedly sexy, feminine way is an enjoyable added touch.

GROSS (***): *Star Trek's* first time-travel episode, and pretty much a winner. It's interesting to watch Kirk's naïveté in beaming Captain Christopher aboard, needing Spock to point out the impact such a "visit" might have on history. Kirk and company's efforts to erase all evidence of their sighting on Earth are fairly suspenseful, and the episode is only marred by the denouement, in which the *Enterprise* travels back in time to its initial arrival and beams Captain Christopher back into his own body before he saw the starship. An inventive idea, but it makes absolutely no sense. A nice turn by guest star Roger Perry as Christopher, who's told by Spock that he will make no significant contribution to history but then learns that his yet-to-be-conceived son will play an integral role in the space program.

TOO SHORT A SEASON

(TNG)
Original Airdate 2/8/88
Teleplay by Michael Michaelian and
D. C. Fontana
Story by Michael Michaelian
Directed by Rob Bowman

The Enterprise *responds to a hostage situation on Mordan IV, where the lead terrorist, Karnas (Michael Pataki), demands that negotiations be handled by the seventy-year-old Admiral Jameson (Clayton Rohner). The admiral, it's revealed, was on that world four decades earlier and negotiated another hostage situation, which ultimately resulted in decades of civil war. Now Karnas wants revenge against Jameson, but fate may have beaten him to the punch. Jameson has taken a youth elixir that is rapidly de-aging him, but the side effects could be fatal.*

ALTMAN (*1/2): A talky, high-concept show that the original series would have done far better. Instead of dealing with the implications of the septuagenarian ambassador's return to youth and how it affects the ongoing hostage crisis, we get a lot of talk and never even see the hostages. Clayton Rohner as Admiral Jameson makes it through the show far better than his lousy old-age makeup. The episode ends with the ambassador falling dead, which is about how I felt at the end of the show, too.

GROSS (**1/2): The episode suffers from the fact that it is truly a guest star show, in which the crew of the *Enterprise* does little more than provide transport so that the drama can unfold. To be fair, Clayton Rohner effortlessly

conveys the various characterizations of Jameson, marred only by the fact that the elderly makeup isn't quite as effective as it should be. The notion of aging backward is old hat for the genre.

TRANSFIGURATIONS

(TNG)
Original Airdate 6/19/90
Written by Rene Echevarria
Directed by Tom Benko

An amnesiac alien being (Mark La Mura) is saved from certain death by the Enterprise. *Dr. Crusher then discovers that he is undergoing an evolutionary process.*

ALTMAN (**1/2): Though a familiar story, writer Rene Echevarria brings a fresh approach to the *TNG* characters, redeeming the show's cliché-ridden premise. The episode is filled with a number of enjoyable character bits, including Worf's unlikely tutelage of Geordi LaForge about how to pick up women. Even Beverly Crusher's first romantic entanglement with an alien is well handled. It's a good thing the character bits work because the evolving-alien story line is as tired as it gets.

GROSS (**1/2): Mark La Mura does a nice turn as the seeming miracle worker aboard the *Enterprise*. Through his interactions, a number of significant character moments occur.

TRIALS AND TRIBBLATIONS

(DS9)

Teleplay by Ronald D. Moore and René Echevarria

Story by Ira Steven Behr and Robert Hewitt Wolfe

Directed by Jonathan West

The Defiant *goes back in time to the twenty-third century to save the life of Captain James T. Kirk, who is the target of a disgraced Klingon (Charlie Brill) seeking vengeance. Sisko, Dax, Odo and Worf must stop him without disrupting the time stream.*

ALTMAN (****): The *Trek* thirtieth anniversary celebration ended with a wonderful tribute to the original series in the skillful hands of two of *DS9*'s best writers, Ron Moore and Rene Echevarria. "Trials and Tribblations" is nothing less than a *Trek* masterpiece. Rather than simply exploiting the cutting-edge technology at their disposal, the writers tell a story that is filled with fond admiration for their TV progenitors and succeeds in nearly every area, from special effects to production design to acting. The re-creation of the original sets and Gary Hutzel's exquisite visual effects work well, as the original *Enterprise* and K-7 are breathtaking. It's hysterical when Terry Farrell, dressed in her hot red miniskirt and portraying a Trill obsessed with making love to Klingons, admits to Sisko that she slept with McCoy. Even Michael Dorn's Worf gets a chance to shine when he regales Odo with tales of the great Tribble hunt. The only misstep is an inept Dennis McCarthy score (mandated by Rick Berman), which eschews Jerry Fielding's original score.

GROSS (****): This is a brilliant piece of television, not so much in the plot but in the creative inventiveness that allows a 1996 show to interact with its predecessor from thirty years earlier. The insertion of Avery Brooks and company into "The Trouble with Tribbles" is flawlessly accomplished, providing a great sense of nostalgia with an equally great sense of purpose. What could be nobler than for Sisko to head back into the past in an effort to save the life of Captain Kirk? There are wonderful flourishes throughout, such as Dax recognizing McCoy as someone a part of her had an affair with ("He had the hands of a surgeon," she says with a sigh); the incredible lineup after the K-7 bar fight, which now has O'Brien and Bashir among the *Enterprise* crewmen, with O'Brien actually conversing with Kirk; an explanation for the Tribbles continually falling out of an overhead hatch and hitting Kirk in the head (Dax and Sisko are tossing them aside looking for a bomb); a lame but hysterical discussion of the difference between Klingons then and now; and a final scene between Sisko and Kirk on the bridge of the *Enterprise* that is incredibly well realized (using footage of Kirk from the "Mirror, Mirror" episode). Productionwise, the re-created sets, particularly of the bridge, are a sight to behold; new models of the *Enterprise* and K-7 are gorgeous (leading one to wonder why Paramount doesn't upgrade the F/X in some of the classic episodes à la George Lucas and *Star Wars*). There is also a humorous bracketing sequence involving the Temporal Police, who are questioning Sisko as to why he went back in time and what changes in the time stream, if any, he may have made. These are very funny, self-mocking commentaries about supposed paradoxes that surround every time-travel story. Even more impressive, the producers were able to get actor Charlie Brill to return to the Klingon role he played three decades earlier. Kudos to everyone involved. See also "The Trouble with Tribbles" and "More Tribbles, More Troubles."

and intense feeling this episode demands.

GROSS (***): Whereas *Star Trek VI: The Undiscovered Country* brought audiences into the Klingon judicial system, "Tribunal" enters the Cardassian world, as O'Brien is quite literally fighting for his life. While Sisko and Odo attempt to learn the truth behind the weapons shipments to the Maquis, O'Brien becomes increasingly desperate in his attempts to prove his innocence in a system that finds people guilty no matter what they do. Look for a nice turn by Fritz Weaver as O'Brien's designated lawyer, Kovat.

TRIBUNAL

(DS9)
Original Airdate 6/6/94
Written by Bill Dial
Directed by Avery Brooks

O'Brien is arrested and brought to Cardassia to stand trial for smuggling weapons to the Maquis. Behind the scenes, Sisko and Odo investigate and learn that the Cardassians themselves were involved in the smuggling to help fuel the conflict.

ALTMAN (**1/2): A show that has kafkaesque aspirations plays out surprisingly conventionally, with a predictable deus ex machina resolution. Despite such nice flourishes as an Orwellian monitor screen in the center of the Cardassian capital, the attempt to provide an incisive look at a totalitarian culture doesn't work. Dark lighting doesn't translate into the dark

TROUBLE WITH TRIBBLES, THE

(TOS)
Original Airdate 12/29/67
Written by David Gerrold
Directed by Joseph Pevney

An emergency distress signal brings the Enterprise to space station K-7. There, the undersecretary of agricultural affairs, Nilz Barris, is panicking because the Klingons are in the quadrant and he wants the grain in the station's storage compartments protected because it is the only grain that will take root on Sherman's Planet. Kirk is not amused, believing that Barris misused the emergency signal, and he can barely be bothered to post two guards near the compartments. Things get out of hand, however, when Uhura is given a furry Tribble by space trader Cyrano Jones (Stanley Adams), and the creature multiplies like crazy until the Tribbles threaten everyone and everything.

ALTMAN (****): "The Trouble with Tribbles" receives an able assist from William Campbell as Captain Koloth, who gets an unwanted introduction to the cute, furry pets known as Tribbles. David Gerrold's script is not only exceptionally funny but also quite clever in weaving its espionage plot through the light proceedings. Stanley Adams as Cyrano Jones gives a classic performance, and Jerry Fielding's score is unforgettable (unless you're Rick Berman, who apparently had no trouble forgetting it). The show also is a great showcase for the supporting cast, particularly Chekov and Uhura. On videocassette, it's the only love money can buy.

GROSS (****): The episode proving that *Star Trek* doesn't have to be preachy, philosophical or even serious to work. It's an all-out comedy in which everyone stays perfectly in character, thus making the situation even funnier. First-time writer David Gerrold scores a home run in an episode that gives us Klingons, Spock at his driest, Kirk at his most exasperated and, of course, those reproducing fur balls, the Tribbles. First-rate all the way. Take note of the sequence in which Kirk is buried in a flood of Tribbles after opening a hatchway on the K-7 space station. Want to know why Tribbles sporadically hit him in the head? Check out the *Deep Space Nine* episode "Trials and Tribblations" for the answer. See also: "More Tribbles, More Troubles" and "Trials and Tribblations."

TRUE Q

(TNG)
Original Airdate 10/26/92
Written by Rene Echevarria
Directed by Robert Scheerer

An Enterprise *intern named Amanda (Olivia d'Abo) is revealed to be a member of the Q Continuum. Q (John de Lancie) pays another unwanted visit to the ship, during which he confides to Picard that Amanda's parents were actually Q. Amanda must choose between joining him among the Q and death.*

ALTMAN (**1/2): Although this episode boasts one of the most heavy-handed B stories since the "Symbiosis" drug diatribe, in which the Tagrians' environmental imbroglio is depicted, the heart of the story is Amanda's dilemma, featuring some witty and malevolent banter between Q and Picard. The plot echoes that of the first season's "Hide & Q," in which Riker is given the power of the Q, but "True Q" is subtler and more skillfully handled — mostly as a result of some deft writing by Rene Echevarria and the performance of the always reliable John de Lancie, who manages to get better with every outing. In addition, David Stipes's visual effects provide an able assist and some scope to an intimate episode.

GROSS (**): Not one of the strongest Q episodes produced. The acting is earnest enough, but the story itself has elements of the original series' "Charlie X" and *TNG*'s "Hide & Q." A middle-of-the-road show.

TURNABOUT INTRUDER
(TOS)
Original Airdate 6/3/69
Written by Arthur Singer
Story by Gene Roddenberry
Directed by Herb Wallerstein

Kirk finds himself the object of Dr. Janice Lester's hatred. She was once romantically involved with the captain and has been unable to assume a command of her own. Now she wants revenge and has found it in an alien device that can transfer her mind to Kirk's body and vice versa.

ALTMAN (*): Despite this being the single most sexist episode in *Star Trek* history, I almost wish Janice Lester's claim that a woman could never captain a starship had been heeded when they hired Kate Mulgrew for *Voyager*. Alas, it was not to be. It's hard to believe that Kirk, imprisoned in Lester's body, can't convince Spock and McCoy who he is, given all that they've shared in the past. The nonsensical farce is worth enduring, however, just to watch William Shatner cavort through the show as though he's been taken over by an unstable woman. His hissy fits and wildly over-the-top emoting, especially when he screams, "I am Captain Kirk!" and orders the deaths of Scotty and McCoy ("This is mutiny!") are priceless. An anti-classic.

GROSS (*): Remember all those impersonations of a wildly enunciating William Shatner that were the rage a few years back? This is probably the episode that provided the most fuel for that fire. What in the world was the man thinking? Once Lester takes over

Kirk's body, barely a minute goes by that doesn't betray the fact that this is *not* the good captain. The third season of the original series began with "Spock's Brain" and concluded with this turkey — talk about bookends.

TUVIX
(VOY)
Original Airdate 5/6/96
Teleplay by Kenneth Biller
Story by Andrew Price and Mark Gaberman
Directed by Cliff Bole

While beaming back from taking vegetable samples on an unexplored planet, Neelix and Tuvok are combined into one person. Dubbing himself Tuvix, he finds himself emotionally drawn to Kes, who doesn't return his feelings. Quickly becoming a valued member of the team, Tuvix forces the crew members to confront a dilemma when they find a way to separate Tuvix back into Tuvok and Neelix, but Tuvix does not want to be separated.

ALTMAN (**): Ken Biller once again takes a thoroughly untenable premise and perhaps one of the show's hokiest high concepts and actually makes it watchable. The idea of the two being combined into one and the subsequent hijinks are laughable, but Tuvix's desire to live, along with the issues it raises among the crew, is noteworthy. One scene that doesn't work is an unintentionally hysterical "sunshine day" montage in which Tuvix performs his duties aboard the ship under a Janeway voice-over. The show seems like a 1970s sitcom as Tuvix solves everyone's problems, cooks and cleans. It's also a little difficult to believe that Neelix is the only capable chef on board, so when he disappears, the crew is plunged into chaos trying to figure out how to cook in a scene that surpasses even *Star Trek VI*'s Klingon translation for sheer over-the-top stupidity.

GROSS (***): On the surface, this seems like another rip-off of "The Enemy Within," but "Tuvix" manages to explore the creation of a new being effectively and raises the question of whether this hybrid's right to live should take precedence over his component parts. Kudos to guest star Tom Wright, who creates a character embodying the personality traits of both his progenitors. His pleas to remain alive as this new incarnation are extremely touching, and we can see that Janeway's decision is a difficult one.

TWISTED

(VOY)
Original Airdate 10/2/95
Teleplay by Kenneth Biller
Story by Arnold Rudnick and Rick Hosek
Directed by Kim Friedman

A spatial distortion results in the transformation of the structural layout of Voyager. *As the ship is compressed and twisted, the crew must work frantically to stop the process before the ship is destroyed. During their attempts to reverse the distortion, Janeway is disabled by the strange force, Neelix is trapped and the rest of the crew is isolated in the maze of the ever-changing ship. With time running out, the remaining officers hole up in the holodeck bar as the ship begins to close in on them.*

ALTMAN (*): A bottle show of the worst kind, "Twisted" involves the crew in a laborious cat and mouse

game in search of the bridge. Nothing makes very much sense, and the only things that work are a few brief character moments in the wake of Janeway's being sidelined, which show how well the ensemble can work together without her. Unfortunately, there are some dreadful touchy-feely moments in which the crew members confess their admiration for each other. Stupidest line: As *Voyager* is about to be destroyed, B'Elanna Torres asks Chakotay what he's doing, and he answers, "I'm trying to contact my spirit guide." There's also an idiotic B story straight out of *TNG*'s "Manhunt" in which Judy Geeson's holodeck barmaid puts the moves on Robert Picardo's holodeck doctor. Is this someone's idea of humor?

GROSS (*): An episode that's so muddled and confusing that it could have been a third-season episode of the original series — *if* those producers had picked it up. A real disappointment on just about every level.

U

ULTIMATE COMPUTER, THE

(TOS)
Original Airdate 3/8/68
Written by D. C. Fontana
Story by Lawrence N. Wolfe
Directed by John Meredyth Lucas

The Federation gives Dr. Richard Daystrom (William Marshall) permission to hook his state-of-

the-art computer, the M-5, into the Enterprise to prove that a starship can be run more efficiently by a machine than by humans. Kirk starts feeling useless, until the M-5, whose memory patterns are based on Daystrom's, acts without logic, destroying another starship for no reason.

ALTMAN (***1/2): A sensational story in which William Marshall powerfully plays the disturbed Dr. Richard Daystrom and Kirk wrestles with being replaced by a computer. McCoy injects the requisite humanism into the proceedings, which gives the episode its subtext and power. There's some great space battle action, and Barney Russo is a welcome addition as Commodore Wesley. As in the best *Star Trek* episodes, there's a genuine emotional heart to the space action, which is among the series' finest. When Kirk talks the M-5 into self-destruction, it's literally a triumph of man over machine.

GROSS (***1/2): William Marshall's arrogant performance as Dr. Daystrom brings a true sense of power to this episode. The M-5 represents a legitimate threat to the *Enterprise* and the Federation, and its firing on friendly vessels is fairly powerful. Kirk's feeling of losing his usefulness in the face of a supposedly perfect machine is more reflective of the current Internet era than of life three decades ago. What hurts this episode more than anything is the solution of Kirk talking a machine to death. You'd think Nomad or Landru would have gotten the word out. See also "One of Our Planets Is Missing."

UNIFICATION, PART I
(TNG)
Original Airdate 11/4/91
Written by Jeri Taylor
Directed by Les Landau

When the Federation suspects that Ambassador Spock (Leonard Nimoy) has defected to the Romulans, Picard and Data are sent to Romulus to ascertain his true motives.

ALTMAN (***): Spock is back, and Jeri Taylor delivers one of her best scripts for part I, although she's let down by some weak performances, including the insufferable Karen Hensel as a Starfleet admiral in the show's opening teaser. (She makes Fran Drescher sound like an elocution professor.) Scoring an acting coup is Mark Lenard, who returns as Sarek in one of the show's best scenes. Surprisingly, "Unification" features some great comic moments (unlike the dour proceedings of the follow-up). Picard's desperate attempt to communicate with Gowron to borrow a cloaked ship is a classic. The penultimate moment, in which Spock emerges from the shadows in the cliffhanger, gives me chills every time I see it.

GROSS (***): There are a hell of a lot of great moments in this episode: Picard using his "influence" and "gratitude" with Gowron to gain a cloaked Klingon ship; the whole business between Riker and the space junkyard quartermaster; and Data and Picard alone in quarters on the Klingon ship, with Picard trying to get some sleep on the extremely uncomfortable bed, while Data just stands there, staring. The intrigue over whether Spock has defected — despite the fact that we *know* he hasn't — mounts nicely, and the sequence between Picard and Sarek is quite effective. Two complaints: The producers bludgeon the viewer with the fact that Picard and Sarek shared a special bond, and Spock's extremely hyped appearance on the show takes place, quite literally, during the episode's final two seconds. (Note: Spock investigates his father's death in William Shatner's *Star Trek* novel, *Avenger.*) See also "Sarek."

UNIFICATION, PART II

(TNG)
Original Airdate 11/11/91
Written by Michael Piller
Directed by Cliff Bole

Picard, who has found Spock on Romulus, learns that the Vulcan has come to the Romulan homeworld on a secret mission to reunite the Romulans with their progenitors on Vulcan but quickly discovers that he is a pawn in Sela's (Denise Crosby) plans to invade Vulcan.

ALTMAN (**): The conclusion fails to live up to the hype, not only because of a lousy script by Michael Piller but also because Leonard Nimoy sleepwalks his way through the episode, which he probably considered a glorified commercial for *Star Trek VI: The Undiscovered Country.* The episode is overstuffed with subplots between Picard, Spock and Data. Despite the obligatory nod to Kirk, writer Michael Piller stays as far

away from paying homage to the old show as possible, constantly reminding the audience about Picard's place in the original *Trek* mythos thanks to his mind-meld with Sarek. He even has the audacity to bring back Sela, played by the talentless Denise Crosby. "I don't get to write much in this job," the Romulan tells Spock in a quiet moment, completely capturing the mundane level to which this episode sinks. More palatable is an amusing *Casablanca*-like bar sequence involving Riker and a Ferengi scoundrel whose humor seems out of place in one of the most eagerly awaited episodes of the series.

GROSS (**1/2): Clichés be damned, getting here *was* half the fun. Whereas part I is filled with moments of suspense and a great deal of charm and humor, part II just kind of lies there — dark, somber and somewhat depressing. Granted, we're dealing with serious matters, and no one expects them to throw a party for Mr. Spock's return, but a bit more liveliness would have helped the episode. Some of the political intrigue is interesting, but Sela seems out of place. More important, after all the buildup, Leonard Nimoy seems emotionally detached (Could this have anything to do with his playing an older, wearier Spock? Nah!), and there is an annoying tendency to cut away from events on Romulus to deal with the *Enterprise.* I wish someone would tell Michael Piller that it's OK to like the original series and using it only deepens the tapestry that the new series are weaving. See also *Star Trek VI: The Undiscovered Country*.

UNNATURAL SELECTION

(TNG)
Original Airdate 1/28/89
Written by John Mason and Michael Gray
Directed by Paul Lynch

A genetic mutation on an experimental colony begins to age the colonists, and a genetically created being holds the clues to a cure. Dr. Pulaski beams aboard a shuttlecraft to find an antidote, and then she discovers that she has been infected with the malady and is rapidly growing older.

ALTMAN (1/2*): An interminable retread of the original series' "The Deadly Years," in which Dr. Pulaski gets to join the geriatric set. One of the most overused *Trek* gimmicks is resurrected as the transporter helps to restore Pulaski to perfect health using her stored molecular pattern (it happens twice in the animated series and then again in "Lonely Among Us"). Too bad they didn't just check the logbooks and use McCoy's vaccine from the original show. Among *TNG*'s worst episodes.

GROSS (*1/2): Dr. Crusher's second-season replacement, Dr. Kate Pulaski, takes center stage in this episode that satisfactorily explores a mounting antagonism between her and Picard. That's the good news. The bad news is the rest of the episode, which is derivative not only of the original series ("The Deadly Years") but also of its animated spin-off. The ending in

particular, which involves Dr. Pulaski's molecular pattern being locked in the transporter computer, is lifted wholesale from the final animated episode, "The Counter-Clock Incident."

UP THE LONG LADDER

(TNG)
Original Airdate 5/20/89
Written by Melinda Snodgrass
Directed by Winrich Kolbe

The Enterprise *serves as a rescue ship transporting a primitive rural farming community away from their doomed planet, along with an advanced race of clones. The clones, realizing they are nearing their extinction due to a lack of genetically replicable material, plan to copy Pulaski's and Riker's DNA in hopes of restoring their race — in spite of the duo's objections.*

ALTMAN (**): A somewhat silly voyage that, despite turning heavy-handed at the conclusion, is redeemed by its humor and light touch. The show's not very subtle pro-choice message is a surprisingly blatant stand for *Star Trek* to take in favor of abortion rights. For a show that often shies away from controversial social issues (unlike its progenitor), it's refreshing to see *TNG* show its stripes, even if it risks alienating pro-life viewers. Elsewhere, pigs and farmers presiding over a different kind of menagerie on board the *Enterprise* is pretty kooky stuff, but it's rooted in an interesting sci-fi story involving two dissimilar races being forced to come together. The original title was "Send in the

Clones," but it was probably deemed too clever for *TNG*, which, unlike the original series, is creatively bankrupt when it comes to episode titles.

GROSS (**1/2): Surprisingly, the colonist story line is more effective than the science-fiction aspects of the episode. Although the idea of cloning as a means of continuing a race is intriguing, the concept of stealing chromosomes from Riker and Pulaski is reminiscent of season one's "When the Bough Breaks," in which aliens kidnap *Enterprise* children as a means of prolonging their doomed society.

UENGEANCE FACTOR, THE
(TNG)
Original Airdate 11/18/89
Written by Sam Rolfe
Directed by Timothy Bond

Picard mediates a dispute between a pirate band and the Sovereign (Nancy Parsons), the leader of the pirates' homeworld, so that the renegades may return under a grant of amnesty. One of the band's clansmen is murdered by Yuta (Lisa Wilcox), Riker's latest dalliance and the Sovereign's servant, who's seeking vengeance for the destruction of her clan.

ALTMAN (**1/2): An improvement over "The Outrageous Okona," which has its own Trekkian take on space pirates. Unfortunately, the story's resolution hinges on the identification of a one-hundred-year-old photo enhancement, which is a weak plot contrivance in an otherwise competent episode. Particularly memorable is Riker's affinity for the Sovereign's assistant, Yuta (*A Nightmare on Elm Street V*'s Lisa Wilcox), which stirs up jealousy in Troi.

GROSS (***): Beyond the fact that the story line deals with clans and various political factions, it also serves as a commentary on the homeless problem in America. Here we're presented with a group of people who are basically scavengers, taking what they need to survive and so used to this life that they now choose it over living by the rules. Incidentally, Picard has two wild moments. The first is when the *Enterprise* is being fired upon by a Lornac vessel, and the good captain merely waits it out before having Worf disrupt their force screens. It's as though the Lornac ship is a gnat, and Picard is waiting for it to exhaust itself. The other moment is when Riker materializes in the midst of the negotiations and ends up disintegrating Yuta. Picard doesn't even blink.

VIOLATIONS

(TNG)
Original Airdate 2/3/92
Written by Pamela Gray and Jeri Taylor
Directed by Robert Wiemer

A telepathic alien race, the Ullians, who have the gift of probing humans' long-forgotten memories, are being ferried aboard the Enterprise, *when the crew members begin to fall into comas.*

ALTMAN (***): Some strong and innovative direction by Robert Wiemer helps convey this intriguing story of mind rape. The characters' fears and coma-inducing mind-fucks don't say much about the characters themselves, but the surreal dream photography is unsettling and effective. Most memorable are the disturbingly adult moments in which Troi is raped by Riker in her quarters and Dr. Crusher visits her husband's casket with a hirsute Picard. For a show often characterized by its static and lethargic storytelling, the vivid imagery and savvy sci-fi premise are welcome. Less impressive is the standard "Data and LaForge sit by the computer and figure out the plot" wrap-up.

GROSS (***1/2): Welcome to the future! After several soapy episodes in the fifth season, "Violations" is a welcome change of pace, highlighted by an extremely strong science-fiction premise and an allegory taken from today. The very notion of mind rape is a highly inventive concept that is brought to vivid life by director Bob Wiemer, who makes each of Jev's invasions into the minds of others an eerie, unsettling experience. Marina

Sirtis's performance stands out, perhaps because hers is the most violent of the three mind violations we witness. Interestingly, during Beverly Crusher's memory of going to view her late husband's body, she's accompanied by Picard with hair, who bears an uncanny resemblance to Ben Lemon's Jev, making the moment even more frightening. Visually, this show is a delight.

VISIONARY

(DS9)
Original Airdate 3/4/95
Teleplay by John Shirley
Story by Ethan H. Calk
Directed by Reza Badiyi

Through a bizarre disruption of the space-time continuum, Chief O'Brien finds himself projected into the future, where he witnesses his own death and the destruction of Deep Space Nine. When he returns to the present, it's a race against time to stop the future from occurring as he witnessed it.

ALTMAN (***): If you're willing to accept the loopy, *TNG*-like premise that O'Brien is time-shifting into the future and witnesses the destruction of the space station, the story can be somewhat gripping. It's a craftsmanlike, though credulity-straining, episode. There are some nice character moments and a showstopping visual of the station exploding. Ultimately, it would have been nice to see a little more of the Romulans and a little less of the technobabble, but these are quibbles about an episode that is as good as these time-travel shows get.

GROSS (***1/2): Each season, *DS9* seems to go out of its way to make

O'Brien's life a living hell, and "Visionary" is no exception. Not only is this guy taking quick trips into the future, but he manages to see Quark torn up in a Klingon bar fight, his own life coming to an end and the destruction of the station, and he even has the opportunity to bitch at Bashir for not saving his life. The revelation of what is happening to him and how it ties in with the Romulans is extremely well handled. As always, Colm Meaney is splendid as O'Brien, coming across as one of the most human characters in the ensemble.

VISITOR, THE

(DS9)
Original Airdate 10/7/95
Written by Michael Taylor
Directed by David Livingston

An aged Jake Sisko (Tony Todd) is a reclusive writer living in a backwater of the Louisiana bayous when a young woman visits his home. The woman, Melanie (Rachel Robinson), claims to have been caught in a storm but is actually searching for advice from the famous writer and trying to learn why he gave up a brilliant writing career. In a series of flashbacks, Jake tells the story of his father's death, which he wants to share before he dies.

ALTMAN (****): This episode never degenerates into maudlin melodrama but is compelling, sensitive and truly moving, with a tour de force performance by Tony Todd as the elder Jake. Yes, there's probably a little too much technobabble, and there are moments reminiscent of "The Tholian Web," but those things are easily

forgiven considering the depth of genuine emotion mined by writer Michael Taylor and the uncredited Rene Echevarria. I never doubted that Echevarria had the ability to turn out work of this caliber, and it's satisfying to be proved right. If anything, "The Visitor" should show that the best *Trek*s are often the riskiest and most emotional. Easily one of the best episodes of all time, with not a space battle or major action scene in sight.

GROSS (****): The only episode of *Star Trek* to bring tears to my eyes. "The Visitor" is character drama of the highest order, focusing on Jake's lifelong pain as his father is transported to another dimension due to a bizarre accident. With the exception of rare visits from Commander Sisko, who periodically appears in this dimension for a very short time, Jake basically lives his entire life alone, filled with guilt over what happened. Cirroc Lofton does an excellent job as the young, mourning Jake, and Tony Todd is outstanding as the elderly Jake, who is desperate to bring his father back to this dimension. His ultimate realization of what he must do for his father to live is both touching and tragic.

VORTEX

(DS9)
Original Airdate 4/19/93
Written by Sam Rolfe
Directed by Winrich Kolbe

Odo is duped by a man who claims to have knowledge of the shape-shifter's people. Reluctantly, Odo takes the man, Croden, to his planet, where they find his daughter and it's revealed that Croden is considered a criminal because he spoke out against the government. Showing surprising leniency, Odo lets the two of them beam over to a Vulcan ship and safety rather than stand trial.

ALTMAN (***): Although it's sappy and the residents of the Gamma Quadrant seem all too human, there's something strangely compelling about this story. I'm not sure if it's just the 1990s or Michael Piller's emphasis on "family values," but this *Star Trek*, like its progenitors, is clearly a product of its times. Where else could you see an alien murderer turn out to be a simple family man at heart? What strikes me the most about "Vortex" is the impressive scope of the production, which has a feature-film quality to it, with some remarkable visual effects and sets. The brief appearance of the Vulcans also gives the universe of *Star Trek* a refreshing breadth and diversity. Although I still believe that if anything will date the show, it'll be the use of the tired shape-shifting gag, which was old before it was ever used, but the loneliness of Odo's existence as a changeling is well played here, giving the character some depth. Much of the credit goes to Rene Auberjonois, who has excelled in every moment of screen time he's had on the series. The episode was written by Sam Rolfe, the creator of *Have Gun Will Travel*, the brilliant western series on which both Gene Roddenberry and Gene Coon worked.

GROSS (**1/2): Probably most interesting about this episode is see-ing the seemingly incorruptible Odo being tempted by the possibility of meeting others of his kind and learning something of his origins. This aspect of the show, and Rene Auberjonois's quiet display of the character's desperation to know the truth about himself, is rather touching. The rest of the story is pretty standard *Star Trek* fare, although Odo allowing his prisoner to escape is probably as significant a character moment as Data firing a phaser out of seeming vengeance in *TNG*'s "The Most Toys."

WAY OF THE WARRIOR, THE
(DS9)
Original Airdate 9/30/95
Written by Ira Steven Behr and Robert Hewitt Wolfe
Directed by James L. Conway

A fleet of Klingon ships appears around Deep Space Nine. Upon boarding the station, Klingon general Martok informs Sisko and Kira that Gowron has sent him to support the Federation against the Dominion, which they believe has overrun Cardassia. When the Klingons interfere with the normal functioning of the station, Sisko recruits help in the form of Lieutenant Commander Worf (Michael Dorn), who arrives just in time to witness the

Klingon invasion of Cardassia. This prompts Sisko to embark on a mission to rescue Gul Dukat, leading to a Klingon attack on Deep Space Nine.

ALTMAN (**): "The Way of the Warrior" often seems like a jury-rigged attempt to integrate Michael Dorn's Worf into the series rather than a legitimate story that is truly germane to the *DS9* mythos. There's no denying that this two-hour installment boasts some of the most spectacular space battle imagery ever committed to celluloid for a *Trek* series. But that can't compensate for the fact that the consequences of the story are not developed in future episodes, and it's hard to believe that in the wake of the carnage, both in space and on board the station, the Klingons and Starfleet could just agree to disagree and go their separate ways. The only real highlight is Dukat, who is caught between a rock and a Klingon. There's also a ludicrous scene between Dax and Kira in a Bajoran sauna that seems designed only to expose the actresses' considerable assets. Superfluous, sexist and just plain stupid, this episode lacks the heart and soul that has often characterized the often superlative series.

GROSS (***1/2): Deep Space Nine is never a calm place, but the tension intensifies tenfold in this episode as the Klingons decide to help the Federation — whether the Federation wants them to or not. On the one hand, it's disconcerting to see the treaty with the Klingons become so tentative, particularly knowing that Gene Roddenberry felt that the peace between them was one of the most important aspects of *TNG*. On the other hand, in real life things do have a tendency to shift politically, so it's not unreasonable to assume that the Klingons would once again become more aggressive. Michael Dorn's Worf is introduced to the series perfectly, and it seems as though he will fit right in with the cast. Tremendous production values are evident, particularly during several space battles. One suspenseful sequence has Sisko debating with Gowron, emphasizing that they cannot allow themselves to destroy each other while the Founders sit back and watch. After a few tense moments, Gowron backs down. Kudos to Avery Brooks, who began shaving his head at the beginning of the fourth season, which seemed to unleash his passion. Indeed, beginning with the fourth season, it is almost as if a different actor is playing the character.

WAY TO EDEN, THE

(TOS)
Original Airdate 2/12/69
Written by Arthur Heinemann
Story by Michael Richards and Arthur Heinemann
Directed by David Alexander

A group of space hippies attempt to take over the Enterprise so that they can be transported to the mythical world of Eden, a supposed paradise that turns out to be deadly.

ALTMAN (1/2*): Few episodes have aged worse than this story of space hippies who hijack the *Enter-*

prise to go in search of the mystical planet of Eden. It makes *Star Trek V: The Final Frontier* look like Tolstoy by comparison. There's not even much amusement to be gleaned from the inane premise and ludicrous visuals of the flower children cavorting in their tie-dyed wares through the starship and finally onto the deadly planet. If you need a good laugh, listen closely to Adam's (Charles Napier) and Spock's duet on the Vulcan harp. It's a hoot!

GROSS (*): OK, boys and girls, in tonight's episode we will learn that we can't judge a book by its cover. Eden looks beautiful, but it's a bad, bad place. Need another reason to avoid this episode like the plague? Playing his Vulcan harp, Spock has a jam session with the space hippies.

WE'LL ALWAYS HAVE PARIS
(TNG)
Original Airdate 4/30/88
Written by Deborah Dean Davis and Hannah Louise Shearer
Directed by Robert Becker

Captain Picard is reunited with a former love (Michelle Phillips) when the Enterprise investigates the research outpost of Dr. Paul Manheim, whose experiments have resulted in a series of time distortions. If these are not corrected, the very fabric of time will be torn apart, destroying all reality.

ALTMAN (**): *Casablanca* it's not. A nice idea for a romantic yarn involving a woman from Picard's past is undermined by a ridiculous jeopardy plot involving a time-paradox device. If the enigmatic

time distortions, in which entire sequences repeat themselves, were better explained and had more than just a tenuous connection to the romance between Picard and Michelle Phillips's Jenice Manheim, this episode might have worked. As it stands, the story sets up thoughtful situations that are thoughtlessly resolved.

GROSS (**): We get a few insights into Captain Picard's past, and it's nice to give the guy a bit of a romance, but the dimensional rip story line just never comes together. This is probably one of *The Next Generation*'s most forgettable first-season episodes.

WHAT ARE LITTLE GIRLS MADE OF?
(TOS)
Original Airdate 10/20/66
Written by Robert Bloch
Directed by James Goldstone

Nurse Christine Chapel is reunited with her fiancé, Dr. Roger Korby, on the planet Exo III. There Kirk discovers that Korby has been using an ancient technology that allows him to create androids that are exact duplicates of people. He utilizes this technology to make an android of Kirk, with the intention of using the Enterprise to spread this new race throughout the galaxy.

ALTMAN (***): Ted Cassidy as the menacing Ruk and Sherry Jackson wearing a classic William Ware Theiss nonexistent costume as Andrea star in an eerie Robert Bloch yarn. The concept of the bottomless pit and the Old Ones' deadly sentry robots are strangely compelling ideas. Michael Strong is effective as Dr. Korby, who was in the android-making business long before the birth of Dr. Noonian Soong. Not groundbreaking, but certainly entertaining.

GROSS (**): An intriguing Robert Bloch premise is sabotaged by guest star Michael Strong as Dr. Korby, a fatal bit of casting because so much of the episode falls on his shoulders. What's particularly annoying about this episode is the means by which Spock is able to discover that the Kirk on the *Enterprise* is not the real captain. It begins when Korby first duplicates Kirk, and the Kirk android, trying to get into character, utters the line, "I'm sick of your half-breed interference, Mr. Spock." It's repeated when the false Kirk comes to the *Enterprise*, thus revealing to the Vulcan that all things are not as they seem. The problem is that Kirk never would have had such an expression in his mind, even on a subconscious level and even at this early stage of the series. It's completely out of character and destroys all credibility. The late Ted Cassidy is an imposing figure as Ruk, and William Shatner gets to verbally sabotage his first machine.

WHEN THE BOUGH BREAKS

(TNG)
Original Airdate 2/13/88
Written by Hannah Louise Shearer
Directed by Kim Manners

The people of Aldea, who are sterile, kidnap a variety of the Enterprise's *most promising children, including Wesley Crusher. While Picard tries negotiating, Beverly Crusher does her best to discern the reason for the world's sterility.*

ALTMAN (**1/2): Considering *Trek*'s record with kid-driven shows, such as "And the Children Shall Lead," "Miri" and "Justice," "When the Bough Breaks" is surprisingly watchable. Wil Wheaton gives an endearing performance, and the story of a world suffering an ecological breakdown due to its technology is topical and subtle, serving to support rather than overshadow the main story line in which the children of the *Enterprise* are kidnapped by the sterile populace of Aldea.

GROSS (***): Though kind of sappy at times, the episode nonetheless manages to convey a touching tale of a people so desperate to live on that they will go to any extreme. The young performers, led by Wil Wheaton, handle themselves nicely and serve as one of the few reminders that families are aboard the *Enterprise*. In subsequent seasons, this will all but be forgotten. Look for a nice turn by Jerry Hardin ("Deep Throat" on *The X-Files*) as the leader of this alien culture.

WHERE NO MAN HAS GONE BEFORE

(TOS)
Original Airdate 9/22/66
Written by Samuel A. Peeples
Directed by James Goldstone

As the Enterprise *attempts to broach the energy barrier at the edge of the galaxy, crewman Gary Mitchell (Gary Lockwood), a close friend of Kirk's, is transformed into a godlike being who must be killed before he can inflict his power on the universe.*

ALTMAN (***1/2): *Star Trek's* second pilot boasts the action over cerebral content that the network demanded but also provides some heady themes, including an explosive illustration that absolute power corrupts absolutely, as Gary Mitchell goes nuts when he receives godlike powers. Gary Lockwood and Sally Kellerman are wonderful in their respective roles, and there's some ominous foreboding as Mitchell's powers begin to grow and Kirk realizes that he will have to kill one of his closest friends to save his ship.

GROSS (****): The story goes that "The Cage" was too cerebral for NBC, so the network ordered a more action/adventure-oriented second pilot. That's what they got with "Where No Man Has Gone Before," although it still manages to be literate and, yes, cerebral in its exploration of the "power corrupts and absolute power corrupts absolutely" theme. A step closer to the final series it would spawn, this pilot, written by Samuel Peeples and directed by James Goldstone, has William Shatner's Captain James R. (later T.) Kirk replacing Jeffrey Hunter's Christopher Pike as commander of the starship *Enterprise,* and the energy Shatner brings to the role is electric. Additionally, the spark between him and Leonard Nimoy is there from the first frame featuring the duo. Guest star Gary Lockwood, soon to star in Stanley Kubrick's *2001,* does an effective job of gradually changing from an average guy to an arrogant demigod. Look for James Doohan

and George Takei as Scotty and Sulu, respectively.

WHERE NO ONE HAS GONE BEFORE

(TNG)
Original Airdate 10/24/87
Written by Diane Duane and Michael Reaves
Directed by Rob Bowman

A Federation propulsion expert named Kosinski (Stanley Kamel) and his alien assistant, the Traveler (Eric Menyuk), come aboard the Enterprise *to enhance the warp drive. Something goes terribly wrong, and after two warp accelerations, the starship finds itself more than 350 million light-years from home. Reality begins to break down, and the crew's innermost thoughts become reality.*

ALTMAN (***): The real highlight here is Rob Legato's visual effects, which provide a hazy and surreal vision of the end of the universe. Rob Bowman's capable and stylish direction and a churlish performance by Stanley Kamel as the egocentric Kosinski work quite well. Less effective is the gimmicky contrivance of the Traveler and his speech to Picard, when he confides that Wesley Crusher is a "boy wonder" capable of extraordinary things.

GROSS (****): At last, *The Next Generation* shows the audience what it's capable of delivering, providing one hell of an episode in the process. There's hardly a wrong move throughout this imaginative tale, from story to characterization (this should have replaced "The Naked Now" as an introduction to the characters) to unprecedented television special effects. Finally, these are real people whom you give a damn about, with Wil Wheaton's Wesley Crusher being given the opportunity to shine rather than annoy. Thanks to the Traveler, we're given some insight into why Crusher shouldn't be beamed into space and how he will mature into another Mozart or Einstein. Nice guest turns by Stanley Kamel as the arrogant Kosinski and Eric Menyuk as the Traveler, whose prosthetics make him look more like a burn victim than an alien. Rob Bowman makes an auspicious directorial debut. See also "Journey's End."

WHERE SILENCE HAS LEASE

(TNG)
Original Airdate 11/26/88
Written by Jack Sowards
Directed by Winrich Kolbe

The Enterprise *is trapped in a void that serves as a laboratory experiment for a superpower alien being. Nagillum (Earl Boen) is intent on experimenting with the ship and studying the crew's reactions. When Picard realizes that the creature will need to destroy at least half of the crew before attaining its desired approach, he threatens to blow up the ship.*

ALTMAN (**): The best thing about this less than stellar *Star Trek*, which is a thinly veiled attack on animal research, is its moodiness, which can largely be credited to director Winrich Kolbe in his freshman outing. There are some genuinely spooky moments on board one of the *Enterprise*'s sister ships. It's also the first time in the series that a red-shirted secu-

rity guard gets to bite the dust. That helps make up for the shortcomings of this episode, which went into production in the wake of the 1988 writers strike.

GROSS (*1/2): There's a great pre-credit sequence involving Worf and Riker in the holodeck during a training program, but that's about all this episode has to recommend it. Yet another alien wanting to study the *Enterprise* crew and their reaction to various threats is old, tired and boring, although the ruthlessness of this particular alien is a bit unsettling. It's hard to believe that the script was written by Jack Sowards, who penned *Star Trek II: The Wrath of Khan*. Incidentally, the alien Nagillum looks like a cousin of Gizmo, the star of *Gremlins*.

WHISPERS

(DS9)
Original Airdate 2/7/94
Written by Paul Robert Coyle
Directed by Les Landau

A study in paranoia as O'Brien returns to DS9 from the Paradas System, stunned to discover that everyone is treating him like an outsider. He is then determined to expose this seeming conspiracy.

ALTMAN (**1/2): In flashbacks, O'Brien relates how the crew has turned against him. Unlike the best paranoid thrillers, this story is too obvious, as O'Brien discovers the conspiracy quickly and spends the rest of the episode trying to extricate himself from the station. The show's ludicrous revelation that O'Brien is in fact a replicant programmed to kill the attendees at the conference is a gag that probably sounded neat in the pitch meeting but warranted several narrative cheats that seem contrived in retrospect.

GROSS (**1/2): A somewhat intriguing mystery, "Whispers" is helped by the direction of Les Landau, who tries to keep the audience as off balance as the story keeps O'Brien. Thankfully, he avoids most of the clichés that have plagued just about every variation of *Invasion of the Body Snatchers*. If there's fault to find, it's with the revelation at episode's end. Obviously, it was intended to have the impact of a classic *Twilight Zone* episode, but it falls short.

WHO MOURNS FOR ADONIS?

(TOS)
Original Airdate 9/22/67
Written by Gilbert Ralston and Gene L. Coon
Story by Gilbert Ralston
Directed by Marc Daniels

The Enterprise *is literally snared by the hand of the Greek god Apollo (Michael Forest), who has decided that the time has come for humankind to worship him again. Kirk must use the force of the starship, as well as crew member Carolyn Palamas (Leslie Parrish), who is in love with Apollo, to combat his awesome powers and gain their freedom. Finally realizing that the species cannot be forced to worship anything and after the* Enterprise *has destroyed his temple, the source of much of his power, Apollo moves to a spiritual plane, joining the other gods who long ago realized that their time had come and gone.*

ALTMAN (***): The best thing about this episode is *The Manchurian Candidate*'s ravishing Leslie Parrish as the beautiful Carolyn Palamas, with whom the Greek god becomes enamored. Even a god can't keep Kirk's wrath under control when he interferes with his control of the ship. Kirk's sparring with the melancholy Apollo is probably the best thing about the episode ("You want worshippers; you got enemies"), which has some potentially silly moments, including the teaser in which Apollo's hand reaches out and nearly crushes the *Enterprise,* that work surprisingly well. In addition, the easy rapport between Kirk, Scotty, Chekov and McCoy as they contend with their dilemma has rarely been better. Ultimately, the ending packs a melancholy punch. Less palatable, and atypical of *Trek*'s progressive social values, is the egregious sexism of the opening teaser, in which McCoy and Kirk unhappily talk about Palamas's being destined to leave Starfleet when she finds a husband ("I don't think of it as losing an officer, but — wait, come to think of it, I'm losing an officer"). Later, she becomes quite enamored with Apollo, and it takes a passionate speech from Kirk for her to realize that her obligation to the ship is more important than her infatuation.

GROSS (***1/2): There are a lot of goofy elements in this episode (Kirk referring to Scotty as a "sizzlehead" for one), but the notion of these modern mythmakers meeting one of classical mythology's prime characters is irresistible. Michael Forest brings the proper arrogance to his role as a god, and William Shatner manages to hold his own (hey, maybe this was the captain's training session for meeting God in *Star Trek V: The Final Frontier*). Moving beyond a green hand in space — particularly when it's holding and shaking the *Enterprise* — the effects are quite impressive, particularly a scene in which Apollo grows in height to giant size, towering over the *Enterprise* crew members. Leslie Parrish as Carolyn Palamas is kind of bimboish, and, beyond looks, you wonder why the god is so determined to have her. The most surprising moment is when Palamas manipulates Apollo under Kirk's orders, and the god ravages her with a violent storm — obviously representing a rape. Indeed, an early draft of the teleplay concluded with Palamas discovering that she is pregnant with Apollo's child.

WHO WATCHES THE WATCHERS?

(TNG)
Original Airdate 10/14/89
Written by Richard Manning and Hans Beimler
Directed by Robert Wiemer

When the Enterprise *leads a rescue team to a Starfleet outpost that is studying a primitive culture, they inadvertently allow the atheist race to get a glimpse of their futuristic technology and are mistaken for gods. Wary of violating the Prime Directive, but needing to rescue a wounded Federation officer, Troi and Riker beam down in native garb. Riker escapes with the lost member of the science team, but Troi is captured by the Nantokans, who have adopted Picard as their god.*

ALTMAN (***1/2): Among the best of the *TNG* bunch, "Who Watches

the Watchers?" bears the strong imprint of Gene Roddenberry's secular philosophy, which serves the episode well. It's deftly written and presents a genuine quagmire for Picard, which isn't resolved by a simple speech but rather by intelligence, action and sacrifice. There's some striking location photography of the Nantokan village, shot at Vasquez Rocks, and having Riker and Troi go under cover on an Away Team mission is a refreshing break from the usual shipboard bottle shows that characterize many of *TNG*'s seven seasons of voyages. Solid performances by *Dark Shadows*' Kathryn Leigh Scott as Nuria and Ray Wise as Liko, playing a far more sympathetic dad than he did as the murderer of Laura Palmer in *Twin Peaks*.

GROSS (****): The idea of an *Enterprise* crewman and the technology at his disposal being deemed a god can be traced back to the original series' "The Paradise Syndrome," but it is handled fully and maturely in this episode. The basic dramatic impetus is solid, and Patrick Stewart handles Picard's gentle rebuking of the populace's worship nicely. This episode serves as a perfect complement to season four's "First Contact." A job well done by everyone.

WHOM GODS DESTROY

(TOS)
Original Airdate 1/3/69
Written by Lee Erwin
Directed by Herb Wallerstein

The inmates have taken over the Elba II asylum, and Kirk and Spock are captured there by former Starfleet captain Garth, who has acquired the power to change his shape at will. Our heroes do what they must to turn the tables.

ALTMAN (**): Set in an institution for the insane, "Whom Gods Destroy" is a fairly weak Classic *Trek* outing despite a strong performance by Steve Ihnat as the surprisingly charismatic Garth. The legendary Keye Luke also has a small role as the facilities administrator. The usual doppelgänger conflict ensues when we learn that Garth can change his shape to imitate anyone, in this case Captain Kirk. The best thing about the episode is the events hinging on the security code ("queens to queens level three"), which Garth attempts to procure to secure his release. There's also a touching moment at the end as Garth begins to make his return to sanity. He looks Kirk in the eye, after having tried to kill him, and says, "Do I know you, sir?"

GROSS (**): Essentially an inferior remake of "Dagger of the Mind," only this time the chief loon has gotten hold of alien technology that allows him to shift forms. Guest star Steve Ihnat is chewing the scenery from the moment he appears on camera, and when Garth becomes Kirk — well, you can only imagine the histrionics.

Yvonne Craig, best known as TV's Batgirl, is kind of kinky as the green-skinned Marta. Pretty forgettable.

WINK OF AN EYE

(TOS)
Original Airdate 11/29/68
Written by Arthur Heinemann
Story by Lee Cronin
Directed by Jud Taylor

After drinking Scalosian water, Kirk's metabolism accelerates to a different plane of existence on a par with the Scalosians themselves. Their race is nearly dead, and they want to use the Enterprise crew to repopulate their species. While Kirk does what he can to foil these plans, Spock, existing in normal time and space, works with McCoy on a cure for the effects of the water.

ALTMAN (**): The concept is fairly screwy as the Scalosians speed up Captain Kirk in an attempt to turn the *Enterprise* into a deep freeze. Logic goes out the window, but it's sort of fun to watch Kirk's reactions to those around him once he's accelerated and desperately tries to make contact with the crew in normal time. Ultimately, Kirk engages in a quick romance with Kathleen Browne's Deela before, in the show's best scene, Spock joins him after discovering his encoded message and repairs the ship, thus defeating the Scalosians.

GROSS (*1/2): There's not much to recommend this episode, which is high-concept with no content. The whole premise is kind of dopey, and the show is hurt badly by the obvious lack of budget, which doesn't allow for any effects highlighting Kirk's existence on an accelerated plane.

WIRE, THE

(DS9)
Original Airdate 5/9/94
Written by Robert Hewitt Wolfe
Directed by Kim Friedman

Bashir learns that when Garak was a member of the Obsidian Order, he was given an implant that would make him fairly impervious to pain in case of torture. Since exiled from his homeworld and "trapped" on DS9, he has been using the implant to deal with life away from his people. Now it's beginning to malfunction, and it could kill him.

ALTMAN (***): Andrew Robinson is once again exceptional as Garak, endowing his character with noble pathos, and Siddig El Fadil gives an earnest and affecting performance as he pushes Garak into facing his addiction. A well-done, money-saving bottle show.

GROSS (***1/2): A wonderful episode that presents yet another side to Andrew Robinson's Garak and continues to explore the friendship between the Cardassian tailor and Dr. Bashir. Interestingly, even when we think we're learning so much about Garak, we come away from the episode wondering what, if anything, we've truly discovered. From the events of "The Wire," the audience comes to realize that Garak is in constant physical and emotional pain, attempting to survive in a world without his own kind. It's probably similar to the situation in which Mr. Spock found himself in

the original series. Praise to Robinson and Siddig El Fadil for so successfully striking the proper chords in this ongoing relationship.

WOLF IN THE FOLD

(TOS)
Original Airdate 12/22/67
Written by Robert Bloch
Directed by Joseph Pevney

Kirk, McCoy and Scotty are visiting Argelius Two for shore leave, following an accident in which Scotty injured his head. No sooner do they arrive than a serial murderer strikes, and all evidence points to the chief engineer. A mystery follows, in which the crew of the Enterprise discovers that an alien force of pure evil that appeared on Earth in the past has returned.

ALTMAN (**1/2): Although "Wolf in the Fold" focuses on Scotty and it's a bit hard to accept the fact that an accident in engineering has given the amiable chief engineer a bitter hatred toward women, there's some creepy suspense thanks to horror writer Robert Bloch, who puts an interesting sci-fi spin on the historical tale of Jack the Ripper. The unassuming John Fiedler is great casting, making the Ripper revelation far more effective. Look for *ID4*'s Dean Devlin's mom as Prefect Jaris's ill-fated wife.

GROSS (***): Usually when one of our heroes is accused of murder, it's laughable because we are well aware that that person is not guilty. "Wolf in the Fold" actually raises the possibility that Scotty may be guilty of murder, because all the evidence certainly points in that direction. The revelation that the culprit is actually an alien presence of pure evil and that it has been committing murder since its days on Earth as Jack the Ripper is splendid and spookily handled. Easily Robert Bloch's best effort for the series. It's also wild to see character actor John Fiedler, probably best known as the voice of Piglet in *Winnie-the-Pooh*, kick some Starfleet ass.

WOUNDED, THE

(TNG)
Original Airdate 1/28/91
Written by Jeri Taylor
Directed by Chip Chalmers

A rogue starship captain launches a one-man war against the Cardassians, threatening a recently negotiated peace treaty. Picard's assignment is to stop him before it turns into all-out war.

ALTMAN (***): Bob Gunton as Captain Maxwell is one of the few actors who has quietly conveyed the power and strength of a starship captain in only a few scenes as a guest star. He is wonderful in this thought-provoking and surprising *Trek* voyage, which boasts a powerful ending in which Picard is forced to bring in Maxwell despite his realization that Maxwell is right and the Cardassians are rearming to protect a fragile peace. However, throughout the episode, you can't help wondering where the rest of the crew is and what they are thinking. Lip service is paid to a weakened Federation unable to sustain a new war because of the Borg having destroyed most

of its fleet. The Cardassian makeup is superb.

GROSS (***): Some nice continuity with "Best of Both Worlds" highlights this wonderful adventure, in which Picard must stop one of the Federation's own, despite the "rogue" captain's accurate assessment of the situation. Some real tension is evident in this sci-fi take on *Heart of Darkness,* and for a moment or two you wonder whether the *Enterprise* will be forced to destroy a sister ship. Similar situations have no doubt taken place in the modern military, making "The Wounded" an enjoyable allegory. Great interaction between Patrick Stewart and guest star Bob Gunton.

YESTERDAY'S ENTERPRISE

(TNG)
Original Airdate 2/17/90
Written by Ira Steven Behr, Richard Manning, Hans Beimler and Ronald D. Moore
Directed by David Carson

During a conflict with the Romulans, the Enterprise C *is propelled forward in time, and history is changed. The crew is unknowingly thrust into an alternate universe in which the Federation is still at war with the Klingons. Only Guinan suspects that something is wrong and urges Picard to return the*

Enterprise C *back in time, where it will open the door to peace with the Klingons.*

ALTMAN (****): A brilliant show — one of the best time-travel adventures *Star Trek* has ever attempted and one of its best science-fiction ideas. Great production values vividly depict the universe in which the *Enterprise* is at war with the Klingons. The total antithesis of Gene Roddenberry's utopian ethos, it's a fascinating milieu. The character dynamics in this universe as Picard and Riker quarrel over orders are among the many delights. The episode's only weak link is Guinan, who serves as the deus ex machina for setting things straight as the only person to realize that something is amiss. Even Denise Crosby rises to the occasion and gives her most assured performance to date, and *Thelma and Louise*'s Christopher McDonald does well as Lieutenant Richard Castillo. It's a gem.

GROSS (****): If you've ever wondered what *TNG* would have been like if its approach had been more like the original series', you need look no further than "Yesterday's Enterprise." This is one of the best episodes ever produced and a true kick-ass show. The characters are given splendid depth, with the return of Tasha Yar, in particular, being handled with great creative finesse. The crew members of the *Enterprise C* are quite strong as well. Guinan's innate sense that things aren't right stretches one's credulity, but otherwise how would they know that history had been altered? Another valid point is the notion that the Klingons are beating the Federation in their all-out war. After all, they are a race of warriors, while the Federation is a race of explorers. Superb through and through. See also "Redemption."

YESTERYEAR

(TAS)
Original Airdate 9/15/73
Written by D. C. Fontana
Directed by Hal Sutherland

Spock must travel back in time through the Guardian of Forever to discover why he no longer exists in the eyes of those in the present. Arriving on Vulcan, he meets himself as a child and helps the young Spock through a rite of passage. The child is saved by his pet sehlat, but the beast is wounded in the struggle and must be put to sleep.

ALTMAN (***1/2): Dorothy Fontana tells a superbly moving story that not only works as an important lesson for children about losing a pet but also is a compelling *Trek* adventure. It's the best-acted episode of the animated series and one of its most adult offerings. Mark Lenard as the voice of Sarek is most welcome, but the decision to have Majel Barrett provide Amanda Grayson's dulcet tones and the lack of Bart LaRue's distinctive voice for the Guardian of Forever are notable shortcomings. There's some wonderful wit, and the introduction of an Andorian first officer, Commander Thalen, who exists in place of Spock in the alternate time line, is handled deftly and amusingly.

GROSS (****): The perfect animated episode (with the exception of the animation itself), which succeeds by tapping into some extremely popular elements of the live-action series, using them in new ways and as a result providing more resonance than most episodes. It's a shame that this story was never filmed with the cast. This episode represents the best of the series, and it's frustrating that the show wasn't able to find an audience. Check out the creature in the episode: Its voice is the same as Toho's Godzilla. See also "City on the Edge of Forever."

SERIES RATINGS

Series	Altman	Gross
The Original Series	****	****
The Animated Series	***	**1/2
The Movie Series	***	***1/2
The Next Generation	***	***1/2
Deep Space Nine	***1/2	****
Voyager	**	**1/2

CAST MEMBERS' FAVORITES

William Shatner (Kirk)	"City on the Edge of Forever"
Leonard Nimoy (Spock)	*Star Trek IV: The Voyage Home*
George Takei (Sulu)	"The Naked Time"
Walter Koenig (Chekov)	*Star Trek II: The Wrath of Khan*
Patrick Stewart (Picard)	"The Offspring"
Jonathan Frakes (Riker)	"The Offspring"
LeVar Burton (LaForge)	"Second Chances"
Gates McFadden (Crusher)	"The Host"
Marina Sirtis (Troi)	"Face of the Enemy"
Michael Dorn (Worf)	"The Drumhead"

APPENDIX

APOCRYPHA
(The Trek That Never Happened)

1930 — Social worker Edith Keeler is killed in a traffic accident. ("City on the Edge of Forever")

1934 — *Amazing Detective Stories* publishes first Dixon Hill story written by Tracy Torme. ("The Big Goodbye")

1947 — Ferengi ship crash-lands in Roswell, New Mexico, with Quark, Rom, Nog and Odo aboard. ("Little Green Men")

1992 — Khan Noonian Singh rises to power and takes control of a quarter of the Earth ranging from southern Asia to the Middle East. ("Space Seed")

1993 — Genetically engineered supermen take power across the world. The Eugenics Wars begin. ("Space Seed")

1996 — Khan is overthrown and escapes the Earth with ninety-six other genetically bred supermen in the SS *Botany Bay*. (*Star Trek II: The Wrath of Kahn*)

1999 — *Voyager 6* is launched and later becomes V'ger. (*Star Trek: The Motion Picture*)

ALIENATED
(Episodes Involving Alien Possession)

"Best of Both Worlds, Parts I and II" (TNG), "Cathexis" (VOY), "Catspaw" (TOS), "Day of the Dove" (TOS), "Dramatis Personae" (DS9), "Elaan of Troyius" (TOS), "Facets" (DS9), "Fascination" (DS9), "The Game" (TNG), "Is There No Truth in Beauty?" (TOS), "The Lights of Zetar" (TOS), "Lonely Among Us" (TNG), "Masks" (TNG), "The Nth Degree" (TNG), "The Passenger" (DS9), "The Perfect Mate" (TNG), "Power Play" (TNG), "Prophet Motive" (DS9), "The Return of the Archons" (TOS), "Return to Tomorrow" (TOS), "Sarek" (TNG), "The Schizoid Man" (TNG), *Star Trek V: The Final Frontier* (TMS), "Turnabout Intruder" (TOS), "Wolf in the Fold" (TOS)

BAD BORG
(Episodes Featuring the Borg)

"Q Who" (TNG), "Best of Both Worlds, Parts I and II" (TNG), "I, Borg" (TNG), "Descent, Parts I and II" (TNG), *Star Trek VIII: First Contact* (TMS)

BARCLAY
(Episodes Featuring Dwight Schultz as Barclay)

"Hollow Pursuits" (TNG), "The Nth Degree" (TNG), "Realm of Fear" (TNG), "Ship in a Bottle" (TNG),

"Genesis" (TNG), "Projections" (VOY), *Star Trek VIII: First Contact* (TMS)

BOOM!

(Episodes in Which the *Enterprise* or Deep Space Nine Is Destroyed)

"All Good Things" (TNG), "Cause & Effect" (TNG), *Star Trek III: The Search for Spock* (TMS), *Star Trek VII: Generations* (TMS), "Timescape" (TNG), "Visionary" (DS9)

CLOAK AND DAGGER

(Episodes in Which the Romulans Appear)

"Balance of Terror" (TOS), "The Deadly Years" (TOS), "The Enterprise Incident" (TOS), *Star Trek V: The Final Frontier* (TMS), *Star Trek VI: The Undiscovered Country* (TMS), "The Neutral Zone" (TNG), "Contagion" (TNG), "The Enemy" (TNG), "The Defector" (TNG), "Tin Man" (TNG), "Future Imperfect" (TNG), "The Mind's Eye" (TNG), "All Good Things" (TNG), "The Search" (DS9), "Visionary" (DS9), "Improbable Cause" (DS9), "The Die Is Cast" (DS9), "Eye of the Needle" (VOY)

DEBATING TEAM

(Episodes in Which Kirk Talks a Computer to Death)

"What Are Little Girls Made Of?" (TOS), "The Return of the Archons" (TOS), "The Changeling" (TOS), "I, Mudd" (TOS), "The Ultimate Computer" (TOS)

DIXON HILL

(Episodes in Which Picard Appears as Detective Dixon Hill)

"The Big Goodbye" (TNG), "Manhunt" (TNG), "Clues" (TNG), *Star Trek VIII: First Contact* (TMS)

DOUBLE TROUBLE

(Episodes in Which a Duplicate of a Crew Member Is Created or Discovered)

"The Man Trap" (TOS), "The Enemy Within" (TOS), "What Are Little Girls Made Of?" (TOS), "The Menagerie" (TOS), "Mirror, Mirror" (TOS), "Whom Gods Destroy" (TOS), "The Infinite Vulcan" (TAS), "The Survivor" (TAS), *Star Trek VI: The Undiscovered Country* (TMS), "Datalore" (TNG), "Time Squared" (TNG), "Allegiance" (TNG), "Second Chances" (TNG), "Crossover" (DS9), "Whispers" (DS9), "Defiant" (DS9), "Through the Looking Glass" (DS9), "Shattered Mirror" (DS9), "Faces" (VOY), "Tuvix" (VOY)

FOR GOD'S SAKE, STAY OUT OF THE HOLODECK!

(Episodes in Which the Holodeck Malfunctions)

"Angel One" (TNG), "The Big Goodbye" (TNG), "Elementary, Dear Data" (TNG), "Emergence" (TNG), "Heroes and Demons" (VOY), "Homeward" (TNG), "Our Man Bashir" (DS9), "Practical Joker" (TAS), "Shadowplay" (DS9), "Ship in a Bottle" (TNG)

FUTURE'S PAST

(Episodes Involving Time Travel)

"All Good Things" (TNG), "All Our Yesterdays" (TOS), "Assignment: Earth" (TOS), "Captain's Holiday" (TNG), "Cause & Effect" (TNG), "City on the Edge of Forever" (TOS), "Eye of the Needle" (VOY), "Little Green Men" (DS9), "A Matter of Time" (TNG), "Non Sequitur" (VOY), "Parallax" (VOY), "Past Tense, Parts I and II" (DS9), *Star Trek IV: The Voyage Home* (TMS), *Star Trek VII: Generations* (TMS), *Star Trek VIII: First Contact* (TMS), "Tapestry" (TNG), "Time and Again" (VOY), "Time Squared" (TNG), "Time's Arrow, Parts I and II" (TNG),

"Timescape" (TNG), "Tomorrow Is Yesterday" (TOS), "Trials and Tribblations" (DS9), "Visionary" (DS9), "We'll Always Have Paris" (TNG), "Yesterday's Enterprise" (TNG), "Yesteryear" (TAS)

HERE'S MUDD IN YOUR EYE

(Episodes in Which Harry Mudd Appears)

"Mudd's Women" (TOS), "I, Mudd" (TOS), "Mudd's Passion" (TAS)

HE'S DEAD, JIM

(Episodes in Which an Important Character Dies)

"Shore Leave" (TOS — McCoy), "Operation Annihilate" (TOS — Kirk's brother, Sam), "Return to Tomorrow" (TOS — Kirk), "Spectre of the Gun" (TOS — Chekov), "Skin of Evil" (TNG — Tasha Yar), "Reunion" (TNG — K'Ehleyr, Duras), "Unification, Part I" (TNG — Sarek), "Tapestry" (TNG — Picard), Star Trek II: The Wrath of Khan (TMS — Spock), Star Trek VII: Generations (TMS — Kirk), "Lifesigns" (VOY — Vedek Bareil)

HISTORY LESSON

(Episodes That Refer to a Real Event in Human History or Use a Historical Figure in the Narrative)

"Tomorrow Is Yesterday" (TOS), City on the Edge of Forever" (TOS), "Wolf in the Fold" (TOS), "Assignment: Earth" (TOS), "Spectre of the Gun" (TOS), "Requiem for Methuselah" (TOS), "The Savage Curtain" (TOS), "The Nth Degree" (TNG), "Time's Arrow, Parts I and II" (TNG), "Descent, Parts I and II" (TNG), "The 37's" (VOY)

IT'S ALL RELATIVE

(Episodes in Which the Family Member of a Cast Member Appears)

"Journey to Babel" (TOS — Spock's parents), "Operation Annihilate" (TOS — Kirk's brother), "Day of the Dove" (TOS — Chekov's imaginary brother), Star Trek III: The Search for Spock (TMS — Spock's father), Star Trek IV: The Voyage Home (TMS — Spock's parents), "Haven" (TNG — Troi's mother), "Datalore" (TNG — Data's brother), "The Icarus Factor" (TNG — Riker's father), "Manhunt" (TNG — Troi's mother), "Menage A Troi" (TNG — Troi's mother), "Brothers" (TNG — Data's brother), "Sarek" (TNG — Spock's father), "Family" (TNG — Worf's parents; Wesley Crusher's father; Picard's nephew, sister-in-law and brother), "Sins of the Father" (TNG — Worf's brother), "Violations" (TNG — Beverly Crusher's husband), "Homeward" (TNG — Worf's brother), "Half a Life" (TNG — Troi's mother), "Redemption, Parts I and II" (TNG — Worf's brother, Tasha Yar's daughter), "Reunion" (TNG — Worf's son introduced), "Legacy" (TNG — Tasha Yar's sister), "New Ground" (TNG — Worf's son reintroduced), "Ethics" (TNG — Worf's son), "Unification, Parts I and II" (TNG — Spock's father, Tasha Yar's daughter), "Cost of Living" (TNG — Troi's mother), "The Inner Light" (TNG — Picard's imaginary family), "Dark Page" (TNG — Troi's mother, sister and father), "A Fistful of Datas" (TNG — Worf's son), "Firstborn" (TNG — Worf's son), "Bloodlines" (TNG — Picard's son, sort of), "Indiscretion" (DS9 — LaForge's parents), "Family Business" (DS9 — Quark's mother), "The Way of the Warrior" (DS9 — Worf's brother), "The Sons of Mogh" (DS9 — Worf's brother), "Persistence of Vision" (VOY — Tuvok's wife, Paris's father)

IT'S ELEMENTARY
(Episodes in Which Data Appears as Sherlock Holmes)

"Lonely Among Us" (TNG), "Elementary, Dear Data" (TNG), "Ship in a Bottle" (TNG)

IT'S THE ONLY LOVE MONEY CAN BUY!
(Episodes in Which Tribbles Appear)

"The Trouble with Tribbles" (TOS), "More Tribbles, More Troubles" (TAS), *Star Trek III: The Search for Spock* (TMS), "Trials and Tribblations" (DS9)

KIRK CONQUESTS
(Episodes in Which Kirk Is Involved in a Romance)

"Mudd's Women (TOS), "What Are Little Girls Made Of?" (TOS — Andrea), "Dagger of the Mind" (TOS), "The Conscience of the King" (TOS), "Shore Leave" (TOS — Ruth), "Court Martial" (TOS — Areel Shaw), "City on the Edge of Forever" (TOS — Edith Keeler), "Mirror, Mirror" (TOS), "Catspaw" (TOS — Sylvia), "The Gamesters of Triskelion" (TOS — Shana), "By Any Other Name" (TOS), "Bread and Circuses" (TOS — Drusilla), "The Paradise Syndrome" (TOS — Miramanee), "Wink of an Eye" (TOS — Deela), "Elaan of Troyius" (TOS — Dolman), "The Mark of Gideon" (TOS), "Requiem for Methuselah" (TOS — Rayna)

KLINGONS
(Episodes in Which Klingons Other Than Worf or Torres Appear)

"Errand of Mercy" (TOS), "Friday's Child (TOS), "The Trouble with Tribbles" (TOS), "A Private Little War" (TOS), "Day of the Dove" (TOS), "Elaan of Troyius" (TOS), "The Savage Curtain" (TOS), "More Tribbles, More Troubles" (TAS), "Time Trap" (TAS), *Star Trek: The Motion Picture* (TMS), *Star Trek III: The Search for Spock* (TMS), *Star Trek IV: The Voyage Home* (TMS), *"Star Trek V: The Final Frontier"* (TMS), *Star Trek VI: The Undiscovered Country* (TMS), *Star Trek VII: Generations* (TMS), "Hide & Q" (TNG), "Heart of Glory" (TNG), "A Matter of Honor" (TNG), "The Emissary" (TNG), "Sins of the Father" (TNG), "Redemption" (TNG), "Birthright" (TNG), "The Chase" (TNG), "Rightful Heir" (TNG), "Firstborn" (TNG), "Past Prologue" (DS9), "Invasive Procedures" (DS9), "Blood Oath" (DS9), "Crossover" (DS9), "The House of Quark" (DS9), "Through the Looking Glass" (DS9), "The Way of the Warrior" (DS9), "The Sword of Kahless" (DS9), "Return to Grace" (DS9), "The Sons of Mogh" (DS9), "Rules of Engagement" (DS9), "Shattered Mirror" (DS9)

LAUGH RIOT
(Comedic Episodes)

"I, Mudd" (TOS), "The Trouble with Tribbles" (TOS), "A Piece of the Action" (TOS), "More Tribbles, More Troubles" (TAS), "Mudd's Passion" (TAS), "Deja Q" (TNG), "Q-pid" (TNG), "The Nagus" (DS9), "Prophet Motive" (DS9), "Family Business" (DS9), "Our Man Bashir" (DS9), "Trials and Tribblations" (DS9)

MOTHERS' DAY
(Episodes that Feature Counselor Troi's Mother, Lwaxana)

"Haven" (TNG), "Manhunt" (TNG), "Menage A Troi" (TNG), "Half a Life" (TNG), "Cost of Living" (TNG), "Dark Page" (TNG), "The Forsaken" (DS9), "The Muse" (DS9)

OUTBREAK

(Episodes in Which the Crew is Infected with a Rapidly Spreading Disease)

"Babel" (DS9), "The Deadly Years" (TOS), "Genesis" (TNG), "Identity Crisis" (TNG), "If Wishes Were Horses" (DS9), "Learning Curve" (VOY), "Miri" (TOS), "Mudd's Passion" (TAS), "The Naked Now" (TNG), "The Naked Time" (TOS), "Night Terrors" (TNG), "Persistence of Vision" (VOY), "The Terratin Incident" (TAS), "This Side of Paradise" (TOS), "Where No One Has Gone Before" (TNG)

Q&A

(Q Episodes)

"Encounter at Farpoint" (TNG), "Hide & Q" (TNG), "Deja Q" (TNG), "Q-pid" (TNG), "Q Who" (TNG), "True Q" (TNG), "Tapestry" (TNG), "All Good Things" (TNG), "Q-Less" (DS9), "Death Wish" (VOY)

STARFLEET LAW

(Episodes Involving Legal Issues or in Which Characters Play a Judge, Lawyer or Defendant)

"The Squire of Gothos" (TOS), "A Matter of Perspective" (TNG), "All Good Things" (TNG), Court Martial" (TOS), "Devil's Due" (TNG), "Encounter at Farpoint" (TNG), "The Measure of a Man" (TNG), "The Menagerie" (TOS), "The Offspring" (TNG), "The Quality of Life" (TNG), "Rules of Engagement" (DS9), *Star Trek IV: The Voyage Home* (TMS), "Suspicions" (TNG), "Tribunal" (DS9)

STAR TREK FOR ALL OCCASIONS

Valentine's Day	"Fascination" (DS9), "Mudd's Passion" (TAS)
Black History Month	"Past Tense" (DS9)
President's Day	"The Savage Curtain" (TOS)
St. Patrick's Day	"Up the Long Ladder" (TNG)
Arbor Day	"This Side of Paradise" (TOS)
Mother's Day	"Haven" (TNG)
Father's Day	"Family" (TNG), "The Icarus Factor" (TNG)
Independence Day	"The Omega Glory" (TOS)
Halloween	"Catspaw" (TOS)
Thanksgiving	"Charlie X" (TOS)
Christmas	"Tapestry" (TNG), *Star Trek VII: Generations* (TMS; come to think of it, no occasion is worth this)
50th Birthday	"Parallels" (TNG; your birthday can't be as bad as Worf's)

INDEX BY SHOW AND SEASON

THE ORIGINAL SERIES (TOS) — FIRST SEASON

The Man Trap
Charlie X
Where No Man Has Gone Before
The Naked Time
The Enemy Within
Mudd's Women
What Are Little Girls Made Of?
Miri
Dagger of the Mind
The Corbomite Maneuver
The Menagerie, Part I
The Menagerie, Part II
The Conscience of the King
Balance of Terror
Shore Leave
The Galileo Seven
The Squire of Gothos
Arena
Tomorrow Is Yesterday
Court Martial
The Return of the Archons
Space Seed
A Taste of Armageddon
This Side of Paradise
The Devil in the Dark
Errand of Mercy
The Alternative Factor
City on the Edge of Forever
Operation Annihilate

THE ORIGINAL SERIES (TOS) — SECOND SEASON

Amok Time
Who Mourns for Adonis?
The Changeling
Mirror, Mirror
The Apple
The Doomsday Machine
Catspaw
I, Mudd
Metamorphosis
Journey to Babel
Friday's Child
The Deadly Years
Obsession
Wolf in the Fold
The Trouble with Tribbles
The Gamesters of Triskelion
A Piece of the Action
The Immunity Syndrome
A Private Little War
Return to Tomorrow
Patterns of Force
By Any Other Name
The Omega Glory
The Ultimate Computer

Bread and Circuses
Assignment: Earth

The Arsenal of Freedom
Symbiosis
Skin of Evil
We'll Always Have Paris
Conspiracy
The Neutral Zone

THE NEXT GENERATION (TNG) – SECOND SEASON

The Child
Where Silence Has Lease
Elementary, Dear Data
The Outrageous Okona
Loud as a Whisper
The Schizoid Man
Unnatural Selection
A Matter of Honor
The Measure of a Man
The Dauphin
Contagion
The Royale
Time Squared
The Icarus Factor
Pen Pals
Q Who
Samaritan Snare
Up the Long Ladder
Manhunt
The Emissary
Peak Performance
Shades of Gray

THE NEXT GENERATION (TNG) – THIRD SEASON

Evolution
The Ensigns of Command
The Survivors
Who Watches the Watchers?
The Bonding
Booby Trap
The Enemy
The Price
The Vengeance Factor
The Defector

The Hunted
The High Ground
Deja Q
A Matter of Perspective
Yesterday's Enterprise
The Offspring
Sins of the Father
Allegiance
Captain's Holiday
Tin Man
Hollow Pursuits
The Most Toys
Sarek
Menage A Troi
Transfigurations
Best of Both Worlds, Part I

THE NEXT GENERATION (TNG) – FOURTH SEASON

Best of Both Worlds, Part II
Family
Brothers
Suddenly Human
Remember Me
Legacy
Reunion
Future Imperfect
Final Mission
The Loss
Data's Day
The Wounded
Devil's Due
Clues
First Contact
Galaxy's Child
Night Terrors
Identity Crisis
The Nth Degree
Q-pid
The Drumhead
Half a Life
The Host
The Mind's Eye

In Theory
Redemption, Part I

THE NEXT GENERATION [TNG] — FIFTH SEASON

Redemption, Part II
Darmok
Ensign Ro
Silicon Avatar
Disaster
The Game
Unification, Part I
Unification, Part II
A Matter of Time
New Ground
Hero Worship
Violations
The Masterpiece Society
Conundrum
Power Play
Ethics
The Outcast
Cause & Effect
The First Duty
Cost of Living
The Perfect Mate
Imaginary Friend
I, Borg
The Next Phase
The Inner Light
Time's Arrow, Part I

THE NEXT GENERATION [TNG] — SIXTH SEASON

Time's Arrow, Part II
Realm of Fear
Man of the People
Relics
Schisms
True Q
Rascals
A Fistful of Datas
The Quality of Life
Chain of Command, Part I

Chain of Command, Part II
Ship in a Bottle
Aquiel
Face of the Enemy
Tapestry
Birthright, Part I
Birthright, Part II
Starship Mine
Lessons
The Chase
Frame of Mind
Suspicions
Rightful Heir
Second Chances
Timescape
Descent, Part I

THE NEXT GENERATION [TNG] — SEVENTH SEASON

Descent, Part II
Liaisons
Interface
Gambit, Part I
Gambit, Part II
Phantasms
Dark Page
Attached
Force of Nature
Inheritance
Parallels
The Pegasus
Homeward
Sub Rosa
Lower Decks
Thine Own Self
Masks
Eye of the Beholder
Genesis
Journey's End
Firstborn
Bloodlines
Emergence
Preemptive Strike
All Good Things

DEEP SPACE NINE (DS9) — FIRST SEASON

Emissary
Past Prologue
A Man Alone
Babel
Captive Pursuit
Q-Less
Dax
The Passenger
Move Along Home
The Nagus
Vortex
Battle Lines
The Storyteller
Progress
If Wishes Were Horses
The Forsaken
Dramatis Personae
Duet
In the Hands of the Prophets

DEEP SPACE NINE (DS9) — SECOND SEASON

The Homecoming
The Circle
The Siege
Invasive Procedures
Cardassians
Melora
Rules of Acquisition
Necessary Evil
Second Sight
Sanctuary
Rivals
The Alternate
Armageddon Game
Whispers
Paradise
Shadowplay
Playing God
Profit and Loss
Blood Oath
The Maquis, Part I

The Maquis, Part II
The Wire
Crossover
The Collaborator
Tribunal
The Jem'Hadar

DEEP SPACE NINE (DS9) — THIRD SEASON

The Search, Part I
The Search, Part II
The House of Quark
Equilibrium
Second Skin
The Abandoned
Civil Defense
Meridian
Defiant
Fascination
Past Tense, Part I
Past Tense, Part II
Life Support
Heart of Stone
Destiny
Prophet Motive
Visionary
Distant Voices
Through the Looking Glass
Improbable Cause
The Die Is Cast
Explorers
Family Business
Shakaar
Facets
The Adversary

DEEP SPACE NINE (DS9) — FOURTH SEASON

The Way of the Warrior
The Visitor
Hippocratic Oath
Indiscretion
Rejoined
Little Green Men

Starship Down
The Sword of Kahless
Our Man Bashir
Homefront
Paradise Lost
Crossfire
Return to Grace
The Sons of Mogh
Bar Association
Accession
Rules of Engagement
Hard Time
Shattered Mirror
The Muse
For the Cause
To the Death
The Quickening
Body Parts
Broken Link

DEEP SPACE NINE (DS9) – FIFTH SEASON

Trials and Tribblations

VOYAGER (VOY) – FIRST SEASON

Caretaker
Parallax
Time and Again
Phage
The Cloud
Eye of the Needle
Ex Post Facto
Emanations
Prime Factors
State of Flux
Heroes and Demons

Cathexis
Faces
Jetrel
Learning Curve

VOYAGER (VOY) – SECOND SEASON

The 37's
Initiations
Projections
Elogium
Non Sequitur
Twisted
Parturition
Persistence of Vision
Tattoo
Cold Fire
Maneuvers
Resistance
Prototype
Alliances
Threshold
Meld
Dreadnought
Death Wish
Lifesigns
Investigations
Deadlock
Innocence
The Thaw
Tuvix
Resolutions
Basics, Part I

VOYAGER (VOY) – THIRD SEASON

Basics, Part II